COLONIAL
RHODE ISLAND

A HISTORY

A HISTORY OF THE AMERICAN COLONIES
IN THIRTEEN VOLUMES

GENERAL EDITORS:
MILTON M. KLEIN & JACOB E. COOKE

SYDNEY V. JAMES

COLONIAL RHODE ISLAND

A HISTORY

CHARLES SCRIBNER'S SONS, NEW YORK

Jacket illustration, a view of eighteenth-century Newport,
courtesy of the Newport Historical Society.

Library of Congress Cataloging in Publication Data

James, Sydney V
   Colonial Rhode Island: A History

   (Colonial history series) a Hist. of the Amer Colonies
   Bibliography: p.
   Includes index.
   1. Rhode Island—History—Colonial period, ca.
1600-1775.   2. Rhode Island—History—Revolution,
1775-1783.   I. Title.   II Series .
F82.J35   974.5'02   75-9685
ISBN 0-684-14359-3

1 3 5 7 9 11 13 15 17 19 C/C 20 18 16 14 12 10 8 6 4 2

Printed in the United States of America

for

Jean Middleton James
and a silver anniversary

CONTENTS

ILLUSTRATIONS

EDITORS'
INTRODUCTION

The American colonies have not lacked their Boswells. Almost from the time of their founding, the English settlements in the New World became the subjects of historical narratives by promoters, politicians, and clergymen. Some, like John Smith's *General History of Virginia*, sought to stir interest in New World colonization. Others, such as Cotton Mather's *Magnalia Christi Americana*, used New England's past as an object lesson to guide its next generation. And others still, like William Smith's *History of the Province of New-York*, aimed at enhancing the colony's reputation in England by explaining its failures and emphasizing its accomplishments. All of these early chroniclers had their shortcomings but no more so than every generation of historians which essayed the same task thereafter. For it is both the strength and the challenge of the historical guild that in each age its practitioners should readdress themselves to the same subjects of inquiry as their predecessors. If the past is prologue, it must be constantly reenacted. The human drama is unchanging, but the audience is always new: its expectations of the past are different, its mood uniquely its own.

The tercentenary of John Smith's history is almost coterminous with the bicentenary of the end of the American colonial era. It is more than appropriate that the two occasions should be observed by a fresh retelling of the story of the colonization of English America not, as in the case of the earliest histories, in self-justification, national exaltation, or moral purgation but as a plain effort to reexamine the past through the lenses of the present.

Apart from the national observance of the bicentennial of American independence, there is ample justification in the era of the 1970s for a modern history of each of the original thirteen colonies. For many of them, there exists no single-volume narrative published in the present century and, for some, none written since those undertaken by contemporaries in the eighteenth century. The standard multivolume histories of the colonial period—those of Herbert L. Osgood, Charles M. Andrews, and Lawrence H. Gipson—are too comprehensive to provide adequate treatment of individual colonies, too political and institutional in emphasis to deal adequately with social, economic, and cultural developments, and too intercolonial and Anglo-American in focus to permit intensive examination of a single colony's distinctive evolution. The most recent of these comprehensive accounts, that of Gipson, was begun as far back as 1936; since then a considerable body of new scholarship has been produced.

The present series, *A History of the American Colonies*, of which *Colonial Rhode Island* is part, seeks to synthesize the new research, to treat social, economic, and cultural as well as political developments, and to delineate the broad outlines of each colony's history during the years before independence. No uniformity of organization has been imposed on the authors, although each volume attempts to give some attention to every aspect of the colony's historical development. Each author is a specialist in his own field and has shaped his material to the configuration of the colony about which he writes. While the Revolutionary Era is the terminal point of each volume, the authors have not read the history of the colony backward, as mere preludes to the inevitable movement toward independence and statehood.

Despite their local orientation, the individual volumes, taken together, will provide a collective account that should help us understand the broad foundation on which the future history of the colonies in the new nation was to rest and, at the same time, help clarify that still not completely explained melodrama of

1776 which saw, in John Adams's words, thirteen clocks somewhat amazingly strike as one. In larger perspective, *A History of
the American Colonies* seeks to remind today's generation of
Americans of its earliest heritage as a contribution to an
understanding of its contemporary purpose. The link between
past and present is as certain as it is at times indiscernible, for as
Michael Kammen has so aptly observed: "The historian is the
memory of civilization. A civilization without memory ceases to
be civilized. A civilization without history ceases to have identity.
Without identity there is no purpose; without purpose civilization will wither." *

The history of the tiny colony of Rhode Island has been
dwarfed by that of its better-known neighbors. The present
volume (the first scholarly history of the subject since the turn of
the twentieth century) affords ample compensation for this
comparative neglect. Here is set forth a richly textured, dramatic
account of the colony that most faithfully forecasts the pluralistic
society, religious practices, and peculiar brand of democracy that
would characterize the nation of which "the State of Rhode
Island and Providence Plantations" would become the smallest
member with the largest name.

According to Professor James, the colonial history of Rhode
Island has not usually seemed to have "a large significance,"
principally because its pioneering accomplishments have "been
taken for granted." They were, however, neither "foreordained
by some vague whim of fate or nature" nor unremarkable. The
legacy of colonial Rhode Island was, in fact, significant, constructive, and durable.

"Rogue's Island," as the colony was derisively described, was,
in the words of the familiar New England quip, the place "where
people think otherwise." But, as Professor James demonstrates,
some of the ways in which they thought otherwise were of
incalculable historical importance. Though Rhode Island was
regarded by neighboring colonies as a "cesspool of heresy," the
heretics, recognizing that they could not persuade each other,
followed the example of the colony's founder, Roger Williams,

---

* Michael Kammen, *People of Paradox* (New York, 1972), p. 13.

and converted their zeal for proselytism into the practice of religious freedom for all, thus fashioning an enduring American principle. Of similar future significance was their willingness to make bold experiments in government while also accepting the necessity of compromise and accommodation. So, too, did their "irreverent pride in being independent, different, and constantly beating the odds" foreshadow national traits, much-touted as uniquely American.

Professor James's history also affords an illuminating case study in the coming of the American Revolution. There was no doubt that Rhode Island—prizing as it did individual liberty and self-government—would resist Britain's efforts to atone for long decades of imperial apathy by strictly controlling the affairs of her distant colonies. And by brazenly resisting, the small colony played a distinctive and important role in the dramatic series of events that led to American independence, a status that Rhode Island had proclaimed for itself two months before it endorsed the famous Declaration of July 1776. The new state was as "other-minded" as the new colony had been more than a century earlier, and Rhode Island's reluctance to surrender any of its independence to a union of the states promoted, ironically enough, the creation of a stronger central government under a Constitution which Rhode Islanders were the last to ratify.

The history of colonial Rhode Island, as Professor James engagingly and persuasively argues, was a success story. As he says, by the end of the eighteenth century, the national acceptance of ideas like religious freedom, separation of church and state, and the protection of individual rights meant that "the United States was catching up with Rhode Island."

Rhode Island's colonial history, viewed in conjunction with the histories of the other twelve colonies, clarifies the meaning of a revolution whose inception, however fortuitous, produced consequences so momentous that they live with us still.

Milton M. Klein
Jacob E. Cooke

PREFACE

The author of a book has to be prepared to defend his choice of a subject. It might seem that going to all the trouble of writing the volume should earn him an exemption from this requirement, but it never does. The author, in fact, must write each page with an eye toward building the case for the defense. Fortunately, justifying a book about colonial Rhode Island calls for no heroic effort. Still, it is obvious that the subject did not exist until the main events to be reported were well under way. Moreover, the subject threatened to vanish from time to time. The colony actually lost its separate existence for a couple of years in the late seventeenth century and barely managed to regain it. And some people may harbor the sentiment that keeping Rhode Island on the map was a fluke of no importance or even a mistake that encumbered the United States with a wholly unnecessary jurisdiction.

The author's defense, then, may be organized by preparing answers to the question, "Why is there a state of Rhode Island?" No single answer will do. Merely to get started it is necessary to explain the circumstances that allowed the first English settlements, the motives of the settlers, and the process of joining the earliest towns into a colony of Puritan heretics. Then there must be explanations of how that colony withstood the attempts to merge it with larger jurisdictions—and why the attempts were made. Giving a good account of these matters, it turns out, entails explaining the distinctive traits and the local patriotism that set Rhode Island apart from the rest of New England. When they appeared, the special characteristics and pride in them gave final proof that colonial Rhode Island was indeed a subject that someone could write about.

There is a danger, however, that the distinctive features may be treated too simply. The words "except in Rhode Island" spring too readily to the lips when uttering general remarks about colonial America. In many respects New England was homogeneous; in many others, Rhode Island was not. It is necessary to see the exceptional qualities of the heretic colony in perspective against diversity within its borders, against its conformity to regional patterns, and against the presence of variation throughout the region. If this delicate task of judgment can be performed, then a harder one may be undertaken: evaluating the extent to which Rhode Island shared characteristics with the other English colonies in North America. Fortunately, the historian of colonial Rhode Island need not climb to such heights of discrimination and may feel that duty has been done by offering a few thoughts to guide others.

Anyone who sets out to study colonial Rhode Island feels a number of special pains and pleasures. Among the pains, foremost is the irksome incompleteness of the documentary record, which rules out careful investigation of many subjects, such as demography, and shrouds in darkness important parts of the legal history and the development of the colony's leading port. The situation has to be treated as an intellectual challenge if it is not to induce despair. Another kind of problem comes from the tendency in the past to write about Rhode Island and its leading citizens so as to make a case for or against them. This inheritance has left a spate of topics vexed by polemical distortion and has posed questions on which subsequent writers are expected to take sides. It sometimes seems as though writing a history of colonial Rhode Island consists of presenting a series of new briefs in all these disputes; that there is nothing else to be mentioned. I have tried to break out of this trap—being in it is like being locked between parallel mirrors. It is often necessary to cast aside old arguments merely to escape the limits they have imposed on what conclusions might be reached and what subjects might be investigated. Discussion of Roger Williams, for in-

stance, has been carried on in terms that keep drawing historians
back to evaluating his relations with magistrates and ministers in
Massachusetts to the exclusion of attention to his life in Rhode
Island. Likewise, the colonial paper money, one of the few things
commonly mentioned as products of the eighteenth century, has
been treated ordinarily as a moral rather than an economic
subject. Readers of this volume will find the first attempt to treat
it as both an economic and a political topic. It should not have
waited so many years.

Still, the historian should not whine overlong. If the study of
colonial Rhode Island is trammeled in controversies, it benefits
from the interest they rouse. Besides, the writer need not fear the
wrath of ancestor-worshipping fanatics ready to pillory anyone
who says they were not descended from saints and heroes. The
peculiar local relish for discovering scoundrels in the family tree
and reversing other people's judgments, in fact, allows the writer
a comfortable freedom to speak his own mind. If anything, this
history will disappoint those who delight in finding rascality in
the olden days. Now that Rhode Islanders are as diverse in
ethnic affiliation as they once were in religion, the great majority
without colonial ancestors to cherish may see social and political
conditions in the colonial past that were forebears of those in the
present.

The greatest pleasure to the historian comes from acknowledging gratitude for help received in the long, usually dreary, toil of
compiling information and fashioning it into a book. This
volume, which is one product of an extensive investigation of
colonial Rhode Island, has been aided by grants from the Social
Science Research Council, the American Philosophical Society,
the Center for the Study of the History of Liberty in America, the
American Council of Learned Societies, the Old Gold Foundation and the Graduate College of the University of Iowa, and the
National Endowment for the Humanities. I have also received
considerable assistance from the staffs of the Rhode Island
Historical Society, the Newport Historical Society, the John
Carter Brown Library, the John Hay Library, the Rockefeller
Library, and the State Archives—all in Rhode Island. Among
the many courteous and helpful people at these places, I would

like to mention the late Mary T. Quinn, for many years the archivist in the State House in Providence, who was more than generous in sharing her vast knowledge of the documents under her care. I would also like to thank Albert T. Klyberg, Noel P. Conlon, Mildred C. Tilley, and Nathaniel Shipton, of the Rhode Island Historical Society for many courtesies, tips, and encouraging words. Joseph K. Ott of the same institution graciously gave his indispensable advice on selecting pictures of Rhode Island furniture to adorn this volume. Gladys Bolhouse at the Newport Historical Society has kindly rendered essential services, as have Chester Oakley and James Coogan in showing me the way around court documents.

My work has been advanced and guided by many other people. I would particularly like to acknowledge the aid of William G. McLoughlin, Virginia McLoughlin, Norma Rainone, and Winifred Barton. I have learned much from Oscar Handlin and Samuel Eliot Morison and hope that this book will merit their approval.

Iowa City   SYDNEY V. JAMES
October 15, 1974

COLONIAL
RHODE ISLAND

A HISTORY

1

INTRODUCTION: ABOUT BEGINNINGS

Rhode Island was founded in 1636, it is customary to say, when Roger Williams and a few other outcasts from Massachusetts crossed the Seekonk River and started building Providence. Frequent repetition has made this proposition seem like a simple fact, but it was far from that. The choice of date is surely arbitrary, for what Williams did in 1636 cannot be separated from what he did earlier and later. Moreover, the establishment of Rhode Island was a process, including the formation of a cluster of towns, not just one, and gathering them into a colony with a character of its own. Nobody set out to do all that in 1636 and nobody could be sure it had been done until about seventy years later. Half the colonial period had gone by before Rhode Island was indelibly on the map—that is, before it enjoyed a flourishing local patriotism and achieved internal order, reasonable immunity from the territorial ambitions of its neighbors, and safety from British plans to merge it with a larger colony. Founding was not fully accomplished in a year or even in the lifetime of any of the first settlers.

Williams had a large part in achieving the final results, but it has not always been recognized. The first historian of the colony, John Callender, wrote in 1738 to commemorate what he regarded as the centennial year. He thought the arrival of Anne Hutchinson and her numerous followers, two years later than Williams, truly launched the colony. In Callender's day, common sense could readily find reasons for assigning primacy to these people. Their towns on the island of Aquidneck, Newport and Portsmouth, were still the center of wealth, population, culture, and government in the colony. Such was their importance that their decision to accept the custom of calling Aquidneck the Island of Rhode Island, a custom of obscure origin, provided the common name for the whole colony. So when a Newport man chose the formal designation that appeared in the royal charter of 1663, "the English Colony of Rhode-Island and Providence Plantations, in New-England, in America." Williams' town was given second place, where many Newport people then and later thought it belonged. Antiquarians without Callender's sense of proportion have argued in a different way, proposing that the arrival of the first English family in the colony's territory, a couple of years before Williams, should mark the founding of Rhode Island. Unfortunately for this notion, the patriarch of that family, William Blackstone, moved into the wilderness to get away from a community, not to start one.

Mr. Blackstone was born to be a footnote on history. A kindly but eccentric clergyman of the Church of England, he disliked the confinement of human society and set up housekeeping in the New England wilderness—in Boston before the Puritans, in Providence before Williams. He left Boston when the population grew too dense for him, partly as the result of his generosity in sharing the fresh water from his spring. Besides, he was not keen on Puritans. He took his family and library to a forest in what is now the town of Lincoln, near the river that bears his name. He planted orchards, in which some cherished varieties of apples were developed. His new neighbors did not crowd in upon him. Occasionally he went to the village of Providence, sometimes to expound the teachings of his church. To attract an audience at first he tossed apples to passersby. He attained minor fame by riding a bull, for want of a horse, on his journeys to town or his rarer excursions to Boston. Unfortunately his library was burned during King Philip's War shortly after Blackstone's death in 1673. His experiences illustrate the falsity of beliefs that Indians were automatically hostile to Europeans. Fascinating as Blackstone may be, attempts to make him a major figure have come to grief. For example, the poet Conrad Aiken tried to make him the prototype of the American who shunned the settlements and pressed westward into the wilderness. The result was a bad poem. The fact must be faced: Blackstone did not start anything.

Roger Williams, by contrast, not only established a town but did much to create a colony. He recognized the commercial opportunities of Narragansett Bay and in his early trading ventures there gained the respect of the local Indian sachems, who later gave him land when he needed a place of refuge and at his behest gave more to others who had to leave Massachusetts or Plymouth for refusal to abandon their convictions. Thus he brought to the shores of the bay, people who, in spite of their many differences, ultimately banded together to preserve freedom from the religious regimentation imposed by law in the neighboring jurisdictions. He secured the first English grant of territory and authority for these people in the patent of 1644 issued by a parliamentary commission. He did more than any other man to establish a government under this document and to put it back together when it broke apart. Certainly he deserves his honor.

Vital though Williams' role was in founding Rhode Island, it was that of a broker between great patterns of events and special circumstances. The calculations of the sachems, who had their own reasons for welcoming settlers, together with the awesome religious storm known as Puritanism that swept people to New England and winnowed out the ones who fled to Narragansett Bay, put a distinctive population of spiritual extremists in the colony. English policy, for all its twists and turns, threw protection over them for a few crucial decades before it swung around to favor larger colonial jurisdictions. And always there was the propitious geographical setting that pulled the Rhode Island towns together and let them become a significant center of commerce in the Atlantic trading world of the colonial period.

In the beginning there was Narragansett Bay, a network of channels and coves formed as the glaciers retreated and the Atlantic washed into the deeper grooves in a landscape resembling a vast rough corduroy. Tireless waves softened the outlines with beaches and sand spits. Rivers and brooks carved valleys leading to the salt water. Elsewhere on the terrain, geological

debris left by the glaciers formed fanciful ornaments of hills and
ponds on top of the bedrock, itself a crazy quilt of ancient
formations.

In the middle of the mouth of the bay is Newport harbor. Near
the open ocean but sheltered from the winds and waves, enjoying
the safety of an island situation, with moderate tides and without
a river to create a bar across its entrance, this deep inlet was an
ideal basin for the sailing ships of the colonial period. The waters
of the bay provided easy communication between Newport and
lesser havens on the perimeter. Small seaworthy craft brought
Newport's wharves, urbanity, and cultural riches within the
range of a great part of nearby Massachusetts and Connecticut
as well. Larger vessels ventured upon the ocean to commercial
centers all around the Atlantic, exporting the products of
southeastern New England and bringing back goods to sell in the
territory served by Newport. The bay, then, was a setting that
drew together the people around it—or at any rate, drew them
together in an age when commerce was the source of great
wealth, and transportation by land was costly and slow.

The bay did not bring together the Indians who lived by it,
except to fight over possession in the century before the arrival of
the English. Things may have been peaceful among the forebears
of these natives, but little is known about their lives in the long
years before the first reported visit by Europeans.* This was the
expedition in 1524 under Giovanni da Verrazzano, an Italian
captain sailing under French sponsorship, who was financed
mainly by Italian businessmen in Lyons. He and his men spent
two weeks at Newport or exploring Narragansett Bay. They

---

* There is no reason to credit the romantic fantasies of Viking settlements. It
may be harmless to believe, as some do, in a vanished empire of Norse colonies
covering coastal New England, but the "evidence" for its existence is nothing
more than the faith of the believers. They persistently ignore the suspicious
sparsity of hard archeological remains and clutch at farfetched comparisons
with Scandinavian structures to convince themselves that the base of an old
windmill, built for the original Benedict Arnold in the seventeenth century, was
actually an old watchtower of a Norse community living on the site of Newport
three or four hundred years earlier. With one such monument to the fantasies
supposedly established, all sorts of oddly shaped rocks and modern trash turn
into "corroboration."

found two populous conglomerations of villages, the Wampanoags on the east and the Narragansetts on the west, locked in
rivalry over the islands in the bay and the coasts on either side.
The explorers' hosts were Wampanoags, who had recently seized
Aquidneck from the enemy, but the roving sailors encountered
no hostility from the defeated side. Verrazzano's praise of this
location inspired no further interest in France. Nobody reported
the news from Narragansett Bay for quite a while.

Exploration in this area by Europeans remained desultory at
best until the seventeenth century, and even then the voyagers
unearthed little information of historical value. The expedition of
the Dutchman, Adriaen Block, in 1614, for instance, resulted in a
rather good map but not much else except the application of his
name to an island. Some English captains managed to perpetrate
high-handed outrages on the native inhabitants of southern New
England which made them understandably distrustful of strange
foreigners. Ironically, some of the most offensive deeds of these
explorers, kidnaping Indians, were motivated by eagerness to
learn about the people in New England with a view toward
commerce with them. Under questioning the captives indeed
supplied information, although it did little to encourage trade;
the interrogators did not care to ask much about the fortunes of
the feuding tribes.

When the *Mayflower* passengers founded Plymouth in 1620
they unavoidably had to learn a great deal more about their new
neighbors than the explorers ever did. The Pilgrims established
their town in a place where a Wampanoag village had been
wiped out by a pestilence that swept the New England coast in
the winter of 1617–1618. The sole survivor, Squanto, had been a
captive across the sea for three years when the epidemic struck
and made his way back just after it had done its deadly work.
From him the immigrants learned that the Wampanoags had a
high sachem, Massasoit, or Ousamequin, as he was generally
known in early Rhode Island. Ousamequin welcomed the
newcomers as potential allies against the traditional enemy. His
people had been losing ground, but it cannot be said whether this
was due to the recent plague or earlier defeats in war. Though
Ousamequin and his successors kept their headquarters by

Narragansett Bay, they had only legalistic claims to the islands in it and the mainland on the west. The Pilgrims more or less fell in with Ousamequin's plans and presently found themselves regarded as foes by the Narragansetts, although the enmity did not lead to war.

The Plymouth settlers were fortunate to keep peace, because the Narragansetts were then a formidable people. They were the largest tribe in the region, perhaps a fifth of the Indian population of southern New England—they may have numbered as many as 5,000, three or four times the strength of the Wampanoags. Yet, hemmed in by aggressive neighbors, the Narragansetts occupied a fairly small territory, extending twenty miles or so west of their bay and fifty or sixty miles northward from the Atlantic Ocean. Thus they lived in a concentration as high as any north of the Aztec lands and the pueblos. Travelers reported them as fine physical specimens. Like most of the tribes of coastal New England they knew how to avoid the seasons of starvation that weakened some Indians farther north or inland. The Narragansetts, in addition to hunting and fishing, raised corn and a few other crops. They had devised ways to preserve and store food to assure a supply the year round.

They had an organization tight enough to make their numbers felt. The basic social unit was the village, of course, and at least as the English understood the situation each village had a leader. Above these local men or women, and receiving tribute from them, were the principal sachems, who were usually men. Legend traces the royal family that produced these chiefs into the sixteenth century, and perhaps earlier, to a great progenitor, Tashtassuck. Frequently two members of the dynasty ruled at once with one as the senior partner. It may be that the rise to preeminence of the house of Tashtassuck provided the organizational strength to turn back the Wampanoags. It is impossible to determine precisely what powers the principal sachems wielded, but they obviously had a strong hand in war and diplomacy, enforcing law, and assigning land. Some, perhaps all, of their powers were exercised with the advice and consent of a tribal council. Each village had its land, but the sachems could turn it over to English settlers, who then had to make provision for compensating the villagers.

Clearly in 1636 there was no sparsity of inhabitants near Narragansett Bay to lure European immigrants. Quite the opposite, the region had an uncommonly dense Indian population. So it is necessary to fathom the sachems' reasons for letting in newcomers. On the Wampanoag side the thinking is easy to deduce. Ousamequin first let Williams occupy the frontier against the rivals, then granted land that his tribe claimed but no longer controlled. It is harder to puzzle out the calculations of Miantonomi and Canonicus, the wise and canny leaders of the Narragansetts, who actually made room for the first four Rhode Island towns.

The Narragansett sachems quickly perceived the threat lurking in English colonization. They promptly showed their resentment when their hereditary enemy found an unforeseen ally in Plymouth. They became deeply alarmed when the Puritans began to pour in during the 1630s. Then it became necessary to define relations with the foreigners. Traditional Indian diplomacy failed; the outlanders did not know the protocol. Painfully, sometimes with the aid of Roger Williams, the Narragansetts reached a shaky understanding with Massachusetts. This was possible because both sides, for a few years, feared the Indians farther west, especially the Pequots and their cousins the Mohegans. The Puritans and Narragansetts in 1636 were maneuvering toward the agreement that allied them briefly in war against the Pequots the next year. Danger on the west made it useful for Canonicus and Miantonomi to improve their safety on the east.

Accordingly, when Roger Williams sought permission to occupy land at the head of the bay, the two sachems gave him a generous tract. He had previously won the confidence of Canonicus and Miantonomi (and Ousamequin too), probably during his trading expeditions to the bay a few years earlier. He learned their language, both to carry on business and to preach Christianity, and as a result became useful in diplomacy. Installed at Providence, he began to act as intermediary between

Massachusetts and the Narragansett sachems. He served both parties well, especially during the Pequot War, but afterwards could not stop the growth of convictions in Boston that the Narragansetts were ceaselessly plotting against the colonists. His honest efforts, however, earned the sachems' gratitude over and over.

Canonicus and Miantonomi rewarded Williams, most richly in the years when his services brought success, by giving land on their eastern borders to English settlers. Having given him the site of Providence, they gave Prudence Island to him and Governor John Winthrop of Massachusetts, perhaps in the hope of strengthening the ephemeral alliance. Then at Williams' prompting they gave Aquidneck to the followers of Anne Hutchinson and later still provided him with a place for a trading post on the west side of the bay. (Williams always gave lavish gifts to the sachems in return, probably in keeping with their customs, but he surely was correct in his claims that their esteem for him made them willing to grant the land.) By these donations the chiefs secured access to trade with the English and set up a barrier of Europeans against the Wampanoags. Within a few years the Narragansetts solidified the buffer zone by selling territory (claimed by the Wampanoags) to other newcomers who created settlements south of Providence. Thus it is quite realistic to think of the colony of Rhode Island as in part a product of Narragansett Indian policy.

More was needed, however, to make a single colony out of the frail string of settlements stationed between the rival tribes. Before commerce drew the towns together they were buffeted into federation by the mysterious workings of the religious revival called Puritanism. The first English Rhode Islanders were eccentric or ultraradical Puritans of bewildering diversity. They squabbled heatedly among themselves. There is much truth in the old New England quip that Rhode Island is where people think otherwise. At the outset the Rhode Islanders thought otherwise in so many ways as to make cooperation among them all but impossible. Their tiny communities and churches were constantly split over new doctrines. By and large their beliefs were equally horrifying to orthodox Puritans in the nearby colonies, who began foisting a unity on Rhode Island by defining it as a cesspool of heresy and treating it accordingly. The heretics learned that they could not shout each other down and followed Williams' lead in converting their zeal for untrammeled spiritual exploration into a policy on which they could unite: religious liberty for all.

In England the strange progress of the Puritan Revolution lifted to power men who, surprisingly, applauded the experiment in freedom near Narragansett Bay. To the dismay of Massachusetts, English officials granted a patent to the heretic towns in order to stymie the orthodox neighbors as much as to provide a basis for government in Rhode Island. Successive upheavals in London brought to office only men who protected the new colony, however feebly. (More surprising still, Charles II after the Restoration continued to protect the heretics; he had his own reasons to annoy Massachusetts.) Thus the Rhode Islanders, in the larger history of the Puritan movement, kept being herded together. Most of them learned to accept their fate.

Slowly acquiescence gave way to approval. The patent of 1644 that officially created a colony gratified Roger Williams and a number of other men who wanted to safeguard religious liberty and turn back a tide of disorder in their towns. It took them three years to persuade their fellow townsmen to join in forming a government, however, and it fell apart after two more. Negotiating reunion took even longer. The royal charter strengthened the government but not enough to stop some designing citizens from encouraging neighboring colonies to disregard Rhode Island and extend their jurisdictions to Narragansett Bay. The neighbors did so on several occasions, meeting little opposition from England. Gradually, enough Rhode Islanders began to rouse themselves to save their government. Zeal for keeping it increased when the ardor to preserve freedom of conscience was reinforced by a desire to keep the colony's land so that the insiders could get it rather than the outsiders.

A substantial devotion to independent government had appeared by the time English policy turned sharply against it. The monarchy of James II in 1686 reduced Rhode Island to the status of a county in the Dominion of New England ruled by a governor at Boston. Upon the overthrow of King James, a band of Rhode Island men took the risk of resurrecting the charter government without authorization from London. The gamble succeeded, but opposition persisted for several years at home and in the imperial capital. By the end of the seventeenth century, however, Rhode Island had the loyalty of the bulk of its citizens. The colony even got the left-handed backing of those who despised its government; instead of conniving to incorporate the territory in an adjoining jurisdiction, they fell to grumbling about the amateurish officials elected under the charter and their low social tone.

A true patriotism finally came to prevail in the early eighteenth century. It sprang up like a sea breeze as Newport's commerce at last began to thrive and the growing city, to serve its own interests, reshaped the government and economic life of the entire colony. The town's business, always seeking new ways to make money without increasing exports and never quite able to shake off the dominance of Boston, relied on a series of risky expedients that were made possible by Rhode Island's semi-autonomous position in the British empire. Newporters lived well, however, thanks to an abundance of energy, wits, vigilance, and sharp practices. With the town's success came the high society and culture that gave the colony a real capital, not just a secondary distribution point. Here was a new triumph but one with familiar traits. Like the older struggles to keep liberty of conscience, create internal order, preserve an independent government, and win the boundaries promised by the charter, achieving Newport's prosperity was an uphill battle against myriad adversities. The gains of one day could not be regarded as solid; they had to be won again the next. Other places might settle into assured positions and revere traditions or ancestors; Rhode Island, scrambling to stay on the map or cut a figure in trade, remembered its struggles and adversaries. The new loyalty, however, was not a bundle of grudges, nor a revised version of Williams' solemn dedication to a cause, but an irreverent pride in being independent, different, and constantly beating the odds.

This unifying exuberance seemed to be stifled when Providence challenged the supremacy of Newport and the colony broke into warring parties. Yet even amid the fiercest rivalry the contestants would subdue their political brawls to join in fighting the British government whenever it tried to encroach upon what they regarded as their charter privileges. A Providence clergyman dubbed the partisan strife, with its peculiar and quite minimal ground rules, "Rhode Islandism," but the term might stand as well for the distinctive ways of the colony, its brash pride, and its notorious tendency to assume that anything goes in dealings with outsiders. And just below the surface was a gleeful relish in the fast footwork, the daring, the stratagems that had kept the colony alive. When outsiders sanctimoniously denounced the place as Rogues' Island, insiders did not necessarily feel insulted.

Once the chief source of danger to independent self-government shifted from neighboring colonies in the seventeenth century to British imperial authorities in the eighteenth, Rhode Island was well versed in the tactics it needed. The menace of royal interference with charter privileges seemed trifling for a while. Then the international wars from 1739 to 1763 enticed the colony into closer relations with the monarchy and inevitably into obedience to imperial policies. Instead of relaxing with peace, London's wartime embrace surprisingly began tightening into a stranglehold; Rhode Island resisted stubbornly and brazenly. When the ministers of George III forced a showdown, the colony, soon joined by twelve others, cut the slender ties with the king and in a burst of enthusiasm hailed partnership in an indissoluble United States of America.

The war to defend the new nation against British plans to restore colonial governments kept Rhode Island constantly on the edge of the main engagements and soured its devotion to the federal union. Never the scene of crucial battles, never the focus of fighting at sea, the state suffered sporadic attacks, an intermittent blockade, and a long, if incomplete, occupation by British forces that Congress seldom thought important enough to combat. The ordeal of war frayed Rhode Island's attachment to the federal union, and the state finally reached the ultimate in autonomy in 1789, when its efforts to cure its own postwar ills cut

it off from the United States, which had been reorganized under
the new federal Constitution. Defiant disdain for this newly
strengthened neighbor could not last, but for a brief bittersweet
interval Rhode Island reached a complete, if bizarre, expression
of its independent spirit only to ratify the Constitution somewhat
reluctantly in 1790.

When Rhode Island joined the United States for the second
time it gave up some of its cherished independence and began
moving into an era when industry supplanted commerce as its
leading source of wealth. It kept the revered charter, however,
and remained New England's enclave of people who thought
otherwise. Its distinction of being the smallest state with the
longest name bore witness to its special past in two other ways. Its
size commemorated Rhode Island's success, unique among the
five clusters of English settlements south of Massachusetts, in
surviving as a separate jurisdiction. Three others were aggre-
gated into Connecticut in 1662, and Plymouth was merged with
Massachusetts in 1691. The heretic colony alone preserved
autonomy. The long name, the State of Rhode Island and
Providence Plantations, reflected the variety among the heretics
—and by mentioning only two elements scarcely did justice to
the original diversity. Forming these headstrong people into a
colony and keeping its separate government required decades of
struggle that often seemed to be unavailing. Roger Williams may
be honored as the principal founder of the colony and its leading
architect and builder for many years, but others furnished the
site and materials. The first visible results appeared in 1636, but
construction went on for years under new guidance after
Williams' death. There was a long way to go when English
people first began setting up towns around Narragansett Bay and
finding reasons to join them in a federation.

2

COMMUNITIES OF OUTCASTS

The four original towns of Rhode Island—Providence, Portsmouth, Newport, and Warwick—came into existence during the decade beginning in 1636. They were all founded so that their inhabitants would not have to live with other people. The first settlers of Providence and Portsmouth were banished from Massachusetts, or went with those who were expelled, because they would not abandon or keep silent about beliefs that were causing turmoil in the Puritan communities. The exiles, it turned out, disagreed among themselves and sought peace (with only moderate success) by founding two more towns. Obviously, the first Rhode Islanders were not easygoing people.

On the contrary, they were as resolute and uncompromising as any of the Puritans who fled the hostile policies of Charles I to create a New England. Though Puritanism was primarily a vast upsurge in piety, a yearning to know God and do his will on earth, and so ostensibly indifferent to its surroundings, it actually sought to reform the world in which it flourished. It aimed at restoring religious discipline in human lives, which had grown lax under ministers who devoted themselves to climbing the hierarchical ladder to richer or less onerous positions, while turning nothing more than a sad smile on the straying sheep in their flocks and ignoring the great numbers who neglected worship altogether. The Puritan standard of discipline was strict, condemning frivolities and time-wasting that most people thought innocent or trifling. Because the bulk of the clergy in the Church of England, led by the archbishop, preferred to fight

Puritanism rather than ungodly living—King James, who was the Supreme Governor of the Church, positively encouraged desecration of the Sabbath with sports—Puritans concluded that the episcopal hierarchy was innately corrupt. It was a carry-over from popery and would have to be overthrown before the right sort of discipline could be extended over the whole population.

The concept of a godly discipline was suffused by a passion among Puritans, distinguishing them from most reformers on the continent of Europe, to strip religion down to what they thought essential: prayer, the struggle to understand God's will and creation, a few simple ceremonies, and a life of useful work. Contentment in the world was abomination. Reliance on beauty in worship was an abhorrent distraction from the inner workings of devotion and the study of doctrine and theology. There could be no compromise, no tolerance for allowing those with little aptitude to shirk the intellectual effort and rely on pious feelings aroused by inspiring architecture, statuary, paintings, music, incense, lavish vestments of the clergy, pageantry, or even rhetorical pyrotechnics in sermons. The passion in its early vigor condemned paganism wherever a Puritan detected it, whether in the names of days and months, the celebration of Christmas, or the solemnizing of marriage by clergymen. The arts, like weddings, might be good in themselves if kept in their proper role in secular life. So with sex, liquor, games, gold, or luxuries—all good as part of God's creation and good for mankind when rightly enjoyed. Rigorous religious discipline would strive to hold all things in their proper places.

While there was a core of agreement in the Puritan movement, especially on what needed correction, many different points of view kept developing on how to proceed, and so the emigrants to Massachusetts included people with a variety of hopes for the reformation of church and society. They agreed more on what they opposed than on what they favored. The process of giving shape and order to the institutions of church and state and of defining religious orthodoxy was a process that repeatedly left behind embittered dissidents with strong opinions. Moreover, the spiritual fervor characteristic of Puritanism constantly propelled some of the most devout to excesses condemned as heretical by the rest—toward beliefs in the possibility of total purification of the church or of individual conduct, the hope of casting aside human authority and accepting only divine rule, or even of receiving direct revelations from God, which proper Puritans believed had ended with completion of the Bible.

Dealing with dissidents and extremists figured heavily in the early history of Massachusetts. Detecting such people was easy to do because they ardently advanced their views. As a result they created commotions that seemed to jeopardize the welfare of the colony, and so should be stopped. The authorities in Boston insisted that they respected liberty of conscience and only prosecuted threats to the public peace or stubborn refusal to abandon dangerous errors when they had been exposed. In the high tide of Puritan excitement, however, unorthodox opinions usually created turmoil, so liberty of conscience was for those with acceptable convictions or unusually close mouths. As orthodoxy became well defined, religious freedom in Massachusetts was increasingly a freedom to conform or get out. Some would not willingly do either and were expelled.

Roger Williams was the first prominent exile. This brilliant and versatile man had been born in 1603 or thereabouts into the family of a London merchant of modest fortune. After his father's death he became the protégé of Sir Edward Coke, the notable champion of the common law, who arranged for continuation of Williams' education, ultimately completed in Pembroke Hall of Cambridge University. His views began to shift toward Puritanism, so he accepted no public pastorate but took service as chaplain to an aristocratic family for a year until he departed for New England, arriving in 1631. For five years he labored in trade, in the field, and also in the pulpit, when a congregation would take him on his own terms. The terms were hard, because he was already developing extreme beliefs on how to purify a church, and on other topics, too.

For five years he generated controversy in Plymouth and even more in Massachusetts, from which he was banished. The reasons for his expulsion have been debated ever since and probably cannot be determined so well as to end the discussion, because no one today can know all of his side of the controversy from his own words. He wrote about his views at the time, but crucial documents have disappeared. What survives are a few statements by him, some statements by his opponents of what they thought he believed, and the pamphlet battle he carried on with the Boston minister, John Cotton, several years later. By that time Williams had modified his position, and circumstances had changed so as to make both writers dwell almost exclusively on the question of religious freedom.

Events leading to the banishment were rather more complicated. Williams did not seek simply freedom to believe what he chose; rather, he wanted to persuade everyone in the colony to espouse new religious duties. Beginning shortly after his arrival, he propounded inflammatory opinions from time to time. He insisted that the Puritan churches in Massachusetts should resoundingly repudiate the Church of England, although the prevailing theory held that in New England the immigrants were showing how to redeem it by creating truly reformed congregations within the fold. He opposed using governmental power to enforce the first four of the Ten Commandments except when breaches threatened the civil peace. This view was held in principle by many other Puritan ministers, but he insisted on a thoroughgoing implementation of it while others were willing to endorse laws to punish blasphemy or to require attendance at worship and paying taxes to support churches.

Williams attacked cherished customs in his fervor to guard pious practices from profanation. He thought joining in church fellowship and all acts of worship, in which he included taking oaths to enter public office or give testimony in court, should be done only by those who had experienced the stirrings of saving faith—that is, had grounds for thinking they were by God's choice predestined for heaven. It followed that traditional churches, where everyone in the parish attended services, should be abolished in favor of gatherings of the supposed elect. It also followed that traditional family devotions should be ended, if only because small children could not know whether they were elect or not. And further it followed that traditional use of oaths in government should be abolished.

Williams held that the Massachusetts Bay Company and its

settlers had sinned in accepting a royal charter that used some impious phrases and purported to give title to land that actually belonged to the native inhabitants. He claimed that the Puritan immigrants could expiate their sin only by getting a revised charter or by returning to England and denouncing their wrongdoing in accepting the original one.

Puritans had rejoiced in a reputation for exacting scruples and a passion for cleansing the churches of Christ from worldly contamination, but Williams outdid the rest. In general his aim was theirs, so they were highly susceptible to arguments like his on particulars. He was not contentious by disposition, but his fervent sincerity drove him to argue his views, and his extraordinary capacity to love his fellow man made him all the more convincing.

Between 1631 and 1635 Williams was a center of controversy in Boston, Salem, Plymouth, and then Salem again. When he finally accepted a call to the ministry at Salem, where he persuaded the church to repudiate the Church of England, he put himself in a position where he could carry on his campaign in ways that forced a showdown. When he was summoned by the Massachusetts legislature to answer for his alarming opinions, the other ministers met and decided that his views justified his removal from the pulpit. In the face of pressure from the clergy and the magistrates, Williams was almost invulnerable, because everyone endorsed the independence of the churches, but he could not prevent the legislature from refusing a grant of land to the town of Salem while hinting that the decision might be reversed if a new minister replaced Williams. Indignant, the church authorized him to send letters to the other churches in the colony, asking them to reprimand the legislators; but the letters went to the ministers, who did not even report them to church meetings.

Williams then asked his church to repudiate the others for renouncing the principle of congregational autonomy and conniving with the government to subdue it. The majority of the church would not go that far, and Williams was once again hailed before meetings of the legislature and the other ministers to answer charges that he denied the legislature's authority in ecclesiastical matters and that his recent letters had been seditious. Of course he had vigorously denied the legislature's authority and written the offending letters, and he defended himself steadfastly. He had a good case: leaders of Massachusetts had originally proclaimed the freedom of the churches from governmental control and upheld church autonomy, although they were watering down their views by 1635; the legislature had been guilty of an underhanded attack on the church of Salem. Yet for refusing to admit fault or abandon his beliefs that threatened turmoil in the colony, Williams was sentenced to banishment.

The intention was to send him back to England, especially after it became known that he thought of settling south of the border near Narragansett Bay, where he could be a fountain of sedition. Before he could be sent overseas he fled secretly, prompted by new moves by the Massachusetts officials and a tip from Governor John Winthrop. Strangely, the two men held each other in high esteem, however much they disagreed— strange, because Williams in this period of his life was constantly driven by his convictions, no matter where they propelled him, while Winthrop characteristically had a sense of how far one could go with principles in a world of imperfect human beings.

The fugitive struggled through the wintry wilderness to take refuge with the Wampanoags, whose sachem provided him with land on the east bank of the Seekonk River. There Williams was soon joined by a few other men, one of them banished also and most of them from the Salem church. They began clearing land and planting fields, but Governor Edward Winslow of the Plymouth Colony heard about it and sent a message protesting that they were in his jurisdiction, which would cause ill will between his colony and Massachusetts. He insisted that the refugees "remove but over the river," where they would be as free as the Plymouth colonists, and then they could all live as "loving neighbors together." Williams obtained Ousamequin's consent to the exchange and received land rights from the Narragansett sachems who actually controlled the disputed territory before he led his tiny community across the river to establish Providence.

According to legend the removal began when Williams and a

Compass and sundial owned by Roger Williams. *The Rhode Island Historical Society.*

couple of companions embarked in a canoe on the east bank of
the Seekonk and paddled across, where several Narragansetts
watched from a slate rock that lay next to the water. Williams
called out, "What cheer, netop," the common English greeting in
the pronunciation of the time sounding reasonably like the
Indian salutation, "Watcheamo," while "netop" was Narragansett for "friend." The voyagers proceeded south without landing,
however, rounded the tip of the long ridge that constitutes the
east side of modern Providence, and paddled north to arrive at
their destination, the sweet spring that flowed at the foot of the
west side of the ridge.

During the next four years the new town grew to a population
of around one hundred and took the pattern of settlement that
persisted for almost a century. Most of the houses, shortly
connected by the Town Street, were built along the foot of this
ridge to the east of the "Providence River," the short passage
between the head of Narragansett Bay and a cove (long since
filled in) where the Moshassuck and Woonasquatucket rivers
reached salt water. Stretching up the side of the hill were lots for
gardens and orchards. Across the crest of the hill a tract was
cleared, fenced, and cultivated as a common field for many years.
Around the cove were marshes in which grasses grew that could
be made into hay for the livestock. In the cove were patches of
reeds used for thatching roofs. A short distance to the north the
Moshassuck River rushed down through a small valley where
dams could be built to harness water power to turn the essential
grist mills and sawmills. Increasing population slowly led to
house lots on the west side of the cove, but for many years the
most significant location of residences away from Town Street
was the cluster near the Pawtuxet River, just above its arrival at
the bay. Chronically the home of headstrong men, this hamlet
sought but did not achieve separation until the creation of
Cranston in 1754.

Almost as soon as Roger Williams had been banished, a new
dispute began to brew in Boston, one that would soon drive a
larger number of people to seek refuge near him. This was the
event known as the Antinomian Controversy, which swirled
around Anne Marbury Hutchinson, a brilliant, magnetic,

strong-willed woman. The term Antinomian, meaning "against law," was applied to her by her opponents who accused her of teaching that those singled out for salvation by God need not worry about failing to lead moral lives. She taught no such thing, but her enemies insisted that her ideas logically led to that conclusion. The daughter of a stiff-necked upright Anglican minister who was no Puritan, she married a man who generally has been supposed rather spineless, although little is known about him except that he advanced the family standing through success as a merchant before his wife prevailed upon him to emigrate to Massachusetts. This she did because John Cotton, the Puritan minister who had brought solace and inspiration to her, was forced to flee from old to new Boston. The Hutchinsons followed.

Cotton touched off something of a religious revival in his new church. As the excitement mounted, Anne Hutchinson held meetings, attended by a growing number of people, where she explained his sermons. Trouble grew out of his reaction to theological tendencies he found prevalent in Massachusetts. Cotton insisted on the standard Puritan or Calvinist doctrine of salvation in all its force and simplicity: God under the Christian dispensation or covenant has chosen to give grace (won by Christ) to a predetermined assortment of human beings; as they discover it in their lives (the conversion experience), these people know the saving faith that it enables them to have; salvation is the reward of faith alone; nothing anyone can do will obtain it or forfeit grace. The simple doctrine of predestination had a logical tendency to imply, especially to people not in a state of religious excitation, that there was no point in trying very hard to be virtuous. To overcome this implication, Cotton found, his brother ministers were advising their flocks to practice prayer and holy living in order to cultivate a preparedness for the discovery of grace and to look for a decline of sinfulness as one of the signs that they had undergone a genuine conversion experience. The ministers carefully steered clear of saying that human effort could win grace. They preached that the whole race was innately corrupt and unable to do anything meritorious by God's reckoning. Still, they came close to saying that people could help themselves toward salvation. Cotton inspired new fervor by his reassertion of orthodoxy, but Anne Hutchinson carried his emphasis to dangerous extremes.

She quite logically insisted that if free grace and the inward sense of it were all that mattered, the slightest reliance on preparedness and efforts to avoid sin tended to put faith on man's merits instead of Christ's. Those who failed to perceive this were returning to reliance on good works, which all right-minded Puritans regarded as a defection either to Catholicism or the heresy of the Dutch Protestant theologian, Arminius. As popularized, her judgment was that the Massachusetts ministers (except Cotton and her husband's brother-in-law, John Wheelwright) were preaching under a "covenant of works." Actually, as became clear later, she asserted that they preached the true "covenant of grace," but not as clearly as Cotton, because they were like the apostles before Christ's ascension. That is, they had not been touched by the Pentecostal fire, the power of the Holy Ghost. She did not say that a minister should preach only as the spirit moved him, but she implied something like that. Standard Puritanism held that a minister must be one of the saved and have a proper university education for his profession, but like everyone else he was to rely on the Bible as the only revealed Word of God. At the time Hutchinson was understood to deny that the ministers of the "covenant of works" had felt the inward power of grace, a serious accusation indeed.

Contrary to what was alleged against her, however, she did not denounce ministers for preaching the force of moral law, including the obligation to obey civil law. She in fact regarded the moral law as eternally binding, because it was decreed by God, even though obedience or disobedience to it would not affect anyone's chance of getting to heaven. Nevertheless, she was accused of denying the binding quality of law on those with grace, and hence her enemies branded her an Antinomian, one against law.

Hutchinson and her disciples made a partisan attack on the other side as they defined it. Although over half of the Antinomians were Bostonians, they visited different towns to question the ministers and expose their failings before their congregations. The controversy became political, dividing officials of the colonial government into opposing sides. Further damage was portended when some Hutchinsonians refused to serve as soldiers against the Pequots, because the chaplain was their leading opponent.

The other side struck back. In a series of preliminary moves, prominent Antinomians were maneuvered into taking open stands; their backer, Governor Henry Vane, was defeated for reelection in 1637; a few important men were disfranchised or banished; and the ministers defined a long list of errors held by Anne Hutchinson or likely to proceed as corollaries from what she held. Then the government moved against Hutchinson herself.

The trial technically was on fairly minor charges—that she traduced the ministers (except Cotton and Wheelwright), held improper meetings, and encouraged those who had signed a petition defending Wheelwright after a sermon by him had been declared seditious. Throughout the proceedings, however, wider questions were introduced about disrupting social harmony and teaching heresy. Hutchinson adroitly defended herself. The dramatic climax came when she suddenly admitted that she distinguished between ministers like Cotton and the rest by divine revelation. She went on to tell how she had been directed by God to follow Cotton to Boston, where she would suffer, but would be delivered as Daniel had been from the lion's den. Proper Puritans believed there had been no direct communication with God since the Book of Revelations, however ardently they yearned for it. In a mixture of horror at her claim and glee at her admission of what had long been suspected, the court let her speak on the subject as long as she would. Cotton tried to repair the damage by drawing out some vital distinctions: pointing out that the revelations had been in the tolerable form of verses of Scripture prompted divinely in her memory, he proposed that the deliverance she expected was probably thought of as coming also in an acceptable form, the providential—i.e., through operations of the usual natural processes—rather than

miraculous. But she had used the words, "an immediate revelation," and when questioned had explained that she meant, "By
the voice of . . . [God's] own spirit to my soul."

If she believed that she received knowledge that way, she was
an abomination in the eyes of proper Puritans. Holding that
immediate revelation was impossible, they concluded that anyone claiming it was accepting whim, insane imaginings, or the
prompting of Satan. Experience had shown, moreover, that belief
in direct divine communication led to wicked acts. In the
shocking case of the German Anabaptists of Muenster, a case
that all other Protestants took as the conclusive proof, the final
result was slaughter of their enemies under the delusion that God
commanded it.

After deliberations on a few more subjects, the court banished
Anne Hutchinson. The punishment was harsh for the deeds she
had been accused of, but not for her heresy as she disclosed it. Yet
she was not before the court on charges of heresy. Nobody could
say that the trial had proven wrongdoing on her part, let alone
criminal acts, so she asked, "I desire to know wherefore I am
banished?" Governor Winthrop dodged the legal point by
replying, "Say no more; the court knows wherefore and is
satisfied."

Following the trial the Massachusetts authorities took action
against many other Antinomians. Some were disfranchised; more
were disarmed, presumably to prevent them from rebellion or
vindictive actions against the triumphant opposition; a few were
banished. Anne Hutchinson, after remaining in custody for a few
months, was tried for heresy by her Boston church. After
exploring many topics, on some of which she had been thinking
out new ideas since sentenced to banishment, she was excommunicated as much for pride as for any precisely definable
heresy. The record of this event reveals a variety of accusations,
including a repeated allegation that her concept of grace would
lead to unbridled sexual promiscuity. Some errors she denied
ever holding, others she professed to renounce. Her repentance
was deemed hypocritical, however, and some of her denials were
deemed outright lies. There was a strong suspicion that she
secretly harbored heresies that had not been brought to light.

Without specifying which errors were the grounds for the action, or the weight assigned to her suspected lies and pride, the church excommunicated her in March 1638.

As the full-scale attack on the Antinomians proceeded, they had to decide what to do. Many made peace with the authorities and deserted Hutchinson. Some followed Wheelwright to New Hampshire. But a much larger group, over eighty men and their families, went to Rhode Island. The organizers, William Coddington, William Aspinwall, and John Coggeshall, drew up a compact forming a body politic, signed at Coddington's house on March 7, and with Roger Williams' help obtained the island of Aquidneck (or Rhode Island) from the Narragansetts. They began moving almost at once, building a town called Pocasset, later renamed Portsmouth, near the north end of the island. Aspinwall shortly made peace with Massachusetts and returned, but others kept joining the new settlement.

Coddington soon became the leader of the group, though not unchallenged. Unique among the founders of Rhode Island, he had been a high official in Massachusetts, serving as magistrate and treasurer of that colony when no older than Roger Williams; Coddington was a man of consequence. His family, though it aspired as he did to standing in the landed gentry, had been in commerce. Beyond his self-importance, the trait that reaches across time from the few documents revealing anything about his ideas or personality was a deep desire for mystical communication with God. Perhaps stirred by John Cotton, this aspiration became a counterweight to his pretensions—in the end, as a Quaker, he looked back to a time, perhaps badly remembered, when he and other Puritans had shared a profoundly affecting sense of the radiation of divine power on their lives. Nevertheless, he always regarded himself, with some justification, as socially superior to anyone else in Rhode Island, although his occupation there was not so much the country squire he yearned to be as the rather frustrated merchant he actually was.

The Antinomian refugees included men with a variety of occupations. There were craftsmen, farmers, servants, and seafarers among them, as well as an innkeeper and a physician. Still, the most conspicuous element was the group of merchants. They brought wealth, far greater than there was in Providence, and ambitions to found a center of commerce. The community at Portsmouth took shape, however, as an agricultural one, with a common field or pasture at the north end of the island just beyond the cluster of houses. Allocation of land, and soon the placement of dwellings, spread around the coast, drawn by the need for water transportation. Apart from lingering preference for living in a compact village, only the ferry to the mainland and the original common field preserved a geographical focal point.

Many of these people, surprisingly, manifested no unusual religious zeal. They behaved like ordinary hard-working Puritans in Massachusetts. A sizable number, however, continued the restless quest for novelty launched by Anne Hutchinson. Free to go their ways, they tried out still more of the excesses Puritanism was prone to. A few began to favor preaching under the direct impulsion of the Holy Spirit. Some proceeded to true Antinomianism, regarding all the acts of a regenerate Christian as controlled by God, and therefore not to be judged accurately by mere human concepts of morality or legality. John Winthrop back in Boston kept hearing about new errors coming up like weeds in Portsmouth, probably more than actually were there, and recorded them solemnly in his diary.

The squabbles over these doctrines, added to the ambition for commerce, and perhaps personal conflicts long forgotten, resulted in the division of the community with Coddington leading the way to found Newport. The obvious appeal of the harbor, curiously neglected when settlement began, drew the merchants and many of the city-oriented artisans. All the same, the apportionment of land provided many farms of middling size and gave the leading men enormous estates which they generally put in the hands of tenants for development. The best-known of these properties was Richard Harding's, which was named Hammersmith Farm; it later passed into the hands of William Brenton. The new town from the start had its center around the brook running into the harbor, with buildings slowly extending south by the water's edge and northeast inland. The first settlers gave themselves allotments of various sizes, but each man's grant

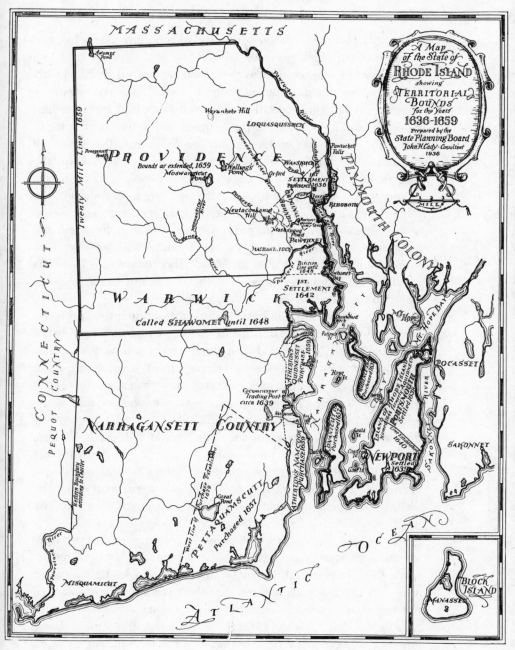

A Map
of the State of
RHODE ISLAND
showing
TERRITORIAL
BOUNDS
for the years
1636-1659
Prepared by the
State Planning Board
John H Cady · Consultant
1936

MASSACHUSETTS

CONNECTICUT

PEQUOT COUNTRY

PLYMOUTH COLONY

PROVIDENCE

Bounds as extended, 1659
Moswansicut
Pond

1st
SETTLEMENT
PROVIDENCE 1636

REHOBOTH

Pawtucket
Falls

WARWICK

Called SHAWOMET until 1648

Division
Line until
1648

1st
SETTLEMENT
1642

NARRAGANSETT COUNTRY

Cocumcussoe
Trading Post
circa 1639

ATHERTONS NARCOOK PURCHASE 1659

PETTAQUAMSCUTT
Purchased 1657

NEWPORT
settled
1639

PORTSMOUTH
Settled
1640

POCASSET

SAKONNET

MISQUAMICUT

ATLANTIC OCEAN

Twenty Mile Line 1659

Wayunkeke Hill

LOQUASQUSSUCK

BLOCK
ISLAND

MANASSES
3

The Rhode Island Historical Society.

ordinarily included a house lot by the harbor, a meadow lot, and a much larger tract of arable land.

Among the Portsmouth settlers there appeared Samuel Gorton, who had been expelled from Plymouth for stirring up a commotion with his doctrines. Massachusetts had to catch him before it could get a turn to prosecute him. He had been born in the same level of London society as Williams, the realm of substantial storekeepers; upon emigration he settled in the Pilgrim town, where he began drawing away part of the congregation into a separate meeting. When driven out, he joined the Antinomians, where he brewed up more controversy. It has always been hard to pin down his beliefs, mainly because his published writings attacked his enemies without declaring more than a few of his own ideas, but also because his followers regarded his teachings as esoteric knowledge not to be disclosed freely to the non-initiate.

Gorton called himself simply and grandiloquently "professor of the mysteries of Christ," but he was regarded as a Familist, a forgotten term that once chilled the blood of ordinary Puritans, because it meant someone who believed in mystical communion with the Holy Spirit in such measure as to transform the entire life of the believer, even so much as to make possible a life without sin. Strictly speaking the label did not apply; Gorton was not among the followers of the Dutch mystic, Henrik Niclaes, who called themselves the Family of Love, a movement that spread to England, where it was driven underground after 1578. However, if Familist meant only a broad agreement with the distinctive beliefs of Niclaes, then Gorton roughly deserved the label.

Yet he followed nobody: he created his own sect, and it barely survived his death, so greatly did it depend on his personality. Little of that personality can be discerned across the centuries, although there are clear signs that the man was warm-hearted, hot-tempered, energetic, irrepressibly cocksure and jaunty, pugnacious, endowed with a scathing humor and political horse sense, capable of attracting passionate disciples, and yet a person manifesting the greatest tenderness toward his friends and neighbors and given to spending hours in meditation and religious ecstasy. Loathed and detested by many in his day, he inspires a different feeling in modern times: virtually everyone who tries to learn about him finds out little but nevertheless becomes fond of him.

Gorton was an ultra-Puritan so far from the center as to oppose most of what passed for Puritanism. He was against all formality or ceremony in worship, against the sacraments, against territorial parishes, compulsory attendance at church, taxes to support religion, and against a college-educated clergy. He believed ministers were appointed by God and preached only under the immediate impulsion of the Holy Spirit. They might profit from knowing the Bible in the original languages, to get closer to the meaning of the texts, but should disdain all theological systems. Any human interpretation of Holy Writ was bound to be limited by circumstances of the times or the mind of the interpreter, while the spirit of God speaking in the Word remains ever the same and "is a thing too sublime to be congealed into ink, too secret to be printed upon paper, too precious to be piled up in libraries, and of too prince-like a spirit to enter into contract with, or be subservient unto any school of humane learning." God's ministers accepted no pay and were responsible to no organized church.

Indeed, any human contrivance or authority in religion was wrong. The pious should get together as they pleased to pray and await outpourings of the Spirit. All might voice the messages of the Spirit, men and women alike (Gorton was emphatic on equality of the sexes), though the divinely selected ministers were those most frequently favored. If religion was rightly under God's direction, a holy order would prevail and the spiritual needs of everyone would be satisfied from the infinite divine source. Though Gorton believed in predestination, he opposed Massachusetts Puritans by insisting that the ministry was for all mankind and that God's unity and covenant were with the whole human race, resulting in "the law of God written in man's heart in the act of creation," which made the path of virtue both knowable and mandatory for all.

It may have followed—Gorton's words sometimes led that way—that secular government was evil and unnecessary. The

Massachusetts Puritans took him to believe that, and he baited them saucily by tracing the authority of their government, in terms that could apply to all governments, to human will, which he said meant Satan in the final analysis. He also insisted, however, that civil government in New England could derive its authority only from England and that the common law was the birthright of every Englishman. In practice, then, he stopped well short of advocating the Christian anarchy that he often seemed to favor.

No one can say just how many of these ideas he spread in Portsmouth. He probably encouraged the Antinomian tendency toward religion based on direct communion with the Holy Spirit, which was taking the form of "prophesying" by anyone who felt called upon to speak. He also quarreled with the people in Newport who were opposed to this kind of thing, as well as with Coddington, who could have been antagonized either by Gorton's attacks on human authority, his defense of the common law against attempts to substitute scriptural law, or merely his personality. At any rate, the quarrels became violent, and Gorton was finally whipped and banished from Portsmouth. Followed by several new disciples, he headed for Providence. There again he got into disputes and made converts. Williams regarded him with deep misgivings. The episode came to a climax over enforcement of laws, suggesting once more that Gorton's views on civil government led to trouble. The Gortonists ultimately sought the sensible solution of founding their own community.

After failing to get peace by moving to Pawtuxet, just beyond the southwest edge of town, Gorton and his friends in 1643 bought a huge tract from the Narragansett sachems, the Mishawomet or Shawomet Purchase, running twenty miles west from the bay south of Providence. They no sooner began building houses and clearing fields around Warwick Cove than their recent quarrels with the Pawtuxet neighbors returned in a new form. Some of these enemies arranged to put themselves under the government of Massachusetts, obtained commissions as peace officers and tried to hail the Gortonians into court. Then the local Indians in the villages led by Pomham and Socononoco protested the Shawomet Purchase and in turn sought Boston's protection to get a hearing for their grievances. When these moves drew nothing but scornful replies from the Gortonians, Massachusetts sent a force of forty men to capture the alleged offenders and carry them off to trials for contempt of authority, resisting arrest, and uttering blasphemy.

Several were released or given light punishment or bound to servitude, but Gorton and six others, narrowly escaping death sentences, were put in irons and distributed around Massachusetts to perform hard labor. They proved more dangerous than tractable, scouting the doctrines they heard in sermons and the government that forced them to listen. The Boston authorities, seeing nothing ahead but a plague of Familist heresies, banished the Gortonists in the spring of 1644, forbidding them to return to Pawtuxet or Shawomet, which Massachusetts then claimed. So the returning men took their families to Aquidneck. Although Roger Williams soon brought an English patent embracing his town, plus Portsmouth, Newport, and the Gortonists' territory in a single new colonial jurisdiction, Massachusetts produced a rival patent and, along with Plymouth, sent armed forces against the Narragansetts. Gorton and two of his disciples hurried off to London to secure from the mother country explicit assurances of protection, with which one of them, Randall Holden, returned in 1646. (Gorton stayed a few years more to fight the anticipated complaints from Boston and to associate happily with like-minded Englishmen.) With the encouragement Holden brought, the Gortonians finally began the permanent occupation of their lands around Warwick Cove.

The little town there grew slowly, requiring two or three decades to reach fifty families. The house lots at the head of the Cove made a town center. Newcomers who did not acquire a stake in the Shawomet Purchase lived on the west side on the edge of a large tract, the Four Mile Common, set aside to absorb such people. Warwick Neck to the east of the Cove was for the purchasers and their successors. There they created common fields and pastures, taking advantage of the many geographical

features that facilitated fencing out predators and closing in
livestock, and set about providing themselves with the necessities
of life.

Nearby remained the villages of Pomham and Socononoco.
Though the Gortonists tried to live at peace with these neighbors,
and Gorton himself inspired awe among them as he roamed
through the woods communing with the divinity, a rash of
incidents forestalled harmony. Livestock got into the Indians'
crops, Indians killed stray cattle, Englishmen cheated Indians in
trade. Occasionally there were fights, and once Englishmen even
robbed a native grave. Between Pomham's people on Warwick
Neck and the Narragansett village to the west of Four Mile
Common, the Gortonians felt hemmed in.

With the founding of Warwick, the original Rhode Island
towns had been launched. The outcasts had founded communities, but they were beset by many troubles. Religious disputes
continued, though the main ones had been resolved by with-
drawal to new locations. It remained to be seen whether the
heretics around the bay would ruin themselves in disorder, as
their enemies predicted, or would achieve the peace their
inhabitants wanted.

3

THINGS OF THE SPIRIT

After all the excitement over religion that had produced the communities around Narragansett Bay, one would expect the settlers to have been more energetic in setting up churches than surviving evidence reveals they were. To be sure, more was done than was recorded. People in each new town gathered for worship. They organized churches, perhaps in a few places drawing up "covenants" declaring basic doctrines and the rudiments of church government. However, they did not preserve these documents, if there were any, or any others worth mentioning. Keeping archives simply did not concern them.

Rather they wanted the living reality of devotion, exaltation of the soul, and Christian fellowship. Some held that the ministry, if properly carried out, spoke the message of the Holy Spirit to those gathered at a given place and time and so would be priceless to those who heard it, but not worth preserving because it would be irrelevant or unnecessary for any later occasion. The churches as institutions, furthermore, were somewhat fragile; they were constantly rent by disagreements as the settlers, away from the constraints of Massachusetts, kept discovering new ideas. Some native groups slowly attained stability during the seventeenth century, but the most remarkable success in ecclesiastical organization came when Quaker missionaries inspired the creation of a firm structure for those most prone to disarray, the believers in direct inspiration from the Holy Spirit.

Between the beginnings and the achievement of stability there was a period of effervescence, when many were prospecting the outer fringes of Puritanism. They found gold—or dross, depending on whose view is believed. They enjoyed a few years of excited intercourse with like-minded people in England during the Puritan Revolution but then returned to the status of weird sectaries in a remote corner of the New World corresponding only with equally obscure denizens in the shadow of the official Church of England. In the aftermath of this exhilarating interlude Rhode Island found its own world of discourse. Torn between the thirst for "openings" of the Holy Spirit and determination to follow the Bible down to the last tittle, religion in the colony found its own dynamic. Before things settled down, however, there were many years of wandering and ferment.

In Providence, the followers of Roger Williams organized to put into practice the ultimate purification of the church that their leader had been advocating. Only those with reasonable hope of salvation should be included; there should be no compulsory attendance or other governmental support. In fact, the purity of the church could be ensured only by ending the traditional effort to use religion to unify and discipline the whole community. Soon the worshippers in Providence became convinced that they had found another error to uproot: baptism should be for the putative elect only, which ruled out infants, whose spiritual fate was unknown. They resolved to start afresh, with rebaptism for the members. Williams, who did most of the preaching, went along with this new turn of events, to the horror of his old friend John Winthrop, but soon struck out on another new path. He left the Providence Baptists to uneducated ministers and new quarrels over ceremonial practices, especially the practice of laying on of hands, which they carried on in a zeal to find the absolutely correct interpretation of the Bible. Many if not most of the neighbors lost touch with organized religion.

Williams' new ideas were more radical than ever. He questioned the organization of a church that proposed to exert discipline over the members, unless it had a delegation of power from Christ or his apostles. Believing that the chain of succession of apostolic authority had been broken by the errors of the papacy centuries earlier, he concluded that no real church could be set up until God arranged a new delegation of power. He

drifted out of church fellowship and embraced startlingly tolerant views: though he denounced the gods and ceremonies of the
Narragansetts, he regarded their religion as suitable to them and
no worse than bogus forms of Christianity, which meant
practically all that existed. Accordingly, he foreswore his earlier
zeal for converting the natives of North America and his earlier
finickiness over joining in devotions with the unconverted. At
length he was willing to preach to anybody who would listen at
his trading post near Wickford and to pray with anybody. He
became a Seeker, one who tried to live a humble and pious life
while waiting for God to sponsor a fresh start for the Christian
church.

The Antinomians started without a clear desire to keep
religion apart from the secular community. Portsmouth voted to
build a meetinghouse, although it never carried out the plan.
Presumably the settlers met for worship but did not form a
church. Quite possibly they hoped to attract John Wheelwright
as their minister; if so, they were disappointed. He remained in
New Hampshire and gravitated back toward Massachusetts
orthodoxy. Without a minister to stabilize a creed, religious
beliefs in Portsmouth were free to proliferate. Anne Hutchinson,
surprisingly, lacked determination or skill to create an organization and even began to lose religious leadership. Gorton probably
stole the limelight by claiming to preach by immediate inspiration of the Holy Spirit, and presently others took up this form of
"prophesying." The town became a hotbed of new doctrines.
When the Newport founders departed in 1639 there was nothing
left but a formless weekly gathering to hear these witnesses of the
Spirit.

There was no force to bring together a solid fellowship. After
Gorton was driven out in 1641 there was less variety, but little
remained of the concerted zeal that had created Portsmouth.
The next year William Hutchinson died, and the year after that,
perhaps baffled by the disintegration of her religious movement,
his widow moved to the Dutch colony of New Netherland, where
she and all but one of her family were slaughtered by Indians.
Today a quiet river and a hectic highway in Westchester County
incongruously commemorate the last refuge of the first great

woman of English America. The tragedy of her life, perhaps, was her inability to build where there was nothing to tear down. Yet the judgment should be rendered tentatively. She emboldened many to grasp the psychological comfort of confidence in their predestination for heaven, to throw off the self-restraint of Calvinistic Puritanism and claim the possibility of direct communion with God that they thirsted for, but they may have been unwilling to accept the guidance of a woman in the creation of a church and community, where they needed her leadership even more. When the commanding figures had left the scene, the Portsmouth Antinomians continued their informal worship, with an occasional tour of duty by an uneducated Baptist minister, until Quakerism arrived and attracted many people twenty years later.

Those who departed for Newport included the people with firmer hopes for organized religion and more conventional ideas about its place in the community. They obtained the services of Robert Lenthall, a properly educated Puritan minister lately in the pulpit at Weymouth, Massachusetts. He may have leaned toward Antinomianism. In any event, he preached and taught school in Newport only a few years before returning to England. There was no proper successor until the physician John Clarke began taking the lead in what soon became a Baptist church. In Newport, too, controversies over ceremony broke out among the Baptists, and a group appeared that counted on immediate inspiration to supply "prophesying." After some uncertainty, several of the leading citizens settled for this religion of the Holy Spirit and advanced to views that made them ready converts to Quakerism. Without fanfare, Newport had abandoned the ways of Massachusetts by giving up the ideal of making town and congregation a unity served by a minister to teach the young and admonish the adult.

Once the Gortonians were in a town by themselves, the result was an elaborate irony. They ceased to stir up contention, which was remarkable in itself. They also had what functioned as a town church, although on principle they resolutely organized no congregation, exerted no ecclesiastical discipline, and rejected any sort of partnership between religion and the secular commu-

nity. Gorton taught them that he was the mere instrument
whereby the Holy Spirit spoke to them and that any number of
others might play the same role, yet his personality proved in the
end the sole source of unity. After he died there were no
successors and the flock drifted toward the Baptists or Quakers. A
few forlorn Gortonists could be found for another century, but
they lived on the memory of the leader and could not say what
he had preached except that it bespoke such a luminous
understanding of God as to pass beyond human comprehension.
In 1771, the last Gortonite, John Angell of Providence, showed a
visitor three books by the long-gone master and said they were
"written in heaven, and no man could read and understand
them unless he was in heaven." This man venerated Gorton as
constantly full of tears and so holy that it could be said that
"indeed he lived in heaven." When memory of his power faded,
his sect vanished.

Small wonder that ordinary Puritans in Massachusetts regarded Rhode Island as a cesspool of vile heresies and irreligion.
Within a short time all the towns had adopted religious liberty as
the only practical policy, leaving zealots to wrangle over
doctrines and ceremonies, with all contenders far beyond the
limits of respectability as reckoned in the neighboring colonies.
People proposed ideas that denied the significance of good
conduct for God's elect, denied predestination, denied the
possibility of organizing a church, and denied the authority of
ministers and magistrates. Nobody defended infant baptism, the
use of religion to benefit human society, the value of a university
education for ministers, or the wisdom of confining political
rights to the godly. Some even denounced war as unchristian,
and so many thought it sinful to take oaths to serve in public
office or give testimony in court that the colony from the outset
never required them—this in an age when conscientious refusal
to take oaths by Quakers elsewhere was enough to create a
political furor. Worse, a substantial number of Rhode Islanders
believed in immediate revelation from God. Almost as bad, a
great number neglected religion completely, and the whole lot
was probably sliding into ignorance and illiteracy.

In this compendium of depravity, the outsider could see sure signs of approaching chaos, and certainly there were ominous discords. But the scandalous points on which people in the Rhode Island towns agreed—religious liberty, disconnection of secular authority from religious support, disuse of oaths and infant baptism, opposition to a traditional clergy—gave both a general policy on which they might unite in a single colony and a distinctive tone. They disputed questions of their own, not ones posed by Massachusetts any longer.

For a brief interlude this little world of ultra-Puritans enjoyed open and profitable intercourse with important outsiders. One way or another the Rhode Islanders had arrived at points of view like those of many small sects in England. The Puritan Revolution gave these sects a chance to grow and multiply, to challenge traditions maintained by ordinary Puritans, and the Rhode Islanders quickly got in touch with like-minded people in the mother country. Roger Williams, Samuel Gorton, and John Clarke, fresh from the wilderness, moved easily into the company of the sectaries and the patrons of religious freedom among the great, such as John Milton and the Earl of Warwick. If these colonials wrote with a view to gaining official favor for their towns in political matters, they spoke to major questions of the day in the mother country—liberty of conscience, the nature of the true Christian church and ministry, the function of government. They entered the lists of controversy against formidable opponents, as though they belonged there. Gorton ministered to a sympathetic sect for some time; Clarke took an English pulpit for many years. The colonial pariahs thus gained a sort of respectability and shared the solicitude shown to the radical English sects by some of the more liberal Puritans who came to power under the Long Parliament, notably Sir Henry Vane, the erstwhile Antinomian governor of Massachusetts.

This agreeable situation did not last. Cromwell curbed some of the wilder sects, and then the summer days of radical Puritans and ultra-Puritans in England came to a decisive end with the Restoration of Charles II in 1660. The last flare-up, the little uprising of the Fifth Monarchy Men proclaiming King Jesus the true monarch, hastened the repression. (William Aspinwall, one of the original Antinomians, was a sympathizer though not implicated in the event.) Once again the Rhode Islanders were quaint sectarians cut off from the main currents of life in the mother country, and Clarke, after great success as the colony's agent, left London to resume preaching in Newport.

By that time Quakerism, the last significant product of the Puritan movement, had spread into the colony. In 1656 Massachusetts banished Nicholas Upsall, a convert who presently took refuge in Aquidneck, to be followed at intervals by various others who voluntarily sought freer air. The English missionaries who arrived the next year found converts almost waiting for them. When the first persecutions began in Massachusetts, Gorton recognizing kindred spirits, wrote to the suffering Friends offering a refuge in Warwick. He, like the Antinomians, agreed with the Quakers' reliance on the divinely implanted Light Within. He also saw them as essentially in agreement with him on the ministry and the repudiation of sacraments and ceremonies. Ultimately, however, he found points of disagreement that ruled out his affiliation with the Quakers. The former Hutchinsonians, at least those who had taken to "prophesying," and even more those who had begun to repudiate oaths and war, needed little persuasion that the Quaker message was as it claimed to be, the ultimate Truth. They lacked a dominant figure like Gorton to hold their fidelity to another fellowship. Many, if not most, of the dwellers in the populous towns of Aquidneck quickly became Friends. Some of the principal men at Newport, such as William Coddington and Nicholas Easton, embraced the new religion. Mary Dyer, who had gone with her husband to England, became a convert and minister there, returning to Rhode Island in 1658. Soon there was no other sort of public worship in Portsmouth.

The inauguration of Quaker worship was soon followed by organization of the distinctive style of Quaker meetings for the conduct of church business. Probably in a simple form at first, there may have been a monthly meeting on Aquidneck by 1660 and a yearly meeting soon after. The yearly meeting was a gathering that Quakers from all parts of New England might attend to hear each other's "openings" from the Holy Spirit and to deliberate on matters of good order and sound principles among themselves. There were several such meetings in the region, but the one at Newport in June quickly became the one at which ecclesiastical business was transacted, leaving the others simply for worship and fellowship.

After a visit by George Fox, the founder of Quakerism, in 1672 the Aquidneck Friends adopted more and more of the institutional practices worked out in England. They created an amazingly intricate ecclesiastical structure in which many took part, although it was mainly conducted by an inner core of stalwarts. There were officers to keep watch over the members, to prevent their sliding into wickedness, if possible, or if not, to urge repentance. Ultimately the yearly meeting issued an elaborate code of conduct to be observed. Other officers kept meeting-houses and graveyards in good order or managed endowments. Ministers were "recognized" when it became clear that God had chosen to entrust them often with savory words at meetings for worship. Efforts were made to encourage educating children. Throughout the year there were special committees to handle a great variety of church business, from ascertaining eligibility for marriage to providing for the Quaker poor or petitioning a government. At Fox's behest, record-keeping began on a large scale. From the voluminous documents which resulted we can see a complex system for regulating the life of the Friends, a system that required great amounts of time to operate but which could create a nearly self-governing community of Quakers. Quakerism thus provided many times over the institutional solidarity the Antinomians had so obviously lacked. The strength of the fellowship was proven by some schisms over obscure disagreements late in the seventeenth century. After prolonged labor, these differences were almost perfectly reconciled.

The new Friends did not withdraw into a private world, however, except to maintain security and discipline in their lives. Quakers gave each other preference in trade, but they freely dealt with outsiders in business and public affairs. So many Friends occupied high offices that historians, uncritically believing some accusations made at the time, have written of their "controlling" Rhode Island by 1670 or of a Quaker party capturing the government a couple of years later. There was no such party, however, although there may have been something of a religious block vote. Quaker officials as far as one can tell, felt scrupulously bound to act for the whole colony and injected their special principles, such as pacifism, into public affairs in no doctrinaire fashion. They rejected the use of oaths and the expensive pageantry of government normal in the seventeenth century, but these were hardly controversial matters in Rhode Island. At most they may be accused of a disposition to seek compromise and subdue conflicts on a few occasions when firmness might have been prudent, but they never wavered on protecting religious freedom.

Quakerism gathered most of the Rhode Islanders who inclined toward mystical Christianity, as contrasted with those who rejected all thought of direct communion with God and sought religious truth by striving for the most exact reading of the Bible. Christians taking the mystical path expected revelation beyond Scripture and counted on the Holy Spirit to provide ministry and even daily guidance for all believers. Outside the Quaker fold there remained the Gortonians, basically a cult around a magnetic leader, plus those who disagreed with Friends by maintaining the doctrine of predestination and by disdaining elaborate ecclesiastical organization, and people who cherished the Protestant sacraments of baptism and the Lord's Supper. The Baptists who relished "prophesying" sometimes organized ephemeral churches of their own and sometimes remained among congregations with a predominant emphasis on living according to the Bible.

The biblical literalists, in general, were at the opposite pole from the mystics, but there were many intermediate positions. The Biblicists believed that Holy Writ completed divine revelation; their goal was to restore religious life to the condition of the early Christians. Consequently, they searched the Book of Acts and the Epistles in the New Testament relentlessly to find direction for religious fellowship. Eschewing the encrustations of interpretation left on these writings by centuries of theological discussion, they read Scripture in a direct and unsophisticated way. Because they agreed with the observation that infant baptism was not mentioned in Holy Writ, they rejected the practice, but accepted the reading of certain hazy texts to mean that Jesus endorsed baptism of adult believers by total immersion. So by and large the Biblicists in seventeenth-century Rhode Island were Baptists.

The Baptists, however, readily fell into disagreement over many other points. Sooner or later they divided over such things as the lawfulness of war and oaths, the ceremony of foot washing, the need to sing psalms as part of worship, and the degree of tolerance to be observed toward those on the other side of these issues. The first point to produce schisms was the laying on of hands. Reading Hebrews 6:2, some Baptists concluded that every believer before admission to full communion should go through a ceremony in which the pastor or some other brother placed his hands on the head of the initiate and spoke some appropriate words to signify the power of the Holy Ghost being extended over the new member of the church. The practice appealed most strongly, but not exclusively, to those who counted on the Holy Spirit to supply ministry and regulation to the flock, but the controversy was over what Scripture prescribed. In Providence the majority, including Gregory Dexter and William Wickenden, agreed to the need for laying on of hands, so the minority withdrew in about 1652 to form a separate church under Thomas Olney that lasted almost seventy years. A similar schism occurred a few years later in Newport, where the minority that separated to form the Second Baptist Church under William Vaughan, an obscure worthy who may have been an Oxford man, was convinced of the need for laying on of hands, while the majority thought it optional and remained under the pastoral care and preaching of Obadiah Holmes, Joseph Torrey, and John Clarke.

Because the advocates of laying on of hands insisted on six basic points of faith and practice—the others being repentance, faith, believer baptism, resurrection of the dead, and the Last Judgment—they became known as Six Principle Baptists. Ordinarily they rejected the doctrine of predestination and instead believed that anyone might be saved, although not all would, and that a believer might fall from faith and so forfeit salvation. This view was called a doctrine of general redemption, so its advocates were also called General Baptists. Thus they were distinguished from Calvinist or predestinarian Baptists, who were also termed Five Principle Baptists because they adhered to the five essential points of Calvinism, including predestination, as defined at the Synod of Dort in 1619.

The Baptists were further divided by controversy over a point raised by an English immigrant, Stephen Mumford, who arrived in 1664. Mumford argued that the seventh day of the week, not the first, still should be consecrated as the Sabbath. Hence those who agreed with him became known as Seventh Day Baptists or Sabbatarian Baptists. His most important converts were William Hiscox, who became a venerated pastor, and a carpenter named Samuel Hubbard, who had moved to Newport in 1648 to enjoy religious liberty. The Sabbatarians tried to remain in the First Baptist Church, but Holmes and Torrey finally provoked a showdown in 1671. The disputes concerned the significance of the Old Testament law and the Ten Commandments in the Christian dispensation. The Sabbatarians insisted that one could not discard part of the fourth commandment without denying all ten; the other side maintained that ignoring the Christian reshaping of the Hebrew tradition amounted to a return to Judaism. John Clarke attempted to reconcile the opposing sides, trying to persuade the Sabbatarians that a distinction should be drawn between the Jewish moral and ceremonial law, with the moral eternally binding, while the ceremonial was to be replaced by Christian improvements. His efforts led only to controversy among his own side. Holmes flatly said the Sabbatarians were deserting Christ for Moses and told them, "You are deluded and ought to be made sensible of it." Hiscox protested, "Must we be forced to walk by your legs and see by your eyes?" Acrimony mounted, and the Sabbatarians, as they saw it, withdrew to form a new church; as the other side saw it, they were "not of us" and had to be regarded as out of church fellowship.

The Seventh Day Baptists, through Hubbard's numerous relatives, spread to Westerly, where they were the only people maintaining Christian worship for many years. They even made converts in adjoining Connecticut.* They all tried to remain in

---

* Most of these converts were members of the Rogers family of New London, who separated into a tiny but durable sect of their own, known as Rogerenes.

one fellowship, experimenting with novelties in organization, such as holding general meetings every eight weeks alternately at Newport and Westerly, until the impracticalities became too great and they divided into two churches. Though manifesting such solidarity among themselves, they continued to think of their communion as remaining within a loose association of Baptists of all varieties.

This sentiment was not always reciprocated, but it made some sense. The different varieties shared a number of tenets in the face of general opposition by outsiders. They insisted on baptism by immersion for believers, and believers only. They ordained pastors (or elders) but opposed a paid or a learned ministry. They opened the pulpit to as many brethren as proved to have a gift for preaching. They practiced the same sort of church discipline. They opened membership only to those who claimed to be believers as a result of a conversion experience, whether they thought of this category as determined by predestination or simply by repentance. In addition, in their devotion to Scripture as the infallible guide to faith and practice, they kept worrying over the same doubtful points and shared a feeling, arising from the confidence that all these points could be settled, that any mistake might be fatal and so all were equally important. In this common attitude, of course, lurked the determination to insist on any controverted topic to the point of shattering a church.

If the idea is not pushed too far, it is helpful to see the two broad types of religion that developed in seventeenth-century Rhode Island, biblicist and mystical, as stemming respectively from Roger Williams and Anne Hutchinson. From Williams came the determination to purify the church, bringing it into conformity with the divine intent as learned from the revealed Word of God, forever completed in the Bible. From Hutchinson came the exciting hope that the Holy Spirit continued to inspire mortals and would supply direction to the devout in their daily

---

They opposed public prayer, but became better known for their insistence on faith healing, going so far as to excommunicate one man who went to a doctor after his foot had been run over by a cart. The Seventh Day Baptists, more than the Six Principle Baptists, had a marked propensity for experimenting with faith healing.

life as well as in their churches. Both these leaders departed from
the fellowships they launched, leaving their followers to settle
their own affairs. Loss of leadership surely resulted in accentua-
tion of certain traits—a drift toward the humdrum and the
narrow-minded among those who repudiated divine inspiration,
a drift toward spiritual anarchy among the Antinomians until
curbed by the personal force of Gorton and the ecclesiastical
heavy machinery of the Quakers.

Most of the time no one said or wrote much about the tension
between the two sides. It may well have aroused passions that
spilled over into political disputes, where one may catch glimpses
of it in the sneers of Olney against Wickenden or the antagonism
in Newport. It came into the open on one memorable occasion—
the debate between Roger Williams and three Quaker missionaries in August 1672. Quite possibly he undertook this confronta-
tion because it could be with outsiders; previously he had
avoided expressing his abhorrence of mysticism and had labored
to encourage neighborly feelings within the colony.

Williams sent a written challenge to George Fox, who left
Newport before receiving it, but John Stubbs, John Burnet, and
William Edmundson agreed to debate Williams' fourteen points.
The result was exasperation and ridicule for the elderly founder
of Providence, who could not make the Quakers stick with
rational argument. They would launch into exhortations as they
felt moved by the spirit or break into his chain of reasoning when
offended by what he said. The Friends and some of the Baptists
in the audience would taunt him with being an "old man" and
audibly approve his opponents. To be sure, his points were
framed in the antagonistic manner that was normal for theological debate in the Reformation period, and he set out to
demonstrate that Quakerism was a fraud and abomination, not
merely a mistake.

Still, the very style of his opponents must have proved, at least
to Williams' satisfaction, that the Friends were adrift from the
anchor of religion, the careful reasoning from the Bible, and were
in their ignorant enthusiasm a prey to their own imaginings.
Williams maintained that they made the Word of God mean
whatever they liked and pretended that without it they could

gain by direct revelation all that was in it and more besides. Thus, they set human whim above divine truth. They could not talk sense about Jesus Christ, his crucifixion, and resurrection, because they talked also of a Christ within that was both a Second Coming and a constantly repeated crucifixion. They fancied they could be free of sin, as though they were not real human beings. They belittled sin by treating it as something that could almost be shrugged off, and so belittled God and made of Christ's crucifixion a silly farce. They undermined the order of society by contemptuous behavior toward superiors and rude behavior toward equals. Williams largely voiced a reaction to the Friends that any ordinary Puritan would applaud—and many did—but he added his own special denunciation of Quaker presumption in setting up churches without a visible, tangible, new authorization from Christ. And besides, he was not standing as the champion of ordinary Puritans. Rather, he spoke mainly for Rhode Island Biblicists, adding what was in effect a warning to them of the consequences of forgetting the tradition of rational interpretation of Scripture. The record reveals no effect of his admonition or his strictures on Quakerism, which flourished the more mightily after 1672.

Even if it is reasonable to think of two primary forms of religion in early Rhode Island, it would be a mistake to overestimate the clarity of the distinctions between them. There were many Baptists who agreed with Quakers on ministry guided by the Holy Spirit and on the moral evil of war. Church discipline was practiced in similar fashion by the various communions. If most Baptists were slower to admit and quicker to expel members and the Quakers by contrast prone to embrace people without drawing sharp lines between an inner circle and the rest, the Sabbatarian Baptists stood somewhere in between. The mystical element read the Bible in much the same way as the Biblicist and expected to draw from it the pattern for the church as well as an index to the validity of latter-day inspiration. In a larger sense, moreover, the religious groups of the colony were alike in their differences from traditional Christianity. They rejected the heritage of ceremony, learning, and hierarchy. They went well beyond the ordinary Puritan horror of using beauty or magnificence to evoke piety. Following what they believed was scriptural precedent, the Rhode Island Christians did not even sing Psalms and they met in fields or private dwellings. Before the end of the seventeenth century, they erected only a few meager buildings: a few small Quaker meetinghouses, a Baptist meetinghouse, and dressing rooms for baptismal ceremonies. They all allowed women to participate in church affairs to an unprecedented extent—the Baptists letting both sexes vote in church meetings, the Gortonians insisting that they and God recognized no distinction between the sexes, and the Quakers welcoming some women as ministers and all as full members of meetings for ecclesiastical business until they set up meetings for women alone. The churches around Narragansett Bay were thus much of one mind on many points in their departures from tradition.

The departures were not purely radical, however. After the early years, the burdens of the Christian heritage of learning and elaborate organization of ecclesiastical authority no longer had to be thrown off because the Rhode Island settlers had left them behind. Solemnity and magnificence in the church were no longer appealing either to mirror and sustain the majesty of the state or to counterbalance it. Secular authority struggled along on a modest scale and so did religious. Neither could afford more grandeur. The Rhode Island Christians adjusted their churches to their lives. They ended up with simplicity, plainness, home-grown preachers, detachment from power and the trappings of power—altogether a modest do-it-yourself style of religion suitable for straightforward people in a society where all worked hard and even the wealthiest were people of modest means by Old World standards.

4

THE SECULAR ORDER

People dwelling in the early Rhode Island towns, regardless of their part in the development of the Puritan movement, nevertheless devoted far more effort to things of the flesh than of the spirit. They had to obtain the necessities of life no matter what else had to be postponed. Moreover, they did not consider bare existence to be sufficient. Roger Williams expressed a fear, common in seventeenth-century America, that a hard-won civilization would be lost in the wilderness. The descendants of rude Britons of yore, civilized by God's mercy, "were now come into a wild and savage country, without manners, without courtesy, so that generally, except you begin with a 'what cheer' or some other salutation, you had as good meet an horse or a cow." There had to be ways to keep what he called "civility," the panoply of cultural refinements, social order, morality, and laws —the elements that raised people above the level of barbarians.

Civility came high: even Bibles had to be imported. To pay for it, there had to be production of marketable wares and channels of trade to export them. There had to be government to make and enforce laws, and so there had to be taxes and politics. To enjoy commerce and government, it soon became clear, there had to be a definite place in the English system of colonial administration and law. Though nobody wrote about the intended social order, everybody probably assumed that there would eventually be specializations of occupation and gradations of rank and wealth. Luckily, it was not vital that all these things be achieved with equal success or all at once.

At the outset, a few essentials were uppermost in the settlers' minds, and they set out to found communities where each family could provide most of its own wants. Each town was located near a source of fresh water to drink and a harbor of salt water to keep a sea road to the outside world. Nearly all the families cleared fields, raised crops, set out orchards, and kept livestock. They produced their own food, the fibers of flax and wool for the basic clothing and bedding, leather for shoes and harnesses, and lye and fats for soap. Houses, wharves, and ships had to be constructed. Building materials were reasonably plentiful: trees for boards and beams and shingles, trees for pitch, clay for making bricks and stuffing chinks, stones for foundations and chimneys, a little limerock for mortar, and rushes for thatch roofs. The houses needed beds, chairs, tables, chests, crockery, pans, candles, buckets, and many other utensils. The settlers could produce almost all of what they used, although they had to apply a great deal of labor and use at least the rudiments of a great many skills to convert raw materials into what they wanted and needed. There were only a few obviously specialized occupations, those of the men who set up and operated sawmills and grist mills. Each town needed these facilities and arranged to put the necessary water power sites into the hands of those who could use them.

There was no desire to attain self-sufficiency by accepting the primitive style of life that local resources could sustain. On the contrary, it was assumed that from these towns traffic would extend into a wide world of commerce, bringing in many of the accustomed appurtenances of life. Glass windows and iron tools, for instance, were not to be forgotten—nor paper, books, gin, fine cloths, spices and ammunition, to say nothing of cordage and sails for ships.

The overriding problem was finding products to ship out in exchange. Roger Williams led the way in buying furs from the Narragansetts, but the swamps and forests west of the bay did not shelter enough animals to make the business profitable for many men or for very long. From the outset the traders knew that they could win a ready market for the domesticated species. Accordingly, the settlers began raising flocks of all sorts on the islands and on the peninsulas, which could be made almost as safe from predators. Shippers exported live cattle and horses as well as barrels of pickled beef and pork. Soon they were sending out boards and timber, some garden produce, cheese and butter, a little flour, and even tobacco. They learned from pioneer Massachusetts merchants where to find markets: nearby coastal towns, the Newfoundland fishing fleet, and the Caribbean. Traders around the bay, however, generally got imports from the Old World by way of Boston, and so they resentfully saw a great share of their profits flow into pockets of wholesalers to the north. The main avenues of Rhode Island commerce were set for over a century within fifteen years of the founding of Providence. If the Newfoundland trade lost importance, it was replaced by commerce along Long Island Sound to New York and trade with the Carolina colonies as they developed.

Though trade was early recognized as essential to the welfare of the colony, it did not yield the profits during the seventeenth century to raise up any stellar merchant princes. Rhode Island was still too small a base for great fortunes. A few Antinomians who arrived with ample capital did very well, especially if they combined raising with exporting livestock, but from the start rivalry for business curbed the gains of all who entered the field. A surprising number of the first settlers became traders at least part-time—half a dozen in Providence, fewer in Warwick and Portsmouth, a substantial cluster in Newport—and many more dabbled in small ventures. Others tied their lives to commerce by fitting out or commanding vessels that carried the goods. In the welter of striving a few men garnered moderate wealth, notably William Brenton, Richard Smith, and various members of the clans of Hutchinson, Coddington, and Arnold.

These local merchants faced sharp competitors, in spite of feeble attempts to exclude them by law. Enterprising men from Massachusetts, Plymouth, and Connecticut sought to do business in the Rhode Island towns or among the nearby Indians. Dutchmen based on Manhattan entered the bay also, some actually residing for long periods in the English towns and conducting enough commerce with New Amsterdam to lure several Rhode Islanders into taking their trade there, too. Dutch fishing expeditions showed that another commodity for export lurked below the waves, although the catch never approached what was taken off Nova Scotia. The Rhode Islanders held their own and repaid the outsiders by pushing into the neighboring colonies, but the success was hard won and never secure. Fortunately, making a living and establishing commercial connections did not depend heavily on governmental support or guidance.

Governmental control did matter, however, for the agricultural towns. The infant communities confidently parceled out land and set up common fields and pastures, steps that were easy to take and at first provoked no opposition. Just as confidently, but with less success they set up regulations for agricultural villages—methods to get the men together to clear and plant the common fields, rules on fencing land, branding livestock, putting rings in the noses of swine to keep them from rooting up crops, and so forth. Regardless of regulations, however, some men would not do their parts, others stole cattle, and unringed pigs got into gardens. When such things happened it became necessary to enforce the rules.

By what right did a town compel a man to work, punish a thief, or assess fines and damages on the owners of wayward hogs? Who was to determine the truth or falsity of charges made by one man against another? These were questions the settlers had not needed to ponder before leaving England, where public authority was taken for granted, whether its legitimacy came from local custom or the crown. In the beginning the Rhode Island towns had no ancient usages and no grant of powers from the king, so they had only such authority as the townsmen agreed to say they had.

It followed that disgruntled persons could easily withdraw from an earlier agreement, quarrel with the terms, or deny on principle that such an agreement could create genuine authority. They seldom repudiated the whole sweep of town action, for that was not natural for seventeenth-century Englishmen, who accepted as matter of fact the age-old self-regulation of agricultural villages throughout the mother country. Rather, malcontents characteristically denounced only the town's arrogation of judicial powers. They insisted that the judges who levied fines and ordered the seizure of property or the jailing of men, acted without real authority. The power to take life, liberty, and property in England came from the king, not the village, and was exercised by judges who were gentlemen or aristocrats of a ruling class sanctioned by countless years. When no such men were on the scene, there was no automatic substitute for them.

The Antinomians tried to avoid trouble by forming an agreement before they began setting up their town. Like the Plymouth Pilgrims who drew up the Mayflower Compact and the founders of some of the Connecticut towns, the Hutchinsonians relied on the power of men to form what amounted to a social contract to create society, supposing that when the body politic had been conceived it could proceed at once to self-regulation. In the Puritan understanding government was necessary, and upright men would willingly submit to just laws as part of practicing virtue. Divine standards of justice were eternally valid, so all that was needed, in theory, was the consent of every man to form a body politic, which could then determine by majority vote how to make and enforce applications of basic principles of right.

Coddington and his colleagues, however, did more and less than they acknowledged when they organized their community. Though they agreed in their compact to be a body politic under the kingship of Christ and to abide by the laws found in the Bible, they chose Coddington to rule as judge, an omnicompetent chieftain in the style of the ancient Hebrew officers given that title, while their town meeting quickly began smuggling in the legal procedures and concepts of England. Altogether, it was quite a mixture. Moreover, leaders of the new settlement adopted social gradations that had no place in the theory of the social compact. Instead of all adults, or even all men, being parties to the covenant, only the inner circle of men signed and obtained political rights as freemen in the new town government. Others were admitted as mere inhabitants. The apportionment of land favored the freemen. Coddington's position, one cannot help thinking, also reflected social and economic rank. As the richest man and the only one of the permanent settlers who had held office elsewhere as a magistrate, he was as near the traditional image of the English gentleman as could be found and so deserved the job of wielding power.

The new town government quickly proved unstable. The freemen chose elders to assist the judge but required all these officers to report their doings quarterly to the town meeting for review. The town's decision to hedge the judge's power alluded to the possibility of using subtler scriptural interpretation or divine revelation to set the officials straight. Conflicts soon built up over land and the teachings of Samuel Gorton, upon which Coddington, the elders, and a few of the freemen framed a new compact and left to found Newport.

Portsmouth had to reorganize. The remaining freemen chose William Hutchinson (Anne's husband) as judge and scrapped divine law in favor of English, but this solution was undermined when the inhabitants organized what may have been a rival town meeting and tried to obtain a fairer share of land. The freemen then came to terms with Coddington and a number of the inhabitants of Portsmouth. Coddington went over to English law, proclaimed subordination to King Charles I (who probably never heard about it) and erected a government over the two towns. When this was done the Portsmouth freemen received land benefits and their new friends among the inhabitants became freemen and received land. Briefly the new system promoted order, the more so after Gorton defied Coddington and was expelled and after William Hutchinson died and his family moved to New Netherland.

The island commonwealth or state acted energetically for almost three years and then weakened, keeping only its judicial functions in vigor. Though this government professed allegiance to the king of England, it proclaimed more loudly that it was "a democracy or popular government," explaining that this was true because "it is in the power of the body of freemen orderly assembled or major part of them to make . . . just laws by which they will be regulated" and to choose their officials. By way of adding tone to the new regime the freemen voted to uphold religious liberty and adopted the soap-opera motto, *Amor vincet omnia* (love conquers all). They also chose a long slate of officials, including some with power to parcel out land in each town,

though this attempt to suppress the uppity inhabitants quickly
failed. More effective were the governor and two assistants from
each town. These five, in addition to other duties, served
individually as justices of the peace and collectively as the bench
of the island's high court. This form of government resembled
more than any other the one used in Plymouth a few years
earlier, yet the Aquidneck men set a pattern of their own that
was later adopted and gradually reshaped into the government of
Rhode Island.

The island commonwealth was no pure democracy, to be sure,
not even as close to one as the colony later became. With
Coddington and a few others chronically in the powerful
positions the government in fact operated rather like an oligar-
chy. The proportion of men with the vote, while impossible to
calculate exactly, was probably close to half, a level that was
high for the time but no prodigy of egalitarianism. Moreover, the
freemen backed the wealthy coterie in power and let slip the
popular control of legislation while continuing to honor the rich
men as judges.

Providence did not begin with a written compact. Williams
and his first companions reached some sort of understanding to
regulate their affairs in general meetings of male heads of
households. With a shrewder sense of history than Coddington's,
Roger Williams relied on what he thought were laws of human
society more than on facile theories of consent. Families were the
natural social units, so should be the building blocks of a
community. If the community had no indubitable source of
superior authority—no biblical law or immediate revelation or
authority by rank for Williams—then the householders should
act as equals. About all they could do was agree to make
decisions by majority vote. If they needed to judge a dispute, they
could resort to arbitration, because that method had been
acceptable in all civil societies known to the founder of Providence, and so must be in harmony with principles of justice
common to all mankind. Unfortunately, he could think of no
means to enforce rules on a stubborn violater except an attack by
the rest of the householders. Moreover, human experience
provided no way for single men to be integrated into a polity

based on family units. Apart from theoretical puzzles there were practical ones of rivalry over land rights and political ones of dealings with the Indians and admission of new settlers.

Williams began tackling these problems in 1638 by means rather like a social contract. He set aside some land for the original settlers, the Pawtuxet reservation, in order to lessen their reluctance to admit later refugees from persecution. After that the town required newcomers, whether married men or single, to promise obedience to town rules before they could take up residence, vote, or obtain a share of the community's remaining land. In 1640 the system was refined into the Combination, a compact to be signed by all who wanted a voice in town meeting. (A couple of women signed, but it is unlikely that they got the vote.) Once again Gorton supplied one of the conflicts that tested the arrangements, yet after he had left there were other quarrels that left Providence in an incurably discordant state for years. Some of the men in the town despaired of forming a solid government on the power of consent. They dreamed of a governor appointed by the king or put themselves under the authority of Massachusetts, which had a royal charter.

The Gortonists, when they founded Warwick, profited from what had gone on in the earlier towns. They confined themselves to the rudiments of setting up an agricultural village and said they would have no real government until they got a delegation of authority from the mother country. The practicality of this procedure was not tested, because the community was scattered by the Massachusetts invasion and not reestablished until the delegation of authority had been made.

In different ways the settlers of Providence, Portsmouth, Newport, and Warwick came to the conclusion that sound government could not be built with materials available among themselves. Authority based on biblical law, divine inspiration, superior rank, consent, and universal principles of justice abstracted from the annals of nations—all had proved insufficient. There remained the possibility of deriving legitimacy from an acknowledged sovereign state, the kingdom of Great Britain, and in different ways the four communities fell back on that method. The island towns resorted to English law in routine legislation and litigation, while their collective government proclaimed its subordination to the king. Gorton flatly denied that there could be government without powers derived from the king or law unless adapted from the common law. Ultimately Roger Williams too concluded, as had some of his neighbors earlier, that the troubles of Providence would have to be overcome by attaching its government to England's.

As it turned out the towns after some traumatic years gathered under a shelter of authority granted by the mother country. Agreeing to do so took a long time and by no means cured all of their ills, at least during the seventeenth century. Whatever they wanted, the towns were told by London to join as local units under a central colonial government of their own. This plan was implied in the patent of 1644, which was authorized by Parliament during the English Civil War, and specified by the royal charter of 1663.

A colonial government paramount over the towns, however, did not suit Rhode Island in all respects. Such a regime conceivably could solve the most vexatious problem of the early years, establishment of a judiciary with powers derived from above rather than from the townsfolk themselves. Under both documents the Rhode Islanders took great pains to create such an arm of government, but kept weakening it by allowing towns to set up their own courts or by contesting the rulings of the colony's tribunal. The town governments, for all their turbulence, each in its own way developed basic institutions, staked out large fields of operations, and wanted from a central government backing with an aura of superior authority rather than new rules for all to follow. Moreover, many of the citizens, as radical in politics as in religion, tried to bring into use daring ideas about the exercise of the body politic.

Apart from adjudication, therefore, the role and conduct of the colony's government had to be thrashed out in a series of ugly incidents. The constitutional arrangements were changed several times in major ways and oftener in details. At every occasion the towns kept asserting their importance. Localism, protean and puissant, steadily subverted the intent of the patent and charter. Only the frightening consequences of obliterating the colonial government—subjection to one of the orthodox Puritan regimes and loss of the territory given by the mother country—forestalled the crumbling of Rhode Island. The colonial government, accordingly, after finding its first function in creating a judiciary, found its second in dealing with, generally staving off, the outside world. The towns were left to handle their own affairs with little interference from above.

The long process of forming a colony of Rhode Island under the English aegis began in 1642, when Roger Williams agreed to go to London as agent of his own town and the island commonwealth to seek a charter. Already the Puritan Revolution was under way in England, and by the time he reached London the king and Parliament were fighting a civil war. Williams sought out influential friends and men in high places who might have sympathies for religious liberty and the radical beliefs that flourished among his constituents. He found such men, fortunately, in the parliamentary commission in charge of colonial affairs. There sat Sir Henry Vane, plus Oliver Cromwell and enough others, including the lord high admiral, Sir Robert Rich, Earl of Warwick, to reach the necessary number to issue a patent.

To prepare his way Williams published his little book on the Narragansett language and customs, *A Key into the Language of America*, and a defense of religious liberty. The first aroused a surprising amount of favorable attention while the second publicized religious persecutions by Massachusetts, which was also seeking a grant of the Narragansett Bay region and had many more influential friends than Williams could muster.

After careful diplomacy Williams won the rivalry and in 1644 carried back a patent giving powers of civil government to "Providence Plantations in the Narragansett Bay in New England." This document put within one jurisdiction the islands in the bay, Providence, and the lands of the Narragansett Indians—and so by implication the Gortonite tract. It allowed the English settlers to form a government along lines of their own choosing, to make decisions by majority vote (of the white men with the franchise, as surely was understood), and to enact laws for civil government, provided their terms were as harmonious

A KEY into the

LANGUAGE

OF

AMERICA:

OR,

An help to the *Language* of the *Natives*
in that part of AMERICA, called
NEW-ENGLAND.

Together, with briefe *Observations* of the Cu-
ſtomes, Manners and Worſhips, *&c.* of the
aforeſaid *Natives,* in Peace and Warre,
in Life and Death.

On all which are added Spirituall *Observations,*
Generall and Particular by the *Authour,* of
chiefe and ſpeciall uſe (upon all occaſions.) to
all the *Engliſh* Inhabiting thoſe parts;
yet pleaſant and profitable to
the view of all men :

BY ROGER WILLIAMS
of *Providence* in *New-England.*

LONDON,
Printed by *Gregory Dexter,* 1643.

with English law as the circumstances of the colony would admit. The only power reserved to the mother country was the right of the parliamentary commission "to dispose of the general government" of the colony "as it stands in reference to the rest of the plantations in America."

The patent gave the colony ample authority, seemingly all that the settlers could wish, but it had shortcomings. The document lacked royal approval; in 1644 one had to choose between Charles I and Parliament, and Parliament had the power in colonial affairs. Possibly the absence of provisions for a form of government also impaired the value of the patent. Setting up a constitution by majority vote with English permission was not much different from setting one up that way without it. All the same Williams had good reason for satisfaction with his efforts.

When he returned to New England in the autumn of 1644, he found that his work would not please everybody. Massachusetts was predictably hostile to the patent and its bearer. The officials at Boston grudgingly gave him safe conduct through their jurisdiction only because instructed to do so by powerful men in London. Williams' reception changed when he reached the east bank of the Seekonk, where he was met by a flotilla of fourteen canoes to escort him with jubilation across the water to Providence. Yet the patent was not greeted with joy on Aquidneck, where Coddington and a substantial number of others spurned what they reasonably might have hailed as the answer to their prayers.

Coddington's motives were far from clear. He loathed the thought of being in the same colony with Gorton—at least, so the island governor said to outsiders. He managed to endure the Gortonian refugees as temporary neighbors during their exile from Shawomet. Conceivably he feared losing power, but by a prompt embrace of the patent he stood to gain. Instead, he looked for ways to keep the Aquidneck towns an independent commonwealth.

Coddington sought the protection of Massachusetts or Plymouth. He broached the possibility of an alliance on vague terms in secret correspondence with John Winthrop. This overture touched off a train of unwelcome events. Neither neighboring colony would consider any formal tie with Aquidneck except annexation by consent of the freemen. Plymouth sent a man to see what could be arranged and perplexed the situation by laying claim to the Gortonite tract on the strength of old Wampanoag rights. Massachusetts soon claimed the whole territory covered by the Providence Plantations patent by virtue of a dubious patent to the same region (signed by an insufficient number of the parliamentary commissioners, bearing a false date, and lacking the proper seals) belatedly sent by the colony's agent in 1645. Coddington feebly reasserted his original idea, while the two orthodox colonies fell to contesting each other's pretensions.

The avidity of Massachusetts and Plymouth produced reactions that brought support to the patent both in England and Rhode Island. Gorton and two of his followers, Randall Holden and John Greene, hurried to London to seek explicit confirmation of their safety from Massachusetts, which they got from the Earl of Warwick and the parliamentary commission. When they returned (separately) with safe conduct passes they barely made it through Boston, but Holden could triumphantly lead the Gortonians' reoccupation of the Shawomet Purchase, where they gratefully named their community after their protector.

While these emissaries were away, Williams began organizing a government under the patent. With the cooperation of several men in Portsmouth and Newport he set up a tentative regime. It could be no more than a rehearsal until a majority of the voters in the towns joined to set up a government. Probably fears of the neighboring colonies were generating consent to unite the communities around Narragansett Bay. The island colony, its legislative arm already withered, began to capitulate in 1646. After preliminary negotiations with the Williams side over the constitution of the new government, the basic code of laws, and plans to grant charters of incorporation to the towns, the Coddington regime laid down its powers. A majority of the freemen of the colony met in 1647 at Portsmouth to carry out the terms that had been arranged.

That assembly began by imitating the founding of the Aquidneck commonwealth but went on to more adventurous measures. The freemen resoundingly declared that their new government would be "DEMOCRATICAL, that is to say, a government held by free and voluntary consent of all or the greater part of the free inhabitants." They called upon each other to sign a pledge (no oath, of course) to join in forming a body politic, uphold individual rights and liberties, preserve the form of government to be established, and endorse the new table of laws. The freemen themselves in a General Court or Assembly were to enact legislation then and later.

They decided to elect a slate of eight officials, mainly to form a judiciary. The eight included an all-purpose chief officer called the president, an assistant from each of the four towns, the general recorder (or secretary), the general sergeant, and the general treasurer. Only the latter had purely administrative functions—and very little of those, as the colony had no funds in the early years. The president and assistants each had powers as magistrates and together composed the bench of the Court of Trials, for which the general recorder served as clerk and the general sergeant as sheriff. In later years the freemen added a general attorney and a general solicitor, thus reemphasizing the importance of judicial functions in the central government. These officers were all chosen for one-year terms. Though they might be reelected at the annual Court of Election, they often were not.

The code of laws was an ingenious document and radical in some ways. It covered criminal, civil, and constitutional topics, with heavy emphasis on judicial procedure, but nearly nothing on commerce or the law of property. Most of the provisions were drawn from English statutes, though a preamble identified three sources: Scripture, especially the teachings of Saint Paul; "the common right among common men"; and English common law. With one qualification these were authorities that standard seventeenth-century thinking held were not in discord but supplemented each other. The Rhode Islanders brandished a banner of radicalism by couching the second in unusually egalitarian terms, yet they really adapted the traditional concept of "right reason" to convictions (later made perfectly respectable by John Locke) that any man could figure out the basic principles of justice. If the ordinary citizen felt doubt, the Word of God was there to resolve it. Still, the principles had to be elaborated to cover all the mundane applications in order that people might know how to behave, and Englishmen fondly believed that their national laws were so faithful to ultimate standards as to be almost as authoritative as the Bible on true justice and quite ideal on how to achieve it in practice.

In spite of the initial hopes, legislation by the freemen failed to work. After a year they consigned their power almost entirely to elected representatives, six chosen by each town. These men, sitting as the Court of Commissioners, tried to preserve a voice in lawmaking for the freemen by several forms of initiative and referendum, but they all proved impractical.

If these measures failed, others succeeded all too well in distributing power downward and inadvertently sapping centralized authority. Ominously, the colony gave rights to the towns without earning their support in return. In the second year, the legislature strengthened town governments by granting charters of incorporation allowing them to design their own institutions and operate their own courts. Another measure prescribed the election of town councils (rather like the boards of selectmen in Massachusetts) to assume various functions, among them organization of militia units, though the councils neglected many of their duties and took to themselves the powers of probate courts. It was even decided to let the island communities keep a scaled-down version of their inter-town government if they liked, a possibility scuttled by Portsmouth.

Nor did strengthening the towns solidify public authority. The towns did not always choose all the required officers; sometimes the men they chose refused to serve. Soon the Court of Commissioners began writing desperate new laws to provide special means of putting men in offices. In 1648 Coddington declined election as president rather than face charges against him by some fellow citizens of Newport and resumed secret dealings with Massachusetts and Plymouth. The colony's government was collapsing; the breakdown was delayed briefly by excitement over discovery of what was thought to be a gold mine and by Coddington's departure for England.

Nevertheless, Rhode Island tumbled into chaos. Internal squabbles broke out in the towns and sometimes pitted the local authority against that of the colony. Several of the Pawtuxet men still claimed to be in Massachusetts, and Warwick feared another military expedition from Boston. Suddenly Coddington returned with a document from the Council of State in England naming him governor of Aquidneck for life, with complete judicial powers. Thereupon three of his former friends rushed to London to get the grant annulled. Then the mainland towns, believing that the island towns were reestablishing their separate commonwealth, installed Samuel Gorton in place of Nicholas Easton, the Newport man who had been elected president, and sent Roger Williams off to England to seek reconfirmation of the patent of 1644. Easton had no notion of stepping down or joining Coddington, so there were three governments instead of one— two claiming jurisdiction on Aquidneck, one of them based on the same patent of 1644 that the mainland government thought it was using. At Newport the rival regimes came to blows, one man actually being killed in a fracas over possession of a house.

Undoing this confusion was not the work of a day. William Dyer, one of the Newport agents, returned from London in September 1652 bringing reconfirmation of the original patent. He and the bulk of the islanders took this as support of Easton's government. So did a minority in the mainland towns, but Gorton and a majority believed they were conducting the true continuation of the colony's original government. Coddington intrigued with the Dutch for military support and sought aid in Boston. A meeting at Portsmouth in March 1653 failed to accomplish much except to ensnarl Warwick in a quarrel between those who favored reunification on any terms and those who wanted it only on their own. Grimly, two governments continued on the scene while Coddington still hoped to revive his.

Easton's regime on Aquidneck gradually came to prevail, as it almost had to by weight of numbers and wealth. A few Warwick and Providence men abandoned the mainland government, with more joining them after a deal was struck over a lawsuit that had produced an elaborate conflict of jurisdictions. When Roger

Williams returned in 1654, he persuaded most of the rest of the population on the mainland to reunite with the islanders. He accepted election as president and spent the next three years clearing away the many remaining causes of discord. With the aid of an appeal from Oliver Cromwell, Coddington was brought around to abandoning his patent and accepting office as a representative of Newport in the Court of Commissioners. Numerous minor issues that had been attached to the dispute over the division of government were either resolved or referred to deliberation on their merits.

The most difficult problem was the persistent affiliation with Massachusetts by several Pawtuxet men and the related ill will between them and the Gortonians. The Warwick people made claims for damages done to them by Massachusetts, which provided both a bargaining point and a pretext for taking the dispute before Lord Protector Cromwell. Luck, however, supplied the key to resolution. A small-time trader named Richard Chasmore, alias Long Dick, who had consorted with the Pawtuxet malcontents and been in various scrapes since 1648, was observed by Indians in the act of buggering a heifer on two occasions in 1656. Williams reported this news to the authorities in Boston, asking what they intended to do about such depravity among their adherents. He instigated prosecution under his own government's authority when action was slow in coming from the north. When a posse from Massachusetts tried to arrest Long Dick and was prevented by a number of Providence men, the malefactor was dealt with by the Rhode Island government. After this demonstration of where power lay, the Pawtuxet men lost interest in protection from the neighboring colony, and Massachusetts stopped trying to use them to stretch its boundaries.

By 1658, fourteen years after Williams had secured the patent, there finally was a government embracing the four original towns in the colony, a government that did not face any significant partisans of a rival regime. Crucial to this hard-won success was the demonstration of power to make and enforce laws, to create an acceptable judicial system, and to provide satisfactory bases for town authority. Also of obvious value was support from the radical Puritans in England during the time of the civil war and the Cromwellian Protectorate. And it should be added that the Rhode Islanders who took their pleas to London carried out their missions with skill.

It is likely that Massachusetts came unwittingly to the aid of the fragile government of Rhode Island by persecuting the Quakers who sought to spread the glad tidings of their new faith. Eccentric and obstreperous though these missionaries were in some cases, when they defied banishment, Massachusetts treated them with severity beyond anything visited even on Gorton. Not only did the Puritan magistrates prove anew their hatred of heretics, in case Coddington or anybody else in Rhode Island had imagined a change of outlook, but they dealt as harshly with Quaker converts from Newport and Portsmouth as with those from England. Mary Dyer, once Anne Hutchinson's most devoted follower, kept returning to Boston to bear witness for Quakerism and against persecution until on her fourth appearance there she achieved martyrdom by hanging in 1660. Plymouth and New Haven were almost as harsh as Massachusetts. Rhode Islanders learned once more that preservation of religious liberty clearly required upholding their government against the territorial ambitions of its neighbors.

One further element should be mentioned in accounting for the survival of government under the patent of 1644: the sudden scramble for land west of Narragansett Bay, with Rhode Islanders hurrying to head off outsiders with stronger backing. Even though the Indians remained numerous, they were beleaguered from outside and weakened from within by disputes over the succession to Canonicus and Miantonomi, both dead by 1647. The colonies that ringed Rhode Island's borders (and challenged them) in 1643 formed a confederation, known as the United Colonies, with the plain intention of dividing the refuge of heretics. Though Massachusetts, Plymouth, and Connecticut could not agree on apportioning the spoils, they could unite in bearing down on the Narragansetts, whom they regarded as dangerous, perfidious, and altogether too congenial with the likes of Roger Williams and Samuel Gorton. By 1656 these Indians were at the mercy of the armed forces intermittently sent to cow them. The United Colonies decided that the Narragansetts had committed various outrages and assessed fines upon them.

The sachems had to sell lands to raise money, and they easily found buyers. Among the interested parties was a large syndicate of partners, including officers who had led expeditions against the Narragansetts or assessed the fines. These men set out to acquire as much as possible of the tribal territory. Known as the Narragansett Proprietors or the Atherton Syndicate, the partners soon acquired claims to nearly all they sought. Rhode Island flatly refused to honor these transactions, so the Proprietors embarked on what turned out to be a seemingly endless career of undermining the colony's jurisdiction. Whenever there was an attack on Rhode Island's independence, they were among the assailants. Their persistence for half a century, indeed, provided the continuing element in what was otherwise a changing assortment of purposes for ending Rhode Island's separate existence. At first they relied on Massachusetts or Connecticut to back their plans by asserting authority over the Narragansett lands. If these designs were to be stopped and speculators in Rhode Island towns to have a chance, the Rhode Island government would have to vindicate its jurisdiction as specified in the patent of 1644. Realizing this, the ambitious men of Newport, Portsmouth, Providence, and Warwick discovered another reason to uphold a single and separate government for their colony. They organized to buy land from the Narragansetts and to use their government to back the resulting claims. They could hardly guess that they were launching half a century of wrangling, but the onset of the rivalry for the Narragansett country enabled the government of Rhode Island to survive the death of Cromwell and the Restoration of Charles II without any challenge to its legitimacy.

The revival of the monarchy did, of course, throw the colony's government into peril. The patent had not been issued by the king, and the colony had been just as partial to the Protectorate as the rest of New England. Knowing the need for royal favor, Rhode Island proclaimed Charles II within three months of learning that he had regained the throne—no speed record, but quicker than the neighboring colonies—and professed joy over the turn of events. The town of Warwick, so it was said, dutifully tore out of its records the first page, on which there was a flowery tribute to the regime of Oliver Cromwell. The colony, however, for several years did not get around to revising the terms of its laws or its substitutes for oaths of office to invoke the name of the king.

Nor did it act quickly to seek royal authorization for its government. Rhode Island sent no money or instructions to its agent in London, John Clarke, until the end of 1661, when it sent only a pitiful sum. The sluggishness, he claimed in exasperation, kept him from getting a charter before the Connecticut agent, John Winthrop, Jr., obtained one for his constituents. Delay wrought far-reaching mischief by allowing creation of a boundary conflict that plagued Rhode Island for years. Winthrop, as much for his partners in the Narragansett Proprietors as for his colony, quietly managed to have Narragansett Bay made the eastern boundary of Connecticut. Clarke did the best he could: he petitioned for a charter, waited for funds, kept an eye on Winthrop, and protested the Connecticut eastern line as soon as he heard about it. His prompt appeal to the king got the Connecticut charter called back temporarily by the lord chancellor, the Earl of Clarendon. That gentleman held conferences with the two agents, yet soon allowed Winthrop to send the document to Hartford and promised Clarke only to treat Rhode Island fairly when it pressed its petition.

Clarke was furious and for half a year made no progress. A first attempt at arbitration miscarried, and he failed to get a hearing before the Privy Council. If a rascally adventurer named John Scott had not stirred up trouble in Long Island, which wanted to be in Connecticut, and in New Haven, which wanted to be left out, Winthrop might have resisted a settlement. To curb Scott's machinations, he had to come to terms with Clarke. So the arbitration in April 1663 succeeded, with Winthrop conceding the Pawcatuck River as the eastern line of Connecticut in exchange for agreement that all private property rights in Narragansett country would be honored by Rhode Island and that the Narragansett Proprietors and those who bought their land would be allowed to choose Connecticut jurisdiction if they preferred it. Winthrop and others privately assumed that an arbitration award could not legally touch a charter issued under the Great Seal.

Clarke feared as much but with Winthrop's help proceeded to obtain a charter for his colony in the grandiloquent name of the Governor and Company of the English Colony of Rhode-Island and Providence Plantations, in New England, in America. After Winthrop's departure, Clarke managed to remove from the draft of the document any allusion to a choice of jurisdiction for people in the Narragansett country, but kept the other terms of the arbitration award in the text that received official approval in July 1663. The charter also prescribed an eastern boundary for Rhode Island so as to include land extending three miles east of Narragansett Bay (somewhat vaguely described) and east of the Blackstone River as far as a line running north from the falls at Pawtucket. Thus Rhode Island acquired claims to territory previously thought to lie in the Plymouth Colony.

The Rhode Island boundaries remained in dispute for years, however. Connecticut repudiated the arbitration award, saying it had not authorized Winthrop to make any concessions. It tried to annex the Narragansett country for forty years and then tried to arrange compromises until finally overpowered by a ruling of the Privy Council in 1727 endorsing an agreement the two colonies had reached (briefly) in 1703. Rhode Island's eastern limits remained in controversy even longer. The colony did not even attempt interference when Plymouth and Massachusetts granted land and organized towns east of the Blackstone River and Narragansett Bay. Finally appeals to the Privy Council resulted in a line drawn by a commission in 1741 and ultimately surveyed in 1747.

Though the boundaries specified in the charter led to decades of controversy and litigation, the provisions on government and law were shortly put into effect. Unlike the first patent, the royal charter of 1663 prescribed a form of government. It differed from the constitution worked out in 1647 and 1648 primarily by enhancing the powers of the magistrates. The rights to operate a government and dispose of the colony's land were given to the governor and company as a corporation—that is, to the freemen.

The corporation would be self-perpetuating both because it had powers to elect officers regularly and because it could admit new freemen. Under the new form the freemen every May elected a governor, deputy governor, and ten assistants. These officers all had powers as justice of the peace and were generally called magistrates. Every May and October, or oftener if necessary, the magistrates were to meet with deputies from the towns in a General Assembly. Newport could send six representatives, the other original towns four each, and subsequently created towns, two. Any action of the Assembly required the assent of a majority of the magistrates. The Assembly was empowered to set up courts, enact laws, and choose such other officials as might prove useful, although between its sessions the magistrates by themselves had power to adopt military measures and appoint officers for the public safety.

Under the charter, Rhode Islanders received welcome assurances of good standing among English Americans. They were guaranteed rights to travel and carry on business in the other English colonies, regardless of old sentences of banishment. They were given rights to fish off New England. They could engage in commerce with other ports in the king's dominions. The monarch declared that the territory of Rhode Island should not be invaded by armed men from neighboring colonies without consent of the local officials. In other words, Massachusetts was not to arrest any more heretics outside its borders, and theoretically, the United Colonies were to stop intimidating the Narragansetts.

The charter also laid down a few fundamentals of law for Rhode Island. Existing statutes and practices were to continue in force until changed. As before, any new colonial legislation was required to conform to English law as nearly as circumstances would permit. The terms of land ownership were to be the same as in the king's manor of East Greenwich, thus providing the colony with the most attractive variety of land tenure in English law—attractive because it was the kind with fewest medieval features. Somewhat loosely, it was said that Rhode Island land was held in "fee simple"—that is, full ownership subject only to paying taxes. The people in the colony should enjoy all the rights of natural-born subjects residing in the mother country, plus, of course, complete liberty of conscience. The charter declared that all people in Rhode Island should "freely and fully have and enjoy his and their own judgments and consciences in matters of religious concernments, . . . they behaving themselves peaceably and quietly and not using this liberty to licentiousness and profaneness, nor the civil injury or outward disturbance of others." King Charles endorsed the colonists' proposal "to hold forth a lively experiment that a most flourishing civil state may stand and best be maintained, and that among our English subjects, with a full liberty in religious concernments." Thus the freemen of the colony were given ample powers to govern themselves under their own laws.

When the charter arrived in Rhode Island, it was put into use at once. The provisional slate of magistrates named in the document met with deputies from the towns in a General Assembly that convened at Newport on March 1, 1664. They found clauses with ambiguous wording and important features of governmental structure on which the charter gave no directions. Setting most of these ticklish points aside for later deliberations, the Assembly ruled only on the ones that had to be decided before the May election. The gathering also resolved to keep the sensible scheme of geographical distribution of the magistrates used in making the first list: five from Newport, three from Providence, and two from each of the other towns. For the time being this rule prevented the Aquidneck majority among the freemen from picking all twelve from their own ranks and made sure that there would be magistrates in every community. The plan endured over thirty years before it was modified to give seats to a few new towns. The Assembly considered a bicameral organization but decided against it; advocates of that procedure did not get their way until 1696.

Within the elastic terms of the charter, the Assembly shaped the colonial government. In the early years fairly simple patterns were devised, giving one cluster of functions to the magistrates alone and another to the General Assembly. The magistrates served as the Council of War, as the bench of the Court of Trials, and as an informal advisory committee for the governor in emergencies. The Assembly, in keeping with the new document, was more than a legislature. It chose various civil and military officers and served as a court of appeals. It decided on the policies to be followed in dealings between Rhode Island and England or other colonies. It responded to a great variety of requests for attention to local and private desires, and so issued many orders and rulings on specific matters in addition to general laws. To help carry out the work of the central government, the old administrative and legal officers were kept, but most of them were chosen by the Assembly rather than by the freemen in the general election.

Development of constitutional arrangements under the charter continued to elevate the importance of the towns as opposed to the colonial government. Though Newport in most respects was the capital, housing the main offices and supplying the chief officials most of the time, the other towns kept asking to play host to sessions of the General Assembly and the Court of Trials. By the eighteenth century these organs of government itinerated among four or five locations. The original towns insisted on keeping the privileges given in 1648, although they gave up town courts (Warwick not until 1674) when they were assured of resident assistants as judicial officers. The first few new towns, all the same, got the right to choose their own magistrates. The exercise of probate jurisdiction by the town councils had to be sanctioned by law and made uniform throughout the colony. The Assembly at first tacitly, then explicitly, gave towns the power to admit freemen and to see to local defense and also gave the militia companies the right to elect their officers, in spite of the clear language in the charter giving these powers to the Assembly itself. The legislature found that it could prescribe civil officials to be chosen by the towns and stipulate their duties, but could not compel action on these decisions. Nor could the Assembly actually resolve the towns' internal disputes, even when called upon to do so. Towns without penalty disregarded laws on many subjects, from collecting taxes to recording land titles and vital statistics. In fact, town government proceeded largely on its own, conducting public business of many kinds, while the colony feebly tried to manage what was left to it.

If the new government of the colony under the charter turned out to be more of a federal structure than the centralized regime of the governor and General Assembly prescribed by the document, the alteration at least stemmed from important realities. The towns had come first, obviously. Diverse in origin, some of them had been founded because the first settlers could not live harmoniously in the others. They had their special ways, although they shared a basic reliance on meetings of the freemen, plus a few essential officers like a treasurer and a secretary, and an executive committee that had been shaped slowly into the town council. But they cherished localism and, far from parting with it in accord with the charter, insisted that it be further honored by the central government. Moreover, the concerns of local jurisdictions were sufficiently distinct from what the charter officers did to justify leaving the two levels loosely connected. The essential functions of the central government were to create general laws and the courts to apply them and to deal with the outside world in relations with England and the neighboring colonies—and in these external affairs to transact quite limited business. The economic life of the colony in the seventeenth century, when it was not a village matter, was beyond the control of the central government because it was in the English commercial web, where commercial law, custom, and personal connections, even more than Parliament's new acts on trade and navigation, regulated what people did.

Though town life and commerce proceeded largely on their own and the government of the colony had only limited power to guide or aid them, at least there was a fairly stable central authority in Rhode Island within a few years after the charter arrived. Considering the events of the preceding decades—the turmoil, the schisms in colony and towns, the frequent changes of constitutional arrangements—there had been ample reason to fear that stability could not be achieved and that the colony would either split or be absorbed by its neighbors.

Ironically, modern analysts have looked at these early years of discord and uncertainty and proclaimed the discovery of a precocious dedication to democracy, constitutional guarantees of individual freedom, limited government, and popular sover-

The home of an ordinary rural family in early Providence: the Thomas Clemence house (1680), now in Johnston. *Providence Journal-Bulletin Photo.*

eignty. In one form or another these concepts were all there, to be sure, and being used as much to heat up hostilities as to seek ways to achieve the general happiness that everyone wanted. But the exploration of ideas that enjoyed a wider vogue in later times was done only partly out of deep convictions; in the wilderness, detached from all other communities, the Rhode Island settlers were forced to try whatever theories they could devise to create a society and live together with their antagonistic views. They discovered and tried to use virtually all the generic types of theory on the origin of law and authority, but none proved satisfactory until it became possible to use the most conventional for the seventeenth-century Englishman, the popular acceptance of a charter of privileges granted by the king.

Likewise, the guarantees of individual freedom were made in terms that were common to English thought of the day. The ideal of limited government as it was manifest in seventeenth-century Rhode Island had a solid ingredient of radicalism, preserving religious liberty, but beyond that rested on jealousy among the towns, localism, and a shrewd realization that the charter, if it was to prove an effective bar to further exercise of royal power, would have to be treated as a constitution prescribing a government of limited powers and prohibiting what it did not authorize. Only the dedication to freedom of religion and its corollary, separation of church and state, were truly radical concepts. Goals of Williams and his followers, they were at first only expedients in the island towns, but soon became the grand principles, the anchor of hope and purpose, for the colony. Trivial though the disuse of oaths of office may seem to later generations, it marked a high point of thoroughgoing secularization of the state that has been abandoned in modern times.

The advanced ideas did not ensure a harmonious society or a strong government, but they made it possible to form a colony. It remained to be seen whether the colony, a patchwork of compromises, accommodations, and daring experiments, could survive its internal fractiousness and the designs of outsiders.

5

LAND, POLITICS, WAR

Hardly had the colony of Rhode Island been created than it broke apart; no sooner was it put back together than it entered a complex of strife that imperiled its very existence for half a century. Those who struggled to preserve it often must have doubted that they could succeed. If they looked back over the years before 1658, with settlers numbering only a little more than one thousand, they saw a record of riots and bloodshed, schisms in churches, the sundering of towns and even the colony itself into rival governments, intrigues with neighboring authorities, plus manifold disputes over land and the foundations of government. If so few people could quarrel that much, what would happen when there were more? Contention, rare just after the reunion, broke out again a few years later. It was hard to be an optimist.

Even the royal charter had little influence on the internal turbulence and less on the ambitions of neighboring colonies to gain control of the land the king had said was Rhode Island. Connecticut would not acknowledge any modification of its royal charter setting Narragansett Bay as the eastern limit; Massachusetts and Plymouth intermittently raised less substantial claims to parts of Rhode Island. The royal commission sent in 1664 to examine and settle various controversies in New England generally upheld Rhode Island's views on boundaries and Indian affairs, but the neighboring colonies refused to accept these rulings. Ultimately the other New England colonies conducted their strategy in King Philip's War so as to create occasions to invade the lands of the Narragansetts and reduce the tribe to a trifling remnant consisting of those who had contrived to remain neutral and a few others who had not been slaughtered, starved, driven to flight, or sold into servitude or slavery.

Why was early Rhode Island prey to such internal discord? The first settlers had shared the ill will of Massachusetts. Once they had sorted themselves out according to their different persuasions, they might have held together at least in the separate towns. Roger Williams, like John Winthrop before him, expected religious dedication to cement a community, to make its members "loving neighbors," who could ease their conflicts by Christian forbearance and underlying good will. Things turned out differently.

One source of trouble lay in the religious ideals the settlers espoused. They deliberately subverted one of the traditional bases of social cohesion by cutting off the secular order from the support of union in church. Instead of an all-embracing institution teaching reverence for government and exemplifying in its own organization an orderly pattern of authority, the Rhode Islanders created exclusive fellowships that militantly left secular affairs alone. Religion, by the reckoning of most Christians and the wisdom of the ages, had gone haywire. Uneducated men and even women preached, pretending to utter words furnished by the Holy Ghost. Cranks and fanatics multiplied, producing weird and dangerous new doctrines, while far too many people used their freedom as liberty to shuffle aside all duty to the divinity. The weak and distracted governments could not curb sinful behavior and the churches flatly renounced their traditional obligations to hold everyone in line by teaching the young and reproving the adult. When one religious fellowship, the Society of Friends, finally began to give such benefits to a large number of Rhode Islanders, it did so only for its own members, which tended to separate them from the rest of the populace as a people apart.

In addition, secular society was prone to discord because it lacked either a traditional order with gradations in rank buttressed by differences in wealth and occupation or an alternative pattern that everyone accepted. Rather, there were plans and expectations, both egalitarian and customary, that had not yet been fulfilled and so lay open to challenge. To shape the communities, apart from a few regulations and fragmentary expressions of policy, the founders used allotment of land. This method of guidance provoked opposition regardless of the objective. Tradition called for a diversity of occupations fitting together to form an interlinked whole, with dignity for all, but with wealth, honor, and power distributed unevenly in accord with the deserts of each calling. This complex concept could not be represented in one dimension, whether on a scale of wealth or acres. When reduced to such simple terms, even as a device to get a community started, the ideal was falsified into an arbitrary scheme to impose invidious distinctions of rank where none had an obvious foundation, even if the intention was to draw a diagram of the interdependence among members of a community. A vision of equality also aroused resentment. A sense of fairness backed those whose contributions of time, money, wisdom, bravery, or special skills gave grounds to expect uncommon rewards.

So apportionment of land soon drew fire, whatever the design. If real property was the key to rank in the New World, as it generally had been in the old, everyone was tempted to get as much as possible at the outset. Why should any man be content with his lot—in either sense of the word? Simple land hunger, an age-old passion in rural England, broke loose in Rhode Island. It lacked its old curbs, the differentiation of ranks that thwarted inordinate ambition and the sheer difficulty of gaining much where all the soil was owned. These circumstances had prevented land lust from disrupting society. In the young settlements, however, there were only minor confinements: the plans of the founders and self-restraints arising from a sense of decency or duty to accept one's place. These were easily overcome, once men learned the tactics of self-seeking suitable to the new situation. The result was an era of grasping for land on a constantly widening scale, a time of ferment that forestalled the solidification of a social order.

The turmoil got started in divers ways. On Aquidneck the founders planned communities with traditional gradations from gentleman to servant. The levels were initially marked out by the amounts of land given to the various settlers—from several hundred acres to none at all. Those in the upper half of the spectrum were to have political rights, the rest would not. The levels were assigned roughly in accord with rank held previously in other places, but a few men, selected mainly on the basis of wealth, were to be lifted to the status of gentlemen and rulers. There were no settlers of genuinely high birth to begin with; Coddington exploited his slight advantage to the fullest, but he was not so far above the rest as to preclude jealousy. The other prospective gentlemen had even less basis for their intended status. A small number of men, by virtue of special occupations, such as miller or boatman, stepped easily into traditional places in the social order. The rest could well question the positions marked out for them. As they all attacked the forest on almost equal terms to clear fields and build houses, there were no tangible realities to justify the future inequalities. In Portsmouth some of the men given little land and no political rights clamored for higher positions and brazenly set up their own meeting to seek their goals. Their success showed how fragile the original plans really were, how hard it was to exclude assertive men from a voice in the affairs of the community. Quite possibly the persistent egalitarianism of Gorton's beliefs emboldened these dissidents.

In Providence, by contrast, the conflict seemed to begin over religious liberty, but came to rest on land. Williams wanted to keep the town open for victims of religious persecution. To do this he espoused an egalitarian social policy: let everyone who was admitted have the same shares of land—a package of allocations including a house lot, meadow, crop land, and privileges to use the commons. His earliest companions, however, wanted special consideration. After heated exchanges with them, Williams agreed that part of the town should be set aside for them (and himself), leaving the rest to be divided up among the first settlers plus a growing number of other people. Still the townsfolk were not satisfied. Some newcomers were admitted only to quarter-share rights; ultimately admissions with full land allocations were stopped after about one hundred had been made.

The experience of Providence, the demands of the first arrivals for unique advantages, proved to be a sign of the future. Before merchants amassed riches and the men with vast estates improved them to support the positions of landed gentlemen, the most plausible claims for preferential treatment by the towns were getting there first and contributing to the costs of the initial purchase. Later settlers received land gratis. Why should not the first receive special benefits? They organized in all towns to make sure they did. Whether called purchasers or proprietors, they secured rights that others, in theory, could not get. By 1658 the towns were acting as partnerships in developing original purchases, with the original purchasers or their heirs the chief beneficiaries. Nevertheless, the implied social ranks, proprietors above the rest, failed to materialize. There was no way, not even generous grants of land, to guarantee superior wealth or standing to first planters or their children. Some divided their rights among their heirs, others sold theirs either to each other or newcomers. Configurations of landholdings kept changing. Eventually, mercantile fortunes or money-lending or the improvement of large tracts created a wealthy element that put the social hierarchy in order, but this did not happen until the eighteenth century. During the seventeenth, only a few attained precarious perches at the top of the ladder, and so everyone pushed to get ahead.

And push they did, together or individually, for much or little, for town lands or the colony's. While the social order remained in flux and public land lay available, any tactics might be employed in the quest for acres: individual machinations, clandestine dealings with Indians, concerted efforts through or in defiance of government, resort to the favors of other colonies that claimed jurisdiction over the territory of Rhode Island, even fraud and extortion. Mere purchase was surely common, but it promised rewards on a modest scale. When achieving the coveted position of gentleman seemed possible by getting great expanses of land, the most ambitious were ruthless enough to trample down anyone else and shrewd enough to combine forces in effective ways with a few other aspirants.

Roger Williams saw the land lust overpowering public spirit and lamented it and fought it but with little success and few to help him. "God land," he feared, would be as baleful an idol to his fellow citizens as god gold had been to the Spanish. Devotion to the new idol surged up everywhere in 1656—in the towns, in the affairs of the colony, and in the plans of outsiders who wanted the territory of the Narragansetts. Eventually the various ambitions got intertwined to an extent that imperiled Rhode Island by threatening to tear it apart from within or dismember it for the profit of the neighboring colonies.

In the towns the passion for land had some constructive results. Providence and Portsmouth began systematic recording of deeds and town allotments. All towns laid out public roads. They began to locate precise boundaries of original purchases from the Indians and the lines between towns. They recorded and analyzed deeds of these purchases to determine their exact meanings (often stretching the expanse in the process) and the soundness of the title they conveyed. Where the towns discovered flaws, they sought supplementary documents. On Aquidneck, where most of the territory was in private ownership, the freemen made plans for future use of what remained. Providence began getting claims to a huge extension of the original tract. Warwick acquired an appendage in Potowomut across Greenwich Bay. All of these measures entailed complications and conflicts, but proved beneficial in the end.

A long and sometimes acrimonious process began of defining rights in the original tracts. In Warwick, for instance, the shares of the Shawomet Purchase were fixed at seventeen and a segment was set aside for newcomers, so the Purchasers and their heirs (or whoever else obtained ownership of their rights) could have the rest. This remainder included all of modern West Warwick and Coventry, so any share would come to a vast estate, and it was perfectly feasible to sell fractions of shares. The territory itself, however, was occupied by subjects of the Narragansett rulers, people who would have to depart—presumably the original sale obliged them to leave when their rights had been paid for—before white settlers could use it. Some of the newcomers, who wanted a tract of reserve land for themselves, found Indians willing to sell them Meshanticut, a tract stretching north beyond the Pawtuxet River. In the island towns, where most of the original purchases had been parceled out in the first twenty or thirty years, the definition of proprietors' rights in the undivided land caused far less difficulty, particularly in Portsmouth, where following the early disputes most owners of property became proprietors.

Rhode Island men began looking for new territory to acquire, spurred by desire for land, but also by knowledge that the Narragansett sachems were selling. Outsiders wanted all the tribal territory, and the Rhode Islanders wanted to establish their claims first. The Indians were not about to yield immediate possession of any great amount except for some islands in the bay and peninsulas on the mainland, so the rivalry was mainly for options to be used in case the Narragansett fortunes continued to wane. The Rhode Island white men, heavily outnumbered by the red men, could not compel cessions of territory. The most they could do was assert their colony's boundaries, uphold the existing friendship with the Narragansetts, buy land rights, and join the Indians in protests against the activities of outsiders. On the whole, the Rhode Island white men managed rather well in a thorny situation.

The troubles of the Narragansetts stemmed from the suspicions of Massachusetts and the squabbling over succession to the principal sachems' positions after the deaths of Miantonomi and Canonicus. Massachusetts' fears revived after the brief suspension during the Pequot War, inaugurating an ever-widening conflict between the Narragansetts and the United Colonies (New England minus Rhode Island) in alliance with the Mohegans. These partners captured and executed Miantonomi; a Mohegan wielded the hatchet that "clave his head." Canonicus died a few years later in 1647. Several brothers, sons, and nephews of Miantonomi vied for inheritance of power. Among them only Canonchet had real ability. The others tended to improvidence, drunkenness, and early deaths. On their wastrel course, they recklessly sold large parts of their people's land.

Continuing conflict with Massachusetts soon compelled them to sell more. Weakness and folly in the royal house let a cousin named Ninigret, the tough and shrewd sachem of the allied Niantics, rise to eminence in Narragansett affairs. His resistance to the United Colonies provoked sterner measures than ever to stop his buying ammunition from the Dutch, warring against some Long Island tribes, and persisting in plans to avenge Miantonomi. Conferences resulted in agreements that he did not feel obliged to honor because they were signed under duress. The United Colonies tried various means to overcome his firmness, eventually resorting to an expedition against him, which they demanded that he pay for. He had no intention of yielding, but the choice was not entirely his to make. Besides, either defiance or submission would be costly and probably require selling more land. The would-be heirs of Miantonomi vacillated, affixing their marks to new deeds at every turn of policy.

Rhode Island men eagerly plunged in to get what they could. The Indians at first parted with fringes of their territory but presently began selling the rights to great blocks of land. The earliest sizable sale was of Conanicut, better known as Jamestown, which was bought by a company of men led by William Coddington and Benedict Arnold, great-grandfather of the well-known traitor. They obtained their key deed in 1657 and went on to buy up lesser claims. While they were finishing their business, Rhode Island men launched four major ventures to gain claims to the Narragansett lands, three south of the Shawomet Purchase and the other west of Providence.

The most successful was the Pettaquamscut Purchase, made by a small coterie. In 1658 and later they acquired rights to a huge tract of vague extent, roughly the southeast quarter of South County. The core of the purchasers consisted of five Portsmouth men, but they took in two partners, Benedict Arnold and John Hull, the prosperous Boston goldsmith. Arnold was probably admitted on account of his influence in the colonial government, Hull for his money and knowledge of precious metals. The purchasers thought they had a black lead mine and hoped for gold and silver.

Two projects came to very little. With official encouragement a large syndicate, composed mainly of men in the mainland towns, sought land between Pettaquamscut and Warwick. They accomplished nothing except acquisition of a nebulous deed that floated about for many years casting a shadow on later purchases in the same area. A number of men obtained rights that were somewhat less hazy to a tract west of Providence called Westconnaug. The purchasers could do no more than send a man to spend a couple of weeks there by way of asserting a claim.

In the southwest corner of the colony an organization with official blessings did better. Though plans to draw in investors from all the original towns came to grief, a group consisting largely of Newport men acquired a sheaf of Indian deeds by 1660. Their strongest claims were to Misquamicut, the part of Westerly between Weekapaug inlet and the Pawcatuck River, but they could assert rights to everything west of the Pettaquamscut Purchase and north of Misquamicut for twenty miles. The shareholders took turns camping out on their tract until they found some permanent settlers.

These purchases had only modest results in obtaining land for white householders. Conanicut provided pasture for the investors' livestock. Few people went to live with the animals, though by 1679 there were enough to justify establishing a town under the name of Jamestown. The Pettaquamscut purchasers used a fringe of territory next to Narragansett Bay, mainly for grazing land, and began selling tracts for farms. In Misquamicut the promoters planned a town center and dealt out lots to each other, but few went to occupy them at first.

The Rhode Islanders who obtained rights in South County, of course, were actually racing to head off outsiders. So it was no surprise when they stirred up trouble. The Misquamicut case was unusual in that Massachusetts claimed the territory as booty from the Pequot War, a claim upheld by the United Colonies as late as 1658. Massachusetts then authorized local government for the place under the name of Southertown, mainly for the white colonists in the part lying west of the Pawcatuck River. The United Colonies had appointed a Niantic Indian governor, Harmon Garrett or Caushawashott, to do what he could to rule the remaining band of Pequots in the part east of the river. When

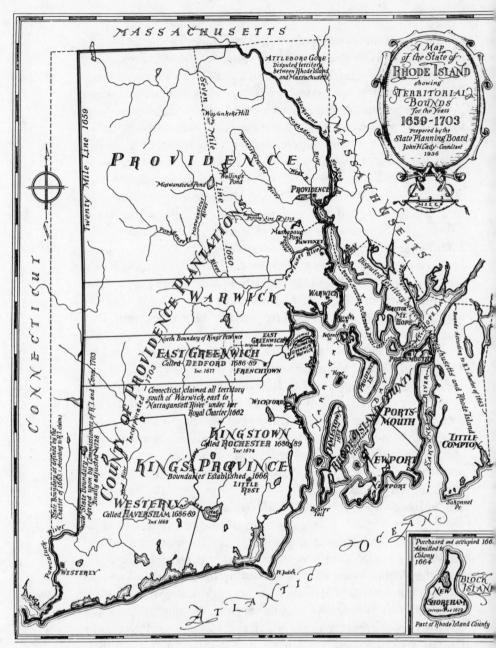

The Rhode Island Historical Socie

the Misquamicut settlers took up residence, Massachusetts sent
the constable of Southertown to arrest them. Two were fined and
held in jail for a year until their sponsors raised money to free
them. The Misquamicut partners promptly sent more settlers.
The Rhode Island government agreed to back this enterprise
openly in 1662, beginning a long series of moves, including
incorporation of the town of Westerly in 1669 to establish the
Pawcatuck River as the western boundary of the colony.

The contest was not really with Massachusetts, however, but
with the Narragansett Proprietors, who would use any colonial
government—or the United Colonies or the court in London—to
get their way. This organization was composed mostly of
Bostonians with associates from Connecticut and Plymouth. The
nucleus consisted of several businessmen and a few officers who
had led expeditions against the Narragansetts. They began
buying land in 1658. Ominously, they took in as partners the
Richard Smiths, father and son, who had been operating a
trading post at Cocumscussoc, successively as partners and rivals
of Roger Williams. The Smiths had a substantial tract nearby,
which they pooled with the first two acquisitions of the Narragansett Proprietors, the northern tract extending north from
Cocumscussoc, and the southern tract consisting chiefly of Boston
Neck. Thus the new combine from the start had claims
overlapping the Pettaquamscut Purchase. Moreover, the Narragansett Proprietors had the enmity, not the blessing, of Rhode
Island.

They soon went on to more extensive dealings in the face of
Rhode Island laws against unauthorized purchases from the
Indians and specific prohibitions against the Proprietors themselves. After the United Colonies in 1660 had once again
overawed the Narragansetts and imposed a fine they could not
pay, the Indians were given four months to raise a great sum in
wampum, provided they mortgaged all their lands to the United
Colonies as surety. The Proprietors then arranged to take the
mortgage, extend the time for redemption to six months, and pay
the fine. They got a receipt for the wampum, but it is unlikely
that they actually paid it to the United Colonies. The Indians
could not redeem their lands in the stipulated time; the

Proprietors said they would give them another five years or more but foreclosed in the spring of 1662, as soon as they thought it reasonably sure that the new Connecticut charter would set the eastern boundary at Narragansett Bay.

Rhode Island, as has already been explained, was at the same time seeking a royal charter to replace the patent, which had been issued under the authority of Parliament during the civil war in England. Though John Clarke could not stop the issuance of the Connecticut charter with the offensive eastern limit, he held Winthrop to arbitration and obtained an agreement to let the Pawcatuck River remain the dividing line in exchange for Rhode Island's allowing any private claims in the Narragansett country and letting the Narragansett Proprietors or those who bought land from them choose which jurisdiction to be under. But Clarke then obtained the Rhode Island charter of 1663 with clauses referring to agreement with Connecticut about the boundary while mentioning nothing about the other terms of the deal with Winthrop. The Proprietors were incensed and, acting on the provisions of the arbitration agreement, held a meeting at Smith's place and voted themselves into Connecticut.

Connecticut promptly set up a government in the Narragansett country. It appointed officers for the little settlement near Smith's trading post, which it named Wickford. It also took over Massachusetts' quarrel with Misquamicut by backing the town of Stonington in granting land and exerting authority in Westerly. The Rhode Island legislature futilely voted measures against the Proprietors and the extension of Connecticut jurisdiction.

A royal commission sent in 1664 to investigate and resolve various disputes in New England heard the contrary claims and backed Rhode Island. It declared the Narragansett Proprietors' claims null, finding that the transactions concerning the mortgage had been fraudulent. It upheld the claims made under Rhode Island, but to solve the jurisdictional riddle posed by the two recent charters declared the Narragansett country to be the King's Province, entrusting it to Rhode Island until further notice (which finally came in 1686).

The commission's rulings served only to provide Rhode Island with new arguments. Connecticut stood on the wording of its charter and found technical flaws in the commission's procedure. The two colonies held conferences to resolve the dispute, but neither would yield enough to satisfy the other. Each appointed its own local officials and jailed the other's. High-ranking officers proclaimed their colonies' authority and planned appeals to the king. The town government of Westerly appeared and vanished like the moon behind broken clouds.

Thus the issue was joined over what was generally called the Narragansett country. At stake was not only ownership of the bulk of Rhode Island's choicest acres but also the character, even the independent existence of the colony in years to come. Land lust, just as it replaced religion as the root of acrimony within the Rhode Island towns, also superseded religion as the chronic source of conflict between the heretic colony and its orthodox neighbors. The contest was long and intricate. It was always political at heart rather than legal, and in many years it was either the main political issue in Rhode Island's internal affairs or intertwined with lesser or greater ones. The contest did not end until trade took the lead over land as the foremost source of wealth and made agriculture the handmaiden of commerce. While it lasted, the contest often resembled a serialized melo-drama, featuring the Narragansett Proprietors as the villains with the old mortgage who appeared at every crisis, schemed with all the other characters, and used every fiendish stratagem to get the poor widow's cottage, only to be thwarted in each episode because the mortgage was a fraud. These arch-villains often used Connecticut as the wicked sheriff to seize the property, but intermittently sought to win over Rhode Island or angled for more powerful backing in London. With the end of the story well known, it is tempting to think that the fate of the Narragansett Proprietors, like that of the stage villain with the handlebar moustache, was never in serious doubt. In the seventeenth century, however, the men with the mortgage often appeared the likely winners. Especially so when their affairs became connected with the even more complex machinations of William Harris, a

Providence man who ironically had played a leading part in extending his town's claims to head off the Proprietors and others buying land west of the original settlement.

Providence in 1656 shared the widespread alarm over outside interests gaining control of Rhode Island territory. It could not stop a sizable purchase of land around modern Woonsocket and could only ignore the enlarged pretensions of the Massachusetts town immediately north. But the Providence townsfolk wanted to get what they could before someone else did. William Harris insisted that the original purchase actually had extended far into the interior. The Narragansett sachems had certainly given the Providence settlers permission to pasture livestock on meadows along the Pawtuxet and other rivers as far inland as they wished. Harris argued that this privilege, combined with terms of other documents, added up to a grant of all the territory between the Pawtuxet and the Blackstone River. All that was needed was to buy out lesser claims. So he negotiated "confirmation" deeds from several Indians.

These measures touched off a terrific row in Providence, especially when Harris' plans for personal gain came to light. Roger Williams opposed the scheme from the start. He insisted that the sachems had given only a moderate tract and their successors would have to grant any additions. By way of compromise, he agreed to help buy enlargements for the town and obtained deeds for the land for which Harris had acquired confirmatory cessions. Seemingly, everyone should have been satisfied, but nobody was.

The personality of William Harris surely embittered the controversy, although his character is now very hard to discern because it was reported mainly by those who hated him. He had lived almost as a recluse, Williams charged, steeping himself in old law books and plotting dark designs. Harris was indeed devious and legalistic, but he was also given to outbursts of religious and political speculations that were Antinomian in flavor. Though no sympathetic traits appear across the centuries, except the deep grief over the death of his older son, Harris had a way of gaining the trust and cooperation of others, if not their friendship or respect. He was at his best in dealing with those he saw seldom, at his worst with those he dealt with directly, especially his more scrupulous Providence neighbors. Williams hotly denounced Harris for his wicked plot to defraud the Narragansetts. Harris protested that he was saving the town and colony from capture of the land by outside interests.

The disagreement grew passionate when questions arose over what was to be done with western town land. If it was part of the original purchase, as Harris maintained, it would be divided among those with proprietors' rights. If it was not, as Williams asserted, it might be divided among the proprietors or, as he preferred, be kept as a reserve where new towns could be created to give refuge to victims of religious persecution. Some of the proprietors, naturally, wanted to have the value of their shares enhanced, but many just as ardently sided with the great founder.

The quarrel came to focus, however, not on Providence proper, but on Pawtuxet, the part of the original purchase that Williams long before had reluctantly agreed to set aside for himself and a dozen other first settlers. That tract became the central issue for three reasons: the opposing theories made a vast difference in its size; its extension was what Harris really wanted; and to get his way he had to overcome the claims of two purchases by Warwick men, which made that town an automatic ally of Williams' side.

The extent of Pawtuxet was indeed a major question. According to Williams' ideas about the original purchase, Pawtuxet was only a few square miles, and the town would get everything west of it when buying additional territory from the Indians. Harris insisted that Pawtuxet extended almost twenty miles inland, just like the rest of the original purchase. Moreover, he maintained that the south branch of the Pawtuxet (Flat River), not the branch flowing out of Ponaganset Pond, was the main stream and therefore the southern boundary of the Providence purchase. Thus he argued that Pawtuxet would embrace modern Cranston, most of Johnston, Scituate, and Foster, plus half of Coventry and part of West Warwick. Any of the thirteen shares would be a baronial estate; Harris and a couple of others who had bought up additional rights could anticipate veritable earldoms. (Harris wrote an elaborate will intended to keep his vast share held by a single member of the family rather than let it be divided among his descendants.) He and his associates thought that they would get no more than their due, while leaving the town plenty of land. Williams and his friends believed the theory of "confirmation" deeds had been a cover for a monumental land grab.

The conflict became complex and bitter and lasted half a century, although resolution began piecemeal after the deaths of the two protagonists in the early 1680s. Harris drew in with him several men who, like himself, had built their houses in Pawtuxet, but unlike him had brought in the authority of Massachusetts against the Gortonians. In fact, his plans probably enticed them back from their secession, although not to cordiality with him—they distrusted each other. Together they kept up the contest in Providence for endorsement of their claims. They sometimes had majorities in town meetings, sometimes set up rival meetings, but could not get a firm and generally accepted vote to define and survey a line that was satisfactory to them separating Pawtuxet from the rest of the town. Even those who liked Harris' theory about the original purchase would not always back him on the southern boundary. He insisted on Flat River and would not budge.

For that reason the Pawtuxet claimants went to court not against their Providence neighbors, but against Warwick men. Harris and his partners started cautiously, seeking to establish rights north of what everyone agreed was the Pawtuxet River. They sued for meadows along it lying south of the Warwick line. They sued for the Meshanticut territory, a purchase by Warwick men that lay immediately west of the original Pawtuxet reserve. By the early 1660s they won judgments at the Court of Trials, but the obstinacy of Warwick, backed by chicanery and loaded muskets, prevented these decisions from being carried out. Warwick, like Williams, believed that Harris had prevailed at court by insinuating himself into the favor of powerful men in Newport, particularly Quakers.

So the battle over the Pawtuxet claims, which had already convulsed the mainland towns, spread into the central government of the colony, producing bizarre manifestations, but no success for Harris. In spite of his choleric and cantankerous character, he did amazingly well in keeping friends on Aquidneck, who frequently elected him an assistant. In the General Assembly he could even get laws enacted that he believed would aid his suits against the Warwick men. The Assembly, however, stepped gingerly when called upon to rule between competing town governments in Providence and the rival slates of deputies they sent, so Harris got no substantial support against his enemies at home.

The struggle threatened to work disastrous effects when it produced a peculiarly unsavory controversy, in which Harris was a key figure, that nearly wrecked the colony's ability to tax. The General Assembly voted to raise £600 to pay the expenses of John Clarke in negotiating the royal charter. As it happened, none of the Warwick deputies had been present when the levy was authorized, and the town refused to pay its share. It protested not only its lack of representation but also the size and purpose of the tax. Warwick accused Clarke of padding his accounts and asserted that he should have charged less for his time because he had been receiving pay for preaching—this smacked of scandal to most religious Rhode Islanders. Besides, he had been the agent sent by the island towns; the mainland had sent Williams. So either the mainland should pay less or the whole colony should also foot the bill for Williams' mission. This response from Warwick, which had most at stake in preserving a separate colony of Rhode Island, was petty and shortsighted, but it gained weight if not dignity from being intertwined with the Harris controversies. The town resented the backing he got from officials on the island in his suits against Warwick interests.

At times tax resistance spread to Providence and stirred up opposition against the charter itself. According to Roger Williams, "Some say they like not some words in the charter; some say they will pay if all do; some are against all government and charters and corporations; some are not so and yet cry out against thieves and robbers who take any thing from them against their wills." He pointed out the benefits of the charter and conceded that "it were to be wished that these dainties might have fallen from God and the king like showers . . . free," but agents had been needed and they had to be paid. Moreover, the government would be dissolved if its authority to tax were destroyed. The General Assembly exacerbated feelings in the mainland towns by calling on William Harris to assist as an extraordinary tax collector.

The controversy came to a strange climax in 1670. The colony's attorney general, as part of launching a suit to collect the tax, tried imprisoning the town clerk and two members of the council in Warwick. The town denounced the law under which he did this as "contrary to all law in England" and vowed to resist. It changed its attitude, however, and began paying the next year when a new tax was authorized to send another agent to London to present the colony's claims to jurisdiction over the Narragansett country, a subject of great interest in Warwick. The plan to send an agent was scrapped, however, leaving the town to protest the abandonment. To a small extent the colony's tax power had been vindicated after eight years of wrangling.

The new plans to send an agent had been fought by Harris, who was turning toward cooperation with those who wanted either to give up fighting the Connecticut claims or to strike a compromise. The Gortonians, knowing the Connecticut charter could be read to include Warwick, would not hear of giving in. When it became clear that Harris had thrown his fortunes in with the Narragansett Proprietors and Connecticut, he lost many of his friends in Newport, who wanted only a few prudent concessions, and the political skies cleared.

Storm clouds gathered again in 1672, however. After a round of negotiations broke down amid accusations of new outrages by Connecticut in Westerly, the Rhode Island legislature passed stringent measures against intrusion and opposing the colony's laws—and also jailed William Harris on charges of treasonous dealings with Connecticut. The sternness provoked a reaction, the election of that year putting into office conciliatory men (often Harris' political friends in the past) and two partisans of the Narragansett Proprietors, Francis Brinley of Newport and Richard Smith, Jr., of Wickford. The harsh laws were repealed, Harris was freed, a new effort at negotiation was launched, and the first two tracts purchased by the Proprietors were recognized as valid by Rhode Island.

This last measure aroused such a clamor, especially when the Proprietors claimed it legalized all their acquisitions, that a new reaction set in. Those who had favored compromise would not go all the way with the Proprietors, so Brinley and Smith refused reelection and froze themselves out of influence in Rhode Island politics. Various others declined to serve. Harris somehow survived the uproar, but generally hardliners returned to office. The colony aggressively tried to set up a town, named Kingstown, in the eastern part of the Narragansett country, as the answer to Connecticut's Wickford, but nothing would keep the new town government functioning.

The stalemate was ended by King Philip's War. When the violence broke out in June 1675, it seemed to be a conflict between the Plymouth Colony and the Wampanoags led by Metacomet, the son of Ousamequin (Massasoit) who had been dubbed "Philip" in a mixture of honor and scorn. The Rhode Island officials thought the trouble should be ended by arbitration and several, including Deputy Governor John Easton, went to propose that the leaders choose impartial men to hear the two sides. This proposal was in harmony with Easton's Quaker leanings, but it came to nothing. In a somewhat less Quakerly fashion, Governor William Coddington offered to aid Plymouth by sending a fleet of small boats to prevent Philip from escaping his home base at Mount Hope (Bristol) while other forces reduced him to submission. This plan failed, though Rhode Island vessels helped by rescuing Plymouth men, and Philip escaped.

The conflict spread, aided by the ill-conceived actions of Massachusetts. That colony, as usual uneasy over the Narragansetts, sent a small delegation to exact promises to remain neutral and to refuse to harbor Wampanoags. Guided by Roger Williams, the emissaries had a satisfactory conference with Ninigret and the other important sachems in June. Soon reports circulated that Wampanoags were being protected in Narragansett villages all the same. English settlers began fleeing to Aquidneck, and the Rhode Island government resolved on neutrality. Small armies from Connecticut and Massachusetts converged on Wickford to demand new promises from the Narragansetts. After a discussion the Indians agreed on July 15 to give hostages and promised delivery of Wampanoag fugitives or their heads in exchange for a bounty.

After these dealings had been concluded, many of the Wampanoags eluded the Plymouth troops and headed northwest, keeping well north of the head of Narragansett Bay. Small forces of men from Providence and Rehoboth, aided by Mohegans in the service of Massachusetts, pursued the fleeing Indians and forced a small battle twelve miles beyond Providence. Once again Philip escaped, at the cost of abandoning ammunition and supplies, and led his men into central Massachusetts while Weetamoo, the squaw sachem of Pocasset (Tiverton) led her part of the Wampanoags, plus women and children from the other parts, to seek refuge among their ancient enemies, the Narragansetts.

Her arrival caused consternation among her hosts. Ninigret and some other principal sachems tried to remain neutral. They vainly devised stratagems to induce the embarrassing Wampanoag guests to surrender to the Rhode Island authorities on Aquidneck. Massachusetts, however, insisted on having them delivered as captives to its own officials. In October the sachems agreed to do that by the twenty-eighth of the month but failed to make good their promise. Ninigret held firm in determination to keep his people out of the war, but Canonchet and others began to waver. Possibly, as believed at the time, Narragansett warriors had already been volunteering in Philip's service. Acting on the conviction that the Narragansetts were deceitfully promising peace at parleys while actually preparing to fall on the English, the United Colonies in November assembled a force to compel them to abide by the earlier agreement, or failing that, to wage a preventive war. Governor Coddington, though invited to add his colony to the coalition, would go only so far as to provide vessels to transport the troops from outside. Tacitly he permitted military action by these forces on Rhode Island territory.

Very quickly the United Colonies assembled a force of roughly

Portrait of Ninigret by an unknown seventeenth-century artist. This oil painting, one of the few made in colonial America depicting an Indian, is sometimes said to show the first Ninigret, who died in 1676 at an advanced age. More likely, it shows one of his heirs, perhaps one of his two grandsons, who were successively sachems of the Narragansetts between 1722 and 1745. The sachem wears the crown made of a belt of wampum. *Museum of Art, Rhode Island School of Design, Gift of Robert Winthrop.*

eleven hundred men under Governor Josiah Winslow of Plymouth. Massachusetts supplied nearly half the troops, Connecticut
almost as many (one-third were Indians), and Plymouth the rest.
An advance contingent carried by Rhode Island's ships, crossed
from Rehoboth to establish a forward base at Wickford early in
December. The rest of the force moved by land making small
forays against clusters of Indians as they proceeded. The notion
of negotiating apparently was discarded in favor of waging as
destructive a campaign as possible. The Indians retaliated with
skirmishes of their own, one of which nearly wiped out the tiny
Pettaquamscut settlement.

The United Colonies' troops gathered there by the ruins on
December 18. The next day they marched inland over Tower
Hill, guided by a Narragansett traitor, heading for the Indian
stronghold on an island of solid ground in the Great Swamp
north of Worden's Pond. Cold and stormy weather had culminated in snow and bitter cold, freezing the swamp sufficiently for
the men to advance across it. They came upon a formidable
barrier: a wall of stakes surrounded by piles of brush and tree
limbs, with several structures like blockhouses from which the
defenders could fire on the attacking troops. Inside were
dwellings for more than a thousand Indians, plus stores of food
and ammunition. The invaders, however, had been led to the one
incomplete segment of the fortifications. The forward units
attacked at once but were twice driven back. When the whole
force arrived another assault was launched. Agonizingly the men
forced their way into the stronghold, moving ahead among the
huts with heavy casualties until someone put the torch to the
village. Unknown numbers of the inhabitants were burned alive,
while many fled northward over the swamp.

Having run out of their own provisions and destroyed the
Indians', the army had to set out for Wickford before sunset.
Some of the dead were left (to be buried later by Ninigret's
people), but the rest and the wounded were carried back to
Wickford. The bulk of the army staggered into camp in the early
hours of December 20. Soon the wounded men who could be
moved were transported to Newport for care. Provisions ran short
in Wickford, too, in spite of modest efforts by the United Colonies

to send supplies and the thorough foraging by the troops, who found hidden Indian stores or sacked villages. (The hunted Narragansetts resorted to raids, too, notably the one on Pawtuxet.) The Connecticut men were especially discontented and wanted to go home. Feeble gestures at negotiation with the Narragansetts came to nothing. By the end of January 1676, however, Winslow was prepared to pursue the enemy. Without catching up with the main party of Narragansetts, he followed them into central Massachusetts before shortages of supplies forced him to give up and send the units of his force back to their homes.

The campaign had resolved the uncertainty of the Narragansetts' policy. They had to be what they had been made, enemies of the United Colonies. Ninigret and the Niantic segment of the tribe remained almost neutral, so Canonchet became the foremost leader of the embittered warriors who ranged in Massachusetts. Many Narragansetts, perhaps mostly women and children, nevertheless remained in their homeland while the main events of the war, viewed in terms of strategy, took place elsewhere. After the complete evacuation of Wickford, a series of Indian attacks hit the settlements next to the bay. During March, Smith's trading post was burned, then the nearly deserted buildings of Warwick, and finally Providence, where about thirty men remained as a garrison. They were helpless against the force that struck on the twenty-ninth of the month. Roger Williams' appeals failed to save the houses. Most went up in flames, including his.

Connecticut set out to wage counterattacks. With the aid of allied Indians (Mohegans, Pequots, and even some Niantics), expeditions ravaged the villages and supplies of the Narragansetts. One raiding party captured Canonchet in April 1676 and turned him over to Connecticut Indians who executed him. Another gunned down the old queen, Quaiapen, a sister of Ninigret and widow and successor of a Narragansett sachem, along with scores of her people. The perpetrators of this massacre in June went on to kill or capture sixty-seven Indians on their way to make peace with the colonial authorities. The Connecticut forces spared nobody and took hundreds of captives, a large number of whom were later sold as slaves. By the summer, many of the remaining Narragansetts were fleeing to surrender at Aquidneck and Providence, where they were subjected to servitude. Others silently filtered through the forests to New York. Except for Ninigret and those who had stuck by him in his equivocal policy, the Narragansetts had been driven from their homeland.

The men who had gone to Massachusetts to join the fighting there during the spring of 1676 hardly dared return. Some tried to find safety by joining their old enemies and new comrades in arms, the Wampanoags, as they headed home, only to find that the Sakonnet branch of that people, under the squaw sachem, Awashonks, had agreed to help the English in exchange for permission to keep their lands. As a result, in the campaign to hunt down Metacomet, who was the symbol if not the leader of the warfare, the Indian peoples who lived around Narragansett Bay were finally exterminating each other. During July and August the campaign was pressed, using Aquidneck as base much of the time, from which parties went to corner bands of the enemy. Captain Benjamin Church was the most famous English leader, but he received help from Rhode Island men, notably Major Peleg Sanford and Roger Goulding. On August 12 Church's force, divided with half under Goulding, surrounded an Indian camp at Mount Hope and opened fire just before daybreak. In the ensuing battle one of the Indians in Church's service shot Metacomet. Church had the body quartered and carried the head back in triumph to Aquidneck. Yet the process of hunting down the natives of the Wampanoag lands continued into the fall.

King Philip's War ruined the Indians of southern New England, but nowhere more suddenly and decisively than around Narragansett Bay. The Wampanoags practically vanished from their strongholds, allowing the Plymouth Colony to sell Mount Hope to a group of purchasers who soon founded the town of Bristol. Other English colonials began developing rights in Tiverton and the territory northeast along the Taunton River. Even Awashonks' late decision to turn against her relatives did not save her; she and her small band of followers soon began selling their lands in Little Compton to a company of men mostly of Plymouth, but with some significant Rhode Island investors. The town of Warwick finally had seen the last of Pomham's Narragansett village near the original Gortonian settlement and the Cowesett villages that had barred expansion inland on the Shawomet Purchase. Richard Smith had practically no Indian customers at his trading post. The settlers could return without fear to Wickford, Pettaquamscut, and Westerly. Where recently had lived a confederation of villages with a population far greater than the whites of Rhode Island, a confederation that could send out a thousand fighting men, there remained only a few hundred stragglers who needed Rhode Island's help to save them from Connecticut. The last contenders for the succession to Miantonomi and Canonicus had fallen in the warfare, except for Ninigret, who died without a visible wound in the summer of 1676, leaving a daughter to rule as principal sachem over the pitiful remnant of the Narragansetts until her half brother came of age.

Rhode Island, like Ninigret, had treated the war in gingerly fashion. Willing to provide naval support to Plymouth against Metacomet, to harbor refugees, to tolerate the attack on the Narragansetts in December 1675, and to succor the wounded after the Great Swamp Fight, Rhode Island thereafter wanted to keep troops from other colonies out of its territory but never raised a hand to stop Connecticut's campaigns to exterminate the Narragansetts. The officials in Newport were quick to advocate plans for restoring peace, although they came to nothing, yet executed Indian captives condemned for various outrages and sold many more into servitude or slavery. By the end of the war Rhode Island men, perhaps without governmental sanction, were joining Church's campaign to finish off the Wampanoags, while the officials did nothing to stop the use of Aquidneck as a base for his expeditions. Rhode Island managed to spend little on the war either in blood or money compared with her neighbors, yet stood a chance of reaping a great reward.

It remained to be seen who would gain control of the Narragansett lands. If right of conquest counted, Connecticut had made good its claim, and the Narragansett Proprietors prepared to seize their opportunity. Rhode Island remained determined to stop them, but its ability to do so was still uncertain. The end of the war brought no end to the internal squabbles or the pressures from outside. Significantly, the colony could not prevent Plymouth from taking land east of the bay that fell inside the borders of Rhode Island as stated in the charter. Moreover, the wrangles over Pawtuxet resumed in 1677. The preceding twenty years of strife and maneuvers over land seemed to have accomplished nothing to settle conflicts among the white colonials, while the war eliminated Indian power over the disputed land. Therefore the conflicts were sure to become sharper than ever. Rhode Island had lost its alliance of convenience with the Narragansetts and on its own faced newly strengthened rivals.

6

THE ECLIPSE OF
RHODE ISLAND

The years between King Philip's War and the dawn of the eighteenth century saw Rhode Island in greater trouble than ever. To describe this harrowing time, one thinks of violent imagery, of tempests or white-water rapids, but the central event was a stoppage of the colony's separate government for a few years, so the metaphor should be drawn from astronomy: a total eclipse. After ominous foreshadowings, the charter regime was snuffed out by the royal hand; the colony was swallowed up in the Dominion of New England—from Rhode Island's point of view a Greater Massachusetts—like the sun in old myths being eaten by a savage beast. In the darkness new and distrusted men took power. Then a small revolution in Boston smote the beast. The old government reappeared feebly, but for several years it remained in a shadow, unable to exert power over its whole territory and menaced by revival of the beast. At length the danger was dispelled, and the charter government began to shine with new luster.

King Philip's War left Rhode Island badly damaged. Most of the human habitations on the mainland were charred ruins. A few structures survived in Providence and Warwick for the refugees to use as shelter while rebuilding. South along the bay nothing usable remained except perhaps for part of the walls of Richard Smith's trading post. The Indians had fared far worse; only a few hundred of them remained alive and free in the wreckage of their villages.

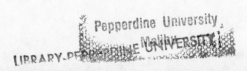

This spectacle of misery did not deter resumption of the old wrangling over land. On the contrary, destruction of the native inhabitants opened the door to English settlers in the interior west of the bay, so rivalry over claims grew hotter than ever. The Pawtuxet men and the Narragansett Proprietors, baffled by the Rhode Island government, sought royal intervention on their behalf by every conceivable means and so began forcing the colony into frequent dealings with London. Other subjects soon rose to greater importance in the official transactions of Newport with London, but for thirty years the disputes over territory bedeviled all the rest, rendering the more painful Rhode Island's uncomfortable transition from relative isolation to full immersion in the affairs of the empire.

The Narragansett Proprietors and the Pawtuxet men, in loose alliance, had begun their appeals to the king before King Philip's War. Their agent, William Harris, journeyed to London while the fighting still raged and brought back orders from Charles II for a special court to hear appeals from Rhode Island courts in suits that Harris had lost and to hear his claims that officials refused to carry out decisions he had won. The governors of Massachusetts, Plymouth, Connecticut, and Rhode Island were directed to choose two judges and four jurors apiece. This tribunal was ready to act in November 1677 and had powers to hear all sides, render judgments, and order that they be carried out. The court ruled for Harris on claims to the extension of the Pawtuxet reservation, an extension that infuriated most people in Providence and virtually all in Warwick, because it was to give him Meshanticut and some meadows south of the Warwick line. The court, however, like most people then and since, found the issues confusing. It tried vainly to distinguish Harris' quarrels with Providence from those with Warwick. It ordered execution of its judgments at first only to the extent of running a line between Providence and Pawtuxet, which seemed to be the key to resolving all other disputes on the Providence side, and set aside for the time being the question of which was the mainstream of the Pawtuxet River, a key to settling matters on the Warwick side. The two keys, however, had to fit locks on the same door: the western part of the line separating Providence from Pawtuxet was to be drawn so as to cross a point midway between the Pawtuxet and the Woonasquatucket rivers. Nobody could determine the point without deciding which river was the Pawtuxet, and Harris would not settle for its being anything other than the tributary from the south known as Flat River. Thus the court's caution accomplished nothing.

In fact, the evasive conduct allowed Harris' opponents to stage a remarkable defense. Though comic in many ways, it succeeded. Warwick, fearing the worst, promptly sent agents to appeal to the king and filed a suit that kept Harris pinned down in Rhode Island for a few months. He bitterly coined the term, "War-wickeds," for his enemies to the south. Providence, led by Roger Williams and Arthur Fenner, planned to run the dividing line so as to shrink rather than enlarge Pawtuxet. Harris protested, but when the court reconvened, one Connecticut judge was absent, so the two Rhode Island men withdrew, asserting that nothing could be done without a full bench. The rest upheld Harris on all points but decided to refer the whole business to the king. Harris dashed off to London.

Soon he and the Warwick emissaries were back, but with hopelessly contradictory orders from the capital. The Warwick men had obtained an order halting action on all disputes pertaining to their territory until the Privy Council could hear the case. Harris, working through the Committee on Plantations, had obtained several royal orders. One directed the governor and council of Plymouth to settle his controversies over the Warwick line. The officials in London were confused because the Warwick men presented their plea as one regarding their town; Harris said he was concerned with Pawtuxet, and no one understood that the Warwick claim conflicted with Harris'.

Harris got other orders, too. He triumphantly flourished one to the governor and council of Rhode Island to carry out all but one of the judgments of the special court regarding Providence. (The other was left to be reviewed by the elderly governor of Plymouth, who died before he could figure out what to do.) The Rhode Island magistrates held still another hearing, announced that the king's orders would be obeyed, and appointed a certain John Smith to act as special marshal to accomplish the business.

The magistrates had received assurances from the Warwick agents that the necessary English officials accepted the Providence view on how to run the Pawtuxet line. So Smith called Harris to meet him at various landmarks on the line and went to the locations as determined by Providence. He could not find Harris. That baffled man, of course, waited somewhere else. When he caught on to this game, he vanished into the forest, while Smith told the governor and council what he had done, and they wrote King Charles that they had tried their best to carry out his orders.

Harris surfaced again reviling Smith and the magistrates for their trickery and proclaiming that he was about to sail for England to denounce them and serve as agent for Connecticut and the Narrangansett Proprietors. On his way he was captured by Algerine pirates and held for ransom. Connecticut gave some money. Mrs. Harris borrowed more, and finally he was freed. When he reached London in the fall of 1681, he lived only three days. Within a couple of years the town of Providence and the remaining Pawtuxet claimants struck the beginning of a compromise. The Plymouth magistrates in exasperation tossed the Warwick disputes back to the king. Harris' surviving partners began to think they could succeed only by a swift, silent petition for a royal patent giving them the lands they thought rightfully theirs.

In the Narragansett country, too, the end of King Philip's War inspired new zeal by the opposing sides. Rhode Island rushed to put settlers on the territory. The General Assembly instigated a plan, carried out mainly by a group of Warwick men, to create a town just south of the Shawomet Purchase. This was the first time that the governor and company actually conveyed rights over any of the land given them by the charter. They authorized the town of East Greenwich, granting five thousand acres and then more to those who would settle there. By April 1678 the town government was in existence. The next year the town of Westerly ended a decade of submergence under Stonington, Connecticut, and reappeared briefly as a local government under Rhode Island. This sign of effectiveness plus the rapid establishment of East Greenwich gave Rhode Island a strong advantage in thwarting the plans of Connecticut and the Narragansett Proprietors.

Those gentlemen reorganized in March 1677 to take advantage of the concession just wrung from the remaining Narragansetts to reconfirm "all their former grants and conveyances of lands" and all their agreements with the United Colonies. To the confusion of the Proprietors, Connecticut demanded that they sell out their rights in the controversial old mortgage as a condition of reasserting its jurisdiction. Rhode Island demanded that all claimants present their deeds to the General Assembly for review and possible disallowance. The Proprietors liked that no better. So they appealed to the king, who asked all parties to submit their claims to him for adjudication, pending which action the rulings (in favor of Rhode Island and against the mortgage) of the royal commission of 1664 and 1665 should stand.

Against such reverses, the Proprietors scored a few gains. In 1679 they came to terms with the Pettaquamscut purchasers, dividing the territory the two groups disputed. Though Harris lost his papers when captured and died before he could present the Proprietors' claims in London, other agents managed to obtain a royal order directing Governor Edward Cranfield of New Hampshire to head a commission to resolve the controversy over the Narragansett country. Cranfield, like some other royal officers involved in this appeal, wanted money—a few thousand pounds as a gesture of appreciation from the winning side. He saw no need to restrict the numbers of the grateful and so gave out a preliminary surmise that all the lands within Rhode Island's borders lacked sound title. He then journeyed to Smith's reconstructed trading post near Wickford to await presentation of evidence to the contrary.

The next events put little in his pocket. The General Assembly refused to honor his summons to exhibit the documents on which the colony's and towns' lands were claimed. Instead, the Assembly appointed officials for its theoretical town of Kingstown (to lend color to the assertion that Rhode Island maintained local government there) and then convened a mile away from Wickford, where it ordered the royal commission to depart the jurisdiction on the grounds that it was a riotous assembly. This order was delivered by the colony's sergeant, escorted by a troop of mounted guards. Only delegations from Westerly and Warwick appeared to display deeds to Cranfield.

He waited two days, retired to Boston, heard the Warwick and Westerly claims, waited longer, and then declared that Connecticut and the Narragansett Proprietors must be right, because Rhode Island had nothing to say for itself. In a burst of magnanimity, he and his colleagues announced that the original purchase of Providence, as well as the two other towns that had been defended, should not be called in question. Though the Narragansett Proprietors spared no expense to win a favorable response in London to the rulings of the Cranfield commission, they were wasting their money. Nobody was taking the commission very seriously. Other events were transpiring that demanded greater attention and gave the Proprietors brighter hopes.

The preparatory moves were palpably being made to redesign the entire colonial governmental system in New England. A shadow began to spread across the region. Rhode Island was at most a minor element in these events. The focus of royal attention was on Massachusetts, where Boston, the great center of commerce for the whole region north of Chesapeake Bay, was treating the English trade laws with less respect than the king's officials thought due. Behind the English frown lay a fear that Boston was essentially an economic rival to London and Bristol and would have to be kept in a subordinate place by parliamentary law. Edward Randolph, who had been investigating the situation since 1676, alleged that smuggling was so rife as to deprive the royal coffers of over £100,000 every year. This estimate came from a fevered brain, but there was no denying that the Bostonians dodged duties to some extent and did so with an annoying air of self-righteousness. Moreover, Massachusetts had refused to allow appeals in litigation to the Privy Council, had played its own game in extending its jurisdiction northward, and had often responded tactlessly to communications from the imperial officials. Whatever the substance of its wrongdoing, Massachusetts was under disfavor.

Randolph wrote reports that led to a suit against the

Massachusetts charter in 1683. Most of the charges were farfetched and some pertained to matters already settled, but the essential accusations were behaving autonomously and failing to enforce the trade laws. Massachusetts made no defense and, while the judicial machinery slowly turned, royal officials brought actions against Connecticut and Rhode Island. The shadow deepened.

The General Assembly in Newport tried less in the way of defense than of precautionary measures. As the demands appeared for compliance with the trade laws, the colony prescribed penalties for those who misbehaved toward royal customs officers, but set up its own device, the naval office, to patrol obedience to the English trade laws—that is, to keep enforcement as much as possible in local hands. The General Assembly made other gestures of cooperation with London before and after expelling the Cranfield commission, but probably without real hope of staying the hand of royal policy. To greater purpose the colony legislated on town government, generally giving or confirming powers. The strategy was to put whatever seemed possible into the control of towns so that less would be lost with the charter. When it became obvious that the charter was doomed, the General Assembly somewhat churlishly repealed its only tax, the liquor excise, and the prohibition on selling firearms to the Indians.

The new royal plan unfolded under a new and widely feared king, the Catholic James II. He set out to extend the Dominion of New England, a vast viceregal government, over the seaboard from New Jersey and Pennsylvania to Maine. Massachusetts and the King's Province in the Narragansett country fell under the new regime at the beginning of 1686; the darkness spread across the rest of Rhode Island over a year later, after the installation of Sir Edmund Andros as governor with his capital at Boston.

In the twilight at Newport the General Assembly chose not to resist, although it protested legal attacks on the charter and appealed to the king to confirm the colony's privileges in trade and religious freedom. The colony's seal was broken, but Governor Walter Clarke refused to make good on the promise to deliver up the charter. By June 1687 Rhode Island was submerged in the Dominion of New England. The eclipse became total.

Though Andros soon received instructions to preserve freedom of conscience, otherwise his rule brought extensive change. All the town governments were greatly reduced in powers if not extinguished. The colony became a county administered by a court of General Quarter Sessions and Inferior Court of Common Pleas composed of ten justices headed by Francis Brinley. This court was under the governor and council in Boston. In spite of its grandiose judicial name the county court performed a large variety of tasks beyond adjudication, making regulations for towns, appointing constables, planning a procedure to keep roads repaired, and imposing taxes.

The Dominion did not last long enough to reduce its government to a system. The governor and council made rules on town governments and commissioned justices of the peace with powers partly independent of Brinley's court. At least in Providence, Warwick, and Portsmouth, town meetings were held in defiance of Andros' directive limiting them to gatherings to elect the authorized officials. The governor and council, and sometimes the governor alone, also stepped into the quarrels over land.

Andros handled these disputes rather inconsistently, which may be a way of saying that he tried to be fair. The Narragansett Proprietors believed their hour of victory was nigh. Before Andros arrived several of the partners were made justices of the peace for the territory they claimed, one of them soon presiding over the county court that replaced the colonial government that had fought them. The Proprietors brought in a group of French Huguenot settlers to found a town just north of Wickford. When the East Greenwich people protested infringement on their territory, the Proprietors confidently appealed to Andros. To their surprise, he imposed a compromise in that conflict. To their horror, he undertook to examine the claims of the Proprietors and declared them insubstantial—he backed the long-standing Rhode Island position point by point, adding his endorsement of the ruling by the royal commissioners of 1665 that the famous mortgage had been an utter fraud. The Proprietors then secretly sent agents to London to petition for a royal charter for their claims, a plan that had nearly succeeded when a revolution interrupted governmental action in England.

Elsewhere Andros acted less decisively. He was instructed from London to look into the practice of towns holding common lands in New England and to work for a revision of land tenure to require annual payments to the Crown, known as quitrents, although they were not really rents as much as fixed automatic taxes. Portsmouth submitted a plan for confirmation of land titles in the town, presumably on a footing agreeable to Andros, but nothing came of it. Some Warwick interests offered to pay quitrents if he would confirm the claims disputed by Harris. The Pawtuxet men, however, also asked his endorsement, so he had to look into the whole long controversy, which delayed a conclusion until it was no longer in his power to make one.

Andros' authority proved fragile. New Englanders objected to paying taxes unless their representatives had voted for them, and they had taken care to leave no standing laws that he might simply perpetuate. As resistance to the Dominion began to spring up in Massachusetts, Rhode Islanders joined in. They refused to pay taxes levied by the county court; the constables would neither call town meetings to elect men to apportion taxes nor collect the levies that the court specified. Before other measures could be tried to break the tax revolt a band of armed citizens in Boston overthrew the Dominion and imprisoned Andros in April 1689. (A few months later he escaped and fled to Newport, perhaps expecting loyalty there; if so, he was disappointed. He was held in jail until officers from Massachusetts came to get him.) Five days after the rebellion in Boston, the Rhode Island men who had last been in office under the royal charter took the lead in calling a meeting of freemen to deliberate on restoring the independent government of the colony.

In response to this invitation a number of the freemen gathered in Newport on May 1, 1689. They approved an ingenious declaration that the privileges of Rhode Island had been confirmed by the king after the Assembly's decision not to resist absorption in the Dominion of New England, and therefore it was right to resume government under the charter after the

Dominion collapsed. They then decided that all the officers of the colony's government at the time of its eclipse should hold their places again. The charter was brought out of hiding. Governor Walter Clarke, a Quaker, resigned a few months later rather than take charge of war measures, but not until he had authorized proclamation of the new sovereigns in England, William III and Mary II. Deputy Governor John Coggeshall picked up the reins and soon sent a petition to the monarchs professing the colony's loyalty and asking confirmation of its old charter.

Though out of the darkest hours of the eclipse, the colony was still in the shadows. Restoration of the charter government could not be accomplished merely by a few votes and proclamations. Some men feared to hold office lest they be declared at fault in the event the Dominion was restored—as King William in fact wished it could be. Attendance at the General Assembly fell off; some towns refused to take any part in the restoration. By February 1690 it was hard to find a man willing to serve as governor. Finally the aged Henry Bull accepted. Taxes proved very hard to collect. The affairs of ordinary citizens were being obstructed, as wills remained unprocessed by probate courts and land titles could not always be recorded. With one thing and another to cope with, it took six or seven years to put the colony back together.

A small but influential group of men appeared who openly and doggedly opposed return to the old form of government. They wanted a stronger control from England, curbs on the power of the freemen, whether in a separate Rhode Island with a governor and council appointed by the Crown or merger with a neighboring colony having such a regime. These men collaborated with those who held the same views in Connecticut and sought backing from imperial officials.

The Rhode Island royalists, as they may be called for convenience, wanted to keep the government set up for Rhode Island under the Dominion of New England with themselves in control, until the monarchs could say what they wanted for the future. At one time two of the royalists, Richard Smith and John Fones, proposed a conference of delegates of the towns between

the Blackstone and Connecticut rivers to organize a force of
rangers, ostensibly to guard southern New England against
Indian attacks, but possibly to do more. The town council of
Warwick saw in the proposal a scheme "to subvert the present
government at least on the mainland and set up another by the
sword." When royalists rescued a prisoner in Kingstown and said
they would answer for their acts to Francis Brinley and John
Fones, justices appointed under the Dominion, the Rhode Island
magistrates saw behind the episode not only defiance of the
restored charter government but also signs that the Narragansett
Proprietors were behind the trouble.

The monarchy, however, did not rush to embrace these Rhode
Island friends. In fact, scarcely a word arrived from London for
many months. With the onset of war between England and
France in 1689, transatlantic shipping was risky, because the
French for a few years ruled the waves. Besides, the administra-
tors in London were too busy to concentrate on the government
in an obscure colony.

Rhode Island on its own faced the enemy. A fleet of French
privateers descended on Block Island in July 1690, pillaging and
terrorizing the inhabitants. A party of the marauders landed to
reconnoiter or raid Newport two days later but withdrew when
discovered. The governor and council, acting as a council of war,
commandeered two sloops and within three days outfitted them
with the guns, ammunition, provisions, and men needed to send
them against the foe. The crews contained a strange assortment
of Newport men including some seamen, leading citizens, Jews, a
shipbuilder, white and Indian servants, and a doctor. The lead
vessel of this pair, *Loyal Stede*, was commanded by Thomas Paine,
a renowned pirate or privateer captain who had retired to live in
Jamestown.

Meeting the French coming back from New London, the
sloops boldly engaged the enemy in a battle that lasted several
hours just off Block Island, where the anxious inhabitants
watched. Although a second round was expected in the following
morning, the French sailed off to the south; to evade pursuit,
they scuttled a slow-sailing prize ship laden with wines and
brandy. She nosed down in the water until almost perpendicular.

The brave Rhode Islanders could not manage to salvage any of the cargo and sadly watched her sink. In spite of this vigorous response in Newport to the attack, the Block Islanders feared another raid and wanted aid. They did indeed suffer two more French landings and barely prevented a fourth. They warned that they would have to look elsewhere if Rhode Island could not at least send money to help pay for their defense.

The military organization of the colony was actually in disarray. Some men in the militia contested the restored charter government. The General Assembly could assert its authority but not make its rulings stick. The first order to arrive from the sovereigns made things worse, because it gave Governor Sir William Phips of Massachusetts command of Rhode Island forces. He proclaimed his authority; then the governor and council, as a council of war, protested against it and issued orders to the militia units. Some officers refused to obey, other officers obeyed only to face noncompliance by their men. The Council of War next resorted to powers recently granted by the General Assembly to appoint officers it hoped would be loyal. Phips replied by providing a leading royalist, Peleg Sanford, with a stack of blank commissions to be issued to officers expected to acknowledge Phips's authority.

Though few took Sanford's commissions, clearly the colony could not endure rivalry over control of the militia. The General Assembly sent an agent, Christopher Almy, to carry its protest to the officials in London. Almy succeeded beyond hope. By December 1693 he could rejoice in an astoundingly favorable opinion by the Crown's attorney general, Edward Ward, who blandly ignored much of what had happened in recent years and declared that no suit against the Rhode Island charter had been carried out in proper legal fashion, and so the colony's privileges remained unclouded. The only encroachment on local control of the militia, he said, could be the requirement to furnish a reasonable quota of men, or even the whole force in case of extreme danger, for service outside the borders during time of war under a royal commander-in-chief. Ward's opinion gained royal approval and was used in drafting the message of Queen Mary to her loyal subjects in Rhode Island in August 1694.

Though the General Assembly took its time in furnishing quotas and at first disputed their size, it chronically relied on Ward's opinion and the queen's message both in arguing against the repeated efforts to turn over control of the militia to Massachusetts governors and in defending the continued force of the charter.

Royal endorsement of the charter government, so slow in its coming, arrived on a scene of drift into discord and chaos. The Assembly was limping along with rare appearances by deputies from the towns in the Narragansett country and Jamestown, places where town government under Rhode Island had ceased. Even Providence and Warwick had been paralyzed for some time. Futilely the Assembly had tried measures to centralize control over taxation and the militia to accomplish what the towns could not or would not do. The General Court of Trials, if one can believe its records, did not sit from the abandonment of the charter to 1693.

The scene changed quickly under Queen Mary's smile. Westerly gave up dickering over defection to Connecticut. Kingstown functioned as a Rhode Island town for the first time beginning in about 1696. East Greenwich resumed local government. The dramatic highlight, however, came in Jamestown, where on orders of the General Assembly, Governor Caleb Carr and Assistant Samuel Cranston called a meeting to reestablish town government. The magistrates read Ward's opinion, the queen's letter, and the town charter. Then the little throng chose Carr as moderator, and he presided over election of the civil and military officers for the town. The eclipse was nearing its end.

There was still much to do to put the colony back in working order. Tax collection had to be improved. The central treasury took in money from the reinstituted liquor duty but otherwise was at the mercy of the towns. They often failed to do their part in gathering revenue from the property taxes levied by the Assembly. Increasingly stringent laws to require town action had little effect during the 1690s, virtually none in places where boundary claims were in dispute. The Assembly assigned each town an amount to collect, so each one wanted to apportion it over the largest possible territory. Refusal to pay automatically brought action on any contested claims or reconsideration of earlier adverse rulings. Warwick and Providence both wanted Meshanticut within their borders; all the towns in the Narragansett country pushed claims against each other. Moves to draw firm lines began before 1700 but kept foundering because the boundary questions were based on older disputes over land rights. The colony still could not settle those underlying rivalries and therefore could not set durable town limits and crack down on tax delinquency. All the same, though direct levies remained unreliable, what little came in, when added to the proceeds of the liquor excise, enabled the colony to start paying salaries to its officials.

The struggle to restore taxation, combined with the returning loyalty of Jamestown and the Narragansett country, led to the division of the General Assembly into a bicameral legislature. With a full slate of deputies in 1696, for the first time since the attempted creation of Kingstown almost thirty years before, the twenty-eight town representatives were numerous enough to demand a separate organization. Because they obtained the power to elect their own speaker and otherwise act like a junior House of Commons it is quite likely that an analogy was drawn with the English Parliament, especially on the point which the deputies won giving them exclusive power to initiate money bills. In any event, division into two houses was clearly associated with measures on taxation.

Another adjustment to the larger number of towns came in the judiciary. The old rule for selecting magistrates from the four original towns was modified, but still several new ones were left without justices of the peace unless they elected officials called wardens who had the same powers, as was done in Jamestown and Block Island. Instead of giving every town an assistant—there were not enough to go around—or insisting that all the new towns elect wardens, the Assembly began appointing justices of the peace, first for towns without resident magistrates, then for the heavily populated original towns as well.

The work of restoring internal order to Rhode Island was interrupted by a new controversy over the colony's obligations to the Crown. When Rhode Island refused to send him its quota of forty-eight men, Governor Benjamin Fletcher of New York complained to London, adding remarks on other shortcomings. His report touched off an exchange of letters between Governor Walter Clarke in Newport and the new advisory commission on American affairs in London, commonly called the Board of Trade. The board brushed aside Clarke's excuses about the pressing need for all possible men to defend his colony and growled about Rhode Island's disregard of the trade laws and its hospitality to pirates.

The war and Governor Fletcher's administration both ended soon enough to let the quota controversy simmer down. The accusations concerning pirates, however, remained lively and were soon linked to charges of improper dealings with privateers. The linkage was natural. Pirate and privateer did the same things, capture ships at sea and raid coasts, but the pirate acted without sanction of law and would steal from anyone at any time, while the privateer had a commission from a government to seize or destroy property of an enemy during time of war. Often, but not always, privateer cruises were planned to be short, to seize enemy ships known to be nearby; pirates normally roamed long and far, but otherwise fitting out for an extended privateer cruise looked the same as preparing for piracy. And who could tell what a privateer might do once over the horizon? Several captains embarking on legal ventures persuaded their men, or were persuaded by them, to turn pirate.

Opponents of the charter government in Rhode Island insisted that it amiably allowed pirates to take vacations and refit their vessels at Newport. Ironically, the first known incident of this sort occurred under the Dominion of New England, when an obscure Captain Peterson was in port. Suspicions about his purposes were reported to a grand jury, which took no action, allegedly because several of its members were friends or relatives of men in Peterson's crew. Later there was talk of the shady past of Thomas Paine and refitting at Newport by such men as the mysterious Captain Want and Thomas Tew, who may have been a local son. Reports had it that Tew in 1693 brought in £8,000 as his share of plunder in the Indian Ocean, while his men of course had still more to spend. Small wonder that they were welcomed after another cruise in 1694.

Beyond tolerating pirates and their gold, the Rhode Island officials were accused of cloaking them with commissions as privateers. Several pirates certainly got such commissions in Newport. One of Tew's men may even have obtained two in 1694, under one of which Captain Joseph Farrow (or Faro) sailed for Madagascar, then a scene of pirate havens, and fell in with the notorious Captain "Long Ben" Avery. Another man who took a commission, William Mayes, either was captured by Avery or freely joined him. Whatever the truth of the matter, it was hard to explain why the Rhode Island privateer was sailing off Madagascar unless to turn pirate or buy pirate plunder.

Enemies of the charter government did not stop with accusations of coddling pirates, but also argued that Rhode Island had no power to issue privateer commissions. Before the 1690s, the colony had issued them only during the Interregnum in England, so the question of legality had not arisen. The first cruises against the French in King William's War, beginning with *Loyal Stede*'s, had been directly sponsored by the colony, which was undoubtedly legal. Beginning in 1693 or 1694, however, Deputy Governor John Greene signed commissions for privateers. (The governors, who were Quakers, did not sign such documents, presumably for reasons of conscience.) His authority was soon challenged.

Some cruises under the colony's authorization aroused no controversy. Legend has it that the brothers William and John Wanton, both in their early twenties, began their spectacular rise to fame and high office by organizing a band of about thirty friends, who sailed out of Newport armed with nothing more dangerous than pistols and by a clever stratagem captured a large pirate ship in 1694. The story continues that three years later they took a French privateer by means almost as makeshift and thereby enhanced their renown and greatly enriched themselves.

Greene's conduct in issuing commissions fell under attack in connection with charges that the colony acted illegally in declaring prizes brought in by privateers to be legitimate seizures. Granting commissions and ruling on the legality of captures were both elements of admiralty jurisdiction, which Rhode Island claimed to have by its charter and the royal officials said it did not. The local opinion took shape in Newport when a Jamaica captain brought in a vessel, requesting the usual judicial action to declare it a legitimate prize won by his privateer company. There was no admiralty court to handle the business, so the General Assembly voted to let the governor and council in their capacity as high court assume this added competence until further word came from London. This home-made admiralty court continued to function, much to the delight of the citizens who profited from the influx of prizes. When further instructions arrived, giving jurisdiction to a judge with powers delegated by the High Court of Admiralty in England, the colony's officials protested that this step encroached on the charter privileges and refused to abandon their makeshift arrangement of 1694. Rhode Island officials persistently denied any wrongdoing, and the controversy remained to precipitate the next crises for the charter government.

No one, fortunately, was singling out Newport as peculiarly depraved. The two other northern ports then beginning their sudden rise, Philadelphia and New York, were also accused of coddling pirates. Governor Fletcher of New York himself was recalled to face, among several charges, allegations of more numerous and flagrant acts of favor to pirates than could be brought against any combination of officials in Newport. New Jersey was notoriously the resort of lawless sea raiders when they wanted an interlude of tranquility. And a good deal could have been said about Boston, Bermuda, and points south.

Altogether, it is likely that Rhode Island privateer commissions were abused and that the officials who granted them had reason to suspect they might be. For a port on the make, however, the advantages of plunder on the high seas, legal or illegal, were so great as to mute scruples. A few undoubted pirates settled down in the colony, but so did some untainted privateer captains and many other honest people. With the facts unobtainable, there is no telling how much booty in the form of coin and goods entered the Newport economy and how much of a discount the people of the colony enjoyed when buying captured rather than legally imported articles. In some measure, however, privateering and piracy surely helped stimulate Newport at a crucial time when locally owned vessels were few, shipbuilding just beginning, and legitimate trade uncertain or worse.

Royalist enemies of the charter government made the most of the situation. They were rewarded with a commission to one of them, Peleg Sanford, as judge of a local Court of Vice Admiralty authorized in England. The commission arrived just as Governor Clarke came under new pressure to enforce the English trade laws. Royal orders required him to give bond for faithful enforcement; a parliamentary statute required him to take an oath promising enforcement. Clarke refused. As a Quaker he would not take an oath. When Sanford appeared with his commission, Clarke urged the General Assembly to repudiate it as inconsistent with the charter; if the deputies tolerated this invasion of their privileges, "he would take his leave of them, and there would be no more choice or election according to their charter." He would not administer an oath to Sanford to enter his new position. In dismay Jahleel Brenton, who had not been a royalist and who had represented the colony in London and won the confidence of officials there so well as to be appointed collector of customs for New England, wrote the Board of Trade recommending that Clarke be summoned to explain his conduct to the Privy Council.

In this minor crisis, wily old Walter Clarke again resigned. The General Assembly chose as his replacement his nephew, Samuel Cranston, the remarkable man who led the colony for almost twenty-nine years, annually reelected until his death in 1727. (Clarke kept his hand in as deputy governor from 1700 to the end of his life.) The Assembly probably did not realize that it was inaugurating a new era—surely could not guess that it was selecting the man who was to hold office longer than any other chief executive of an American colony or state. Cranston, however, proved to be what Rhode Island needed. The eclipse was finally over.

7

CRANSTON, THE EMPIRE, AND INTERNAL ORDER

Governor Samuel Cranston presided over a transformation of Rhode Island from a beleaguered cluster of villages to a flourishing agricultural province organized to aid the growth of Newport's trade. He did not launch new policies as much as extend, elaborate, and carry out those that had been sketched a few years before he took office. His outstanding accomplishment, the key to many things that followed, was to bring his colony into a working relation with the imperial government in London while preserving its charter privileges. As he succeeded in doing this, it became possible to bring internal order to the colony and start settling old disputes with its neighbors.

With hindsight, one can see that events had already started to move in directions that became significant during the Cranston years. Strengthening and centralizing the colony's government, separating towns from the management of common lands, systematizing law, even introducing traditional forms of Protestant Christianity and reviving interest in learning—all had begun, although they had not proceeded far enough to yield many effects. Nor in 1697 was there any reason for confidence that the direction would remain steady or that the colony could keep its own government. Visible to the discerning were changes of even greater importance: the population was growing at a much faster rate than ever before, and shipbuilding was booming, with many vessels staying in Newport ownership. The town was suddenly beginning to fulfill its hopes of being a major center of trade.

During Samuel Cranston's long tenure of office, Rhode Island was reorganized to support Newport's commercial ambition. Obstacles to expanding settlement were cleared away to increase the port's hinterland. Roads were pushed into the interior, often over local objections, to facilitate taking products of the countryside to a spate of new commercial centers around the bay, at which the goods could be loaded on small craft for transfer to Newport. Laws were enacted by the colony and the towns to regulate commercial life. Raiding at sea, mostly legal, brought in goods and coin needed for the rising port. Ultimately the colony inaugurated a daring policy of creating paper money to supply a medium of exchange needed by the port. Rhode Island energetically extended its jurisdiction, although it won little of its territory still held by Massachusetts until somewhat later.

If these changes were conceived in the interests of an aggressive trading center, they were nevertheless congenial to the other towns in most respects, because the aspirations of Newport could be fulfilled only by development of its hinterland. To be sure, there were violent quarrels and embittered losers; some private ambitions were thwarted in the reordering of governmental affairs. As will appear, the Newport leadership took care to aid local interests on one side while attacking on another, to seek compromises, and to avoid showdowns. On the whole, political skill kept internal grievances from building into powerful combinations. As general prosperity advanced, individual rancors could usually be rendered powerless until they ceased to matter.

Who deserves credit for Rhode Island's transformation? Sad to say, so little information survives to afford glimpses into the way people worked with each other that one must use imagination more freely than is desirable. The brilliant accomplishments of the long Cranston administration surely were not the work of a single mind. Indeed, the records reveal a group of men who constantly took major public responsibilities before the political upheaval of 1714 and 1715 shifted the alignment. All, from Samuel Cranston down, remain shadowy figures. Who has heard of Isaac Martindale, Joseph or Nathaniel Sheffield, Giles Slo-

cum, Weston Clarke, or Henry Tew? A few are less obscure—
Walter Clarke, Joseph Jenckes, and John and William Wanton
—because they served as governor before and after Cranston.
One may speculate on Henry Tew's kinship with the pirate,
Thomas. The names of Nathaniel Sheffield and a few other
figures in this group appeared among the crew of *Loyal Stede*;
several were in seafaring or trade. But in reality they are little
more than names on paper, and few papers survive from this
period, practically none to reveal the personal concerns or
characters of these men.

Such evidence as there is shows Cranston constantly at work.
He was everywhere, serving as chief executive, president of the
Council of War, chief judge of the Court of Trials, moderator of
the Newport town meeting, presiding officer of the town council,
promoter of civic betterment, committeeman for assorted tasks,
spokesman for the colony in some delicate negotiations, and
prime mover in four or five landowners' organizations. It may be
fair to picture him as the doge of a nascent New England Venice.

Samuel Cranston was born at about two o'clock in the
morning on Saturday, August 7, 1659, according to a record he
cherished. His father was John Cranston, a Scotsman with skills
as a physician and surgeon, who had been slightly involved in the
affairs of the Narragansett Proprietors but had changed his
leanings and later served as governor. His mother was a sister of
Walter Clarke. Samuel, as a youth, became a sea captain and
earned a reputation for bravery. Later he settled down as a
merchant but never became very rich or fond of luxury, probably
because he was engrossed in the public business, for which he
received little pay. He married a woman whose parents were
Thomas Hart, another Newport shipmaster, and Freeborn
Williams, the second child of Roger. (Freeborn Hart, when
widowed, married Walter Clarke, thereby making that man
Cranston's stepfather-in-law as well as his uncle.) Thus Samuel
Cranston, though obviously the leader of Newport, had a
convenient marital tie to the first family of Providence. He also
assimilated for a time some of the Clarke Quakerism and was
occasionally said to be a Quaker. In fact he associated fully with
no communion, though when an Anglican church was built in

Newport, a pew was reserved for him, and he took his children there for baptism.

If these details suggest the behavior of a natural-born politician, a one-man balanced ticket, it is a relief to learn that he had some personal interests. Curiously, he went in for astrology. The precision of his birth date, like his own notations of births of his later children, served to aid in determining extraterrestrial influences. Towards the end of his life, like many Rhode Islanders since, the governor took an interest in genealogy. He inquired about Cranstons in Scotland, corresponded with a minor laird to whom he claimed kinship, and found an elderly lady who procured for him a coat of arms.

Governor Cranston may have been a trifle pathetic in seeking to identify himself with an aristocratic British family—he counted for more in the world than the laird ever did—but his attempt reflected an element in his thinking that had greater importance. He was the first governor to regard his position as one requiring him to steer Rhode Island as a province of the British empire.

He was almost the first who had reason to see it that way. During much of the seventeenth century, ties with the mother country were slender. The half-forgotten settlements around Narragansett Bay occasionally reminded London of their existence by seeking a charter or appealing disputes over territory for royal determination. Men like William Harris and Randall Holden gained the ear of high officials without much delay or expense, in all likelihood because they were quaint and backwoodsy characters. They were given virtually anything they asked, even when one sought the undoing of what another had just won. Probably no one at court thought it worthwhile to learn much more than what the emissaries said about their affairs before granting these boons. There was too little commerce in Rhode Island to worry anyone in England, no royal governor to send reports or receive instructions, no minister of the Church of England to correspond with the bishop of London.

When Rhode Island seemed to require attention the simple course was to throw it in with Massachusetts. The Dominion of New England failed, but afterwards in London it looked as though a few minor measures could accomplish all that really needed doing around Narragansett Bay—appoint a customs collector, an admiralty judge, and give the governor of Massachusetts authority to command the militia in time of war. Annoyingly, the tiny colony balked. A few of its citizens who yearned for closer ties to the monarchy—and for power—railed against this stubbornness. Whenever possible they told the king's men that the local officials were ignorant bumpkins, mere Baptists and Quakers, who should be brushed aside. Walter Clarke, keen enough when it came to the seventeenth-century business of fending off the designs of Massachusetts and Connecticut, lacked the suppleness and breadth of vision to deal with Whitehall. Samuel Cranston lacked these qualities at first but gained them quickly.

The first order of business was to extricate Rhode Island from the dilemma posed by English policy in an era of international war. For Rhode Island the new measures to replace the Dominion of New England appeared to pose an impossible choice between tolerating encroachment on the charter privileges and refusing obedience to all demands of the imperial officials. It was useless to grumble in private that the mother country had not lifted a finger for her New England colonists in King Philip's War and to protest in public that she called on Rhode Island to supply land forces to Massachusetts or New York without offering compensatory protection at sea. Regardless of how fairness might be reckoned in Newport, when the colony rejected the commissions of Governor Phips of Massachusetts and Governor Fletcher of New York to command the local militia or refused to call up a small squad for their service, the resistance courted new legal action against the charter and renewed internal division. Failure to keep a separate provincial government could lead to the stifling of religious freedom and the promising commerce of Newport.

The way out of this trap, put in bald terms, was to do most of what the imperial officials asked while doggedly opposing the governmental changes they thought were necessary to get it done. Rhode Island agreed to send soldiers for the imperial wars while denying the validity of any commission to an outsider to take command of the militia; it accepted an admiralty judge appointed in London while defending the admiralty powers of the colonial magistrates; it revised the laws and administration of the colony, conceding a right of appeal from the local courts to the royal Privy Council, while insisting that no essential change was being made because none was needed. Officials in Newport took conspicuous action to defend the coast and prosecute pirates. Sensibly, the Cranston administration attended to the substance of complaints against Rhode Island, denying steadfastly that the complaints had weight, as a means of staving off plans to remedy the ills by altering the foundations of the provincial government.

Upon assuming office Cranston confronted the second of three emergencies that were essentially the same. They all centered on a commission to a governor of Massachusetts giving control over the Rhode Island militia; in all three the local royalists denounced the charter officials as unfit to govern and called for a change in government; in all, the royalists pushed validation of the Narragansett Proprietors' claims. The second emergency was the most complex. As has been mentioned, Walter Clarke resigned rather than take the oath to enforce the trade laws or administer the oath to Peleg Sanford as admiralty judge. In addition, Richard Coote, the Earl of Bellomont, came over as governor of Massachusetts (and New York and New Hampshire as well) with a commission empowering him to command the Rhode Island militia in time of war. Soon Edward Randolph, surveyor of customs for America, inspected the colony and sent a highly critical report to the Board of Trade.

Randolph clearly got most of his ideas from the local royalists. He claimed that the replacement of Clarke by Cranston was a typical Quaker subterfuge to install a man without scruples about oaths but otherwise change nothing. Rhode Island, Randolph claimed, harbored pirates; in fact, Cranston and the Clarkes profited from piracy and connived at the recent release of men jailed on suspicion of piracy. Other complaints from the royalists and Jahleel Brenton also reached the Board of Trade, especially ones alleging inadequacy of the colony's laws and bias in its court. The board decided that Bellomont should question the Rhode Island officials, obtain copies of official documents for transmission to London, and generally look over what was going on around Narragansett Bay.

Cranston clumsily tried to head off adverse results of the inquiry, if not the inquiry itself, by writing to the Board of Trade on the main topics of investigation. His protestations, apologies, and copies of official papers only made things worse. The board sent back a stern reply declaring that the documents were neither complete, legible, nor such as to bear out his assertions. What he reported revealed a shocking laxity in the conduct of government that should have been punished and surely would have to be corrected.

Bellomont finally reached Rhode Island with his entourage in September 1699. He asked about court actions in which favoritism was alleged, about pirates, about the assertion of admiralty jurisdiction, enforcement of the trade laws, the administration of oaths, the militia, conflicts between the laws of the colony and the laws of England, and about a swarm of specific allegations. He conferred with some leading royalists, notably Francis Brinley and Peleg Sanford. Perhaps to his surprise these men urged on Bellomont the claims of the late William Harris and the still lively Narragansett Proprietors. Unable to get satisfactory answers about oaths and the trade laws, unable or unwilling to adjudicate the controversy over the Narragansett country, Bellomont solemnly departed, leaving Brinley and Sanford to pester Cranston for a full copy of the colony's laws and the official records.

Bellomont, in fact, did not wait for the documents. Before they came to his hands he wrote his report, charging twenty-five "irregularities and maladministrations" ranging from using a shortened form of the official name of the colony and neglecting to evangelize the Indians, through biased or ignorant judges and protecting piracy,* to a cluster of deviations from the terms of the

---

* Bellomont's accusation on piracy seems to have stung Cranston, who had already taken steps to make Newport inhospitable to lawless sea raiders. Even while Bellomont was writing a critical report to the Board of Trade, Cranston was aiding him and Peleg Sanford in the prosecution of James Gillam, a pirate who had put in at Boston after looking over Newport and deciding not to tarry.

charter. He also asserted that the charter gave no authority to impose taxes, erect an admiralty court, inflict the death penalty, or let the militia companies elect their own officers. The guiding idea behind these accusations was a belief that the colony's government had the same standing in law as a municipal corporation in England. Though palpably unrealistic, this notion had been used before by Randolph in concocting charges against Massachusetts and Rhode Island. Probably Randolph supplied it to Bellomont.

The earl also parroted the royalists' contempt for the officials. The attorney general was "a poor illiterate mechanic," the magistrates were "generally Quakers and sectaries, . . . illiterate and of little or no capacity," the deputy governor was "a brutish man, of very corrupt or no principles in religion." This band of clowns naturally neglected good form in the conduct of government, a situation that might have been merely sad if it had not sprung from systematic exclusion of "several gentlemen most sufficient for estate, best capacitated and disposed for his majesty's service." He meant Brinley, Sanford, and company. He was completely deceived by them except in regard to the Harris claims and the Narragansett lands, subjects on which he had sense enough to retreat into the role of fact-gatherer.

In actuality the royalists had been called upon to assume

Cranston helped search for the loot of Captain William Kidd, who had been sent out by England to attack pirates at Madagascar and had been accused of turning pirate himself. Bellomont had put Kidd in jail and may well have been framing him in order to get part of the wealth the captain had brought back from wherever he had been. The Massachusetts governor by turns accused Cranston of keeping a share of confiscated pirate booty and of warning pirates when admiralty court officers at Newport sought warrants for their arrest, thus giving them time to escape. Altogether, Bellomont's strictures on Cranston were inconsistent and ill-grounded, and perhaps were contrived to divert attention from less savory proceedings in his own jurisdiction. Still the strictures hurt, and Cranston was soon outdoing himself to take vigorous action against pirates. He did not get a dramatic climax to his efforts, however, until 1723, when he served on the bench of a special court to try Charles Harris (no relation to William) and his crew, a notoriously sadistic lot. Following a sensational trial in Newport, twenty-six men were hanged there after elaborate pageantry before a huge throng.

public responsibilities quite often. Sometimes what they did in office, as when Brinley had been an assistant, gave good grounds for their return to private stations. The wealthy and compara- tively well-educated were chronically expected to undertake public responsibilities, however, and received many chances to show what they could do. The complainers wanted more power than they deserved, and their snobbery and pettifogging betrayed their modest merits. In political intelligence, they were no match for Walter Clarke, to say nothing of Samuel Cranston.

But what was the governor to do when the powerful earl sided with the local opposition? For the time being he could only stall, offer apologies, and make gestures of compliance with what was asked of him. In reality the laws were almost as disheveled and incomplete, the judges as ignorant, and the conduct of official business nearly as amateurish as had been alleged. These things could not be cured in a hurry. One small step was possible at once, accepting the appointment of an admiralty judge for the colony, William Atwood, whom Cranston swore in personally in October 1701.

The governor could also look for a way out of the debilitating contest with Connecticut, which was dragging on remorselessly in a succession of alarms, parleys, and displays of power. In search of an agreement on the boundary, Cranston appealed to Colonel Fitz-John Winthrop, the proud and wealthy governor of Connecticut who was also one of the Narragansett Proprietors. In this letter, one of the few to convey a sense of Cranston's personality when he was in his prime, he argued that the two colonies were actually as one when it came to preserving their privileges and must save them together. To give force to his ideas he naturally turned to imagery of seafaring: the two colonies were the halves of one ship. He wrote, "our contending doth lay us both open for others to take the greater advantage against us" and "to strike at our charters. Perhaps you think there is no danger of yours, so you will do your endeavors to overthrow us and thereby strengthen yourselves. But I would pray you not to flatter yourselves with such expectations, for you may assure yourselves that if we split you will sink, for we are both upon one bottom, and I am apt to conclude [there are] as many rents and leaks on your part as on ours, if not some trunnel holes open."

It followed that he and Winthrop, as "the chief or head pilots" of the ship, must rally their people "to labor for their own preservation and safety, and not to delay till we split upon the rock or fall into the quick sands." The pilots should forget personal profit. Winthrop was rich enough to "lay aside all interest." If he could find a way to settle the old quarrel between the two colonies and free them to prepare their defenses against the French and Spanish it would be an achievement that would "make him happy in the world to come and his name famous to future generations." Cranston concluded the fervent, yet calculated, appeal: "Let me entreat Colonel Winthrop to propose some way to accomplish all this. I know he can do it. And let us make our names famous as instruments to promote so good a work."

Unmoved by this eloquence, Winthrop sent back a reply that was mostly noncommittal, but protested the arrest of a Connecticut man by Rhode Island officials, acting west of the Pawcatuck River. "It seems wonderful to me," he wrote, "that at the same time when your Honor insinuates for proposals to prevent animosities . . . you should nevertheless detain under extravagant bonds one of our people . . . within our known and undoubted bounds." Connecticut was in no mood to yield an inch. The two colonies went on arresting each other's local officials.

Cranston seemed to be getting nowhere, but luck was with him. Bellomont, constantly hectored by Brinley, was just beginning to take up the cause of the Narragansett Proprietors when an untimely death removed him from the scene. Back in England, a new turn of the political wheel dislodged his backers from influence. So the second emergency fizzled out miraculously. The planets may have been favorably aligned over Cranston's cradle on that night in August 1659.

The third crisis built up all too soon, but this time Cranston was ready. The new governor of Massachusetts, Joseph Dudley, arrived at the start of Queen Anne's War, bearing the usual commission to command the Rhode Island militia and also one as vice admiral with power over the ports and what maritime forces there might be. He appeared with a retinue at Newport in September 1702, presented these documents to the local officials, and had himself sworn in by one of his own retainers. Cranston and some of his council attended the ceremony but did not assist. Instead they reiterated the long-standing argument that Dudley's commissions were of no effect because in violation of charter privileges. When Dudley ordered the Aquidneck regiment of militia to appear before him for review, the highest officer, Captain Isaac Martindale, refused on the grounds that he received orders only from the governor and council or the General Assembly. Dudley tried the mainland regiment, getting a fair turnout at Kingstown. Cranston and the council rushed over to upbraid the officers, then sped back to the assembled deputies, who added their voices to a choir denouncing Dudley's pretended authority. Dudley retreated to Boston, where he penned a report essentially like Bellomont's, only longer. As might have been expected, there was a new flare-up of controversy with Connecticut.

Cranston knew what to do. He called on the Assembly to appropriate money for military expenditures in aid of the queen's war against France and Spain and for representation of the colony's interests in London. Instead of sending a special emissary in the fashion of times past, the colony relied on its new agent residing in the imperial capital. He was William Wharton, a solicitor with close ties to William Blathwayt, the dominant figure on the Board of Trade especially when the Tories were in ascendancy. Though Dudley's allegations were repeated and amplified in 1705 with the concurrence of the governor of New York, Rhode Island depended on a trained legal mind to reply to the charges and state its case to the board. The result was a collapse of sweeping accusations into a few minor technical points and the dismissal of the theory that the colony had the same place in law as an English municipality.

While Wharton was drawing the fangs of the hostile reports, Cranston wrought a miracle: he won an acceptable compromise with Connecticut in 1703. (It did not last, but it set this old contest aside at a crucial time.) Precisely how he did it can only be guessed. Cranston was in cahoots with James Fitch, a rival of

Governor Fitz-John Winthrop of Connecticut for office and land, also with some of Winthrop's in-laws in a massive family fight over an inheritance, and with Quakers protesting Connecticut's intolerance. Moreover, Dudley himself in effect lent a hand by his contempt for the Narragansett Proprietors and his ardor to overthrow the charter government of Connecticut, which he detested more than Rhode Island's. Just how these pieces fitted together—whether all of them in fact did figure in the puzzle—cannot be determined. Whatever lay behind the event, in May 1703 the Rhode Island negotiator, Joseph Sheffield, won a concession from the beleaguered Connecticut officials for a boundary line approximately where it was later fixed. The two colonies promised in vague terms to accept private property claims, however derived, on both sides of the line. The language was artfully chosen to let the Narragansett Proprietors think they had won at last, so they raised no objections until they learned better, when it was too late.

This agreement had a substantial foundation in the successful assertion of Rhode Island local government in the disputed region. Strong measures had stopped a tax revolt in 1699 and fostered general acceptance of tax obligations. Action to draw precise boundaries for Westerly and Kingstown was slowly overcoming the last local quarrels but did not produce results until the winter of 1703–1704, on the heels of the agreement on the colony line. Thereafter, Connecticut could not undermine the authority of those two towns any more.

While dealing with Dudley and Fitz-John Winthrop, Cranston and the General Assembly were preparing Rhode Island to make a good showing in Queen Anne's War. To begin with they planned defense against raids or invasions by the French and Spanish. New laws provided for organizing town watch and scout forces, previously managed by local officials on an improvisatory basis. The Assembly in 1701 also enacted the first explicit authorization for military discipline in the militia companies, which were grouped into two regiments, island and mainland, under majors appointed by the Assembly. The colony recruited and maintained a small garrison for the fort at the mouth of Newport harbor and half of a force to guard Block Island. The

Assembly presently balked, however, at proposals to construct other fortifications. Nor would it end election of militia officers, in spite of the repeated criticism that the practice ran contrary to the charter, probably for fear that interference with this popular procedure would dampen military ardor among the men. Luckily, after the fracas over Dudley's muster at Kingstown, there was no further competition against the authority of the colony's officials over the officers.

Cranston's next move was to show good faith in Rhode Island's assertion that it would furnish a quota of men in aid of the war against France. When Dudley backed off from insisting on his authority to take over the militia, Cranston and his council promptly sent a contingent of men for a prospective expedition in the summer of 1704. The following February the General Assembly endorsed this action by voting to raise a company of forty-eight men to be constantly ready for service under Dudley. Two years later the Assembly added authorization for a vessel to be requisitioned, fitted out to transport the men, and take part in any likely engagement against the French. As it turned out, that summer's campaigns accomplished little against the enemy, but military zeal remained unquenched in Newport.

All this martial bustle afforded evidence that the colony felt a patriotic fervor, contrary to what had been said against it. Governor Cranston, putting the best face on things, reported to London in 1708 that the men were constantly ready "upon any alarum or other expedition or service, to repair to their ensigns at their respective places of rendezvous, to attend such orders as they shall receive from their superior officers, etc., the which obligations and orders are upon all occasions very cheerfully and readily obeyed and complied with." Possibly so. He said nothing of exemptions for pacifists, of which the colony had many, but rather expatiated on the array of ammunition each man was to provide at his own expense. Artfully the governor steered his report to the conclusion that local defense of the individual towns against small raiding parties was about all Rhode Island could manage with its small population, limited resources, and long coastline.

The very next year, however, the colony demonstrated again

its ardor to outdo itself in the queen's service. The Assembly rushed to support a projected invasion of Canada. This expedition miscarried, but the organization for it was used to raise a new force—some ships, plus four times the Rhode Island quota—for the invasion of Nova Scotia. One ship was lost, but Port Royal was captured and renamed Annapolis Royal. Again in 1711 Rhode Island supplied men and ships for the invasion of Canada. This effort met disaster in the Gulf of St. Lawrence. Though the colony's contingent in these last two campaigns was small, about two hundred soldiers, it must be remembered that this number amounted to almost one-seventh of the males of military age (16–60) and could be mustered only by enlisting Indians and by requiring each town to furnish a certain number of men. Thus Rhode Island showed it could rally to the queen's cause without its militia being put under the command of a royally appointed official.

The colony also plunged into privateering and sea warfare with considerable success, though Governor Cranston failed to keep all of what he thought were his powers in this arena against challenges by Dudley. The outbreak of Queen Anne's War signaled the fitting out of privateer voyages. The declaration of war arrived at Newport on June 25, 1702. By July 6 William Wanton, Isaac Martindale, and John Scott were ready to send out *Greyhound.* Cruising in the Gulf of St. Lawrence, this brigantine captured three French vessels laden with fish, which were brought back to Newport in September. Dudley tried to obstruct Cranston's assumption of admiralty jurisdiction over these prizes and tried to brand Wanton a pirate. The Rhode Island governor nevertheless continued issuing commissions to privateers, and more prize vessels filled with fish and other goods came to Newport to be certified as legitimate prey by Cranston's admiralty court. The governor dutifully reserved a tenth of the value of the prizes for the queen, asking and eventually getting permission to use part of the royal tithe to fortify Newport harbor.

Dudley would not abandon opposition and got his way point by point. In 1704 Cranston stopped asserting his colony's power to try suspects of piracy and soon yielded to an admiralty judge with an English commission the right to hear claims to vessels captured at sea. Even after these steps backward, Cranston could not stop objections to his issuance of privateers' commissions, although he came close. Admiralty Judge Nathaniel Byfield refused to condemn a prize sent in by Captain John Halsey, who had sailed under Rhode Island authority, because the commission had been signed after the Privy Council in London had declared that the Governor of Rhode Island had no power to issue such documents. The prize was a Spanish vessel with a valuable cargo of wine, brandy, sugar, and other merchandise. The Boston merchants who had financed Halsey were not about to forego this profit, and one of them was an admiralty officer with responsibilities for prizes. He backed Cranston and prevailed upon Dudley to join in asking Byfield to proceed. The judge submitted to pressure, his feelings reportedly soothed by a bribe. Thereupon Cranston issued a fresh commission to Halsey, who captured more vessels, took them to be declared prizes at Brava in the Cape Verde Islands under the friendly Portuguese flag, but then for some reason turned pirate and set sail for Madagascar. Cranston stopped issuing commissions to privateers. Possibly no one asked him for one after the Privy Council's ruling rendered such a document dubious in law. In any case, the colony had not been able to keep the admiralty powers it claimed under the charter.

Thereafter Cranston distinguished himself in the war at sea by vigorous dispatch of hastily armed vessels to attack French marauders. These ventures occurred several times, once after a new attack on Block Island, with good results on most occasions.

Nimble policy in Newport, of course, did not by itself deflect the arrows of Bellomont, Randolph, and Dudley. The attack on Rhode Island was only a part of a campaign against chartered and proprietary colonies that had been going on for a long time. The vigorous phase of 1696 to 1707, staged by the new Board of Trade, included efforts to get action by various means, even parliamentary legislation voiding the old grants. Being an assault on substantial interests, it drew great opposition from those directly threatened and also from leading Englishmen who feared or condemned any attempt to tamper with rights to property or privileges. At times William Penn or the charter government of Connecticut faced the heaviest fire. As Cranston pointed out in 1701, it was necessary for the beleaguered colonies to stick together in the time of peril. When parliamentary action failed, when opposition stymied efforts to assert royal prerogative to change colonial governments, and finally when William Blathwayt and three other men were dismissed from the Board of Trade in 1707, the whole campaign withered away. Rhode Island certainly benefited from being only one of several colonial governments under duress. Still it had to hold its own without direct aid from the others.

Seen from London, Cranston merited respect for his skill in parrying the thrusts at the charter privileges and his wisdom in realizing that his colony must yield some voluntary cooperation with the imperial government. Seen from Newport, he deserved credit for much more: by turning back the intrusions of Bellomont and Dudley, he undercut a dangerous internal faction and did so while gaining all but total victory in the long struggle for the Narragansett country. Moreover, while these events were going on, the colony took giant steps to bring order to the laws and local government, its commerce expanded, and even war turned profits. The early years of the Cranston administration brought quite a change to Rhode Island's prospects.

The government of Rhode Island during the Cranston years underwent a thorough overhaul. The internal workings and the laws were revised to bring order and system to the province and to give the central government the scope of control specified for it in the charter. The colony weathered attacks on its privileges until an outpouring of zeal in Queen Anne's War and a change of policy by her ministers made it possible for Rhode Island to set a new course in its relations with the mother country. These dealings with Great Britain, however, though they "anglicized" the province in many ways and geared it to the empire, served to shield self-government while the Cranston administration made it effective. Indeed, without the internal reconstruction, keeping the charter privileges would have been neither possible nor worthwhile. Though much was said about saving the charter as if it was an end in itself, the ultimate purpose of self-government was to foster the commerce of Newport and, by extension, the prosperity and cultural autonomy of the whole colony.

If the colonial government was to be used for Newport's ends, the General Assembly first had to gain the full authority that the charter had assigned to it. Quite a gap had to be closed when Cranston took office, even though the Assembly in the time of his predecessors, Caleb Carr and Walter Clarke, had launched some promising measures that he continued. To curb disorder within the colony many things were necessary: to finish establishing the Assembly's tax power; to compile the laws, enact more to cover all essential subjects, and rewrite the old statutes to make them technically adequate by English standards; to stop the conflicts over land, so that chaos and squabbling over property rights would cease impeding settlement and generating political disruption; to end quarrels over town boundaries and bring town governments under a uniform regulation by law; to improve the workings of the colony's central government itself and to extend its control over the military organizations of the towns. In short, much of the disarray left by the seventeenth century had to be put to rights. To accomplish this business, the General Assembly had to subdue independent power exerted by the towns and landowners' organizations and secure control over many parts of public affairs that had been only nominally subject to its rulings.

The ailing tax power, of course, had been under treatment for several years. There was no difficulty in restoring the liquor duty or imposing a new one on slaves. Nor did the colony meet resistance to port fees. The old property tax was another matter, however. Often resisted or ignored in the seventeenth century, it remained hard to collect in the eighteenth. The General Assembly determined a total amount to be raised and on the basis of rough estimation of taxable wealth assigned shares to the towns. They were to apportion the shares among their citizens according to the value of their property. The Assembly specified what assets were to be taxed—land, livestock, or whatever—but left the towns to choose officers to do the work of assessing and collecting. Town treasurers, in theory, would ultimately deliver to the colony's general treasurer the money or its equivalent in commodities, such as grain or pickled meat. There had been provisions in law concerning town procedures, but towns had not always followed them, and after restoration of the charter government, noncompliance was rife. Doubt or denial of the Assembly's authority provided ample excuses for tax-dodging in some places, while others refused to pay on the grounds that the town's share was unfairly large or its boundaries were so vague or improperly determined as to prevent spreading the burden among a sufficient number of citizens.

Step by step the Assembly fought tax resistance. It stipulated what officers the towns must choose to assess and collect taxes, added provisions for legal action against the officers if they failed to carry out their duties, and asserted a power to appoint such officers if the towns did not elect them. Slowly the towns settled into compliance. After quelling the tax revolt in the Narragansett country in 1699, Cranston pushed for settlement of town boundaries there, with success in a few years. Warwick and Providence went on disputing jurisdiction over the Meshanticut district for some time longer, however, while Warwick balked at taxes. The likelihood of payment rose, on the whole, though slowly. By 1704 the system worked fairly well, but by then wartime expenditures had already made it impossible to finance the government out of revenue even if all the money came in that was due. The colony had to resort to credit, first simply by taking goods and promising to pay later, then by notes to be redeemed out of future revenue. Plans were made to meet these obligations with property taxes in the years after the war, yet the plans were scrapped in favor of a fiscal system based on paper money. Rhode Island greeted the end of Queen Anne's War with a long tax holiday.*

The process of bringing order and adequacy to the colony's laws reached results slowly in the two decades between Bello-

---

* The towns had raised money by property taxes during the seventeenth century and continued to do so in the eighteenth. They faced resistance at times, but seldom widespread evasion. The usual practice was to let town bills pile up for a while and then levy a rate to pay them. During the paper money era in the eighteenth century, the towns received part of the interest on the loans that put the paper in circulation. As a result, some towns as well as the colony stopped taxing property.

mont's visit and publication of the first compilation in 1719. The table of laws sent to Bellomont amounted to little more than a summary of legislation; in spite of Cranston's protestations, Rhode Island's statutes were in a mess—literally so, in that such as existed at all had to be hunted down in a pile of loose papers or where entered here and there in ledgers. A series of committees worked fitfully to make a compilation and eventually produced one in 1707. Before it was made, the General Assembly had passed various measures reaffirming some old laws, repudiating others, and for safety's sake writing (in 1700) a statute announcing that the laws of England would be observed in matters not covered by colonial legislation. When these stopgaps had been enacted, as Brinley complained, no one could tell what laws were in force.

He was no happier with the document of 1707, which was manifestly incomplete and in some passages inaccurate or a clever distortion. As depicted in this text, for instance, town government was defined and regulated by law to an extent quite out of keeping with the realities of 1707, to say nothing of the earlier times when the statutes were said to have been enacted. Compilation was being used as an occasion to overhaul the laws and at the same time to make a blueprint for future practice.

Further work on the laws was impeded by the crush of public business and the lack of lawyers. More favorable conditions prevailed at the end of Queen Anne's War, by which time two attorneys, Nathaniel Blagrove and Nathaniel Newdigate, had drifted in from Bristol, then still in Massachusetts. It must be acknowledged that Blagrove, the pioneer of the Rhode Island bar, was not universally esteemed. On one occasion, Judge Nathaniel Byfield, his Bristol neighbor, accused him of forgery and lying under oath to defraud his wife's children by her first husband. Blagrove was not run out of town after this incident by a pack of outraged citizens; quite the contrary, they elected him their representative to the General Court of Massachusetts, so it can hardly be said that the man was forced to take up practice in Newport. More likely the growing business and absence of other lawyers in that town made it an attractive place for him and later Newdigate.

As they embarked on practice in Newport, both men sneered at the crude procedures they found in Rhode Island courts and in their pleadings introduced technicalities of English jurisprudence. They may not have won many cases that way, but they impressed upon the magistrates, perhaps more effectively than the royalists had done, the need for improving the administration of justice. The lesson was brought home as cases were appealed to the Privy Council: what had gone on in the Court of Trials had to be respectable in the eyes of men accustomed to English procedures. Newdigate eventually was called in to help prepare the publication of the laws in 1719.

That volume carried forward the work of assigning to the General Assembly and its statutes the central and nearly complete authority prescribed in the charter. The laws reflected the direction of change in the conduct of public business, although they still went beyond the facts in depicting an orderly system. Inevitably, there were those who disliked the way things were going.

The angriest were the losers as the old contests over land were settled. The drive to strengthen central authority in the colony, visible by 1719 in general laws to define and limit the functions of proprietors of common lands, had been far more conspicuous in earlier events. A series of measures and manipulations ended the most notable old controversies, tamed or liquidated the proprietors' organizations, and seized the bulk of the Narragansett country for the governor and company of Rhode Island. The colony encouraged but could not force the separation of town government from control of common lands in Providence and Warwick; the proprietors themselves brought about this development by their zeal to shut others out of their affairs. Only in those two places were there extensive undivided lands after 1715, and they were owned by a number of syndicates which with increasing timidity clutched their acres, kept out of trouble, and settled their disputes by arbitration or carefully arranged test cases in court.

Governor Cranston and his friends set the pace in disposing of old contests over land. The quarrels were not completely settled, because in some arenas the governor had no means to intervene, and in virtually all there remained vexatious minor disputes that occasionally flared up into neighborhood squabbles for the better part of a century. The most important effect of ending or subduing the seventeenth-century controversies came in rapid expansion of the settled areas, but other benefits flowed from removing causes of political strife.

The easiest way out of chronic bickering over common land was to parcel it out to individuals. Cranston took the lead in seeking this goal in Newport. The same solution was attempted everywhere on the islands and south of Warwick on the mainland. In all cases there were minor failures, in some the deliberate preservation of tracts for later development as commercial centers. The most spectacular divisions were in the huge Pettaquamscut Purchase, which was almost entirely distributed during a dozen years after 1693. Carving up the small Jamestown commons produced quarrels of appalling bitterness, pitting Cranston once again against Francis Brinley, but the governor turned them into occasions for strengthening the colony's government. He asserted and made good the General Assembly's power to rule on the survey to be used and to have public roads laid out and thrown open. He played a less attractive role in Westerly, where he resurrected the Misquamicut proprietors' organization, which the townsfolk had treated as defunct. The governor and his Newport partners proposed to divide up a large territory. Local opposition halted the plan, and it was abandoned after obscure and probably unlovely haggling. The proprietors from Newport scaled down their claims and sold their shares to Westerly people. The town resumed its habit of treating the undivided land as its own. There was very little left.

The Westerly imbroglio, for all its bad smell, was one of the maneuvers toward Cranston's great triumph in defeating the Narragansett Proprietors and opening South County to the rapid development that made it a thriving agricultural hinterland for Newport. He took office when the Proprietors, as Rhode Island would soon do, were gearing themselves to imperial government. They looked to London for aid more than Connecticut, which had begun to see their ambitions as separable from its jurisdictional claims. The Rhode Island men among the Proprietors

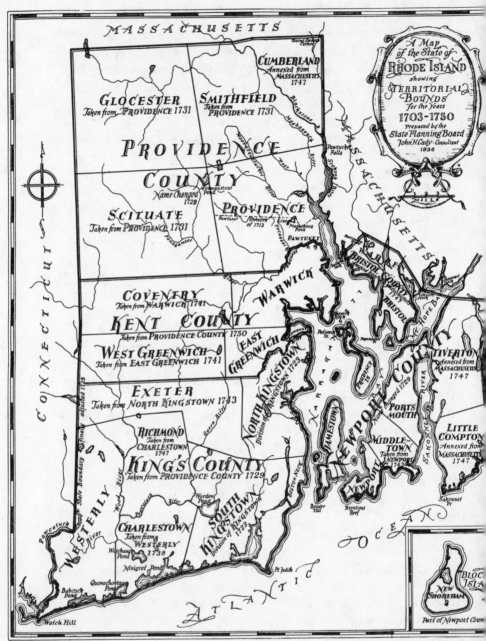

A Map of the State of RHODE ISLAND showing TERRITORIAL BOUNDS for the years 1703-1750

Prepared by the State Planning Board
John H. Cady - Consultant
1936

The Rhode Island Historical So

were generally royalists, who persistently encouraged attacks on the charter government as a means of advancing the claims under the notorious old mortgage. They were slowly winning the support of Bellomont just before his death, but they found Dudley far less tractable. He disdained them and set more importance on quashing the charter of Connecticut than Rhode Island.

Cranston took advantage of the Proprietors' frustration and Connecticut's fears to win the boundary agreement of 1703. Connecticut shortly went back on the deal, but Cranston proceeded as though it was still solid. Under the intercolonial agreement, Rhode Island promised to endorse all private titles to land on its side of the line even if they were derived from Connecticut's authority. Brinley and Nathaniel Coddington, a friend of the Proprietors who was not an outright royalist and had been strung along by Cranston, joyously assumed that the agreement gave the Proprietors all the land they claimed, except for what was held by individuals under title derived from another source. The Proprietors rushed to court to sue for their rights. Cranston, on the bench, gave them reason to expect his support. Panicky men in Westerly thought that he was throwing away their decades of resistance to Connecticut jurisdiction and land grants. Possibly he was looking for a compromise, as would have been consistent with his political style and underlying purposes, or possibly setting up a double cross, as Coddington later charged.

Whatever Cranston's wish, after some hesitation and dickering with Westerly men, he came around to their scheme for gaining a number of ends while trampling over the Narragansett Proprietors. The Westerly design was an intricate combination of letting certain grants under Connecticut authority enjoy the town's blessing, resolving conflicts between these and town allotments by compensation, and getting colonial sanction for grants the townsmen had made to each other in 1692 and for some extralegal purchases from the Indians. Cranston at first interfered with the plan by raising claims under the Misquamicut purchase. After the obscure conflict already mentioned, the Misquamicut claims were given up or sold to Westerly people

while the governor and the General Assembly adopted the
Westerly proposal to hail young Ninigret, son of the original, as
prince of the Narragansetts.

This last device was used to put all the remaining Narragansett territory under the colony's control. Ninigret petitioned the
Assembly for the appointment of trustees to take charge of his
affairs. Among other things, the trustees would arrange compensation to the colony for its substantial expenses on military
defense and its stalwart opposition to the machinations of the
Narragansett Proprietors with their fraudulent mortgage. As the
accounts were cast up, the Indians owed the colony almost as
much as their land was said to be worth. The colony conde-
scendingly set off a small reservation and assumed title to the
rest. (This formula bore a noisome resemblance to the detested
mortgage.) These arrangements were made between 1707 and
1709, and the General Assembly, after reviewing all contrary
claims and allowing a few minor ones, proceeded to appoint a
committee to sell the territory.

The portions for sale were solemnly described as "vacant
lands," in keeping with a theory long maintained in Newport
that the persistence of the Narragansett Proprietors hurt the
colony by preventing settlement in the disputed areas. Actually,
as the sales of "vacant lands" and the earlier sparring over town
boundaries revealed, there were quite a few people living on the
territory. Some had leases from the Narragansetts; perhaps a few
had grants from various pretended owners; others probably just
squatted. The sale of lands legitimized these people—for a price,
of course—and allowed others to move in or enlarge their
holdings, but also permitted a number of Newport and Portsmouth men to acquire large blocks of property.

The sale conveying the entirety of West Greenwich appears to
have been the political pay-off. The tract was nominally sold to
thirteen men, who then took in a total of forty-six others as
partners. Heading the list was Samuel Cranston, but there were
also several trustees for Ninigret, all the members of the
Assembly's committee on "vacant lands," the surveyor, and a few
other important men in the colony. These insiders got shares
bigger than the rest, but even so amounting only to about one

thousand acres apiece. The insiders had not the faintest idea of living in West Greenwich, nor of paying out of pocket for the land.

Rhode Island asked little for its newly acquired land and got less, but it reaped a far greater reward in the rapid improvement of the Narragansett country. The average price for "vacant lands" probably was about 10 *d* per acre. The treasury often took personal bonds as payment instead of cash. The bonds were clumsily drafted, and many signers repudiated their obligations. The costs of suits to collect the promised money further offset the net return to the colony. Still, with titles no longer dubious in South County, people put the land into productive use in about fifteen years.

Dealings with the region vexed by the old Pawtuxet controversy had less decisive results, although the ancient conflicts were put on the path to resolution. As the eighteenth century began, Providence and Warwick were contesting jurisdiction over Meshanticut, the heirs of William Harris and his associates were launching an appeal to the Privy Council, and the Providence proprietors were rereading old deeds to make a claim farther north than ever, just as the adjoining Massachusetts town of Mendon was laying claims farther south. The Assembly wanted Meshanticut in Providence, but Warwick resisted skillfully.

Cranston and his Aquidneck friends moved into this tangled situation with tactics rather like those that they were using in Westerly. In 1707 they revived the Westconnaug proprietary organization, dusted off its old deeds to a fifteen-mile square somewhere west of Providence, and decided to claim the territory between the Pawtuxet River and the north border of modern Coventry. This intervention touched off a panic in Providence, because it took place just as the town was preparing to fight the Pawtuxet case before the Privy Council.

The Westconnaug outfit proceeded cleverly. It took in as partners key men in Providence and Warwick. It fought the attempts of the Providence proprietors to resist its surveyors. And it asserted rights to the area that William Harris had most coveted. Political strength lay on the Westconnaug side; as was presently demonstrated, the challengers from Newport could win a legal test. The Providence proprietors had to yield. The Westconnaug men compromised by giving up some of their northern land. Then the Aquidneck shareholders, except Governor Cranston and a couple of others, sold their rights to people in Providence and Warwick. The buyers thus acquired a new sort of interest in the territory that Harris and his associates had claimed was the westward extension of Pawtuxet.

When the Providence proprietors struck the deal with the Westconnaug claimants, the ramifications went in several directions. Warwick surrendered jurisdiction over Meshanticut; and Providence, over the land along the Pawtuxet River below the north line of the original Warwick purchase. The town boundaries thereby ceased to be a matter of controversy. Implicitly, Providence gave up William Harris' old claim that Flat River was the mainstream of the Pawtuxet, thus ending a long-standing argument.

To the surprise of Providence, Governor Cranston aided the town in its other concerns. He probably called on the colony's agent in London to help fight the Pawtuxet claimants. Their attorney, for whatever reason, realized he could not win. He wrote that getting up a new presentation of the case would be "like dressing a cucumber with oil and vinegar, pepper and salt, and then throwing it upon the dunghill." Forty-seven years of failure would weigh heavily against his clients. At last William Harris' hopes were dashed. The Pawtuxet claimants by 1714 settled for what they could get: a large tract comprising what is now the western half of the town of Cranston and the southern part of Johnston. Moreover, the governor tried to help the Providence proprietors enlarge their holdings to the west and north, using this campaign as an occasion to reopen old boundary disputes with Massachusetts. He got nothing for his pains except an unsatisfactory definition of the line west of the Blackstone River; the best anyone could say of the agreement was that the terms were vague enough to give pretexts for later rounds of negotiation.

Eliminating the major conflicts over land in Providence and Warwick did not bring a dramatic wave of cultivation, as in South County, but only a gradual spread. Much of the territory was rocky and infertile. Furthermore, minor quarrels kept discouraging settlement—disputes, for instance, over an important division line in Warwick, the routes of highways radiating west from Providence, or overlapping allocations made during times of conflict. The Providence proprietors went on parceling out their acres during the eighteenth century and had some left even later. Their most coveted land lay on the waterfront and in the old town commons nearby, territory of special value as commerce began to grow in Providence. All the same, the interior filled up rapidly enough to justify carving three new towns out of the original Providence by 1731.

The main events in ending the disputes over land took place in a short period, 1703 to 1710. The benefits appeared speedily, though many subsidiary quarrels remained to be resolved. Clear titles could be enjoyed nearly everywhere in Rhode Island. Settlement expanded, population increased. In 1700 around seven thousand people lived in the colony, well over a third of them clustered on Aquidneck. In the first half of the eighteenth century, the figure jumped to about thirty-six thousand, boosted by redrawing the boundaries, but apart from that help, still a rate of growth that meant doubling every twenty-four years or so. In addition, stopping the old disputes over the Narragansett country and Pawtuxet put an end to the intrigues and political brawls that had sapped the strength of the colony even when they had not jeopardized its existence. Especially when control of common land was separated from town government, as happened nearly everywhere in the colony, the government, both central and local, gained relief from some familiar sources of discord. Proprietary organizations ceased using towns as their tools. Towns and proprietary organizations alike had to deal with the central government directly; both increasingly became regulated by law.

Burgeoning population and spreading settlement inevitably wrought a transformation in the towns, a transformation that exposed them to uniform regulation by the General Assembly. Towns on the mainland, by virtue of their size, could no longer be communities. The men could not readily gather for town meetings and training days. They often stayed home. The militia companies divided first, the usual reason being that the men in one section found it too troublesome to travel a great distance to the traditional place for martial drill. Then towns were split. By 1723 Kingstown was severed into North and South, but the two parts were still large. In 1731 Providence was quartered; soon Westerly, Warwick, East Greenwich, and North Kingstown were divided. The island towns remained manageable in extent, being unable to grow, but Newport in practical matters became two: an urban or "compact" part and a rural or "woods" part, although a formal separation of most of the woods part as Middletown could not be agreed upon until 1743.

Town government lost one of its basic original functions, the regulation of agricultural villages. Even where common fields and pastures were still desired, townsfolk could not be held to orderly observance of rules. Some men neglected to set up their segments of fence; others encroached; domestic animals got in or out, whichever they should not have done. The derelictions, once major concerns of a community, turned into minor problems, seemingly insoluble, of interest only to that portion of the inhabitants that happened to have rights in these old tracts.

Depredations on common land could not be stopped either. People chopped down trees for bark used in tanning, leaving stripped logs and limbs to rot and impede other users. Special resources were particularly jeopardized—lime rocks, shellfish and seaweed beds, thatch, pine or cedar swamps, sand, and clay pits. Such things could easily be exhausted. Resentment flared against those who exploited the commons for raw materials to produce exports, such as barrel staves or shingles or house timbers, out of what was intended for household use. Neither rules nor self-restraint could curb the ravaging. Perhaps blaming plunder of the commons on those planning to manufacture exports merely named a scapegoat for unscrupulous practices that were rampant. In any event, dividing the common land proved the only way to halt the bickering, and proprietary organizations parceled out the commons for the benefit of their own members regardless of the welfare of other townsfolk.

Very little was left of the original preoccupations of the towns, what with losing their responsibilities for regulating common fields and pastures, acquiring and apportioning land, and creating a judiciary. Instead, the town governments acquired new obligations and enlarged their attention to old ones that had been peripheral but now gained importance. In rural areas it was still essential to keep fences up to standard. In addition, the rapidly increasing web of roads needed upkeep. Bounties were put on various creatures considered destructive—on wolves, as long had been the case, but also on crows and blackbirds, which were believed to eat huge amounts of grain. With dwindling amounts of common pasturage, towns had to set limits on how many animals the inhabitants could turn loose, had to create pounds where strays could be taken, write elaborate laws on poundkeepers' duties and fees, on the control of dogs, and on the ringing of swine.

As towns ceased to be communities in a traditional sense, they became simply units of local government, a conversion symbolized in curbs on their old powers to admit or exclude newcomers. In 1718 the General Assembly ruled that towns might not refuse as an inhabitant anybody owning £50 worth of real estate within their boundaries. They could legally keep out only prospective paupers. By 1724 the Assembly began limiting the towns' discretion in admitting freemen by imposing a uniform property qualification.

The concerns of the town meeting differed from place to place, but the routines of government lost their old local individuality and converged on a single pattern. The pattern directly and indirectly was created by the central government. The round of sessions of the General Assembly and the Court of Trials forced all the towns to hold meetings almost simultaneously to select deputies and jurors as well as to cast votes for the governor, deputy governor, and assistants. By the early eighteenth century the towns also fell into one schedule or another of regular quarterly meetings—the Newport plan was widely adopted—because it was no longer practical to notify the freemen on each occasion. There had to be a time, such as the first Tuesday in certain months, that they could know by referring to the calendar.

More directly, general statutes prescribed what towns did. Acts of the General Assembly specified what might be done in town legislation on certain subjects, such as roads and livestock. The colony directed the towns to offer bounties for the production of flax and hemp and stipulated procedures for choosing officers to administer the reward and determine when a given parcel of fibers qualified for payment. Statutes also began to govern procedure in town meetings, new laws prescribing quorum rules, a list of topics that might be on the agenda only if announced ahead of time, and procedures whereby private citizens could get a meeting called or force the moderator to put a proposal to a vote even when he preferred not to. By the 1730s town government had progressed so far into the impersonal that action had to be taken against fraudulent practices, such as stuffing ballot boxes or falsely claiming property sufficient to qualify as a freeman.

Towns did not always observe laws of the colony, to be sure, and there was no provision for punishing their neglect. They were haphazard even in requiring tavern keepers to pay for licenses. Years dragged by with most places failing to acquire standard weights and measures. Nor did most towns abide by laws requiring them to impose standard sizes of cooperage, inspect packing of commodities or quality of leather, or appoint auctioneers. In reality, most of the laws regulating commercial life were for Newport; other towns were left free to observe such of them as they saw useful.

Town meeting business declined in that it increasingly dealt with matters of regulation and administration rather than central concerns of communities. Even though town meetings stubbornly refused to give up control over disbursing money, by 1730 they did little more than hear and accept a committee report on debts the town had incurred since the last time, and then approve a measure, often a tax levy, to pay what was owed. By and large the town meeting had not been consulted on running up the bills.

Perhaps the most dramatic symptom of what was happening to town meetings was the list of officers chosen annually. During the seventeenth century the roster was short—the clerk, treasurer, sergeant, a few councilmen, a constable or two, and perhaps a surveyor and some fence viewers or overseers of the highways. By 1730 or 1740 the list had lengthened fearfully. Portsmouth in 1738 chose a slate of fifty-two officers, a moderate number for that period—the old ones plus three overseers of the poor, three assessors, six field drivers (to capture stray livestock), a pound-keeper, three viewers of hemp and flax, two corders of wood, two cullers of clapboards and shingles, a sealer of weights and measures, a sealer of leather, a packer, an auctioneer, a town attorney, and a committee of auditors. Most of the additional officers were chosen to carry out laws passed by the General Assembly. The assortment of officers reveals a good deal about the economic life of Portsmouth, but it also reveals how far the town meeting had shifted from being a working organ of government to an agency for choosing those who actually carried out public business.

By comparison, the town councils, being much more suited for administrative functions anyway, grew in importance. From the past they inherited the function of probate courts, which clothed them in the garments of magistracy. If the elected councilmen were not actually considered judges, their conclaves were graced with the presence of men who were, for all magistrates and justices of the peace residing in a town were automatically members of the town council—or rather, they were until town objections spearheaded by Newport, where the magistrates and J.P.'s could easily outvote the elected members, led to changes in the law. Finally in 1733 the Assembly agreed to confine the membership in the councils to the six men elected by the town meeting.

All the same, the Assembly loaded the councils with new duties. They received the touchy problems of laying out highways and regulating dams and weirs on rivers to make sure that no one caught all the fish or prevented their migration upstream. (These topics were so sensitive, in fact, that a few councils shunned their duties and forced the Assembly to make laws on specific roads or rivers.) Councils were entrusted with powers to prevent the influx of paupers and to expel anyone without a legal right of settlement—ordinarily such a right being gained by birth in the town or unquestioned residence there for a year. They had to see to the care of the poor, orphans, and lunatics. In some places the councilmen doubled as overseers of the poor, but in others they merely designated objects of charity, provided the money, and left a panel of overseers to do the rest. In dealing with the poor and newcomers, as with the probate of wills, the councils performed what were seen as judicial functions, and their actions were subject to appeal—the governor and council being the appellate tribunal in most cases.

One mysterious area of the councils' quasi-magisterial power was their control over Indians and the offspring of Indians and blacks. Surviving laws fail to explain what was going on, but town councils in Portsmouth, Jamestown, South Kingstown, and Westerly routinely exerted a great deal of control over these people. (It is tempting to think that everyone involved was somewhat ashamed of what was being done and kept records to a cryptic minimum.) Westerly's dealings with young Ninigret were a special case, surely, but in the other towns mentioned, Indians and mulattoes were commonly compelled to serve as apprentices —that is, as servants—from childhood until the age of twenty-one or twenty-four. In Jamestown the Indians were treated as a group at times, being required to do such work as build a chimney for a watch house or the beacon at Beaver Tail. In Portsmouth a young Indian was sometimes referred to as a "parish child," a term not otherwise in use. Possibly some hereditary condition of servitude was being perpetuated through chronic poverty for the descendants of refugees in King Philip's War.

The most far-reaching powers of the councils were those given them by law for use in times when epidemics broke out. Small pox was the usual disease. When it appeared, councils could commandeer dwellings for isolation of the ill, impose a drastic quarantine, impede travel to almost any extent, and destroy personal property that was suspected of harboring contagion. Though these measures practically never worked, the town fathers persisted in using them.

For all the importance of the judicial attributes of the town councils, the administrative ones were most clearly in the ascendancy. Apart from probate jurisdiction, the councils shied away from the procedures of courts and tended to rely on justices of the peace acting as such to issue warrants or receive evidence of lawbreaking in areas where the councils had responsibilities to make and enforce rules. Town meetings, moreover, fostered the administrative role by calling on councils to serve as executive or interim committees, to draft laws, and to appoint men to undertake tasks the meeting had decided should be performed.

The councils, previously convened irregularly to probate wills or post a watch, by the early eighteenth century were setting up schedules of regular monthly sessions. Often with the town's approval, they used the money paid for liquor licenses as their special fund. Though the fund mainly went for relieving the poor or posting notices, councils encouraged full attendance by buying themselves dinner or bowls of punch. They even began purchasing special seals for stamping official documents. Gradually they were taking on the traits of boards of aldermen.

The militia companies or "train bands" in the towns, like the towns themselves, fell under the regulation of the central government of the colony. Controversy centered on how the officers were to be chosen, whether by the men or the General Assembly. Election by the men was customary and popular, although Cranston insisted it was "repugnant to the express words of the charter and highly dishonorable to the crown and dignity of Her Majesty," Queen Anne. It had been obvious since 1691 that electing the officers could lead to trouble. After a crisis that year over men refusing to serve after being chosen by the Portsmouth company, the Assembly began appointing the majors for the two regiments, giving them authority to name inferior officers as needed. This measure did not prevent the militia response to Phips, Bellomont, and Dudley, but the Assembly would not risk further changes as long as the wars lasted.

For the time being, the hazards were political at the root. The colony's authority remained fragile in all respects for several years after restoration of the charter government. Doubts of its legality, followed by doubts of its correctness in resisting Bellomont or Dudley, prevented a firm linkage in the colony's chain of command. The governor and council could not hope for improvement until they operated an unquestioned regime.

Cranston worked toward that end first and, once he had made headway and the war came to an end, urged appointment of militia officers. The assembly voted to do so in 1713, reciting pertinent passages of the charter, but repealed the law the very next year.

It took Cranston four years to swing the Assembly around again. Then in a comprehensive statute on military affairs which he drafted himself, the officers were made appointive again, and regulations were written for town watches. In addition to these encroachments on local discretion, the law gave overdue authorization for practices that had been carried on for years, putting the governor and deputy governor in the chain of command as colonel and lieutenant colonel respectively, and empowering the governor to commission naval officers and enlist or impress seamen for the colony's service. Unhappily for the aging governor, the Assembly once again returned choice of militia officers to the train bands just before he died, only to reclaim the power once again briefly and for good in 1741.

These reversals probably resulted from a needless effort by the advocates of appointive officers to abolish exemption of conscientious objectors from military training. Rhode Island had a substantial number of Quakers and some pacifist Baptists. They would not serve as soldiers, but they held nonviolence as a personal obligation rather than a political program. When in office, Friends made no effort to impose their standards on the conduct of public business. The causes of the pacifists and the elected militia officers became linked and rose and fell together until the Assembly in 1730 sensibly took back selection of the officers while reaffirming exemption of conscientious objectors from military duties.

The internal reconstruction of Rhode Island during the Cranston administration brought obvious improvements in order. Different branches of public business were put in the hands of appropriate officials or organs of government. By and large the land passed into simple individual ownership. Increasingly comprehensive laws defined the functions of town meetings, town councils, the myriad of town officers, and the remaining proprietors of common lands. The General Assembly could determine town boundaries and get roads laid out and maintained. In short, the colony finally gained the control over local government that the charter had given it. To be sure, when Cranston went to his grave in 1727, much of the reconstruction remained unfinished, and often towns did not do as the law required, but a great deal had been accomplished and more soon followed.

The central government of the colony was reordered also. The formal changes—adoption of a bicameral structure for the General Assembly and the arrangement of sessions of the Assembly and the Court of Trials in a series of different locations during the year—mattered less than changes in the nature and competence of the central organs of government. The General Assembly which had replaced the Court of Commissioners in 1664 was still in most respects a congress of emissaries from doggedly individualistic and mutually distrustful communities—emissaries who met for limited purposes and often found it impossible to carry them out over the disapproval of their constituents. When the towns had been harnessed as fairly uniform agencies of local government and when the number of towns had increased, the Assembly could act on a greater range of subjects, with much greater hope of effect and without much fear that a single community could block the action of the central government.

Though the statement must be made with caution, it is fair to say that the Assembly was becoming more distinctly a legislature. While it retained many of the attributes of an all-purpose, quasi-sovereign body, its function as writer of general laws was on the rise. Even its judicial business was falling under some regulation, only special appeals by petition being left to the full Assembly. In addition, the creation of justices of the peace who were not members of the House of Magistrates began the process of separating the judiciary from the General Assembly.* Still, as

---

* The process advanced more dramatically in 1729, when the Assembly decided to create county courts of record, which began sitting the next year. The bench of the new criminal courts, as in the county justices' courts in the earlier part of the eighteenth century, consisted of the justices of the peace residing within the county, but the Assembly every year chose four judges for

in the past, the Assembly recognized no limit on what it might do in answering individual requests, even when the response meant interference with the legal operation of other organs of government. The changing concept of the Assembly, in any event, was less significant than its increasing capacity to make its will be done, its laws observed.

During the Cranston era there was a growing disposition to treat the charter in the fashion that later Americans would treat constitutions. In fact, occasionally the charter was referred to as "our constitution"—this at a time when the word "constitution" was ordinarily used to mean either of two other ideas. It had often been employed to mean the entire set of circumstances of the colony, as when asserting that a given law was as harmonious with English law as would suit the condition of the colony. "Constitution" also referred in common English usage to the entire complex of laws and institutions, traditions and ceremonies, privileges and precedents, that together made up a government. Significantly in Rhode Island, "constitution" early came to mean the basic document prescribing the organs of government and certain limits on what that government legally might do. Cranston himself fostered this concept, no doubt goaded by the attacks on Rhode Island by Bellomont and Dudley for failing to abide by the literal prescriptions in the charter. The governor's thinking, however, probably contained an ingredient foreign to later American ideas: if the colony lived by the exact wording of the charter, the privileges could not be taken away.

Neither the appearance of the now familiar concept of a constitution nor Cranston's variant on it ruled out reshaping government by patterns not to be found in the charter. Quite the contrary, bicameralism was introduced with other revisions that plainly drew on the English Parliament as a model. Likewise, the office of justice of the peace was imported from the mother

---

each of the new civil courts. These men sometimes held office also as town deputy but tended to have a more secure position as judges by virtue of repeated appointment for long stretches of time. The old Court of Trials was renamed the Superior Court. In 1747 the Assembly reorganized the Superior Court to hold sessions in each county (five in number by 1751) and began appointing judges who were distinct from the upper house of the legislature.

country. The House of Deputies, once it became a separate chamber, imitated the House of Commons by choosing a speaker. How much further imitation went on cannot be determined for lack of evidence. This borrowing was hardly unnatural, but it did evince a conviction that Rhode Island really was part of the British empire and could meet its changing needs by adopting the ways of the mother country.

Unhappily for the historian who feels obliged to explain everything, there are no documents to reveal more than a few thoughts of the men who reshaped the internal order of Rhode Island in the early eighteenth century. Did they think of the manipulation of old land claims as part of a campaign to end old conflicts, wipe out autonomous bases of political power, and make a little money while clarifying titles so the land could be put to use? Did they deliberately foster the revision of town government to build up administrative functions and extend the duties of the councils so as to make the towns effective agents of a central government? Did they plan compilation and technical improvement of the laws to fit with these other changes, to enhance the legislative role of the General Assembly, and to make its dominance in a governmental system more comprehensive? Were their ideas more guided by English examples than by a concept of legally limiting constitutional law? Or were the changes in the landowning syndicates and local government systematic and harmonious only by coincidence—or only in the imagination of the historian? There will never be final answers to these questions, but the reconstruction of Rhode Island, though incomplete and imperfect, followed lines that suggest a vision of rationality and order, a respect for individual rights as distinct from the privileges arising from property, an understanding of the use of law to restrain as well as to expand power, and a strong flavoring in the combination provided by the imported spice of English ways.

8

ECONOMIC POLICIES OF
THE NEWPORT ELITE

Making self-government effective in Rhode Island and preserving it from British restraints both had their ultimate value in
giving the Newport merchants a free hand to use the General
Assembly for their own ends. They wanted to draw upon a
hinterland—the whole colony and as much as possible beyond its
borders—as a source of commodities for export and a market for
imports. To a great extent they succeeded in carving out this
commercial domain by means of sharp wits, daring, energy, and
eternal vigilance, but they needed freedom from interference by
officials they could not control. They also used to great effect
their dominance in their own colonial government, especially to
pry loose the stranglehold of Boston on the whole of New
England commerce. Though they never managed to get more
than a feeble grasp on that golden fleece of British-American
trade, direct traffic with London and Bristol, they contrived to
use the autonomous authority of Rhode Island first to discrimi-
nate in favor of local traders against men from Massachusetts
and then to manipulate the currency to the disadvantage of their
rivals north of the border.

Until challenged by Providence men in the 1750s, leadership
in Rhode Island came from Newport. Even Joseph Jenckes, the
successor to Samuel Cranston, at the behest of the General
Assembly moved to that town from Providence when he became
governor. The colonial leaders, after his election as before, were
Newport merchants who took it for granted that what was good

for Newport was good for Rhode Island—or at least good enough. They quarreled among themselves not on the basic assumption but on how to act upon it. Francis Brinley and the royalists were wrong in tampering with the colony's privileged position in the British empire; Walter Clarke and Samuel Cranston had a much sounder understanding of what Rhode Island needed. Yet Brinley and Sanford, though they had interests in many parts of New England, were still by their own lights trying to advance their interests as Newport merchants. They knew how to make money there and wanted to adjust governmental arrangements to permit them to make more. Likewise, when the Wanton brothers after 1714 allied with men in Providence and Warwick, especially such as had been hurt by Cranston's measures to organize the colony for the good of Newport, these challengers, once in office, took still more daring steps to reach the same goal.

The predominance of Newport interests remained possible, because in a large measure that city's aims harmonized with those of the other towns. Everyone wanted expanded settlement, increased exports, and avenues of transportation connecting the newly cleared farms with a central market. Legislation to secure these benefits was controversial only to those whose private interests it injured. There was little or no opposition to public expenditures for a fort and a lighthouse for Newport; sooner or later the public treasury provided comparable boons to the other towns. Laws to keep out the ships and roving traders from other colonies, though potentially subjecting rural folk to the mercy of Newport merchants, were counterbalanced by projects to draw the business of eastern Connecticut and southern Massachusetts into Rhode Island, often over roads ending at new trading villages on the mainland. Laws to regulate the quantity, quality, and packing of rural products for the benefit of Newport shippers encountered some resistance, but were offset by giving bounties to farmers who brought in commodities the city especially wanted. Nor did opposition rise to stop subsidies for specific enterprises or tariffs to protect nascent industries.

While the economic legislation went no further than these measures, as was the case before 1715, the Cranston administration without opposition presided over a broadly developmental program that was acceptable throughout Rhode Island. Then controversy flared over the most far-reaching plan, the use of paper money to give Newport a currency that could be used to capture business from Boston. Launched by the Wanton coalition that turned out of office most of Cranston's early associates, this device faced a shifting opposition—first rural hostility, then anguished Massachusetts victims, then a growing number of Newport merchants themselves, and finally the imperial officials in London. Yet the Wanton fiscal policy served the Newport mercantile elite quite well for a quarter of a century. Then inherent difficulties in the plan, aggravated by slipshod and corrupt administration, brought a lingering and painful reckoning. The agony came not only from internal conflict within the colony and harsh condemnation in London but also from exposure to a contradiction that had been latent all along in the aims of Newport itself. Breaking free from Boston, if successful, meant assuming a position like Boston's in the British trading world. If such a position could be achieved, paper currency would have to be abandoned to facilitate commerce with the mother country and to reconcile Rhode Island's fiscal practices with imperial policy.

Reckless of the impasse to be reached in the 1740s, Newport and Rhode Island prospered mightily for half a century beforehand. Bringing more land under cultivation, farmers raised production of crops and livestock. Minor commercial villages appeared on the mainland where these commodities were shipped to the avid markets at Newport. The trade of that city expanded enormously. Newport built up its business with the Caribbean and coastal North America, entered the African slave trade, and by the middle 1730s could begin some direct dealings with London and Bristol. Constantly in need of exports, Newport gained at least an equal influence with Boston's in a belt in southern New England from Nantucket through eastern Connecticut. These gains were hard won, but the government of Rhode Island under Governor Cranston did what it could to help.

The earliest measures were blunt and aggressive, to keep out competition from outsiders and forestall English regulation of the port. Port fees at Newport and later at the other harbors in the colony were charged on all vessels not owned locally, except when they arrived only to fit out voyages. In 1699 the Assembly enacted the first in a series of laws to prevent nonresidents from retailing imported goods anywhere in Rhode Island. Aimed at roving traders with merchandise obtained on credit at Boston, the act imposed a tax of 2½ percent on whatever such persons brought into the colony to sell, except products of Rhode Island or a neighboring province. (Introducing New England products would help Newport merchants.) To encourage enforcement of this law, the tax was to be paid into the town treasury where it was collected. Providence, at least, actually charged the duty on wares brought by outsiders.

Restraints on direct British control of the port were ingeniously woven into the very statutes requiring observance of the English acts on trade and navigation. While proclaiming that parliamentary laws were to be enforced, the Assembly made sure they would be administered as much as possible by local officials under local rules. The naval officer, for some time past in charge of this business, was given more control over shipping than the imperial customs officers had. After the Board of Trade stopped threatening the charter, the Assembly set maximum fees for the customs men as well as the naval officer. When officials in London neither objected to these actions nor responded to appeals for customs officers at other harbors in addition to Newport, the colony cheerfully proceeded to establish regulations encouraging local traffic by exempting from fees at the naval office all open boats and lighters plying coastal waters, even if coming from neighboring colonies.

While these measures were being put into use, Governor Cranston wrote a revealing analysis of his colony's commerce in reply to questions sent by the Board of Trade in 1708. Shipbuilding had become a major activity in the preceding decade. There were no figures for earlier years, but since 1698 over a hundred vessels had been built in local yards. Of these more than eighty were sloops, with the rest divided about evenly between the larger categories of brigantine and ship. Most had been sold to outsiders, probably many to Boston rivals, but twenty-seven sloops and two brigantines remained in Rhode Island ownership, all but two or three being owned by Newport-ers. Twenty years earlier men in the colony had owned no more than four or five vessels.

The governor explained the sudden rise of shipping inade-quately, not mentioning where the capital came from, but offered some shrewd observations. The land on Aquidneck had been carved into small farms, so that many sons of the farmers had to take up "trades or callings." Still, frustrated land lust was not the whole story; after all, it could have been gratified by acres on the mainland. Rather, the boys generally wanted to go to sea and their fathers encouraged them. The farmers struggled to lay aside some money, so they could do as the tradesmen in Newport did, "improve it in getting part of a vessel . . . for the benefit of their children that are bred to navigation." In short, the island was alive with ambition to make money in trade.

Already in 1708 Newport skippers had found most of the lines of business that the town followed for years. In describing exports and imports, Cranston pointed out that his colony acquired from Massachusetts "all sorts of European commodities," sending back "butter, cheese, and money." The only other sources of European manufactures were in Chesapeake Bay (along with pork and wheat) and in the British West Indies, whence traders carried English textiles and Spanish and Swedish iron as well as sugar, molasses, cotton, ginger, indigo, pimento, and rum. If Rhode Islanders loaded manufactures at Dutch Caribbean ports in violation of British law, as may well have been the case, the governor saw fit not to mention it. To the Caribbean, Rhode Island shipped provisions, including beef, pork, butter, cheese, onions, and cider; horses; and lumber products such as boards, planks, timbers, and barrels. To the mainland colonies from Connecticut to South Carolina went rum and molasses, butter and cheese. In exchange, these colonies provided wheat, which New England could no longer grow owing to a blight, plus pork and leather, and from the south rice, furs, pitch and other items. Surprisingly, Connecticut sent forest products peculiarly useful in shipping—tar, pitch, rosin, turpentine, and boards—and New

York was the source of rigging. In addition, there were a few special avenues of commerce: with the Madeira and Azore islands for wine (another drain on the supply of cash), with a few places for salt, and with Curaçao for cocoa and pieces of eight. Unfortunately, no statistics, not even estimates, were offered on the volume of business flowing in these various channels.

From the governor's description, several important observations may be drawn. Rhode Island was already bringing in pork and grains and forest products from elsewhere in North America to pour into its export traffic. It even went to nearby colonies to get the timber and rigging for its ships, as well as the biscuit and pickled meat for the crews. Probably distilleries were already attaining a significant place in the manufacturing done in Rhode Island. The shortage of local products could partly be offset if local craftsmen added value to whatever came to hand. But the colony in 1708, as later, still imported rum from the West Indies. Further, as Governor Cranston asserted, the commerce flowed almost entirely in the channels approved by British law. He alluded to one port that might be considered suspect and may well have been discreet on others, but there is no reason to suspect smuggling of any magnitude, unless one believes the nightmares of men like Edward Randolph, who had visions of great clandestine traffic with pirates.

In general, however, the scene depicted by Cranston was quite credible—of a Caribbean trade bringing in some cash and profits in other forms, augmented significantly by North American coastal trade, with the cream skimmed off by Bostonians who supplied the bulk of the European manufactured goods brought into Rhode Island. To Newport's grief, it "never had any immediate or direct trade to or from England" and suffered an adverse balance of payments with Boston merchants that annually took "not less than £20,000 in cash" out of Rhode Island, chiefly to pay for British manufactures.

The governor probably omitted a few topics without any wish to distort the picture. He did not explain how profits arose in the Caribbean trade or how they were used; he said nothing of carrying trade between ports entirely outside the colony; he did not explain what had happened to over seventy vessels built in

Rhode Island. Some of the vessels may well have gone to enlarge the fleet of the Massachusetts competitors, but soon the shipyards around Narragansett Bay were supplying merchants in London and Bristol. The Caribbean commerce in 1708 or not long after was interwoven with a carrying trade between the West Indies and a variety of other places, such as the wine islands, the Carolinas, and even Great Britain. Through this supplementary activity Newport merchants enlarged their profits and converted them mostly into bills of exchange on British firms. Bills of exchange were like checks: orders written by one man instructing a second to pay a third. The second functioned like a bank. All went well if the second had the money and owed some or was willing to extend credit to the first. Such bills were particularly valuable when drawn on someone who could pay promptly in hard money.*

On the subject of slaves Governor Cranston had some surprising things to say. Apart from a single importation of blacks from Africa in 1696, he wrote, all the slaves in the colony or their ancestors had been brought from Barbados. From that island, generally thought to have been an importer rather than an exporter of slaves, Rhode Island acquired "one year with

* The use of bills of exchange seems simple enough, but actually it was constantly subject to failings and abuse. All concerned had to be wary. The value of a bill depended on the writer's knowledge and scruples at the time of writing and on the payer's solvency, existence, and willingness to honor the draft at an unforeseeable time in the future. With the best intentions, a writer could be wrong about his ability to command payment; in emergencies, he might take the risk of writing a bill without much confidence that it would be honored. There was nothing except fear of losing a good name to stop somebody from writing bills that were unlikely to be paid or sure to be protested; the deceit would not come to light until many other transactions had been completed, when it might be possible to make good on the fraud. Payers, even when able and obliged, could refuse to pay on some pretext, if they preferred for the time being to use their cash on hand for something else. Bills, moreover, could be sold any number of times before they were presented for payment. Bills therefore were rated by estimation of their reliability. Possessors of old or dubious ones sold them as fast as possible at the smallest discount they could negotiate. Bills of highest quality might change hands many times; they were as good as coin, and nobody wanted to waste them needlessly in a specie-starved economic world.

another, betwixt twenty and thirty." This he thought was sufficient to supply blacks for the local market, "the reasons of which are chiefly to be attributed to the dislike our planters have for them, by reason of their turbulent and unruly tempers. And that most of our planters that are able and willing to purchase any of them, are supplied by the offspring of those they have already, which increase daily; and that the inclination of our people in general, is to employ white servants before Negroes." The population figures he compiled did not entirely confirm a widespread insistence on white labor. The 220 "Black servants" in Newport comprised a tenth of the population and outnumbered white servants eleven to one. Blacks were even more important in Jamestown, comprising over one-seventh of the small population. Elsewhere, only Portsmouth, Kingstown and Westerly had significant numbers. Still, Cranston's evaluation of the market was corroborated by an event he did not mention to the Board of Trade, the imposition of a £3 per capita duty on slaves. By 1715 the naval officer had accumulated over £289 from this tariff, which probably was not the whole amount paid in, suggesting that only around a hundred blacks had been imported during the preceding ten or fifteen years.

But the outlook was changing. In 1717 there was more than £100 from the tariff in the naval officer's hands. An amendment to the duty encouraged direct importation from Africa, while other new legislation provided the first measure against runaway slaves and forbade importing Indian slaves. In 1729 the Assembly, alleging that "great charge, trouble and inconveniencies" had arisen from people manumitting slaves, ruled that none might be freed unless the erstwhile owner posted bond of at least £100 to indemnify his town in case the freed person became unable to live without charitable aid. Well before that time the duty was not being collected and the attempt was totally given up in 1732, ostensibly in deference to royal policy favoring the slave trade, but probably as much in accord with local preference. White Rhode Islanders thus reconciled themselves to slavery and the slave trade during Newport's rise. Ironically, they did so as the Quakers among them, most numerous in the towns with the highest proportions of black people, went through their first internal controversies over the morality of slavery and agreed to a few points, such as a religious duty to shun the trade.

Along with efforts to freeze out nonresident retailers and the turn toward encouraging slaving voyages, Rhode Island resorted to a great variety of measures to improve commercial life within the colony to the benefit of Newport. Some of these were humdrum devices to foster reliability in quantity and quality of goods, when the volume of trade happily grew so great that buyers needed to know what they were getting without checking up on every item. In other cases, the object was to encourage local production for export or to reduce the need for imports. In still others, the goal was to improve internal transportation.

In order to simplify trade and curtail fraud, the General Assembly promoted standardization of measurements. Though the towns did not promptly observe the act requiring them to choose a sealer of weights and measures, who would be provided with standards equal in size to those used in Boston, little by little compliance spread. Unfortunately, the colony's sealer, who was also Newport's, complained in 1712 that he had only wooden standards that varied deplorably with the weather, so could hardly provide the uniform units expected of him. The Assembly authorized him to procure brass or copper standards. By 1730 uniformity was probably fairly well established, and the Assembly wrote a more detailed law on the subject.

Similarly the campaign moved slowly to put into use standard sizes of cooperage and to require inspection of packing. Although launched in 1705, it succeeded quickly only in Newport, Portsmouth, and Westerly. The goal was to get pickled meat of good quality well packed for export in standard-sized containers. The colony's packer and his deputies elected in the various towns were to stamp properly packed meat and prevent the loading of any other on outbound vessels. The legislation was made more detailed and extended in 1731 to cover fish, beer, and other liquids offered for sale, whether for export or not. At the same time the Assembly extended the control on wooden products from cooperage to cover shingles and clapboards. The law was requested by Newport merchants, who wanted guaranteed quality for export, but it required the towns to impose controls, although Newport was the only one to act promptly.

Beginning in 1707 the colony tried to ensure sound quality in leather and leather goods. Towns producing such wares were called upon to elect a searcher or sealer of leather, who would not only affix his seal to well-tanned hides but also inspect tanneries and confiscate shoddy goods. That this measure was for the benefit of merchants rather than tanners is plainly revealed both by the response—Newport at once chose a sealer, although most other towns did not—and also by the provisions in the law imposing penalties for obstructing searches and allowing merchants to sue tanners and curriers attempting to sell substandard goods.

Bounties, tariffs, and loans on easy terms were used to encourage production of needed commodities, though not with great results. For many years beginning in 1721, the Assembly offered a bounty on hemp in order to reduce the need for bringing in cordage, and soon on flax also. Less effective were bounties on fish, intended to swell exports, and support for sugar refining and the manufacture of nails, firearms, and duck, a fabric used in sails. The only durable enterprise launched by the colony's aid was James Franklin's printing shop. He went to Rhode Island in 1726 with the promise of contracts to print official documents. This work kept Benjamin's brother and former master in business but could not sustain his *Rhode Island Gazette*, which failed after a few issues in 1732. Manufacturing and processing flourished only when they did not need governmental aid. The citizens entirely on their own tirelessly sought new ways to add value to raw materials and invested in distilleries, tanneries, shipyards, brickyards, forges, ropewalks, snuff mills, chocolate mills, candle works, bakeries, and a profusion of large-scale artisans' shops and small-scale cottage industries.

Rhode Island vigorously developed internal transportation in the early eighteenth century. The primary purpose was to draw goods to Newport, the secondary one to obey instructions from London to provide facilities for the royal postal service connecting the colony with Boston, New York, and points south. Both objectives required the development of through routes that were clearly visible, quite a departure from the old ways. Roads had been laid out originally for local use. Many of them could barely be discerned by people who did not know where they were, because owners of adjacent land fenced in segments, allowing travelers to proceed only by opening and closing a series of gates. This was bearable when traffic was light and everyone using the road was part of the system, gaining some land and paying for it by putting up with the nuisance of gates.

With growing business and population, a few roads had to be genuinely public, and governmental authority had to make them so over stubborn local resistance. In Portsmouth, for instance, where an increasing volume of traffic from out of town, including droves of livestock, blundered through the fields to Newport, the ways had to be cleared leading south from the ferries to the mainland. Over the objections of some cantankerous people, the town required landowners to fence along the routes and tear down old gates. The best compensation was a slice of the original road obtained by narrowing it. The same solution was used in other places, at the cost of reducing provender for animals on the way to slaughter, for several through highways. Along the new Post Road from Providence to Westerly the different towns had to be forced by the General Assembly to open the route and keep up bridges across the rivers. Likewise the colony had to compel Jamestown to open roads between the ferries linking Newport to the mainland and had to push through the roads connecting Providence with eastern Connecticut.

To prevent every obstinacy from producing paralysis, the General Assembly wrote a general law. It authorized town councils to lay out roads by impaneling a special jury that could select the route and rule on compensation for private land taken. The actions of the jury and council were subject to appeal to the Assembly, and that body also felt free to order a council to summon a jury to lay out a specific road, but the system at least made possible the opening of several important long highways in the first decades of the eighteenth century.

The major new routes served new activities. The mainland

Post Road linked the towns west of the bay. The Plainfield and later the Killingly roads drew the produce of the interior and of northeastern Connecticut into Providence and, of course, permitted carrying other goods back. The Ten Rod Road (the width to afford food to livestock) similarly benefited Wickford. Lesser highways radiated from other places, such as Warwick and Westerly. These routes ended at harbors from which small craft gave passage to Newport. A few bridges on these main highways, notably Hunt's Bridge and the Pawtuxet River span on the Post Road, were so vital and so expensive to maintain that the colony began to subsidize them. By the middle of the century, the number of subsidies grew to resemble a miniature pork barrel.

Roads to the ferries, and the ferries themselves, constituted a peculiarly important part of the transportation network that could no longer be left to local care. The colony began taking control over ferries in 1696, by requiring all to carry the king's postal service free and conferring a monopoly on the widow Mary Edmonds for service between Providence and the opposite side of the Seekonk River. The colony's power, however, faced the test in Portsmouth. In a long controversy beginning in 1698, the Assembly overrode the town's objections that it had long before started a ferry to the mainland, had given land for a wharf and a place for travelers to await the boat, and had consistently maintained control of the service. Portsmouth did not finally give up until 1727, but raised no objections for several years before that time while the Assembly's committee on ferries awarded franchises to the operators the town liked. The rights to operate ferries between Newport and Jamestown and Jamestown and Kingstown, granted in 1700 to men willing to pay for the privileges, aroused no protests.

By 1702 it was prudent and practical for the Assembly to choose a committee to award franchises. It set the fees to be paid by the operators, the fares they might charge, and the facilities they had to provide for travelers—whether waiting places, taverns, enclosed pasture for domestic animals, or whatever. The system did not work smoothly for several years. Special local interests clamored for attention; the committee occasionally neglected its duties; the franchise holders sometimes did not pay.

By about 1714, however, the committee was functioning effectively, and Rhode Island was in control of these vital links in its transportation network.

By far the most important means the colony found to aid its commerce, however, was the issuance of paper money.* The practice began, as in other colonies, to finance extraordinary wartime expenditures. Rhode Island helped pay for its force in the attack on Port Royal in 1710 by £5,000 in bills of credit. (These were not intended to equal sterling, but rather "current money of New England," officially three-quarters of sterling, although in the marketplace Massachusetts paper money in this standard was passing at about two-thirds.)† They were to be redeemed in coin brought in by an annual tax of £1,000 in each of the next five years. Soon the Assembly issued £8,000 more in bills of credit and presently discovered that the taxes were not being paid and the treasury was spending bills it received instead of burning them. Military expenses were still piling up, and when they stopped, the colony headed into the postwar depression that made ruthless taxation inexpedient both economically and politically.

Moreover, the convenience of having more money in circulation was hard to forego. Rhode Islanders had previously made do with barter and credit for most transactions, with occasional reckonings in silver. Taxes had been payable in commodities; the treasurer could always sell such things to shippers, but rural people could not easily get coin. Everyone kept accounts in pounds sterling or current money of New England, but most people rarely saw any English coin and rated silver or gold, in

* The following discussion of Rhode Island currency relies heavily on the fascinating doctoral dissertation by John Blanchard MacInnes on "Rhode Island Bills of Public Credit, 1710-1755," completed at Brown University in 1952.

† This variant on the English money system went back to the Massachusetts coinage of the seventeenth century which had the same metal but only three-fourths as much of it as in English coins of the same denomination. The difference was justified as an effort to keep silver in the colonies by enhancing its value; by the eighteenth century the difference was kept and widened by the scarcity value of the silver.

whatever coinage came to hand, as so much precious metal. The specially severe shortage of coin during Queen Anne's War drove up the price of silver as it flowed out of New England. Colonial treasury notes, beginning with those of Massachusetts, provided a welcome medium of exchange. Soon the Rhode Island bills of credit, too, proved acceptable throughout New England and so made commerce easier for merchants.

Postwar conditions posed new problems in currency policy. A depression dashed the earlier optimism. People said trade stagnated, and apparently it actually did, so for once the chronic complaints of the merchants deserved credence. Per capita imports of manufactured goods into New England began to decline. The fortunes of Newport seemed likely to take a sudden turn for the worse.

The sad experience of Thomas Richardson gives a glimpse into what happened at the end of the war and how calculations went awry. A Boston Quaker merchant who had long had a Newport partner, Richardson decided to move to the Rhode Island town in 1712. He reasoned that he could make higher profits there if he could arrange direct shipping to and from England, because he could charge less than the usual Newport prices for imports and more than make up the difference by cutting out the costs of transshipment at Boston. He could derive a second advantage by exporting directly to the mother country, fancying that cargoes would be easy to assemble, because Newport sent out "great quantities of sugar, pitch, and tar" as well as "a pretty deal of [whale] oil taken yearly at the east end of Long Island."

By 1714 he found the plan failing. Though locally built ships were a good product to sell to Englishmen, he could not get rigging quickly enough. Nor could he make up cargoes when he needed them. He had to chase after provisions and wool and also after the dwindling supply of furs still being trapped in the Narragansett and Mohegan regions. While scurrying about on this business, he had to pay wages to captains waiting to command the vessels. Even when fishing brought in a big catch, fellow Newport merchants seemed magically to be at the dock with signed contracts to deliver the fish to Boston. Worse, shopkeepers went on buying manufactured goods in Boston, where Richardson strongly suspected the wholesalers were giving special discounts. The discouraged Quaker scaled down his ambitions, put his capital in the Caribbean and coastal trades (like everyone else), and took European wares only on commission and mainly via Massachusetts. His erstwhile partner, Walter Newbury, thought over the prospects and moved to Boston.

One response to hard times, almost reflexive during the eighteenth century and common enough at other times, was to promulgate "industry and frugality." The two made a harmonious pair for the public at large, but not for the importer. Richardson did his part for industry by attempting to set up a shop to bake ship's bread, by encouraging hat-making in Newport, and by promoting whaling among his Nantucket Quaker connections. The normal special twist to industry in colonial New England, however, was to start production of the textiles and hardware that made up the bulk of imports from Great Britain. Such efforts, especially coupled with a little frugality, spelled gloom for the importer.

A turn to industry and frugality therefore meant accepting defeat in Newport's ambitions, a loss of wartime gains, and perhaps more. A daring monetary policy could produce an opposite effect. Unfortunately, very little survives—probably very little was written—to illuminate Rhode Island reasoning on paper money. What remains of New England's extensive public debate on the subject during the colonial period mostly came from Massachusetts pens. Quite likely a version of the Boston controversy agitated Newport. Advocates of paper could argue in both places that trade stagnated and prices fell because money was in short supply and that a distinctive local currency of no intrinsic value would stay in New England even if coin continued its flow to Britain. With more money and rising prices, everyone would buy and produce more; prosperity would inevitably blossom.

Against such optimistic reasoning, doubters could point to the fundamentally fraudulent and immoral nature of declaring paper to have value. They forecast the collapse of the deceit, to the general ruin, sooner or later. Also, the local currency, they predicted, would not have even the desired short-run effect precisely because it would stay on the scene and not be acceptable in Britain.

To meet these objections the friends of paper had long-rehearsed arguments. It would not be worthless if backed as they proposed, either by commodities or land. The disadvantage to the merchant of paper being worthless in England would be more than offset by the stimulation of local production by plentiful money and perhaps also by bounties or direct public investment, which would assure the trader an increased supply of needed goods to ship to the mother country.

British policy also had to be reckoned with. The imperial officials had steadily opposed American tampering with money. Overvaluing silver was bad enough, and a parliamentary act of 1708 was passed to curb the practice. It remained virtually a dead letter for forty years, in spite of clamor by British exporters, but it expressed a policy that was reaffirmed intermittently in statements by the Board of Trade and instructions to royal governors. Cranston's plea in 1708 for permission to overvalue the metal at the rate prevailing in Massachusetts received a sharp rebuke. There was no telling what might be provoked by a more radical departure from a monetary standard approved in London. Perhaps it would be a new attack on the charter.

Controversy over monetary policy very likely entered into or even caused the political upset of 1715 in Rhode Island, but the episode remains mysterious. Seats in the House of Magistrates changed hands in unprecedented numbers, the deputy governor and all but one of the assistants being replaced. Turnovers in the House of Deputies were less sweeping but had begun in the midyear election in October 1714. Many old associates of Cranston were replaced by what appears to have been a group organized around the Wanton brothers and the two Coddingtons, William and Nathaniel, with new allies in Warwick and Providence. The military heroes and others of their family became renowned backers of paper money. The Coddingtons had toyed with royalist views in the 1690s, had backed the Narragansett Proprietors, and had cooperated with Cranston as long as he seemed likely to steer the way to compromise with that interest. Then they denounced him bitterly and helped Providence fight the Westconnaug Proprietors. What the Coddingtons wanted in 1715 is not clear; perhaps it was nothing more than vengeance, but if so they failed to unseat Cranston then or ever.

The governor himself remained cautious on monetary questions, but he never made strong objections to the paper money plans inaugurated in 1715. Nor did he exhibit his old energy for public projects after that year but served increasingly as a presiding figure. Whatever his fears for the charter, it soon became obvious that no one in London was about to trouble Rhode Island any longer and that paper money enthusiasts were in the saddle at Newport.

As the General Assembly framed its plans, the bills of public credit would not after all be retired by taxation, but by issuance of a new form of paper currency. Clearly following the Massachusetts lead of 1714, the Assembly the next year voted to have printed £40,000 in a new type of note to be lent to people of the colony, taking as collateral mortgages on land worth at least twice as much as the amount of the loan. (This type of paper money has generally been called land bank notes, but in the eighteenth century, after other varieties had been issued, it became known as "old tenor," a term derived from phrases used in bills of exchange.)* The borrower would pay interest at 5 percent and had to sign bonds to the colony's treasurer for each of the first five years' interest payments. The loan might be repaid after five years or renewed for five more. To arrange loans the Assembly named a panel of trustees, in later years called the Grand Committee, who were all Newport men, plus two-man committees for each of the towns. Strictly speaking there was no

* The word "tenor" was used in its rare sense meaning "character" or "quality." The other New England colonies also issued land-backed currency of approximately the same nature (or "tenor") as Rhode Island's. After Massachusetts brought out a new kind of currency, later known as middle tenor, the original notes became known as old tenor. Massachusetts introduced a third variety, known as new tenor, which was also issued by Rhode Island. By then, however, "old tenor" was firmly implanted in the Rhode Island vocabulary, and "old tenor" remained the monetary standard in general use except when "current money of New England" (the equivalent of new tenor when its value was sustained) or "sterling" was explicitly stated.

provision for retiring the notes; the statute authorizing them expressed an expectation that interest and principal would be paid on them, so making it possible to take them out of circulation, but set up no timetable for disposing of them. On the contrary, the treasury chose to treat interest payments as current income, in fact as a substitute for taxes. The bills were offered as having a value equal to the current money of New England and, in guarded terms, were declared to be something close to legal tender for all public and private debts.

The purpose of issuing paper money based on land was to supply a medium of exchange for the commercial operations of Newport merchants. The preamble to the act authorizing the land bank alluded to wartime expenses, the scarcity of money, and the resulting stagnation of trade and distress to the agricultural interest. Farmers were not clamoring for the money, however. When the scheme was first promoted in 1713, the Providence town meeting opposed it and voted to tell the General Assembly so. The farmers could pay taxes in kind and obtain imported goods on credit against the day when they had produce to sell, which the merchants were only too eager to get. Only those in commerce needed a larger money supply. The farmers, if they agreed with those in Massachusetts, feared encumbering their land with debt to create this convenience for the traders and rightly distrusted paper money they might receive for their products instead of gold or silver.

Fears that the paper would not retain its announced value proved realistic soon. Rural people hesitated to borrow the bills, and the new money was not universally accepted. The legal tender provision of the original act had to be repealed in 1716. At the same time, Rhode Island approved the already existing use of other colonies' old tenor bills, which for many years circulated interchangeably with its own. Thus Rhode Island entered a New England regional currency pool, an advantageous step because it kept the colony's money acceptable in Boston and insured that its depreciation would be roughly in unison with the bills of the neighboring colonies. The paper lost value slowly at first, and interest was paid fairly promptly. The purchasing power of the notes went down to about 45 percent of face value

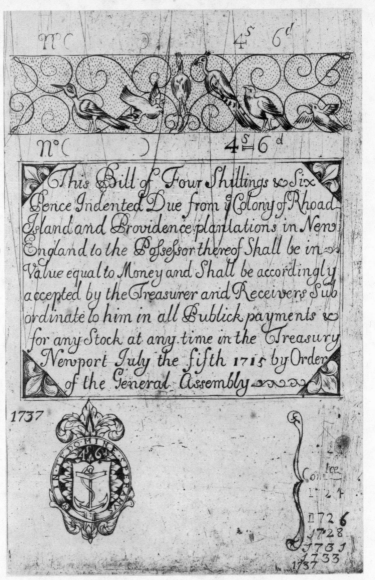

A recent impression from the copper plate used from 1715 to 1737 to print Colony of Rhode Island and Providence Plantations four shillings and six pence public bills of credit. For each emission a date was engraved on the plate. When the bills were received from the printer, they were numbered at the office of the Grand Committee and signed by at least three of the members. Before being put into circulation, the top of each bill was cut off with scissors on a wavy line through the ornamental design. The upper strip, with one notation of the number, was kept by the colony as a stub to preserve a record of the distinctive wavy line that would let the bill be identified when it was paid into the treasury. At least, such was the plan. Office procedures were so slipshod that the system proved faulty. *The Rhode Island Historical Society.*

by 1723, a decline that some considered a reasonable equivalent to a tax.

Demand built up in the commercial circles, as before, for more issues of old tenor currency in 1721 and later years. The bills were not plentiful enough for the colony. Furthermore, they had a way of flowing to Boston, and although Rhode Island retired none before 1728, other colonies did, so the currency was shrinking as population was growing. The land bank of 1721 was to stop this contraction. As a means of providing more substantial benefits to the rural areas than the first bank had done, half the interest money was to be distributed to the town treasuries in the same proportion as the quota of bills available for loan in the town. Otherwise the bank was to be floated in roughly the same way as the first. (On this occasion some of the old Cranston associates, or their sons, were named to the Grand Committee, possibly a sign of political tranquillity or a gesture of reconciliation.) The plan for the bank was soon modified, however.

As the time neared for repayment of the first loan, few wanted to pay. With something like a third of the heads of households in debt to the colony, their wishes had to be considered. Besides, the sudden retirement of £40,000 would shrink the currency available for daily use and require costly measures to recapture the substantial portion of the amount then in Massachusetts. The prospect was too painful to contemplate. Only those few suffering from depreciation and those with moral or theoretical misgivings about land banks cared deeply about retiring the paper. The Assembly in 1724 obligingly enacted the first version of a plan to postpone repayment. As finally worked out, the principal on the loans was to be paid in ten annual installments beginning in 1728. The same timetable was applied to the second bank, so payments of principal borrowed in it would not begin until 1734. The borrowers had to produce special bonds to the first trustee for each of the payments. Further provisions of the revised law gave debtors periods of grace to redeem mortgages after payments had gone into default, so the colony in fact sanctioned even greater delay in repayment. Moreover, no interest was charged on the loan during the period when principal was to be repaid.

Rhode Island went on to issue more bills—a third bank of £40,000 in 1728, then £60,000 in 1731 over mounting opposition. The second of these provided for bounties on hemp, flax, whale oil, and codfish. By that time demand for the money was changing character. Towns with commercial ambitions—Westerly, Warwick, and East Greenwich—called for a new bank, while a coterie of opponents coagulated in Newport. This group included the customs collector, attorney Nathaniel Newdigate, and an assortment of merchants, several of them Anglicans and probably several with aspirations to open direct trade with Britain. They planned an appeal to the Board of Trade, seconded by Governor Joseph Jenckes, who inquired whether his refusal of assent to the act had vetoed it. These opponents even went so far as to talk of Rhode Island's laws becoming subject to review by the Privy Council like those of royal colonies. Deputy Governor John Wanton got wind of these schemes, called the Assembly back into session to hear about them, seized the opposition's papers, rushed some explanatory statements through the legislature, and then returned the papers in a mutilated condition.

Suddenly Rhode Island faced a constitutional crisis. Even the elderly and experienced agent in London, Richard Partridge, feared the consequences. Astonishingly, the Crown's attorney general and solicitor general announced that the charter did not give the governor a veto and that "the crown hath no discretionary power of repealing laws" in Rhode Island. Jenckes tried to rescind his dissent from the paper money act and declined to stand for reelection, pleading advanced years and failing memory. Paper money advocates triumphantly elected the Wanton brothers governor and deputy governor and proceeded in 1733 to celebrate the victory by authorizing the fifth land bank of £104,000. In London, however, the Board of Trade began a long, slow search for ways to stop this sort of thing.* The board faced

---

* In Boston frightened merchants set up a syndicate to issue bills with silver backing, vainly hoping to drive the dubious paper out of use. All that came of their efforts was hoarding of their bills and a steeper rise of the price of silver as the merchants tried to buy enough to expand their operations.

The Colony House at Newport, designed by Richard Munday in 1739 and built during the next few years. A monument to commercial prosperity, paper money, and the architect's taste, the structure was placed with symbolic fitness at the head of Queen Street (now the north side of Washington Square) at the juncture with Broad Street (now Broadway). Queen Street ran straight onto the Town Wharf, soon to be extended and renamed Long Wharf. Broad Street brought overland traffic from Portsmouth and Bristol Ferry. *The Preservation Society of Newport County Photo.*

an all but official apathy on the part of the king's ministers in the Walpole administration; Great Britain, like the rest of western Europe, was suffering a shortage of specie, and so long as gold and silver kept coming in from Boston, few wanted to interfere.

Protest greeted the bank of 1733 and the sixth old tenor bank of £100,000 in 1738, but substantial public works were aided by the money. The fort guarding Newport was completely rebuilt and armed, a pier was extended from Block Island to create a harbor intended as a fishing base, the Colony House was finished in Newport, and a lighthouse erected at Beaver Tail in Jamestown. The New England commercial web, starved for currency by retirement of bills in Massachusetts while population went on growing, eagerly absorbed all the paper Rhode Island would print. Boston merchants cried in anguish but they accepted it. Even some of the opponents of the bank of 1731 immediately took out loans from it.

So far the paper money was a resounding success. Governor Richard Ward, reporting to the Board of Trade in 1741, fairly purred as he defended the old tenor emissions. "Although we were not rich," he wrote, "yet poverty was a stranger among us till the year 1710, when we were called upon to appear in the field of honor and interest of Great Britain. The vast expense of that and other expeditions in the war reduced us to a low ebb, yet we manfully struggled through our difficulties." Having little commerce in the seventeenth century, Rhode Island had little money at the end except what was left of the funds brought by the first settlers. When faced with the steep bills of Queen Anne's War, the colony had no choice but to issue bills of credit and after the war could find no better way to pay the debt than issuing old tenor currency.

The policy had been wise. Boston merchants kept buying all the gold and silver they could get, making paper an essential medium of exchange. So Rhode Island issued more to keep its infant commerce growing. Trade increased, attracting "people of all sorts and conditions to come from all parts and settle among us." They brought useful skills, thus furthering commerce and generating a need for still more currency. By the 1730s the colony was supplying a great part of the medium of exchange for

Connecticut and Massachusetts as well as itself. Rhode Island continued to prosper.

Ward boasted, "We have now above one hundred and twenty sail of vessels belonging to the inhabitants of this colony, all constantly employed in trade; some on the coast of Africa, others in the neighboring colonies, many in the West Indies, and a few in Europe." Without the land banks neither the trade nor the defense of the colony would have been possible. "In short, if this colony be in any respect happy and flourishing, it is paper money, and a right application of it, that hath rendered us so. And that we are in a flourishing condition, is evident from our trade, which is greater in proportion to the dimensions of our government, than that of any colony in His Majesty's American dominion."

Nor did Rhode Island, as some averred, profit at the expense of others. It supplied rum, sugar, and molasses to its neighbors, even the mecca of trade, Massachusetts. It supplied the West Indies with lumber, provisions, horses, and slaves. It supplied Great Britain with ships.

As to the troublesome detail of depreciation, Ward said it was a mere illusion. The Boston merchants were the culprits: by buying up gold and silver to make remittances to Britain they had made these metals "commodities on the same level with common merchandise" and bid them up, adjusting their transactions in paper money so as to preserve their profits. This practice produced a semblance of depreciation in old tenor bills; those who claimed that the huge amount circulated by Rhode Island caused their value to decline were simply wrong. The proof, said Ward, could be seen in the Connecticut money, which stood at the same ratio to silver as did the bills of the other New England colonies, although not £14,000 were outstanding. Furthermore, during the last few years when Newport had begun a small direct trade with Britain, and so to that extent escaped the clutches of Boston, the ratio of the Rhode Island bills to silver had held steady at twenty-seven shillings per ounce.

When Ward penned this panegyric on old tenor money, he was actually pronouncing a eulogy. He wrote to the Board of Trade, but the board wanted a report because questions had been asked in Parliament, originally to bedevil the Walpole administration, about the American paper currencies and what the king's ministers were doing to restrain them. Already Rhode Island had received and heeded royal orders to stop creating the old type of land bank. The paper money of 1740 was new tenor, declared to stand in relation to silver at the rate of 6s 9d per ounce, in line with the parliamentary act of 1708. Ward could offer no new plan to dispose of the old tenor bills; blandly he declared that his colony had already set up the best one it could devise.

Ward's analysis of the paper money had its weak passages, but his claim that the old tenor banks had enabled Newport to rise from bucolic backwater to leading port was accepted ruefully in Boston. The attitude there, of course, was nothing like Ward's smug satisfaction. Anguished Boston importers saw Newport thrive during the depression that spread over most of New England from the late 1720s through the 1730s. With Governor Jonathan Belcher both by conviction and royal instructions insisting on the orderly retirement of Massachusetts bills, Rhode Island provided a fountain of them, supplying over half the paper currency of New England. The Boston merchants could appeal for laws to prevent circulation of Rhode Island bills, but their officials would neither impose such rules nor sponsor a substitute medium of exchange. Boston traders, no matter how much they wanted to, could not refuse the bills. Glumly they agreed to sell goods to Newporters, who by depreciation obtained a discount when the payment fell due. Bostonians could estimate that Newport had before 1730 built and fitted out thirty vessels through this discount and by the simple advantage of having money to buy with. Rhode Island merchants also used their ability to get manufactured goods to dominate the commerce of southern New England.

Even without British intervention, however, the Rhode Island raid on Massachusetts commerce could not have continued as it had been going. The neglected business of retiring the bills caught up with Newport and when broached proved hard. The rate of payments on interest fell off by 1730, and payments of principal soon were in arrears also. The first audit of the Grand

Committee in 1733 revealed alarming delinquency. By the end of the decade only about three-fifths of what was due came in during an average year. Efforts to settle the accounts of the treasurer who died in office in 1729 resulted in bafflement. His bookkeeping did not make sense, and his records of interest payments were in a shambles. Considering the number of mortgages, by 1733 well over a thousand, and the sets of bonds that should have been with each one, orderly filing had been needed at the very least, yet no system had been contrived. No one could find all the papers that should have been in the hands of the treasurer and the first trustee; sets of bonds could not always be matched with the mortgages. There was no routine to keep the officials aware of who owed what each year, so there was no way to dun the laggard. No records had been kept of all the sales of mortgaged lands. Borrowers had left the colony. Town committees had not always sent the various papers to Newport. For several years after the chaos came to light, moreover, little was done about it.

When a new war loomed up, procrastination could go on no longer. Rhode Island eagerly armed for the conflict that broke out in 1739. War meant privateers, high prices for commodities in short supply, and governmental contracts for forces on land and sea. These were all attractive, but the last required public expenditures. Rather than contemplate a tax, many in Rhode Island wanted a new bank. This time the Newport paper money men were fairly well backed by rural towns and a few places that were beginning to see in paper money the means to capture trade from Newport as Newport had from Boston. Imperial policy, however, required that any fresh loans be made in bills guaranteed to keep a value in relation to silver at 6s 9d per ounce. Even if new devices to support the value of the currency were to be tried, there was more opposition to the bank in Newport than ever before. Some members of the Grand Committee opposed it, fearing that Great Britain might find a way to force redemption of old tenor (then at 27s per ounce) at the official rate; besides, they reasoned, if the borrowers could not pay interest and principal on what already was lent, how could the populace pay more? The new loan was approved by narrow

Portrait of a Newport merchant, public servant, and worthy heir to a great name: Thomas Cranston (1710–1785), painted by Joseph Blackburn, ca. 1755. *The Rhode Island Historical Society.*

votes in the Assembly, and the committeemen resigned in protest.

Serious work began on cleaning up the accounts on the old banks, amid charges of corruption and favoritism on the part of the Grand Committee. The Assembly appointed a dreary series of investigatory and audit committees (some of them threw up their hands in horror and resigned), devised new methods to crack down on borrowers in arrears, and kept changing them until a system was created that almost worked.

The first step of sorting out the records was followed by instigating a flock of suits against those behind in payments of interest and principal. This business almost swamped the courts. Revision of the judicial structure and appointment of additional attorneys for the colony yielded only slight benefits. With responsibilities divided among the attorneys, their accounts quickly fell into disarray, and some of them had to be sued to compel restitution. On one occasion an audit committee was sued.

Jahleel Brenton, who had been secretary of the Grand Committee and kept its office in his house from 1726 to 1744, turned out to have been rather slipshod, to say the least, but his negligence remained hidden until his position was redefined and he was required to post bond. He refused, almost bringing the management of the paper currency to a standstill. Soon the Assembly ordered his successor to sue him, but the case was hopeless because Brenton's papers were in such a state that nobody could specify what he was being sued for. After a bewildering succession of arbitrations and audits, his fees for the time he spent on this business were declared to exceed the shortage in his accounts.

With suits going off like a fireworks display, something close to order was achieved by 1750. Receipts of interest and principal reached levels of 90 percent of what was owed. Roughly accurate figures indicated how much would never be collected owing to legal complications. A team of experts—Benjamin Nichols (by then keeper of the Grand Committee), Thomas Cranston, James Sheffield, and Stephen Hopkins—had emerged from the Assembly's numerous committees as the men who could make headway against the currency muddle. This episode, in fact, first lifted

Hopkins into prominence. The Assembly finally began burning large numbers of old tenor bills.

Still, the officials often lacked zeal. One treasurer refused to follow a new procedure to collect interest because it would increase publicity and court costs to the debtors. He preferred threatening suit and letting them pay up quietly. Town committees, guilty of extreme clumsiness, were not called to account except after long delays. Mysteriously, a substantial number of borrowers from the first and second banks, many of them prominent men, never paid any principal and never were sued. Significantly, foreclosing the mortgages, long said to be the ultimate weapon to insure value of the money, was not done— the Assembly never even specified how it might be done until 1754.

If favoritism and administrative bungling that smacked of corruption lasted so long and were curbed with such tenderness and forbearance as the record reveals, the reason probably lay in the attitudes of the Newport merchant patriciate that had operated the paper money business all along. Its members wanted the commercial benefits the land banks had conferred, not the agony of repayment or sheriff's sales of land under foreclosure. They treated each other with a fraternal good will, tolerating bookkeeping in public affairs that they would not have stood for in their own counting houses. They had no wish to squeeze blood out of each other, although in the end they would see others forced to pay. Although three of the men who finally did the dirty work were Newport merchants—perhaps significantly, all were heirs of old stalwarts in Samuel Cranston's early administration—the fourth was the man from Providence who toppled the political hegemony of Newport.

If the great Newport adventure of climbing to the ranks of the major ports was accomplished in great part by a monetary raid on Boston, and if the old tenor currency went (slowly) to the flames in a noisome air of corruption, the gains were real enough. Newport had grown steadily from a population of less than two thousand in the commercial center at the beginning of the eighteenth century to over five in the middle, peaking over nine thousand before the Revolution flushed out a torrent of refugees.

By 1750 the bustling city had opened new lines of trade—some direct importation from Great Britain, the carrying of slaves from Africa to the Caribbean—and built up the old ones. It had carved out a hinterland. Perhaps it was ready to make do without a predatory money system. In any case it had to try, and to try in the face of rising competition from Providence.

9

BABEL ON NARRAGANSETT BAY

Religion in Rhode Island made almost as abrupt a shift in the eighteenth century as government and commerce. The colony experienced all four of the great religious movements in colonial America—Puritanism, Quakerism, imperial Anglicanism, and the revival known as the Great Awakening—but in its own way. Rhode Island began as a bundle of special cases of Puritanism, then gave Quakerism its first great base in North America. When the Church of England launched its effort to win over colonials to its particular form of Christianity and to imperial patriotism at the same time, the Anglican pioneers in Rhode Island had the singular experience of finding themselves in competition with missionaries sent by the official church of Massachusetts. And when George Whitefield brought the Great Awakening to Newport, the various denominations in the colony showed strikingly different propensities to respond, ranging from enthusiasm to distaste and hostility. So the Awakening in Rhode Island was disjointed and scattered, not the mass excitement Whitefield evoked elsewhere. In addition to these variants on the common experience of the English colonies, Rhode Island in the eighteenth century underwent two broad developments that were less usual, the restoration of severed connections with Christian tradition and the divergence of urban from rural folkways in religion.

The break between the seventeenth and eighteenth centuries was softened, mercifully, by the Quaker advance into the colony, which in many ways bridged the gap by continuing the development begun in Antinomianism and at the same time starting the parade of religions sending missionaries to organize churches in Rhode Island. The Friends were only the first to find there people whose beliefs and tastes in worship prepared them to agree with the evangelists. Beginning in 1694 the Anglicans and Congregationalists, half a century later revivalist Separates, Moravians, and other offshoots of the Great Awakening, all found Rhode Islanders to welcome them as the messengers they had been awaiting.

The responsiveness to the missionaries, in a sense, manifested a loss of vitality in the older religious traditions. There was no more exploration of the outer fringes of Puritanism, little more invention of sects. Gone was the old sense of a place in religious history defined by defiance of Massachusetts Puritan orthodoxy as the first step toward restoring a true, original Christian church. Gone with it was the zest for combat over doctrine and the exhilaration of regarding all tradition as questionable. In the eighteenth century different aspects of religious life became the important ones. Doctrinal disputes were rare: some churches, notably the Anglican, took their creeds for granted; in others, only a few cardinal points aroused controversy, especially the nature of conversion and the location of authority within the fellowship. Intense debate, however, raged as often over peripheral matters, such as congregational singing, the laying on of hands, control of church property, and the morality of slavery. The earlier century had been the time of the daring and rash; it was followed by decades of restoring links with the past and the outside world. Where religious life had been overwhelmingly treated as the fervor of the present, it came to be treated as dwelling within tradition and constantly forging links of the past to the future.

In part the seventeenth-century concerns vanished with the original founders. John Clarke died in 1676; within a few years Roger Williams, William Coddington, and Samuel Gorton went to their graves. By their opposition to college education for the ministry, they had done much to forestall the training of successors. No strong new voices rose to rally dedication to the special religious ways that had been worked out in the colony. If the shadowy Baptist preacher, William Vaughan, was in fact an Oxford man, he did not take the part of champion of the local ways either in Newport or before the wider audience of English Protestants. For a dozen years the colony was nearly cut off from the larger world of Christianity except as traveling Quaker ministers came and went and as the several sorts of Baptists desultorily corresponded with people of like persuasion in England.

Moreover, the Baptist and Quaker ways did not satisfy a good many people in Rhode Island, as became clear in the 1690s. Ironically, the novelties offered to slake their spiritual thirsts were religions that anywhere else would have been counted as old, traditional, and conservative in contrast with the eccentric sects nurtured around Narragansett Bay. Conspicuously, the incoming denominations achieved their success where wealth was concentrated—the nascent cities and the two Kingstowns. In these places, Anglican and Congregationalist missionaries rightly sought responsive Rhode Islanders. In Newport and Providence, however, the organization of churches relying on college-educated ministers prompted aspirations among Baptists for more learned preachers, more elegant ceremonies, more beautiful meetinghouses. To some degree all the sects in these urban centers began to appreciate renewed contacts with traditions of learning, to cultivate knowledge and the arts, to use ecclesiastical architecture to express their natures, and to stress measures to ensure the continuation of the church into the future.

The relations between faiths in the colony were less those of contenders for monopoly than those of teams in an athletic league. It might be better to think of two leagues, as the ordinary rural areas stayed with one type of religious organization while the Kingstowns and the cities went in for a more elaborate scale of things. In the rural league competition was mainly between Baptist preachers until revivalism became an issue; the simple country churches brought in only a few practices their ancestors had spurned, such as building meetinghouses. Christians in the wealthier places, however, created a bill of fare from which the worshipper could choose the most appealing level of lavishness in worship and erudition in sermons or find devotion to a specially cherished doctrine. The spate of revivals in the 1740s, Rhode Island's manifestation of the Great Awakening, thoroughly reordered the rural associations, but in the cities merely added some congregations under new denominational labels. In view of the diversity of sects and the paucity of knowledge about their inner lives, the simplest method to use in unraveling events in the religious life of Rhode Island after 1690 is to tour the different churches, viewing their recruitment of members, pastors, and well-wishers, or their triumphs in the competition against each other, rather than their theologies or their spiritual tempers.

The most striking change in the eighteenth century was the entry of the Church of England. Francis Brinley and the royalists deliberately invited Anglican evangelizing as part of the campaign to replace the charter government and put power into the hands of the self-styled social superiors. Brinley approached Francis Nicholson, the old soldier who had become a career colonial official, with good results. Nicholson was a team-spirited if not a devout Anglican, and both donated money and somehow propelled a clergyman named John Lockyer to sojourn in Newport from 1694 until about 1702. He drew enough people to form a church; they built a sanctuary where he officiated but could neither afford a steeple, a full outfit of ceremonial objects, nor all of Lockyer's salary.

An appeal transmitted by Governor Bellomont of Massachusetts led to the inauguration of a subsidy by a new English philanthropic corporation, the Society for the Propagation of the Gospel in Foreign Parts—the S.P.G., for short. This organization in reality was an arm of the Church of England to spread Anglicanism in America, using persuasion and education, but looking hopefully toward public support if not an old-fashioned establishment. The overtones of political purpose—fostering imperial patriotism, aligning the rich and powerful with English policy, undermining the influence of Quakers and Congregationalists—were present but ordinarily muted. The new Trinity Church in Newport thus had a doubly clear political orientation. Queen Anne herself supplied the lack of ceremonial vessels.

The man sent by the S.P.G. to replace Lockyer, James Honeyman, accordingly had the delicate task of escaping the origins of his church without repudiating them. Like a surprising number of the newcomers who cut a figure in Rhode Island culture, Honeyman was British but not English: his family was from Scotland. He managed very well by a combination of tact, winning ways, and longevity. He served nearly half a century and in his declining years could take satisfaction in having built up an Anglican church to an impressive size and elegance, steering it past mere toleration to prestige in the land of Roger Williams and William Coddington. He could quite reasonably regard himself as among the colonial patriciate and could look forward to his family's perpetuation by his son, a leading lawyer.

These triumphs were far in the future when Honeyman arrived in 1704, and he found on return from a journey to encourage the subsidy of the S.P.G. that things tended to slip backwards in his absence. He smoothed over a quarrel in 1709, quite possibly a result of colonial politics, insisted that local disputes be dropped at the churchyard gate, and like Cranston, eagerly embraced the uncontroversial variety of imperial patriotism in supporting Queen Anne's War. He overstepped the limit of prudence by advocating an American bishop on several occasions beginning in 1713, provoking the General Assembly to enact in 1716 an emphatic law against governmental backing of any religious group and reaffirming religious liberty and the equality of all denominations.* Perhaps Honeyman joined the clamor for a bishop only to please the S.P.G. In any event, he toned down his arguments, saying no more of obtaining governmental aid and stressing the need for episcopal authority only to keep good order within the fold.

Trinity Church flourished under Honeyman. It gained financial strength to allow it both to enjoy independence from the S.P.G. between 1720 and 1740 and to erect a new church begun in 1725—the handsome structure still standing, although somewhat remodeled. Honeyman attracted leading people—Cran-

---

* As published in later years, Rhode Island law excluded Catholics from toleration. Like some other provisions in the statute books this was a gesture of compliance with British law. There is neither any record of the General Assembly enacting the provision nor of prosecution under it. If there were any Catholics in colonial Rhode Island, no official notice was taken of them.

stons, Wantons, Coddingtons, Sanfords, Brentons, Bannisters, and Ayraults, and an influential but nearly forgotten man named Peter Bours. Bours, whose name was probably pronounced "Bowers," for years was a leader in the church, the cultural enterprises of Newport, and the General Assembly, where he was often the speaker of the House of Deputies although he was an outspoken foe of paper currency. After 1740 Trinity returned to the S.P.G. for funds to pay an assistant to the rector who would double as a schoolmaster, but the congregation remained an assemblage of the wealthy and prominent.

A short episode in the early years of Trinity Church, the sojourn of the Anglo-Irish philosopher, George Berkeley, not only added luster to the church but gave to Newport a splendid display of the power of Anglicanism to form a link with the cultural refinement of the Old World. In and out of Honeyman's flock arose a redoubled zeal to bring learning and the arts to the aspiring seaport. This effect was not, however, what Berkeley set out to accomplish.

His plan was to found a college on Bermuda, to bring religion, learning, and culture to the sons of colonial Englishmen and the Indian natives. It was high time, he thought, for the Church of England to spread its influence, uplift the provincials, evangelize the natives, and promote arts and letters in America. Too long the colonies had been valued only for their commerce. Berkeley also had a vaster dream. Reviving the old theme of Europe's decay and the promise of rejuvenation in the New World, he wrote his "America, or the Muse's Refuge, a Prophecy." He foresaw a new cultural flowering:

> In happy Climes the Seat of Innocence,
>   Where Nature guides and virtue rules,
> Where Men shall not impose for Truth and Sense
>   The Pedantry of Courts and Schools:
>
> There shall be sung another golden Age,
>   The rise of Empire and of Arts, ...

To America would pass the leadership in culture by the inspiring deeds of her people and the noble hearts of her poets. They would be

> Not such as *Europe* breeds in her decay; [but]
>   Such as she bred when fresh and young,
> When heav'nly Flame did animate her Clay, ...

> Westward the course of Empire takes its Way;
>   The four first Acts already past,
> A fifth shall close the Drama with the Day;
>   Time's noblest Offspring is the last.

His dreams captured the imaginations of men of learning in Dublin and London, great men at court, even the Princess of Wales, shortly to become Queen Caroline.

Scanning the map of British America from Barbados to Nova Scotia, Berkeley concluded that Bermuda was roughly equidistant from all parts, an idyllic island conveniently situated near trade routes. There he envisioned a college to be named St. Paul's, eventually to be surrounded by academies for music, painting, sculpture, and architecture, plus parks, markets, residential belts—a new metropolis. The plans for the ring of faculty houses and gardens make the vision sound like an eighteenth-century precursor of Jefferson's for the University of Virginia. Altogether Berkeley had a grand idea, a magnificent culmination to the Anglican enthusiasm for taking the lead in shaping the culture of colonial America. Or, it would have been a magnificent culmination if it had worked.

Equipped with a royal charter for his college, pledges of private donations, an all-too-misty parliamentary grant of funds from anticipated sale of West Indian land, and an entourage consisting of his bride, her friend Miss Handcock, two or three leisured gentlemen and the painter John Smibert, Berkeley embarked for America in 1728. Landing in Virginia, he found passage on a coastal vessel sailing to Newport, where he proposed to buy a farm to supply provisions for the college while awaiting final arrangements for the subsidy from the royal treasury.

News of his arrival reached Mr. Honeyman in mid-sermon. The rector announced the event, closed the service with a blessing, and led the congregation to the wharf to greet Berkeley. A few months later the philosopher bought his farm about three miles east of town, naming his house Whitehall. He preached frequently in Newport, tactfully staying with topics on which all Christians agreed, and drawing crowds of all persuasions. He may even have attended Quaker meetings, and offered a few words there. At times he journeyed to Kingstown to preach and, with Smibert, to learn something about the Indians at firsthand.

Berkeley drew to himself those with intellectual interests in Newport and for some distance around. His presence proved a catalyst for the coterie of men who formed a Society for the Promotion of Knowledge and Virtue by gathering for conversation. The founders included two young lawyers, two schoolmasters, two merchants, and two ministers—of these, half were in Honeyman's flock, the others being Congregationalists or Baptists. Some of these gentlemen and some of the scenery around Whitehall figured in *Aliciphron or the Minute Philosopher*, a series of dialogues Berkeley wrote during his thirty-two months in Rhode Island. (The work bears about the same relation to the culture of the colony as Dvorak's "New World Symphony" does to that of Iowa.) Thus the philosopher provided encouragement and inspiration to the intellectual life of Rhode Island as it was being revitalized in its eighteenth-century form.

As Berkeley learned how impractical his choice of Bermuda had been and how Sir Robert Walpole was thwarting the parliamentary grant, he toyed with the idea of establishing his college at Newport or New York, but reluctantly concluded that the project would have to be given up. After a tour of Harvard College, he left Smibert to struggle along painting portraits in Boston and returned to London. With the consent of some of the private contributors to the Bermuda College, he donated his farm and eight chests of books to Yale, sent Latin classics which Harvard lacked, and provided an organ for Trinity Church in Newport.

The Church of England with aid from the S.P.G. gained beachheads also in Providence, Kingstown, and Bristol, which was still under Massachusetts rule. The zealot in Providence who advanced the cause was Gabriel Bernon, an elderly Huguenot who had lived for a time in Newport and who manifested a respect unusual among Anglicans for intellectual attainments among the local dissenters. He busily drummed up money from many sources and launched the building of a church before a rector could be found meeting Bernon's specifications. He wanted a man of accomplishment in learning as well as the ministry in order that the Church of England might outshine the offerings of the other pulpits in town. In 1722 he welcomed George Pigot who had once taught school in Newport and had more recently served in the Anglican base at Stratford, Connecticut; he stayed in Providence only until 1727. St. John's (then King's) Church managed tolerably well until 1739, when it obtained its first indubitable star, John Checkley, who had been a controversial pamphleteer and bookseller in Boston before obtaining ordination at age fifty-eight. Checkley's temper mellowed, his interests broadened, but he kept his vigorous mind and flair for words. He lived his last fifteen years serving the Providence church to its great satisfaction. His congregation embraced some of the local dignitaries, as was usual in New England Anglican churches, plus a substantial number of ordinary citizens, but could not boast the eminence of Trinity or, perhaps, even of St. Michael's in Bristol.

The Kingstown Anglicans established St. Paul's church early in the eighteenth century and enjoyed the ministry of two men for brief periods, and Mr. Honeyman intermittently, until in 1721 the S.P.G. sent the redoubtable James MacSparran. A Scotsman reared in northern Ireland, but always a super-Briton, the parson never reconciled himself outwardly to a land of genial religious diversity or attuned himself inwardly to Rhode Island society. His resistance to assimilation, however, enhanced his effectiveness as emissary of the self-defined higher religion and culture. He held himself above the colony and seems to have inspired his wealthy and easygoing parishioners to hold themselves above their neighbors and even somewhat above their human frailties. He also brought in a schoolmaster for their children and taught religion to their slaves.

Unfortunately, MacSparran fell in with the local litigiousness and pettiness, in arrogant hope of securing the equivalent of an endowment. Whatever he may have accomplished in coaching the elite of the famed Narragansett planters, he embroiled his church in one of the classical legal battles of eighteenth-century

"Whitehall," built in 1729, George Berkeley's residence during his years in Rhode Island. The house stands in Middletown. *The Preservation Society of Newport County Photo.*

James MacSparran (1693–1757), Anglican pastor of the Narragansett
country, painted in 1729 by John Smibert. *Bowdoin College Museum of Art,
Brunswick, Maine.*

America. The plan to gain the three hundred acres set aside by the Pettaquamscut purchasers for support of an "orthodox minister" was hatched before MacSparran arrived, but he adopted it. Though the case was built on mundane matters of leases and adverse holding under a variety of claims, MacSparran and his church relied heavily on the assertion that he was "lawfully settled . . . as a minister of the Gospel . . . qualified and approved as the laws of the realm provide and direct," and so deserved the benefit of the land. On his behalf, flimsy testimony was procured to show that the donors had the Church of England in mind all along, but it was also argued that even if they did not, the law recognized no other qualification of an orthodox minister than one conforming to the established church. Actually, all but one of the Pettaquamscut purchasers had favored Massachusetts orthodoxy, and this was easy to substantiate; lawyers opposing MacSparran added that the Toleration Act of 1689 had given certain dissenting denominations a recognition as orthodox in English law.

Out of the several suits and countersuits, the ones that came to be central turned on the question of intent of the donors. Anglicans and Congregationalists from Massachusetts rushed to bolster their respective sides and wield influence in London. In the courts there were repeated rebuffs to MacSparran, who was even abandoned by the S.P.G., but persistently got up new evidence and new devices to bring additional suits. After thirty years of intricate legal maneuvering, the Privy Council ruled decisively against him. Even the Archbishop of Canterbury threw his weight against MacSparran! Finally the old gentleman gave up and in a fine gesture bequeathed his own land as a glebe for his successors.

In addition to serving their own parishioners, the Anglican ministers ordinarily traveled about the colony to preach, teach, baptize, and solemnize weddings. They developed small followings in such unlikely places as Jamestown and Warwick, but not enough to warrant founding more churches. As the existing ones settled into routine they were small, disproportionately favored by the well-to-do, and probably centers of imperial patriotism.

Parallel with the spread of Anglicanism, and for similar reasons, went the introduction of Congregationalism.* A group of Massachusetts ministers launched a campaign in 1695 to take the gospel to "the paganizing and perishing plantations" south of the border. Relays of parsons went to preach in Newport and Providence. Scattered throughout Rhode Island were people who preferred this brand of Christianity to anything organized in their towns, and Newport contained enough to persuade one of the missionaries, Nathaniel Clap, to reside among them in 1696. A committee of Boston ministers had to raise funds to augment local resources there and elsewhere in Rhode Island, acting in much the same role as the S.P.G. did for the Church of England.

Clap turned out to be a Puritan of the old stamp. He held rigid standards for church membership, sometimes to the despair of his Boston backers, and refused to consider forming a church for many years for lack of a sufficient number who could convince him they were probably among God's elect. He preached and taught all the same, but of course would not administer the sacraments of baptism and the Lord's Supper in line with old Puritan convictions that these were functions of a minister, who was an officer of a church, not just a man with the proper training. Eventually he was prevailed upon to organize a church in 1720, but he kept suspending the sacraments out of a belief that there were too few qualified members. The flock grew restive and tried to add a co-pastor, but this only led to a quarrel, review of the controversy by a council of outside ministers, and then a schism. There followed a comic episode with Clap refusing to set foot in the original meetinghouse ever again, while Boston money

---

* The name for this sect of Christianity is hard to select. "Congregationalism" was used fairly commonly, though "Presbyterianism" came into use in the mid-eighteenth century, in spite of the absence of the organizational traits that distinguished Presbyterianism. One could use "Massachusetts orthodoxy" to underline the simple truth that this was religion as publicly supported in Massachusetts, but this gain would be purchased at the cost of suggesting a uniformity of belief that did not exist in Massachusetts and a governmental favor that did not exist in Rhode Island. The Massachusetts standing order, of course, did prevail in Bristol and other towns later transferred to Rhode Island jurisdiction.

was building a new one for the Second Congregational Church. After a sojourn in an unused Baptist building, Clap and his flock occupied the new structure, leaving the old to the schismatics.

The Second Church emphatically embraced an evangelical form of Congregationalism along lines becoming fashionable in Boston. It also insisted that the church rather than the minister pass on candidates for admission to membership. The preacher was John Adams, a minor poet with astounding mental powers. Widely read in nine languages, he had an almost photographic memory and a brilliant command of logic. Such a scholar was never at a loss for words. He was accused, however, of going too far in aping Cotton Mather's florid pulpit style. The man in the congregation who leveled the accusation added that the model was a bad choice, because Adams could not emulate any man relished so little by the people of Rhode Island. They preferred "good practical discourses delivered in a good style." Adams retaliated by preaching his next sermon in mimicry of Clap. Obviously, things were not well in the Second Church. Adams was soon dismissed. He returned to Harvard College to pursue the literary life during most of his few remaining years. A Yale man, James Searing, stepped in and stabilized the church.

With Adams off the scene, the two congregations restored amiable relations. They jointly sponsored a school that had been endowed before the schism. Clap officiated at the wedding of Searing to Mary Ellery. The old bitterness washed away, and Clap served out his life increasingly beloved in spite of his crustiness. Upon his death in 1745, it turned out that he had been keeping church funds and adding as much as he could spare of his salary in a box marked, "What's here contained for piety is all design'd and charity." After deliberation the church raised an equal sum and bought the house and land next door to Clap's, which it then rented, using half the income for the church and the other half to perpetuate Clap's custom of buying and giving away books, "to do good and to keep up a grateful remembrance of him." The house was called Piety and Charity. Under Clap's last associate pastors and his successor, the First Congregational Church, like the Second, had competent but unremarkable leadership. Both attracted many respectable families and a few of the wealthy, including some Coddingtons, Brentons, Sanfords, Ellerys and Vernons.

With minor differences between them, the two congregations installed in Newport were outposts of the Massachusetts standing order. The ties were deliberately kept, and not merely by financial dependence. In the 1760s they were observing days of prayer and thanksgiving proclaimed by the governor of Massachusetts, probably a practice that had been observed all along. The ministers met periodically with brethren from pulpits around Narragansett Bay without regard to colony boundaries. The organization of the religious bodies followed Massachusetts norms, though not required to do so by law. Full membership was allowed to the putative elect, determined as each church saw fit, leaving a large number of people who attended services, owned pews, and contributed money, but did not take communion. Together these faithful nonmembers comprised the congregation, but the men among them, joined with the male members, were called the Society and took up the functions of the parish in Massachusetts—raising money, managing property, and declaring the will of the congregation in choosing a minister.

The two churches did preserve a basic difference of tone, as became clear when they called new ministers in the pre-revolutionary period. After dismissing Clap's successor for drunkenness, the First Church obtained the services of Samuel Hopkins, the brilliant disciple of Jonathan Edwards. Hopkins arrived in 1770, at a time when he was waging theological controversies of major importance on the nature of holiness, the value of sin, and the existence of free will. He had shocked the New England clergy by publishing a treatise entitled *Sin Through the Divine Interposition an Advantage to the Universe* (1759), arguing that wickedness is indelibly evil although God created the world in such a way as to make sin conducive to much good in human affairs. Later he argued with great subtlety the proposition that the human will is free even though strong desires effectually govern what people choose and the desires, being heavily determined by the presence or absence of divine grace, are controlled by God's arbitrary and immutable decision to predestine a few for heaven and the rest for hell. Hopkins, following Edwards, also advanced a disturbing opinion on original sin: denying that there was any such thing in human life, he argued that the unregenerate inevitably allied themselves with the failings of Adam by repeating them. Hopkins was not a man to make things easy—nor yet one to reach radical conclusions.

His views on virtue, in a somewhat distorted form, ultimately became the hallmark of his theology. He took his departure from Edwards' interpretation of God as perfect goodness and his concept of saving faith (the effect of grace on the human heart) as a suprarational and ecstatic acceptance of God's universe. Hopkins, backed for once by plain words in the Bible, said that God is love, or perfect benevolence. So human virtue, the approximation of ultimate holiness, consists of selflessness, a benevolence to all mankind and God's creation as well as to God himself. It followed that men should seek good for each other, which, Hopkins boldly insisted, meant abolishing slavery as well as more conventional endeavors such as spreading the gospel and curbing the ravages of strong drink. In arguing his proposition, however, he deliberately offered a logical absurdity: the regenerate Christian would, without delight to be sure, feel willing to endure eternity in hell if that would redound to the glory of God. Hopkins hastily pointed out that condemning a saint to everlasting torment could not conceivably glorify God, but his argument using the absurd extreme was picked up and popularized. So, it was said, he posed the test to the anxious soul: are you willing to be damned for the glory of God? Anybody who answered "Yes" would escape the flame and so would have to doubt the sincerity of the reply. Thus Hopkins was credited with devising one of the most exquisite psychological tortures ever known. There was something in Hopkins, therefore, that carried forward the spirit of Clap. Hopkins' abstruse and uningratiating sermons also honored the tradition of the founder by tending to drive away part of the congregation.

Hopkins became a resolute patriot during the Revolution and had to flee Newport for a few years. Somehow this experience stimulated a fervent belief that the millennium was about to begin. He penned a treatise on the subject, and when he gathered his ideas into a massive *System of Doctrines*, published in

1793, he added an appendix on the anticipated earthly bliss. According to William Ellery Channing, who revered Hopkins in the manner of a rebellious son, "The millennium was more than a belief to him. It had the freshness of visible things. He was at home in it. His book on the subject has the air of reality, as if written from observation. He describes the habits and customs of the millennium as one familiar with them." Channing added, "Whilst to the multitude he seemed a hard, dry theologian, feeding upon the thorns of controversy, he was living in a region of the imagination, feeding upon visions of a holiness and a happiness which are to make earth all but heaven."

At the second Church the pulpit star was Ezra Stiles, later president of Yale. Stiles was a first-rate preacher and pastor, possessing almost by nature the felicity of expression and human warmth that Hopkins lacked. Urbane and yet doggedly evangelical, Stiles was a huge success. Always tolerant and distressed by sectarian bickering, he was a man to bring people together. His intellectual powers never produced imposing results, largely because he had such an inquisitive mind and framed so many projects that he scattered his energies wastefully. Typical of his conduct was the response to the new Jewish congregation in town. Curious, he attended services, at first looking for abominable errors and ways to expose them in order to convert the flock. Presently he grew intrigued by Jewish traditional learning and made himself a master of Hebrew and a few other Semitic languages to delve deeper and derive the most from conversations with itinerant learned Jews. Stiles had more relish for meeting people than for writing books.

He collected information avidly and with a critical mind. His chief eccentricity, one common in the age, was a penchant for numbers. What he found, salted away in his voluminous papers along with shrewd observations, has drawn readers to his diaries who would not touch a tome of Hopkinsian divinity. The journals reveal a busy mind, an agreeable companion, a personage with a great zest for his fellow men.

The two great pastors of Newport Congregationalism, after some initial edginess, came to admire each other and exchange pulpits. They made an incongruous pair—the big, brooding

Ezra Stiles (1727–1795), intellectual and civic leader in Newport while serving as pastor of the Second Congregational Church from 1755 to 1776, painted in 1771 by Samuel King. Stiles planned the portrait to show his mind as well as his face. The books represent his many interests, including Plato, Livy, Newton, and the Hebrew tradition; the diagram of sun, planet, and comet on the pillar commemorates the study of astronomy; the disc at the upper left diagrams Stiles' theory of the moral universe. *Yale University Art Gallery, Bequest of Dr. Charles C. Foote.*

Hopkins nowhere so much at home as in a cathedral of logic; short and malproportioned Stiles with his bright eyes constantly examining the people or counting the houses in the world around him. Hopkins in a sense could have resided anywhere, but Stiles, as his Yale experience unhappily demonstrated, was perfectly suited to Newport. Together they substantiated the old New England conviction that the Puritan heritage held the torch of intellect, though the Church of England might stage the more beguiling spectacle.

Congregationalist efforts to arouse interest in Providence and Kingstown succeeded less quickly than in Newport. A few preachers visited Providence occasionally at the end of the seventeenth century, but nothing came of their labors. One young Harvard graduate went to teach school, but stayed only long enough to win the hand of a local beauty with a substantial dowry. Between the Baptist first settlers and the Quaker belt spreading north along the Blackstone, Providence was well-nigh proof against Massachusetts orthodoxy.

Only when people from that neighboring province began to move over the line did Roger Williams' old town acquire a population disposed to import the nearby religion. Even then, they discovered in Rhode Island what the first settlers had brought, a defiant individualism that broke through the patterns of inherited decorum and acquiescence to the authority of superiors.

When new attempts were undertaken to promote Congregationalism in Providence in 1721, the result was a contemptuous outburst by some leading citizens, but a Massachusetts émigré, Dr. John Hoyle, helped a committee of Boston ministers to raise money for a meetinghouse; the committee in 1728 finally found a minister, Josiah Cotton. The congregation needed continued financial support from outside and drew a substantial number of its members from those who were moving into town from Massachusetts. Joseph Snow, a son of one of these immigrants, led an opposition to Cotton during the excitement of the Great Awakening. As a result, the small congregation split, with Snow's side forming a new church, the first Congregationalist body established in Rhode Island without financial support from

Boston. Devoted to a strenuously evangelical program, Snow's new group obtained his ordination, even though he was not college-educated, and began to absorb people who were of similar taste in religion, though opposed to infant baptism. In a sense the Providence Congregationalists assimilated Rhode Island more than they intended.

Snow remained a controversial figure. He was not included in the association of Rhode Island Congregationalist ministers when that was formed, nor invited to appear in any of their pulpits. (He did not like them, either.) When Deacon Nathaniel Coggeshall took advantage of Hopkins' absence to invite Snow to fill in at the First Church in Newport one Sunday in June 1771, Stiles wondered uneasily what the regular pastor would think on his return. Stiles had previously heard Snow at the Seventh Day Baptist services, where he was "loud and boisterous." Still, he delivered "many sound truths," and Stiles asserted, he "pretty well understands the Doctrines of Grace and is of a sober, serious, exemplary life." Probably Hopkins' flock enjoyed an agreeable change from the usual fare.

The original Providence congregation struggled along, at times unable to support a minister. Cotton resigned; after an interval another man was found, John Bass, who served seven years. An outspoken enemy of the Great Awakening, Bass went so far as to repudiate predestination and deny that infants were born with original sin deserving hell fire. Firewater was another matter. Bass, needing more income than his church could provide, joined Snow as partner in a distillery and later left the pulpit to practice medicine. After another barren interlude, the church found a successor who stayed long enough to build up a substantial flock. A rich Boston native, Jonathan Badger, who had gained wealth in South Carolina and retired to Providence, tried to get up an endowment, but failed. He donated an organ for the meetinghouse, however, and made sure it was used by playing it himself. This small detail was significant of the higher social tone in the church, the greater attention to decorum, than prevailed in Snow's. In other respects, however, the two were rather alike, becoming neighborhood churches, the original one on the east side, Snow's on the west, appealing to aspiring middle-class families in the commercial development of what is now the downtown area.

Congregationalist expansion into the Narragansett country had two fortuitous advantages: the migration of the father of a trained minister and the donation of the Pettaquamscut purchasers. Samuel Niles, the first Rhode Island son to graduate from Harvard, was born on Block Island—the first settlers were Massachusetts people who did not realize until too late that they were founding a town in the heretic colony—and wrote about New England's wars, the most valuable part being a firsthand account of the capture of Block Island by French privateers. He actually served on his native island as a Congregationalist minister supported by the town of New Shoreham and a grant of land by the proprietors, the nearest thing ever achieved on Rhode Island soil to an established church. However gratifying this approximation of the Massachusetts standing order may have been to him and his flock, there was not so much money in it as to prevent him from following his father to Kingstown. There the encouragement for a young man of the cloth proved even less compelling, so after preaching informally for a few years he harkened to a call from Braintree, Massachusetts. Young Niles enjoyed in Kingstown what little income there was from the three hundred acres devoted by the Pettaquamscut purchasers to the ministry. Further, one of the partners, Judge Samuel Sewall of Boston, gave a small lot on which the local zealots built a meetinghouse.

Niles, however, went to Braintree, Seventh Day Baptists were the only ones to conduct services in the meetinghouse for several years, and the Anglicans tried to claim the ministerial land. When Bostonians resumed evangelical outreach in the 1720s, they sent a man there briefly but did not find a candidate for a steady ministry until 1730. Then Joseph Torrey took up duties as pastor and as anchor to Congregationalist claims to the ministerial lands. No wizard of the pulpit, the best he could do was hold tight on the glebe and preach so listlessly that the Great Awakening rolled by the Narragansett Congregationalists unnoticed.

Things were livelier in Westerly, where a Congregationalist

missionary society sent Joseph Park in 1733. There was another contest over land with MacSparran's Anglicans—a meeting-house on a tract donated by George Ninigret. Park put himself at the head of an Indian congregation of some fifty families that worshipped there but made no headway with the white neigh-bors until he was stirred by the revivalism of James Davenport, whose excesses in attacking enemies of the Great Awakening led to his being declared insane in Connecticut and Massachusetts. Park gathered a church (including several Indian members) and was ordained its pastor. Obscure quarrels broke out. One of the Indians, confusingly named Samuel Niles, began exhorting, was opposed by Park, and withdrew, leading the rest with him. Park engineered dismission of several white church members including his own wife, to form a second church. But then he decamped for Long Island. His church dissolved. The Indians formed their own church under Niles, aided by erstwhile Deacon Stephen Bab-cock, who gathered a church of white people partly from the old flock and partly from revivalist Baptists. Again like Davenport, however, Park calmed down, reconstituted the white church, and resumed preaching occasionally to the Indian congregation by 1759.

The greatest boost to Congregationalism came with the redrawing of the Rhode Island boundary to take in the Attleborough Gore (Cumberland) and the string of towns east of Narragansett Bay from Barrington to Little Compton. At a stroke the number of Congregationalist churches in Rhode Island doubled. They differed widely among themselves, ranging from the troubled and fragile flock living astride the Tiverton-Little Compton line to the solid old institution in Bristol. Some faced the need to cut loose from public support, but a couple had not enjoyed it previously. There had always been so many dissenters to the standing order that they had been able in a few places to block the ordinary use of land and taxes for an official religious society.

Before turning away from the new denominations, three others require brief remarks. They all served to enhance the cosmopoli-tan tone of Newport without affecting other towns. The Great Awakening brought two, the Moravian church, or Unitas

Fratrum, and an intense little Baptist group. The Moravian mission to America was intended to foster an ecumenical amalgam, though it succeeded mainly in provoking firmer denominational lines. Centered in Pennsylvania, it aimed its efforts at white and red Americans of all sorts. Bishop Joseph Spangenberg launched the Newport outpost in 1758, but did not send a pastor until eight years later. The missionary, Albertus Ludolphus Russmeyer, though educated in Germany, spoke fluent English and attracted a fair number of people to his brand of pietism—and quite possibly, to the happy combination he offered of revivalist religion and a more elaborate liturgy than native New England revivalists generally liked. He had some eighteen communicants by 1772, although the flock was scattered after the Revolution.

The revivalist Baptist group was gathered by a somewhat unstable Englishman named Henry Dawson, who arrived in 1769. Roughly Calvinistic in doctrine, he was a separatist to gladden the heart of Roger Williams. He wanted to preach only to the regenerate. With a dozen followers he formed a church in 1771 and put up a meetinghouse soon after. Presently he became persuaded that the sabbath should be celebrated on the seventh day, obtained ordination by some Seventh Day Baptists in New Jersey, and probably faded out of the picture, leaving his converts to gravitate to the old Sabbatarian flock.

The most impressive of these three lesser newcomers were the Jews, who neither sought nor made converts in the gentile population. The first Jews went to Newport in the late seventeenth century as the result of the latter-day diaspora from Brazil following the Portuguese reconquest from the Dutch. A few wanderers dwelt in Newport in sufficient numbers to hold services and buy a cemetery lot. For unknown reasons, the little congregation dispersed by about 1700, perhaps as a consequence of the uncertainties of life in Rhode Island during the preceding decade. A new influx began half a century later; by 1754, the newcomers formed Congregation Nephuse Israel (Scattered Ones of Israel), changing the name ten years later to Yeshuat Israel (Salvation of Israel). The change reflected the growth of numbers and wealth, the sense of finding a home. Jewish merchants were prospering as well as the others, slowly finding their way into the public affairs of the colony.

The congregation began to build a synagogue in 1759, with the help of contributions from Jews throughout the British empire. The donation best remembered, however, came from a Newport Anglican, Peter Harrison, who supplied the plans. He used the fashionable Georgian style adapted to the liturgical requirements of Judaism, producing a splendid result. The plain brick walls of Touro Synagogue enclose an enchanting interior, dedicated finally during Hannukkah in 1763. The newspaper story of this event read:

> It began by a handsome Procession, in which were carried the Books of the Law, to be deposited in the Ark. Several portions of Scripture, and of their service, with a prayer for the royal family, were read, and finely sung by the priest and people. There were present many gentlemen and ladies. The order and decorum, the harmony and solemnity of the music, together with a handsome assembly of people, in an edifice the most perfect of the temple kind in America, and splendidly illuminated, could not but raise in the mind a faint idea of the majesty and grandeur of the ancient Jewish worship mentioned in Scripture.

> Dr. Isaac De Abraham Touro performed the service.

Services were indeed regularly conducted by the hazzan, or reader, Isaac Touro. Though no rabbi, Touro enjoyed respect and had enough learning to be styled doctor of divinity and to teach a great deal to Ezra Stiles. The congregation was led by the parnas, or president, who with a committee of elders was elected annually. There was a shohet (kosher butcher) in town, and the congregation kept a school in an ell on the synagogue. The itinerant rabbi, Haim Isaac Carigal from Hebron, preached several times in 1773, probably hoping that the congregation would urge him to settle, but it could not afford such luxury. Perhaps he strengthened the resolve of Newport Jews to improve religious education, but they were content with a faithful observance of the basics of their faith and its full liturgical calendar. A few among them had some depth in Jewish learning, but Carigal probably did the most for Ezra Stiles, who was

Interior of Touro Synagogue in Newport, designed by Peter Harrison and dedicated December 2, 1763. *Photography by Hopf.*

already making great progress in Semitic studies and inspired by conversations with the rabbi, took a fresh interest in the Talmud and Palestinian antiquity.

Though the Jewish community was taking root in Newport, producing luminaries, such as Aaron Lopez and Naphtali Hart, in the business and culture of the town, the Revolution proved as damaging to it as to the Moravians. Some loyalist Jews left; Lopez retreated to inland Massachusetts and then suffered an accidental death; others set out for New York or New Orleans. By the beginning of the nineteenth century, the second congregation had vanished as completely as the first.

While new religions were taking root in Rhode Island, the old ones continued to develop. The rapid growth of population naturally led to greater members of Baptist churches and Quaker meetings. It is virtually impossible to estimate whether attendance at public worship kept pace proportionally with population—probably it lagged behind—or whether one of the old denominations gained relative to another. The practice of the Baptists of counting only full church members who took communion, and not the habitual attenders at services (who often were just as devoted to the denomination as the "members") was essentially the same as among the Congregationalists. So figures on church members are always surprisingly small. If Stiles' calculations for Newport provide a reliable guide, the members might be a third or less of the adults who came to hear the preacher, and women greatly outnumbered men among the members.

The Six Principle Baptists spread steadily on the mainland, forming churches in the various towns roughly three or four decades after the beginnings of settlement. Sometimes they gathered without ordaining a pastor, letting such brethren exhort as felt able to do so until one or two demonstrated a gift for ministry. A few men, like Daniel Everitt of South Kingstown, Pardon Sheldon in Scituate, and Jonathan Sprague in Smithfield, proved to be especially apt for the pastoral role and attained considerable fame. Others achieved passing notoriety as a result of accusations of immorality or heterodoxy. These rural congregations were simple and unpretentious, in manner and spirit usually very like their seventeenth-century precursors until beset by the Great Awakening.

The Baptists were quite susceptible to the new religious excitement. They had always frowned on the dry and intellectual style of ministry common among Congregationalists, and many of them had confidence that the Holy Spirit worked steadily through believers, whether in preaching, guiding daily life, or in steering the course of churches. Further, Baptist worship had probably been fairly strenuous emotionally, and certainly disdained elegance. So revivalists, who called for a living ministry, reliance on the Spirit, and contempt for tradition and decorum, found Baptists prepared to agree with them.

It was then an easy next step for some to discover a new depth of religious fervor and conclude that the revivalists were right in claiming that most people who styled themselves Christians, including some ministers, had not yet felt the full force of conversion. Having found this new level of religious experience, the converts crusaded to get it recognized as the true standard. Others resisted, and churches fell into dispute or schism—or even broke apart hopelessly. Disagreement could not be treated as just another difference of opinion, because the enthusiasts of the revival commonly took the new rush of excitement to be a major turning point in history, a new reformation, perhaps even the herald of the millennium. On such an occasion doubters were, if unwittingly, trying to hold back one of God's mightiest works.

The quality of the conversion tended to draw Baptists to the doctrine of predestination. The sense of feeling an overwhelming force, a burst of sunshine in what had seemed the night, went so far beyond the old expectations of a religious crisis—discovering the evil of sin, struggling to repent, and learning to rely on God—as to bring out a new understanding of the power of God and the helplessness of man. The sharper this contrast, the more plausible it seemed to understand the convert's salvation as decreed by a divine fiat.

This tendency to predestinarianism had profound effects. It built up both the minor Five Principle Baptist ranks and, when acting in tandem with the sense of advancing a great event, inaugurated several new congregations united around revivalism and Calvinist doctrine, leaving the members free to accept or reject infant baptism. The measure of the force of the Great Awakening in Rhode Island is probably best taken in the willingness of these Baptists to relegate their distinctive tenet to a secondary level. Unhappily they, like their ancestors, were so little concerned with the mechanics of ecclesiastical organization or the writing of devotional literature—and so intensely concerned with the daily realities of religious experience—that very little survives on paper to reveal the inner life of the rural Baptists beyond what figured in specific controversies.

The urban brethren were going their distinctive way before the Awakening and finding another road to convergence with the Congregationalists. In many respects, it was a road to that element in the Puritan tradition that the revivalists opposed. First in Newport, then in Providence, an appetite appeared for learned and salaried ministers, imposing meetinghouses, even organs, and ultimately a college. The English Baptist tradition had valued secular knowledge while scorning a trained ministry. Accordingly, Rhode Islanders who were in tune with their coreligionists in the mother country could, and sometimes did, pursue learning in diverse ways. But the introduction of a ministry more in the standard Puritan style, with the meager trappings of ceremony that went with it, was something else again.

The process began in the old Five Principle congregation where Clarke had preached. After his death, it fell to a low ebb; it managed to build a modest meetinghouse, but for several years it had to rely on the ousted Sabbatarian, William Hiscox, to fill the pulpit. By then he was a man of dignity and study, but his death in 1704 left the church destitute. After ordaining some home-grown pastors and enduring a nasty controversy over Clarke's bequests and a resulting short-lived schism, it formed anew and called John Comer to serve as pastor. He had attended both Harvard and Yale, although he did not take a degree at either. Still, he was the first college-educated Baptist in Rhode Island for many years. He immediately introduced orderly procedures in ecclesiastical affairs, codifying the rules, keeping church records, and hunting down what few there were from earlier times. He drew up a confession of faith, carefully skirting predestination to avoid offense to part of his flock, but found a statement by Clarke stating that he and his brethren had held "that soul-supporting doctrine." This Comer copied into the records. He even persuaded the congregation to sing psalms, something the Second Baptist Church would not do until much later.

All this change, coupled with Comer's "close and searching ministrations," doubled the membership, but distressed a few of the old faithful. Two major contributors closed their purses. As a dispute quickened, Comer suddenly announced his embrace of the laying on of hands as an essential ritual. Soon he went over to the Six Principle church and repeated his efforts to bring order to its affairs and his evangelical zeal for winning new members. Before long, he stirred up controversy by preaching predestination and left on a tour of New Jersey, never to return to a Newport church.

Neither of these two Newport congregations was the same after Comer. The First eventually found in John Callender a Harvard man who graced the pulpit and wrote the first history of Rhode Island. In his day the wealthy London Baptist and patron of learning, John Hollis, donated part of the money to erect a fine new meetinghouse. The Second found a learned, but not college-educated, Englishman named John Eyres to continue the shift to a professional ministry. Significantly, both churches in this period of change encountered grievances on the part of some members who resented the enhanced authority of the elders and the insistence on regulations by the churches. Dissidents angrily asserted the paramount authority of the individual conscience, to which Eyres retorted on one occasion that such principles would "immediately tend to ruin all churches and to preserve all wickedness from censure."

The zeal for learned ministers faded in Newport by the late colonial period. The Six Principle church in particular ceased to insist upon formal training. It expected a good deal of exhorting by the brethren. The socially higher-toned First Church had to wait some years after the death of Callender before it could find a college-bred successor in Erasmus Kelley, who went so far as to introduce the commemoration of Christmas.

The Sabbatarians were lucky to have any preacher whatsoever. Eventually with William Gibson and later with William Bliss, they had respectable autodidacts, and briefly in the Westerly branch they had a young college graduate. Rather one must look for their interest in learning among the laity: the remarkable Ward family sent a boy to Harvard when this was almost unheard of in Newport; he, his father (later governor), and even more, his uncle Henry Collins lent a hand to projects to cultivate arts and knowledge in their city for many years.

Even in Newport, many Baptists retained the old-fashioned distrust of a learned clergy, while others slowly turned toward college training for ministers and laymen in an institution under their aegis. By the 1760s quite a few joined enthusiastically in the plan proposed in Philadelphia for a Baptist college in Rhode Island. The college ultimately sank its foundations on the hill above Roger Williams' old home. This was a fitting place, although local hostility had in 1729 frustrated developments similar to those in Newport.

At that time the old Six Principle church, the only one left in the town, considered installing John Walton as associate to Elder James Brown. Walton was a Yale man and a physician; he favored paying ministers, singing psalms, and relegating the sixth principle of laying on hands to the optional category. Though these were not revolutionary ideas, they stirred up a fierce opposition led by Deacon Samuel Winsor. When Governor Joseph Jenckes, an old Providence man who had moved to Newport on taking office, wrote favoring Walton, Winsor's hackles rose. No matter how many high and mighty people might favor paying the minister, it was the sin of simony to him. Walton suavely called for more rather than less tolerance of internal difference, pointing out the great variety among Baptists on a number of points, and inconsistently urged a hearty condemnation of Winsor's attitude. Thus he probably served only to arouse the old biblicist rigidity of his opponents. After some conferences that Walton thought were progressing to compromise, Winsor won on all major points.

Winsor's outlook dominated for almost forty years; eventually he became the elder of his flock. Over his opposition the church in 1770 was prevailed upon to call as pastor James Manning, the Princeton man who had become the first president of Rhode Island College (now Brown University) and had been doubling as Baptist minister in Warren. In Providence, as in some other places, Baptist laymen—particularly Moses and Joseph Brown— upheld the cause of learning. With the capture of the college, moreover, they wanted to add a meetinghouse of fitting grandeur. The old building, in use during most of the eighteenth century, was soon replaced with the magnificent First Baptist Meeting House finished in 1773, where college commencements have been solemnized ever since 1776. Upon viewing the new structure, Ezra Stiles commented, "It is the most costly and superb edifice of the kind in New England," and added, "This denomination have greatly changed their taste. Ten years ago they would not have suffered a steeple or bell to their meeting houses." Stiles judged rightly from the architecture: the Providence Baptists had made an abrupt switch, suddenly excelling Newport in realigning their church with the traditions of learning and magnificence found among eighteenth-century descendants of Puritans.

One finds versions of these dominant trends even among the Quakers. As they spread from their original base on Aquidneck to inhabit virtually all parts of the colony, they developed new meetings on the mainland—at East Greenwich, South Kingstown, Smithfield, and Providence. Small numbers gathered for worship at several other places. Meetinghouses of appropriate size were constructed in the various locations. There appeared the same sort of division between rural and urban elements that prevailed among the Baptists, though in less extreme form. Rural Quakerism was a religion for the middling sort—poorer in Smithfield, richer in South Kingstown. It proceeded in a rather uneventful way until troubled by a sort of echo of the Great Awakening in the 1760s. Newport Quakerism became more elaborate and had a generous segment of the rich and powerful. By the end of the seventeenth century, its yearly meeting was the one where the central ecclesiastical business of New England was

The triumph of splendor over Baptist tradition: the First
Baptist Meeting House in Providence, dedicated May 25,
1775. Designed by Joseph Brown, a merchant and
scientist, who used drawings in James Gibbs' *Book of
Architecture* and modeled the steeple after rejected plans
for St. Martin's-in-the-Fields in London. The bell bore
the inscription:

> For freedom of conscience the town was first
>   planted.
> Persuasion, not force, was used by the people.
> This church is the oldest, and has not recanted,
> Enjoying and granting bell, temple, and steeple.

From a print by S. Hill, 1789. *The Rhode Island Historical
Society.*

transacted. Accordingly, the new meetinghouse was constructed to accommodate the huge throng that converged there every June. The Newport Friends pioneered in various novelties, such as a school run by the monthly meeting, and had an endowment in land to finance a great part of their expenditures.

If not even the Aquidneck Friends relented in their opposition to college-trained preachers, they developed methods to cultivate the ministry. This was done beginning in 1708 by the appointment of "elders," whose function was to watch ministers and prospective ministers, point out any disposition they had to speak more than the spirit gave them or use unacceptable mannerisms of speech or gesture, head off a drift into eccentric views, and encourage diligent reading of Scripture. The ministers and elders held their own meetings, thus marking out a spiritual elite. These meetings occasionally were called upon for opinions on difficult moral questions, but more commonly imposed a code of conduct on the ministers, a code thought beneficial to their functions, but in some respects designed to require a stricter morality than was demanded of ordinary Quakers.

Along with the institutional means to cultivate ministry and protect orthodoxy went a revived interest in the intellectual heritage of the sect. Quaker meetings arranged the importation and distribution of devotional literature from 1699 on, but the most impressive undertaking was a new edition of Robert Barclay's *Apology for the True Christian Divinity*, the standard theological work on the distinctive Quaker views. Planned in 1727, the project came to completion in time to show Berkeley (if he noticed) which denomination pioneered the publication of theology in Rhode Island.

Nor did the Friends confine themselves to reprinting old treatises. Though they avoided public display of controversial questions, they opened some important new topics through internal discussion. The doctrine of universal salvation, propounded by John Wright of Newport and a number of Bostonians, caused quite a stir in 1739. It was greeted with such horror that no one wanted to write down in detail exactly how Wright advanced the idea. He presently reconciled himself to dropping the subject, saying he had never wished to undermine basic

Quaker principles but had incautiously introduced the concept of universal redemption on various occasions "in private debate or conversation." This was a good deal less than the whole truth, but all concerned were content to drop the controversy with this conciliatory statement.

The more enduring new subject was the moral objection to slavery, which became a burning question as early as 1716, long before it was more than an idiosyncrasy of sensitive individuals of other persuasions. A traveling English Friend speaking against slavery and the slave trade brought debate to its first climax in 1717, leaving the Aquidneck meetings unconvinced and the mainland meetings willing to condemn only the importation of slaves. The Yearly Meeting would go no further than to advise the members to refrain from importing slaves, forbidding the practice only in 1761. By that time, a year after the saintly John Woolman from New Jersey had labored strenuously to convince the New England Quakers that they would inflict misery on themselves as well as the black people by continuing to have anything to do with slavery, fervor built up to shun it altogether. Soon the meetings resolved to require members to prepare their slaves for freedom, to free them at once if able to earn a living, to rear them if young, and to support them if aged or infirm. And of course, no Friend could remain in good standing who took part in the slave trade.

Quaker interest in the arts and letters remained tightly circumscribed by sectarian convictions on what constituted frivolity, waste, and superfluity. Like other heirs of Puritanism, Quakers condemned the dance, imaginative literature, and the stage. But Friends went further, ruling out music and the decorative arts. They opposed ornamentation of useful articles, but differed over what was an acceptable minimum. One does not see in Rhode Island the development of the Quaker style found in Pennsylvania. The great meetinghouse erected at Newport in 1699–1700 was an adaptation of the old Massachusetts four-square meetinghouse favored by the Puritans; there was even a cupola that to visiting Friends in later years smacked of steeple. Berkeley was offended by the fondness for bright colors and heavy silver among the wealthier Rhode Island Friends. He

Religious diversity displayed in a view of Newport in 1740. Prominent public buildings dominate the scene: from left to right, the Quaker meetinghouse with its cupola, the new Colony House (behind the old Town Wharf), the Second Congregational Church meetinghouse, Trinity Church, and the First Congregational Church meetinghouse. The Baptists remained adamantly against steeples or ostentation, so their three meetinghouses do not stand out. Lithograph made by Newell in 1865 (the original painting is owned by the Rhode Island Historical Society). *Newport Historical Society.*

reported a gold teapot prized by one man beyond the limits of good Christianity. No one could accuse Abraham Redwood of austerity in the fine wrought iron gates of his country seat. Quaker zeal began to formulate a code of plainness only toward the end of the colonial period.

Nevertheless, higher education remained tainted with ties to snobbery and the abhorred priestcraft; if it was not infallibly polluting, it was justifiable only in rare cases as preparation for a physician. Not that all Friends shunned the portrait painter or the vanities of Latin and the heathen classics, but not all steered clear of more depraved activities, like fornication and fraud, either. Still, there remained both the old ultra-Puritan belief that useful knowledge, such as science or geography, could be worth pursuing, and the subliminal veneration of college training in the respect accorded to the early Quakers, like Penn and Barclay, who had used it to advance their religion. Slowly, a few Rhode Island Friends took up learned pursuits and began to think a purified college curriculum might be possible. Some of these initially felt enthusiasm for the College of Rhode Island.

The outstanding Quaker minds of the late eighteenth century, Moses Brown and Job Scott, both had connections with the institution, Brown as an ardent backer before he converted from the Baptist persuasion and Scott as a student for a short time, an episode he later repented. To Moses Brown, the change of religion required no profound alteration of his intellectual interests. His excursions into theology and the classics had not been as extensive as his investigations of natural science, and in any case his best efforts went into technology, a field in perfectly good odor. His Quakerism led him to feel he should retire from public affairs and devote his time to religious affairs, but he never retired completely, nor did his new faith demand that he should. Scott, who became a protégé of Brown and a schoolmaster, distinguished himself for religious intensity and a power of expression that made him worth comparing with John Woolman. Job Scott managed less skillfully than Woolman to rein in the mystical impulses. He pursued idiosyncrasies in thought and imagery that disturbed his fellow Quakers. The religious writings of Scott, as a result, were published in heavily revised fashion or not at all.

The bulk of the Friends were quite indifferent to the refinements of learning. The leaders of the meetings periodically looked over the situation and discovered widespread ignorance especially in rural regions—people who were illiterate or nearly so, families without Bibles, loyal meeting-goers who hardly knew what Quakers stood for. During most of the eighteenth century, little was accomplished to remedy these evils. The codified "discipline" of the Yearly Meeting, reduced to a table of "queries" in 1701, gave a résumé of what Quakers should do and avoid doing, simple enough for anyone to grasp. But not all attended the monthly meetings where the queries were read every three months. Surveillance of individuals by officers of the meeting went through periods of lassitude. Distribution of books did no good for those who could not read them. Eventually the meetings had to attack ignorance at the root by promoting education for the young.

For the meetings to see education as a primary goal, it was first necessary to qualify the seventeenth-century understanding of religious fellowship. Then the emphasis had been on believers united in the love of God. Friends might agree that good Christians raised their children carefully to understand religion as well as their numbers and letters and the skills needed to earn a living. In arranging for schooling safe from corrupt influences, Quakers had a primer to use, published in the name of George Fox himself. All the same, the children were not believers, not real participants in the fellowship. Early in the eighteenth century, a distinct change set in. New insistence on marriage within the fold, closer surveillance over children by the meetings' officials, special meetings to instruct the young, demands that parents employ Quaker schoolmasters and schoolbooks, ultimately a campaign to get monthly meetings to establish segregated schools—all these were accompanied by a shift to thinking of Quakerism as hereditary, often expressed in imagery based on comparisons with the ancient Hebrews. Newport Friends quite early started a school, which was held off and on first in the meetinghouse, later in a special building. Elsewhere, no such plan was thinkable until late in the century, and even then Friends were too scattered to make it practical to draw all their children into local schools even if there had been enough masters. So the Yearly Meeting tried to establish a boarding school at Portsmouth just after the Revolution, but it too failed quickly.

In the spiritual life of the Rhode Island Friends, the most momentous event before the Revolution was a revival of religious ardor that flourished in the 1760s. Though intended as a campaign of moral reform and return to the old purity of the founders, the movement went further. It provided the spiritual force to bring a collective condemnation of slavery and the slave trade as well as the zeal for improving the upbringing of children—the reform should be carried forward through the young. A new campaign got started for shunning alcoholic beverages. Zeal for return to the origins of the sect fostered study of its history and teachings. A proposal to bring out a new edition of Barclay's *Apology* won unanimous approval from the Yearly Meeting. Zeal to end laxity of descipline led to expulsion of the lukewarm. Converts had to demonstrate a knowledge of what Quakers should believe and how they should live before being admitted. Among the pared down and purified band of Friends spread a determination to uproot the worldliness, the fondness for costly clothing and furniture, and the love of money and public office that Berkeley had spotted years before.

Gradually the reform movement led to still more profound changes that brought Rhode Island Quakers more fully into concord with Friends elsewhere than they had ever been and united them all in a new sense of their religious mission. Apostles of reform from England and Pennsylvania lamented shortcomings not at first perceived by Rhode Islanders—a tendency to deism and "having so much to do in government affairs." Soon the onset of colonial resistance to imperial government disclosed the dangers of staying in politics and showed the dangers to be the same in Rhode Island as in Philadelphia. In Newport it became plausible to believe that Friends everywhere in America must behave alike, both for their own safety in a time of trouble and to make their example to the rest of the people as clear as possible. As others were putting on the uniforms of revolutionary armies, Quakers must show that they had "enlisted themselves as soldiers under the prince of peace." So consultations were held about bringing the New England discipline into complete agreement with those of the other Yearly Meetings. At the end of the Revolutionary War, Rhode Island Quakers finally decided they should avoid public office.

The belief that Quakers should no longer wield secular authority, paradoxically, sprang from a new conviction that they had a duty to guide the body politic. Gone was the old faith that Quakerism would ultimately prevail as the only true religion, gone the hope that Friends could serve themselves and their society by holding the reins of government, gone too the easygoing assumption of the eighteenth century that a Quaker could hold office with a serene conscience as long as he had nothing to do with oaths or compelling men to serve in war. Instead, there was a new belief that holding office was itself a corrupting form of worldliness, even if it did not mean complicity in war or slavery. Quakers should set an example of utter freedom from secular attachments, should by their actions show their fellow citizens how to love and serve mankind. Even if the corrupt majority should persecute Friends, their suffering would serve to redeem the society by publicizing their example. Hidden in this conviction was the resignation to their religion's forever being a minority sect.

This change of heart signaled the end of Newport Quakerism. Between the exclusion of some who would not go along with the new spirit and the departure of others for Philadelphia or New York, few of the rich and powerful Friends remained. The Revolutionary devastation of the city hastened the process, but already leadership in the Society of Friends was passing to tradesmen, small-time merchants, schoolteachers, or the upstart grandees of New Bedford or Nantucket. The shift was less dramatic elsewhere in the state, but slowly Quakerism ceased to embrace the old portion of the high and mighty. The heritage of William Coddington and the Quaker Wantons faded away. The old meetinghouse in Newport was greatly enlarged, its cupola taken down, and its kinship with its Puritan forebears concealed under a new roof. The huge throng gathering for Yearly Meeting saw by 1818 an imposing structure in the austere plainness of the Pennsylvania Quaker style.

Inspection of the religious life of eighteenth-century Rhode Island reveals a rather abrupt break with the earlier events. Ironically, novelty in the heretic colony was provided by the arrival of the old. First the Anglican and the Congregationalist services began, later the far more ancient Jewish. They brought their respective traditions of learning and ceremony. As they entered the scene, the Baptists and Quakers began to take a kinder view of religious learning and a specially trained clergy and began to put up a succession of meetinghouses, each one larger, costlier, and more lavish than the last.

Religion, which for so long had marked off Rhode Islanders from nearly everybody else, except during the Puritan Revolution, began to create links with the outside again. The Friends began doing this well before the rest, always having ministers coming and going between the various colonies and England, and, after the organization fell into a system, making Newport the center of New England Quakerism. The Anglicans and Congregationalists, however, connected Rhode Island to the great figures of London and Boston. Judaism depended on financial and intellectual support from a far-flung network which brought benefits from several mainland colonies, the Caribbean, London, Amsterdam, and Palestine. Even the Baptists began to form useful institutional bonds with the outside world. The Sabbatarians always had kept in touch with their few brethren in New Jersey and England. The Six Principle Baptists cautiously experimented with conferences and general meetings. The Five Principle Baptists, after the Great Awakening started a local association with fraternal correspondence with others. When they began cooperating with those of the middle colonies to found a college, they made extensive use of the new ties with coreligionists in the British empire. In a broader sense, Rhode Islanders began to be washed by British-American religious currents—the surge of Anglican expansion, the Great Awakening, the reshaping of the Puritan heritage.

Accordingly the salient developments ceased being the lonely struggle to stabilize churches and the invention of new beliefs taking their adherents ever farther into spiritual isolation. By the eighteenth century, new doctrines no longer claimed much attention; instead, the proliferation of denominations and the adaptation of social patterns to them provided the action in the scene.

During the eighteenth century Rhode Island Christians began to sort themselves into religious groups that corresponded roughly with social distinctions. The clearest case was the Anglican church which began with very few avowed communicants and quickly attracted the rich and the powerful in conspicuous numbers. It also could count on the few royally appointed officials and often on those merchants in Newport who tried to enter direct trade with Britain or the country well-to-do who adopted as much as they could of the ways of English rural gentry. It attracted lawyers. The most striking example of the Anglican appeal was in Kingstown, where in 1701 a group of men sought the aid of Samuel Sewell in Boston to start a Congregationalist society, but soon roughly half of them became stalwarts in MacSparran's parish. For them the fine points of doctrine or ecclesiastical structure were insignificant. They wanted a dignified, embellished, worship; in short, they wanted imported wine, not home-brewed Baptism. Quite possibly the Anglican celebration of kingly power and honor to the laws and the wielders of power—in general, the celebration of rank and hierarchy in this world and the next—enhanced the satisfaction they drew from their new affiliation.

Less clearly marked were the other main denominations, but they gradually found their social levels. Congregationalism, to exaggerate somewhat, was for the respectable and substantial who prized education, learning, decorum, and regularity in life and worship. There were more Congregationalist doctors than lawyers. Possibly in the ranks of Newport merchants whose trade was with Boston, one would find a marked inclination toward Congregationalism or the increasingly similar First Baptist Church. Certainly Congregationalism was favored by people who moved in from Massachusetts in the eighteenth century. Dr. Walton in Providence perhaps had bad aim; his sensibilities were with the Congregationalists until the likes of Winsor lost out.

Still, Baptist and Quaker congregations, especially the urban ones, long retained a share of those on the higher rungs of the social ladder. In these denominations the marked shift was toward internal differences between towns, where conformity with the older Christian traditions advanced, and the country, where something like the seventeenth-century spirit persisted.

The Great Awakening, though it brought new ideas about conversion and an upsurge in the doctrine of predestination, revitalized in rural Rhode Island the tradition of unlettered preachers impelled by the Holy Spirit and renewed the old conviction that religion is the fervor of devotion in the present, not faithful conformity with tradition and obedience to the teachings of the learned. The excitement of the revival upset the old distinctions between the different sorts of Baptists, producing bewildering divisions and recombinations among them. In Newport, by contrast, the Congregationalist pastors, though mostly favorable to revivalism, upheld the decorum of worship and yielded nothing to lay enthusiasm. Hopkins and Stiles, both renowned intellectuals, partook little of the spirit of the Awakening, and Stiles quietly turned away from it to seek out a more historical connection with the Puritan origins of Congregationalism. The revival in the city did not throw the old churches into turmoil but introduced new denominations, the ephemeral Baptist flock of Henry Dawson and the somewhat more durable congregation of Moravians.

In eighteenth-century Rhode Island, religious liberty allowed people to gravitate toward the forms of faith and ceremony that satisfied them. The ancient use of the church to bring a whole community together simply did not figure in the scene. So people sought out those places of worship that succeeded in giving meaning to their lives, gave significance to the architecture of their world, defined a community of congenial associates who shared values or aspirations, and ordinarily expected to see their ways carried forward by marriages between their children. Changing fortunes could bring a change in religion: Governor Cranston could stop leaning toward Quakerism and start attending Trinity Church as he became engrossed with the colony's position in the British empire; Narragansett planters looking for a higher-toned religion could set their sights first on Congregationalism and then, with growing prosperity, on the Church of England. Many other examples could be offered. Yet there were always the sociological anomalies, men like Moses Brown, a successful merchant and politician with an appetite for knowledge, who left the Providence Baptists just when they donned the trappings of Congregationalism and joined the Quakers just as they were sinking to a religion of the middling ranks and simple rural people. So religious liberty meant freedom for the thirsting soul as well as the social climber, the seeker of discipline as well as the seeker of solace. Roger Williams would not have counted on more, although he would have wished for better.

10

THE SOCIAL BREEDS AND OTHERS

With all the change that colonial Rhode Island experienced in the eighteenth century—in economic development, religion, and political affairs—small wonder that the quality of life kept changing too. New hopes, fears, envies, and joys replaced old ones. Of course, some staples of human life remained constant, such as disease, malice, death, lust, worry, friendship, or high spirits. Even so, some basic conditions of the seventeenth century faded away as the Indians were killed off and the English colonists ceased to live in communities hugging the bay with forests looming on the land side.

In its early years the colony had lived largely in isolation from the rest of the world. It had created its own eccentric realm of religion, raged over its own quarrels, and dealt with the royal government as with a fairy tale court. The greatest menace had been the ogres in Boston; the greatest passion, the lust for land. In a short time, the Rhode Islanders learned to see their colony as a province in the British empire and to treat London politics as a major factor in their affairs. The monarch's wars brought French raiders to Block Island and Newport, opened opportunities for privateering, and created the hazard of capture by privateers. Imperial policies increasingly hemmed in the growing commerce based in Narragansett Bay. Prosperity in trade, the satisfaction of old aspirations, brought wealth on a new scale, unfamiliar religions and luxuries, a burst of agricultural expansion, a cosmopolitan tone, fears of epidemics, new passions for getting into trade, and novel anxieties over pushing ahead or suddenly failing. The widening social spectrum, the more frequent connections and collisions of the colonials with outsiders, forced attention to rank, especially the ways to measure position in Rhode Island against the standards of Great Britain. Altogether, people in the colony had to think about a much more elaborate social order than before.

The eighteenth-century developments kept bringing new impressions to the senses. The brooding forest fell before the axe, giving way to fields and pastures separated by useful groves. The Indian villages vanished, the Indian trails turned into wide, if miry, roads. The bay filled with sails. Churches and meeting-houses sprang up, some even with steeples to punctuate the skylines of Newport and Providence while the wharves gave pattern to their harbors. Streets were paved and named. The smells of the countryside continued, but the city trades added new ones—from distilleries, tanneries, ropewalks, and the like. The sounds of the commercial bustle added to the variety. Newport started hiring a crier to advertise goods for sale and a bellman to patrol the streets at night. At religious services congregational singing, even choirs and organs, began to embellish the ceremonies. The variety of imported dainties for the table—cocoa, tea, spices, tropical fruits, wines, rum—underscored the cosmopolitan quality of the colony. The newly introduced religions brought new thoughts about the relation of the present to the past, of Rhode Island to the rest of the world.

This burst of novelties bespoke a burgeoning population. Colonial census figures give only rough approximations, almost surely below the actual totals. Casual estimates nearly always ran far ahead of the official numbers. Yet, the totals gathered in Newport from information supplied by militia officers or town clerks probably give a fair picture of the proportions of growth. From five thousand at the time of King Philip's War, the colony slowly increased to six by the beginning of the Cranston administration, to over seven when the governor gathered the first official figures in 1708. The next count reported 17,935 in 1731. After the addition of almost five thousand people in territory acquired from Massachusetts in 1747 the total reached about thirty-two thousand. Then it grew by a quarter in the next

eight years and continued until it neared sixty thousand in the
1770s, a number not reached again until four years after the
Revolution. Thus there was a density of sixty persons per square
mile, a high concentration for the eighteenth century.

Moreover, the distribution kept shifting. The island of Aquidneck had originally contained well over half the people. The
fraction kept dwindling, from about 40 percent in 1700 to 19
percent in 1770. The Narragansett country gained rapidly in the
early eighteenth century, rising from a quarter to a third of the
total by 1755, but the original territory of Providence and
Warwick was right behind, pulled ahead by 1770, and kept on
increasing its share of the total, reaching 40 percent or more by
the end of the century.

Cutting across these geographical patterns were changing
configurations of other sorts. Indians, roughly half concentrated
in South County, were also scattered in the island towns and
Warwick. A substantial number entered the colony with Tiverton and Little Compton. There were about one thousand within
the borders in 1731, at least 1,250 by 1749, and almost 1,500 on
the eve of the Revolution. By that time their intermingling with
blacks produced a recognized and substantial category of mulattoes, which made simple reckoning of Indian population impossible by 1783. Slaves, common in the Kingstowns, were a still
greater portion of the inhabitants of Jamestown and Block
Island, 10 percent or so of Newport and indeed all the southern
half of the colony. In the north they were common only in
Providence. The distribution suggests that black labor was
employed to an unusual extent in tending livestock and various
urban occupations, in comparison with fieldwork and domestic
service. The urban population, however, was probably the most
impressive. Consistently, it verged on a quarter of the total, a
fraction probably twice that in any other colony and even farther
above the average for British America. As Newport declined in
proportion to the entire population, Providence made up the
difference with help from Bristol, Wickford, and East Greenwich.

Perhaps the most dramatic change in eighteenth-century
Rhode Island, beyond the rise of Newport commerce and the
frenetic growth of population, was the increase in sheer variety

among those who lived or sojourned there. The bulk of the population still consisted of farm families living on a simple scale and practicing many trades part-time in a rudimentary way. Such people slowly extended cultivation to the whole interior. In addition, in various parts of the colony, there came on the scene wealthy merchants, military heroes, shopkeepers, prostitutes, dancing masters, full-time artisans, black slaves, Irish servants, great landlords, leisured dilettantes, and the colorful but suspicious habitués of the waterfront.

Most of these new varieties were to be seen mainly in Newport or nearby Portsmouth, until Providence began to attain urban qualities and Bristol was taken over from Massachusetts. The coastal belt of the Narragansett country, however, gained a diverse assortment. It acquired more than its share of ministers and slaves, plus a near monopoly on the landed rich. It also had most of the surviving Narragansetts, under the kingship of Ninigret's heirs. Gradually a few coastal harbors became small commercial centers with artisans and shopkeepers—as at Wickford and East Greenwich.

In addition to the varied spectacle of residents, Rhode Island began to receive many visitors. The stream of traveling Quaker ministers had been flowing for years, and there were a few other people journeying for religious reasons before the Congregationalists and Anglicans launched missionary invasions. Later, George Whitefield landed at Newport for his first tour of New England, and other itinerant evangelists crisscrossed the colony. Commerce brought in people from all over. Other travelers arrived to strengthen their health or gratify their curiosity. Judging from what many of them wrote, Rhode Island early gained a reputation as the garden of New England, with the soil and climate of Aquidneck particularly singled out for praise.

Near the beginning of the eighteenth century, people began coming for the summer—from South Carolina, first to escape the Yamassee tomahawk, later the heat; from the West Indies, to escape ennui. By the 1730s a ship annually transported fugitives from the fevers of Charleston. Later still there was a contingent from Philadelphia. Aquidneck and South Kingstown (then including Narragansett) attracted as permanent residents various men who had grown rich enough elsewhere to retire to the moderate temperatures and congenial society of these fortunate locations.

Both these places were thought to enjoy some of the appealing features of the mother country on a miniature scale, whether in climate, cultivation, or the ornamentation by genteel country seats of the well-to-do scattered among pastures and intensely cultivated fields. Both had their share of horse racing for silver tankards, of family quarrels over entailed estates and other endless lawsuits after the British fashion in the eighteenth century, although South Kingstown probably monopolized what fox hunting there was.

This zone at the mouth of Narragansett Bay had at the beginning of the eighteenth century a comfortable preponderance of the wealth and population of the colony, so it was no wonder that it produced the widest spectrum of ranks and the earliest high society. No information survives to explain how Newport came to have a substantial population of slaves—10 or 11 percent consistently, and a smaller number of Indians—or what work they did. Next to nothing exists about the settlement of artisans on the small lots set aside for them or about the beginnings of shipyards. So little can be known about the transformation of a minor commercial outpost to a major port before the eighteenth century. It is possible, however, to discern some of the beginnings of refinement and pursuit of an elevated social tone.

As early as the 1670s a subtle change began to overtake Newport. Perhaps it may be called the rise of respectability. John Sanford, the man who kept the colony's records, in the middle of his career abandoned the relaxed manner of spelling that he had shared with everyone else and began to practice consistency, nearly always adopting what has been standard ever since. Others manifested the trend by changing their names to more elegant forms: Henry Timberleggs became Henry Timberlake, the Badcock tribe became Babcocks, and the Dunghills dropped the fourth letter. Decorum advanced in religion, followed soon by

the erection of meetinghouses and the accumulation of endowments. Leading the trend were men who later rejoiced over the
Dominion of New England and yearned for a royal governor.

The link between the colony's origins and the resurgence of
respectability lay in the few old Hutchinsonians who had never
quite given up the conviction that they were quite as good as
anyone in Boston and should make their quality obvious.
Coddington's self-esteem bounced back after he lost his patent to
govern during his lifetime. He sternly wrote Governor Richard
Bellingham in 1674 upbraiding Massachusetts for its treatment
of Quakers and reinterpreting the old Antinomian quarrel to
mean that the Hutchinsonians had kept the faith and their
enemies had deserted it. "Forty-five years past," he remonstrated,
"thou didst own such a suffering people, that now thou dost
persecute. They were against bishops and ceremonies and the
conformable priests. They were the seed of God that did serve
him in spirit, then called Puritans, now called Quakers."
Coddington had also brought back from England with his third
wife her young nephew, Francis Brinley, who was bred to
commerce and the social pretensions, but not the religion, of his
foster father.

As the old quarrels cooled among the leading Hutchinsonians,
the Brentons and Sanfords drew together with Coddington.
Symptomatic was Peleg Sanford, who married first a daughter of
William Brenton and second a daughter of William Coddington,
going on to become a royalist and an intimate of Brinley. Peleg
Sanford was a grandson of Anne Hutchinson; he and his brothers
were deeply involved in the web of Hutchinson family mercantile
activities based at Boston. This regrouping in Newport brought
together the wealthier, more rank-conscious, of the old Antinomians and their descendants; the network expanded most conspicuously into restored connections with Boston, but also into other
places by means of new friends and relations in Warwick and the
Narragansett country. Ironically, the people in this concatena-
tion gravitated to the Church of England, except for the Sanfords
and Hutchinsons, who generally leaned toward Massachusetts
orthodoxy. Almost as ironically, this group became the core of
the first Rhode Island royalist coterie.

The turn against autonomy under the charter had its easy stages and proved short-lived. Peleg Sanford, even before becoming governor in 1680, had lent a hand to thwarting William Harris and hoodwinking the government of Charles II. But upon assuming the colony's office he faced the first long questionnaire from the imperial authorities, an early sign that Whitehall intended to gain the knowledge to regulate Rhode Island. Sanford got the point, especially when he served as a justice in the county court under the Dominion of New England and then lost power to the likes of Walter Clarke and his brethren. The lesson was ground in when Clarke refused to swear in Sanford as admiralty judge.

A similar experience impressed the Jahleel Brentons, uncle and nephew. The uncle contrived to get an appointment as royal collector of customs for New England in 1689, underwent the complicated torment usual for such officers—obstruction by local officials and weak support by his superiors in England—and gladly resigned after twenty years. While in office he also served occasionally as Rhode Island's agent in London, steadily moving toward a view that the colony should claim fewer privileges and do what it was told. The nephew and heir finished the process by switching from Congregationalist to Anglican and trying to turn the tables for MacSparran in the Narragansett glebe land case.

By that time the budding Newport swells had long abandoned hostility to the charter government. Led by Coddington's grandsons, they had joined forces with the Wanton brothers, newly rich, ex-Quakers, and newcomers to the colony though they were. Thereafter, the Newport men of social pretension mixed again in public affairs as insiders to the political system. Increasing wealth enlarged the circle of the refined and the possibilities for combinations among the prominent against each other to steer the use of power for private benefit. The younger Jahleel Brenton, in charge of lending the colony's paper money, treated his friends with more than good-natured solicitude when the day came to pay some of it back.

By the time he was doing this, in the 1720s, the Newport gentry was enlisting recruits of diverse character. Abraham

A pioneer of Newport elegance: the Jahleel Brenton house, formerly standing on Thames Street, built about 1720. Probably erected for a man who prospered in the service of Crown and colony, the mansion in the hands of his merchant nephew and namesake housed the offices of the Grand Committee during the many years when he was in charge of lending the colony's paper money. *Newport Historical Society.*

Redwood moved in from Antigua; he was much more given to ostentation, knowledge, and the social whirl than his Quaker precursor, Thomas Richardson. The new customs collector, Nathaniel Kay, easily joined the polite circles, as did the Anglican rector, Mr. Honeyman and his lawyer son. Later Godfrey Malbone from Virginia followed the Wanton path to wealth and eminence, while John Bannister moved in haloed by kinship to the Duke of Newcastle to glamorize his wealth. Local people rose to the upper circles by getting rich and pursuing culture—the Huguenot Ayraults fleeing hostile neighbors in East Greenwich to money and Anglicanism in Newport, the Wards and Henry Collins making headway by various combinations of brains, taste, and political savvy. Toward the end of the colonial period, cultivated and sagacious Jews, such as Abraham Rivera and Aaron Lopez, began to associate with the upper crust. The list might easily be extended.

Altogether the Newport high society was fairly open, especially to big money and a decent show of the tastes of the genteel. It easily comprehended a variety of religious persuasions, provided they were not intense. It even tolerated bankruptcy, notably in the case of Henry Collins, who was protected for years by his creditors while he continued as a leader in civic improvement and the arts.

This is not to say that the upper crust lived in genial harmony. It most emphatically did not; but like other colonial elites, it knew how to carry on its internal feuds and squabbles within limits of self-restraint that forestalled collective self-destruction. In politics it operated in a slightly different arena, one which included the merely well-to-do, the deliberately unpretentious, some rustic gentlemen, and a few purely political animals. By the time a new royalist coterie took form, it consisted not of the rank-proud natives, but of British immigrants, often professional men, who could not forgive Rhode Island for taking satisfaction in going its own way.

Outward signs of high culture, except for new religions, came slowly, even in the category of education, which was more accessible than most. Few Newport boys went to college—a son of Peleg Sanford was the first, but he died in 1721, ten years after graduating. Only a few others resorted to Harvard or Yale during the rest of the colonial period. For most, less schooling sufficed. The leaven of higher education was supplied by men who came from elsewhere, usually to serve as ministers or teachers. The local interest in learning fostered first the Society for the Promotion of Knowledge and Virtue (or Philosophical Club) in the 1730s and the Redwood Library a decade later. These institutions drew on the immigrant educated, bringing them together with native autodidacts. Conversation at meetings of the society, one guest reported in 1744, dwelt heavily on business conditions and the differences among the religions professed in Newport. Quite possibly there was less mutual self-help in education than had been intended. Still, Newport had adequate schools, and there was a good deal of bitterness when Providence won the colony's college in 1770. At that time, it was alleged, about forty boys were prepared for higher learning by study of the classics—the assertion implied that nowhere else in Rhode Island could one find such a number—and so perhaps the town's best course was to set up a rival institution combining secondary and higher education.

Elegant architecture appeared more rapidly than learning. At first, Newporters prudently contented themselves with houses of fairly small dimensions and put their money into building the comb of wharves extending into the harbor. The civic project of greatest size was the Long Wharf, begun in the seventeenth century, rebuilt and extended in about 1700 by a syndicate of leading citizens, and repaired and extended still farther by a new organization after 1740. By the 1720s, however, a few old dwellings were being enlarged, a few larger ones being constructed, and some country seats were going up in the rural parts of town or in Portsmouth or even later on the mainland to the west. With symbolical fitness some of the new town houses of the upper crust were constructed directly in front of the residences of Cranstons and Carrs who were not striving for ostentation. The paper money raid on Boston went into full swing, starting a building boom and emboldening Newport gentility to begin satisfying its aspirations for appropriate surroundings.

The obscure carpenter, Richard Munday, and the even more

obscure Benjamin Wyatt, gave the town's elite their own version of Anglo-American Georgian style. As perceptively analyzed by Antoinette Downing and Vincent Scully,* there was by 1720 a turn toward Renaissance classical models as naturalized in England by men such as Sir Christopher Wren. "Henceforward, structural elements were to be minimized and concealed; buildings were to be conceived in terms of simple rectangular masses, with flat roofs and level cornices, designed to have a center of interest and decorated at focal points with detail drawn from a classic repertoire of ever increasing correctness." Overhangs and steeply pitched roofs went out, casement windows gave way to sash, basic timber frames hid behind ornamental facings, panelling began to spread over interior walls, chimneys sprouted in the middle of the structure instead of the ends. Imposing public buildings went up to punctuate the array of new or newly remodeled residences. The ornamentation and basic style came from classical models, but as Downing and Scully observe, "the tastes of a wealthy seafaring merchant society stamped these new buildings with a provincial and matter-of-fact, almost burgher lavishness. Newport building, like Newport furniture, now developed a quality of intrinsic richness wherein the ornament became an inseparable part of the whole." One might go further and say that ornament, whether in the moldings and decorations of interior woodwork or in the carvings and curvings of furniture, tended to cover whole surfaces. Line and embellishment at times almost fused, giving the Newport classical style a strangely baroque quality.

To say of this local style that it was nouveau riche extravagance would imply vulgarity, but this would be unjust. At most it may be observed that Newport design, like Newport gentlemen, lacked academic devotion to the classics. As a result the style was not simply imported as was true in some of the southern colonies; Newport created its own and did extremely well. Trinity Church and the Colony House by Munday were excellently done. If he and Henry Collins, as legend has it, designed the interior of the

---

* In *The Architectural Heritage of Newport, Rhode Island*, 2nd ed. (New York, 1967), chs. 3 and 4.

Sabbatarian meetinghouse, they used remarkable skill in cramming a wealth of intricate ornament into a small chamber to create a jewel rather than a jumble. The principal designers, moreover, worked with rudimentary sketches rather than complete drawings, relying on a band of artisans to execute the different elements in the structure. These craftsmen had to be fully attuned to the artistic sensibilities of the designers in order to carry out verbal instructions and produce a harmonious result.

With the next generation of the Newport elite came a new designer, Peter Harrison. Fittingly, this young Englishman (who eloped with a daughter of John Bannister after making her pregnant) produced as his first public building the Redwood Library in 1748—fitting because Harrison introduced academic classicism by using the best books then available. The Newport gentlemen who accepted his design were likewise resorting to the traditions of learning. To a degree, Harrison subverted the local style by imposing European standards of taste. He simply combined the floor plan of one structure he found in a book with the front façade of another and the rear façade of a third, adding only a pattern of exterior wood to resemble dressed stone masonry. Inside he similarly drew on what he could find in books on architecture. In later public buildings, he displayed an imagination that could go far from the models he used. For instance, he adapted the façade of a London house by Inigo Jones to design the Brick Market house, omitting two of the five windows on each story to create a building that was higher than wide, altogether unlike the original in basic shape. Harrison's town and country dwellings used a variety of proportions much greater than had been seen before. He subdued ornament: while he increased its use on exteriors, inside he used delicate moldings to outline flat spaces and restrained the amount of showy carving. The effect was more sophisticated than what Munday had designed.

By the time Harrison was at work schooling taste, Newport had changed dramatically from its appearance in 1720. In four decades, say Downing and Scully, it had "changed from a medieval-looking colony of steep pitched roofs, turrets, and overhanging cornices to an urban center with spired churches

The pulpit of the Seventh Day Baptist meetinghouse in Newport, built in 1729. According to tradition, the design was by Richard Munday assisted by Henry Collins. The building has undergone severe treatment: moved twice, its wooden walls enclosed by brick, its box pews dismantled and their walls installed as wainscotting below the chair rail, and occupied as headquarters and then exhibit hall of the Newport Historical Society. The basic beauty survives. *The Preservation Society of Newport County Photo.*

The Redwood Library, designed by Peter Harrison (possibly assisted by his brother Joseph) in 1748. Drawing by Eugène Pierre du Simitière in 1768. *The Library Company of Philadelphia.*

and balconied public buildings. Broad gambrel or gable-on-hip roofed mansions with pedimented doorways, dormer windows, and cupolas stood in state behind fine brick walls pierced by wrought iron gates in gardens filled with rare trees and plants imported from France, the Indies, or England." The Newport patriciate had created its proper setting, only to be challenged for primacy by Providence and to be fatally undermined by the Revolution.

The last two decades of Newport's robustness were nevertheless replete with the trappings of civilized luxury. Gentlemen frequented tavern clubs, kept sailboats for pleasure, and journeyed out to nearby islands for turtle frolics. The town could finally support a newspaper, the *Mercury*, launched in 1758. The pages of this organ, between the ominous tidings of wars, political conflicts, bankruptcies, and currency crises, reported the opening of schools (one by an insolvent merchant), the arrival of a man to teach French, the organization of a class in psalmody, the summer delights of tea houses in the nearby rural area, and the winter delights of Mary Cowley's dancing school. The paper disclosed that a Masonic lodge had been founded and held balls and lotteries to raise money to build "Freemasons-Hall" as a facility for "public entertainments." David Douglass' dramatic troupe presented a series of performances in two seasons with an enthusiastic response. The print shop had playing cards for sale. Horse races (of course, to encourage improvement of the breed) were held on Easton's Beach for purses up to £100. The great challenge was to beat the Bull Horse owned by Giles Sanford, which was attempted by several animals owned by the Gardiner family of South Kingstown. Finally they produced a winner in Cheating Jenny. It was a comfortable life for those who could afford it.

Perhaps the portent of doom for the city's luxurious ease was the fire that gutted the country house of Godfrey Malbone on June 7, 1766. The blaze broke out in the roof and spread quickly. When Malbone realized that the house could not be saved, he ordered his servants to carry dinner to his guests in an outbuilding, observing with gentlemanly poise, "If I have lost my house, that is no reason why we should lose our dinners." If this story is true, the guests must have disputed his logic politely, as most of the furniture was saved. Amidst the surviving magnificence of the gardens, the stone walls remained standing: Newport had its first ruins that natives could show to visitors.

The traveling gentleman found more to see than buildings. Newport achieved a reputation for beautiful and enchanting women. Dr. Alexander Hamilton, a Scotsman residing in Maryland, reported in 1744 that "the young ladies in town . . . are generally very airy and frolicsome." A local physician illustrated the point with "a drawer full of the trophies of the fair, which he called his cabinet of curiosities. They consisted of tore fans, fragments of gloves, whims, snuff boxes, girdles, apron strings, laced shoes and shoe heels, pin cushions, hussifs,* and a deal of other such trumpery." Though Hamilton reported meeting only one woman whose virtue may have been commercial, the town was soon supplied with a brothel run by Madam Juniper, a black woman, with an integrated staff. The doctor, like many another sojourner, enjoyed flirtation with respectable beauties. One summer evening he and a companion found some new friends, "and with them walked a little way out of town to a place called the Little Rock. Our promenade continued two hours, and they entertained us with several songs. We enjoyed all the pleasures of gallantry without transgressing the rules of modesty or good manners."

During the Revolution, the Prince de Broglie reported on the Newport belles in greater detail. He had heard of them from French officers who had been quartered there, all too briefly to suit them. He sought out a celebrated Miss Champlin, finding her quite as admirable as reported, and then the two daughters of Dr. William Hunter. "The elder, without being regularly handsome, had what one might call a noble appearance and an air of aristocratic birth. Her physiognomy was intellectual and refined. There was grace in all her movements." The younger was "a perfect rosebud." He delighted in a score of others as well. But the prince reserved his greatest admiration for Polly Lawton,

---

* Dr. Hamilton wrote a phonetic spelling of "housewife," still pronounced as he spelled it when it means a small container for sewing equipment.

daughter of a laconic Friend. She was "the very goddess of grace and beauty." She dressed and spoke with Quaker plainness and seemed utterly unself-conscious, yet she reveled in the attention of her visitors. The French nobleman wrote, "I acknowledge that this attractive Polly appeared to me the most exquisite work of Nature, and that every time her image occurs to me, I am tempted to write a big book against the dressing, the theatrical graces, and the coquestishness of certain rich ladies much admired in the world of fashion." Perhaps his vision was distorted by preconceptions of the superiority of nature over art or some other form of the world-weariness of the French aristocracy, but he was bedazzled all the same.

Knowledge of the rest of the Newport population tends to be fragmentary. The magnificent furniture draws attention to the makers, as the architecture does to the carpenters, masons, smiths, glaziers, and so on. The *Mercury* calls attention to its publishers, Anne Franklin and her son James, and later to Solomon Southwick. In its pages appeared advertisements for clockmakers and other artisans. The surviving craftsmen's houses give some sense of the scale on which they lived—rather comfortably in the case of some carpenters. Various documents mention officers on sailing vessels. Unfortunately, there is little to reveal the lives of the majority. Considering only the men, those who were the laborers, the servants, the slaves, the aged, and the poor all remain shadowy.

Even so, far less can be known about the children, who were roughly half the total population. Imagination conjures up scenes of schoolrooms, with most of the older pupils boys, of rambles in the nearby fields and orchards, play in the streets and among the traffic on the docks, sporting in the surf, and of delight in toys and stories or purloined apples. A majority of the children, however, probably spent most of their waking time at work. And most of these probably helped their parents. Brooms and pans and spinning wheels were educational toys for little girls. Boys went, when quite young, to help in shops and stores. Many learned the ways of seafaring as early as twelve. Apprenticeship served a variety of purposes—rearing orphans and keeping toddlers in discipline as well as teaching skills to teenagers. And

Rhode Island ships returning from the Caribbean brought the finest close-grained mahogany. From it the cabinetmakers, the most celebrated being members of the intertwined Goddard and Townsend families of Newport, made furniture with a distinctive style. Many of these pieces, recognized as masterworks by the wealthy people who bespoke them, have been passed down through the years with the same care for their condition and the records of their origin that would be given to great paintings. Special features of design —the "block and shell" pattern or the under-cut claws of the feet—distinguish Rhode Island styles. Yet the justness of proportion, the curving lines of a beauty needing no ornamentation, the achievement of both grace and sturdiness in the legs, the sure sense of where to use bold innovation—of such elements the craftsmen compounded the highest artistry.

Desk-bookcase, *Yale University Art Gallery, The Mabel Brady Garvan Collection.*
Desk, *Museum of Fine Arts, Boston, M. and M. Karolik Collection.*
Corner chair, *Mr. and Mrs. Eric M. Wunsch, photo courtesy of Israel Sack, Inc., New York.*
Tea table, *Courtesy, The Henry Francis du Pont Winterthur Museum.*
Side table, *Mr. and Mrs. Joseph K. Ott.*

the children were frequently sick, with many dying in the cradle, or later from the old childhood diseases, from smallpox or tuberculosis or undiagnosed maladies or injuries.

Almost as little is known about the women, perhaps a quarter of the population. This is a result of the condition of society then. The eighteenth century was emphatically a man's age, and in no place more so than one where power was not hereditary. The prevailing theory of reproduction, in the face of abundant folk wisdom about family resemblances, declared the male sperm the "seed" of the embryo, with the female womb providing nothing but a soil in which it grew. This theory was a poetic expression of the role men wanted women to play in all respects. In actuality, of course, women did more to make a community function and contributed more to an embryo than the men liked to think. Still, the female sex was kept rather inconspicuous in Newport's public life. The noteworthy exceptions were a few women in business, who with surprising consistency were not native to the town, and a few in crime, who were as often local daughters as not. The city, unlike some other places in New England, produced no outstanding female Quaker ministers, although it boasted at least its share of those who were gifted and respected.

The dearth of women who made a splash with their talents or personalities may have been happenstance rather than a result of adverse social conditions alone. Women had greater access than was common to spheres normally reserved to men in the eighteenth century. Anne Franklin, an immigrant from Boston, could operate a printing establishment and publish a newspaper without arousing comment; the widow of Sueton Grant, from Scotland, convulsed the courts with suits against her husband's creditors without inspiring more than chortles over how she outwitted the lawyers, including her own who was trying to swindle her. Though females had no say in the Anglican or Congregationalist churches, their importance in the Baptist churches, where they voted in the deliberations of the members in full communion (and they were usually the great majority), and among Quakers, where they had their own officers and meetings for business, gave them a stronger voice in religious affairs than women had in most other places.

Women in Newport, as was true throughout the colony, managed to receive better treatment in law than sometimes has been believed. They could obtain divorces on the same grounds as men. They did so about one-fourth as frequently; the evidence does not reveal whether women sought divorce less often than men, had fewer grievances, or faced heavier burdens of proof when taking complaints to court. (Neither sex shrank from gathering sensational evidence or producing salacious details in abundance to present to the judge and jury.) Women inherited and controlled property; a female Quaker minister gave most of the substantial endowment of the Newport monthly meeting. Though English law generally worked against women, it allowed extensive rights to spinsters, confirmed to widows anything that had been stipulated in wills, and assured to wives whatever had been agreed to in contracts with their husbands prior to marriage. The Friends made a point of requiring women who planned remarriage to get contractual safeguards for the inheritances of their children by a previous husband.

Underneath these formalities, however, lay a bedrock of custom that assured a social importance for women. By and large, they were expected to be versed in the skills of their husbands and to carry on the family business when the husbands fell sick or died. In short, most Newport women as a matter of course had a share in what was customarily men's work, and those who had the greatest share were ordinarily the ones most like their menfolk, the artisans and shopkeepers who remain as faceless in the record as their wives.

This is not to say that women had no special work. As was common before the industrial age, maintaining the household was a drudgery measured mainly by the size of the house. The care devoted in wills to clothing, bedding, and furnishings showed how valuable these things were and how much time a woman spent on spinning, weaving, sewing, mending, washing, and cleaning. She also had the endless chore of preparing meals and preserving foods when they were available against times when they were not. Unless she could afford servants or slaves, a wife's duties grew greater as her husband's wealth increased. The poor could frequent taverns, the rich could stroll with visiting gentlemen. Between fell the majority. Furthermore, the pace of women's work differed from men's. Wealthy merchants kept short hours except when something special, such as a ship to be fitted out, required a burst of activity. Many other occupations were sporadic or seasonal. Women's labor was incessant, symbolized by the distaff, the wand to hold the fibers when working at the spinning wheel.

In the wealthy rural area near Newport, there flourished two sorts of community. One of these is fairly easy to describe. On the rest of Aquidneck and the neighboring island of Jamestown were a mixture of substantial farmers, more often Quakers than anything else, and a few rich people. The good soil of Portsmouth and Middletown, already subdivided into small holdings, yielded garden crops and fruit, while the thinner soil supported the livestock that provided meat and dairy products. Local opinion has always insisted that the island corn is sweeter, the milk and cheese richer, than any other in New England. A distinctive feature of the terrain on these islands was provided by the windmills, which supplied power to grind grain for a region almost devoid of water power. Though Portsmouth failed in the attempt to start its own commercial center, the townsfolk had long been improving their income by investments in overseas trade or land on the mainland, so they drew rewards from the colony's expansion. Probably poor white people were rare in rural Aquidneck compared with other places, but before the Revolution there were surprising numbers of black slaves and Indians in some servile condition. Together, the non-white peoples comprised over 20 percent. The heavy concentration on Jamestown suggests that slaves were employed to tend the livestock, although they occasionally had many other occupations, such as ferrymen or domestics.

The more challenging region was the Narragansett country stretching from Wickford to Westerly, including the "palace" of the Indian prince in Charlestown. An argument has long been going on over whether there were Narragansett planters, rich slave-owners presenting the nearest equivalent to the Virginia gentry to be found in the north. The argument is downright weird, because nobody has made a case for their absence, yet those who produce the evidence of their existence seem fearful that it will not be believed. One source of trouble is lack of a sense of scale. How much land constituted a plantation? How big was big? How many slaves amounted to a large number? Another trouble comes from the declining size of landholdings. Unlike the Virginians, who often acquired extra plantations in the interior of their colony, the Rhode Islanders gained nothing significant after buying tracts in the "vacant lands." In later years they divided their acres among their heirs. The process started with the Pettaquamscut purchasers: as they sold their lands to others or divided tracts among their heirs, the holdings could never be as great again. So one gets the impression of a landed gentry on the decline from the hour of its birth. Yet the measurement of acres meant little at first because only about two thousand settlers lived there along with five or six hundred Indians. The vast holdings were mostly unused. There was a middle period in the process of subdivision, roughly the first half of the eighteenth century, as the population grew to about thirteen thousand, when the land was coming into production and was still owned in large chunks by a few dozen men, as well as in small chunks by many more. During this period existed whatever there was of a counterpart to the southern plantation gentry.

The importance of owning great tracts of land should not obscure the value of location and political connections. Nigh unto Newport, the Narragansett country was intimately connected with that port and its leading citizens. Some Narragansett gentlemen became prominent Newport lawyers. Some Newport patricians, such as Francis Brinley, had huge estates on the mainland. A few Narragansett gentlemen were always to be found among the colony's leading officials. There was a steady interchange between the two places.

The details of getting and improving land are often beyond discovery. Little evidence survives, what with the early confusion over jurisdiction, the later burning of town records in North Kingstown, and the deliberate obfuscation of what was done to gain territory from the Indians after 1707. Yet much of the economic base of rural wealth can be discerned. Various heirs of

Pettaquamscut purchasers and Narragansett Proprietors developed great estates. So did some who merely bought from such people, such as the prolific Hazards and Gardiners. There are bad odors of defrauding the Indians in the affairs of others, however, such as the Stantons and Champlins.

Merely holding title to land (or having claims by some illegal lease from an heir of Ninigret) did not make anyone rich. The Indians had cleared a great part of the territory, however, so it was possible to bring in livestock without investing more than the price of fencing. The increase of the flocks did well for the Richard Smiths in the seventeenth century and probably for many other families. With such a start, further development was comparatively easy. One method was even easier for those who could afford to be patient: they leased land to a tenant whose obligations consisted of clearing fields, building fences and outbuildings, planting orchards, and delivering a fixed share of the increase in the livestock. As Newport commerce expanded, practically any farm product would command a good price; while the paper currency was expanding, the taxes were ridiculously low or totally absent, so prosperity in the Narragansett country was all but automatic. Conversely, when commercial expansion slowed, taxes resumed on a normal scale, paper money loans fell due for repayment, and holdings became smaller, the good times faded away quickly.

While the living was easy, a few dozen families lived very comfortably. Their houses were not huge by standards of the day—a large one was fifty feet square with two stories. They devoted little to learning or artistic refinement. Like the Virginia gentlemen with whom they have been compared, their greatest intellectual attainments were in the law. In religion, they often preferred the Church of England, although quite a few joined the Congregationalists or Quakers and a small number ranked among the Baptists. Generally, however, they lavished more devotion on the rustic amusements of hunting and fishing than on divine worship. Like the rural well-to-do throughout colonial America, they made a virtue of hospitality as part of the struggle to stave off boredom and isolation. They made the best of events, such as weddings and holidays, court days and town meetings.

One should not be content with a picture of amiable eighteenth-century country gentry on a modest scale. The Narragansett country was noted for its eccentrics as well as its friendly gentlemen and handsome women. Travelers found pranksters, cantankerous squires, and taciturn innkeepers. Moreover, South Kingstown provided a textbook of political fraud and malfeasance in office, generally the work of scions of the leading families. In addition, the Narragansett gentry provided all of the truly outrageous counterfeiters of Rhode Island money in the Greenman and Potter rings. The latter was led by a member of the colony's committee to issue the money; he obtained control of the plates and tricked his colleagues into signing the bills he struck. Another notorious counterfeiter (this time of coins) was a silversmith from the same locale. These criminals were scarcely punished, and their sins were quickly forgiven by their neighbors.

All was not entertainment and skulduggery, however. One sign of aristocratic traits in the Narragansett country was the interest in careful breeding of the all-important livestock. Though various men began early to plan bringing in and preserving the best strains, probably no great success was achieved until the early eighteenth century. Nothing was done about the swine or the few goats. When butter and cheese became major money-makers, however, good breeds of dairy cattle were introduced. Draught horses had been one of the first exports, and some pains were taken to prevent deterioration of the stock. No one can figure out precisely when the Narragansett pacers appeared or how they first came into existence—the best guess is that the progenitors were from Ireland—but the fame of this breed has overshadowed the greater economic significance of the draught animals. The pacers were small beasts for luxury transportation. Their natural gait, akin to a rack, was extremely comfortable for the rider. The demand welled up, the breed was cultivated in a few other places, and a purchaser from Cuba bought all he could get; by the end of the colonial period the pacer was almost extinct in the Narragansett country. By the end of the eighteenth century, there was only one left. In many ways the career of the pacer paralleled that of the Narragansett gentry.

In the land of the Narragansett gentry: "S.W. View of the Seat of the Hon. Henry Marchant, Esq., in South Kingstown, State of Rhode Island," pencil sketch about 1790 by unknown artist. Marchant was a Newport lawyer and patriot who in the days of his prosperity owned a country villa, as men like him had often done before. *The Rhode Island Historical Society.*

Tending the houses, stables, dairies, gardens, fields, and orchards were various kinds of subordinates. Tenants were probably more important than records reveal. There were also hired hands and indentured servants, plus Indians who could have been either indentured in the usual sense or in consequence of debt—a sort of peonage. The slaves, however, have claimed the most attention. Various estimates of their numbers have been offered, some so extravagant as to be absurd. According to the colonial census reports, which are probably low, slaves in the Narragansett country numbered 111 in 1708, rose to over eight hundred by 1750, peaked somewhere above a thousand several years later, and then declined.* Almost half at any time were to be found in South Kingstown, which contained about a quarter of the colony's black population. Even in that town few people could own large numbers of slaves, rarely as many as fifty on one property, because the total did not far exceed four hundred at the greatest, and they never amounted to more than 17 percent of the inhabitants. Most owners must have held between one and five. By the time of the Revolution, Quakers were freeing their slaves, and after the war a new state law began gradual emancipation, which gave liberty to more than half by 1790.

Local tradition, as in most other parts of colonial America, held that the conditions of slavery were milder in the Narragansett country than elsewhere. There may have been some truth in this claim; though many bondsmen surely were constantly subject to their owners' orders, a few records present a system of requiring each slave to perform certain tasks—tend so many horses or sheep, make so many cheeses per day—beyond which the slave had no further duties. This type of management allowed slaves to use their remaining time as they pleased, and

---

* The census reports on black people are particularly suspect. For instance, there is not the faintest reason to believe that black Newporters declined from 220 to 110 between 1708 and 1749, only to rise to around eight hundred in 1755. The number given for 1749 is the implausible one; otherwise, statistics indicate a black population comprising 10 or 11 percent of the city's inhabitants. There was no incentive for the citizens anywhere in the colony to make known the numbers of their slaves, who either were or might become taxable property.

some raised crops for market. Something of a slave society developed, with an annual festival in June reminiscent of the Roman Saturnalia, when the slaves in each of the Kingstowns elected a governor to serve as their judge and spokesman during the ensuing year. The candidates drummed up votes well in advance; the balloting was carried out amid lavish pageantry; afterwards came a day of feasting and athletics.

The Indians remain even less well described in surviving documents. Dr. Alexander Hamilton in 1744 visited the reigning prince in Charlestown, where he had a commodious house near the Post Road. The doctor reported, "He possesses twenty or thirty thousand acres of very fine level land round this house, upon which he had many tenants and has, of his own, a good stock of horses and other cattle. This king lives after the English mode. His subjects have lost their own government, policy, and laws and are servants or vassals to the English here. His queen goes in a high modish dress in her silks, hoops, stays, and dresses like an English woman. He educates his children to the belles lettres and is himself a very complaisant mannerly man. We paid him a visit, and he treated us with a glass of good wine." The prince was George Augustus Ninigret, the queen was Sarah, a woman of high birth. They sent their son to England for an education. Their people numbered about a thousand, most of them dwelling nearby. The couple brought an interlude of respectability to the royal house of the Niantics, between the extravagances and sexual adventures of the two previous princes and the lawsuits and drunkenness of the successor.

Early in the eighteenth century, of course, the Narragansett Indian lands had been reduced to a small extent. Unofficially, Ninigret II and his son, Charles Augustus Ninigret, had parted with more, by unrecorded sales and leases. Many of their subjects had fallen into servitude or wasted lives of poverty and debauchery. They began consorting with black slaves, producing an unknown number of "mustee" offspring, who floated in ill-defined status around the great landowners. The tribe retained some identity, although its council of elders often lost its ability to guide the princes. As a result, there were a few efforts to stage palace revolutions to replace the wastrel sachems with a young son or nephew. The most elaborate of these took the form of contesting the inheritance of Thomas Ninigret, son of George Augustus, through the colonial courts. The challenge probably had the ulterior purpose of putting more Indian acres into the hands of white men. One way or another, the royal family kept falling into debt and ending up with less land, while their subjects drifted away from their reservation and into the unhappy lives of the downtrodden.

The rest of rural Rhode Island was a region of small farms. Settlement slowly blanketed the land, although the Providence proprietors had unoccupied acres even at the end of the eighteenth century. The northern mainland region had fewer people than the Narragansett country at the beginning of the century and remained behind until about 1770, when the population reached over twenty thousand exclusive of the residents of Providence. Rivers with the meadows and relatively fertile adjoining land, with sites for mills or fords, drew people before the rocky uplands. The long roads into the interior encouraged belts of settlement. Most of the people who took up the land were ordinary yeoman farmers of New England with their families. Their lives were a routine of work regulated by the seasons. Farm technology remained rather simple in the eighteenth century. Care over breeding livestock, getting the best varieties of seed, or fertilizing the soil were mainly refinements of the nineteenth century. Later, too, were the intricate needlework, pickling and preserving, and proliferation of gadgetry that came to characterize rural New England. In the eighteenth century, textiles were simple, stock bred as it would, an eight-fold yield of corn was common, pickled pork constituted a principal source of protein, and a few basic implements were all most families had. The style of life allowed a surprising amount of indolence for the men in some seasons and surprisingly little work for the children.

Most farms produced livestock and small amounts of grain or dairy products for market, but there were a few specialized cash crops. In Warwick and elsewhere, a low grade of tobacco was grown for export to slaves in the West Indies. Sale of the leaf was said to bring in the difference between being able and unable to pay taxes. Around Bristol and a few other towns, the green onions, then as now called rareripes in Rhode Island, were raised for a large market. Some people grew flax and hemp, especially when the colony offered a bounty. Many brought in money by converting trees to useful goods—firewood if nothing else, but also timers, shingles, clapboards, barrel staves and ends, or less often furniture. The profusion of part-time trades and small-scale retailing can scarcely be enumerated. On Block Island fishing— and some would add, despoiling wrecks—helped add the vital income that spelled the difference between a primitive subsistence farming and the ability to pay taxes and buy the essentials for a decent life, such as ironware, fine cloth, rum, and East India goods.

Among the rural population the spectrum of wealth ran wide. In every town there were paupers and families teetering on the brink of poverty. Widows with few acres and several small children could look forward to misery: if the boys and girls were indentured, as the town council often insisted, the land would go to waste; if they were not, the land would probably be sold to pay for rearing them. Either way pointed to a bleak future. The same prospect existed for men who were disabled by disease or injury, leaving them incapable of supporting their families. The old and sick sometimes reduced themselves to poverty by their best efforts to provide for their own needs. Some families chronically proliferated scions without enough land or wits to make a living.

The blighted lives of the rural paupers can only be glimpsed in the town council records, with their bare notations of efforts to force people to take in their poor relations, or failing that, of grudging expenditures to support old people or orphans in foster homes, payments for shirts, bedding, a doctor's visit, or the ultimate disbursement for a coffin. Before town aid was provided, the councils expected the applicant to promise to the town what remained of his or her property. When death ended the unhappy life, the council with grim thoroughness made lists, with each item appraised, of the few shabby garments and perhaps a little bedding and a few personal articles like spoons or keepsakes. The eighteenth century stared unblinkingly at disease, destitution, and death. In fairness to the councils, it should be added, however, that caring for the poor ran up the bulk of the town tax bills.

At the other end of the scale were a few men owning great estates and more commonly an assortment of go-getters. Clever traders in land could gain at the expense of their neighbors. Millers and blacksmiths could do well. So could retailers who knew how far to extend credit, how to drive hard bargains, and how to market the country produce they normally took in exchange for the wares they sold. A smart shopkeeper like the Baptist pastor in Warwick, John Gorton, owned a small vessel in which he did his own transportation of goods to and from Newport and other places around the bay, throwing in a little preaching wherever he got a chance. Even in the late seventeenth century there were small fortunes to be made in money-lending. They rarely come to light, but some members of the Arnold family of Pawtuxet clearly had gone into this business by 1680, probably with profits from furs. They did very well indeed, although their neighbors learned to hate them. Later, small ironworks began to succeed. By the late colonial period they became especially attractive, although the smell of profit from the blast furnace brought in outside investors who outnumbered the rural entrepreneurs.

Binding the parts of the colony together during the eighteenth century were several new market centers. Portsmouth, which failed to create one, nevertheless explained most clearly what was in everyone's mind. The town in 1694 planned a tract of small lots to secure "the great benefit and profit that may arise to every freeholder . . . by settling tradesmen and propagating a manufactury, which way hath been the only means and motive of enriching most rich places in the world." There were to be wharves on the Sakonnet River shore, a town house, and a schoolhouse, but after many frustrating years, Portsmouth remained hopelessly rural.

Similar plans beguiled people in many other towns. Some came to little. The tract of small lots set aside in the Pettaquamscut Purchase did not stimulate a compact village, but a few hamlets eventually sprang up as rural prosperity gave occasion for them, at Tower Hill, Little Rest (later changed dull-wittedly to Kingston), and even near Point Judith. Nor did Block Island develop much of a town center. Hopes for creating a good harbor, by building a pier out into the ocean or digging a channel to a convenient pond, could not be realized for very long at a time. The piers washed away, and the price of keeping a channel open proved prohibitive. Much of the time shipping to the island stopped short in the ocean, leaving passengers and cargo to be transferred from the shore to the vessel (or the other way around) on small craft. Such conditions thwarted the establishment either of a trading village or a fishing base. Nor did several schemes for commercial development in Warwick enjoy more than trifling success.

Yet secondary commercial centers appeared in more favorable locations. Pawtuxet, though inland, finally became a real village, profiting from its place by the road crossing the nearby river. Westerly produced a little town center where the Misquamicut proprietors had hoped for one. At the ferry landing on the east side of Jamestown, a small business district slowly took shape. Lodowick Updike, on land he inherited from Richard Smith, promoted a much more successful port village at Wickford. Updike laid out lots, which he began selling early in the eighteenth century. This port, with the Ten Rod Road to draw traffic from inland, thrived as a point for transfer of goods going to and from Newport.

The development of the East Greenwich waterfront, however, was more imaginative. Unpromising though the place was as a port, the town proprietors reserved the eastern tip of their grant until about 1711, when they began offering small lots on conditions designed to ensure commercial use. The proprietors received some of the lots as dividends, but their committee gave away the rest to people who would pay one shilling toward the expenses of surveying and would promise to build a house above a minimum size set by the proprietors. The committee changed the details of these rules a few times, but maintained the basic requirement of erecting a house within a short time or forfeiting the lot. By 1725 the policy was achieving success. It was possible to find a man to use the lot specifically set aside for a shipyard.

Soon the busy village acquired those bookends of humanity, a schoolhouse and a graveyard. By 1752 the committee and the proprietors enjoyed the still more delightful experience of arguing over regulation of wharves and whether to let a rich citizen and his partners monopolize the best site. When development had reached the point where wharves were that valuable, the commercial center could be certified successful. Still, it was a sober community of hard-working Quakers and Baptists, devoting itself to dealings with the rural hinterland on one side and Newport on the other. Today it appears to spill across the town line into the Cowesset section of Warwick. In fact, the Shawomet proprietors had made plans for a little port there before East Greenwich was even founded, and the newer town by its astute policy snatched the prize from the older. The triumph was sealed by erection of an impressive courthouse after East Greenwich became the shire town of Kent County, which was separated from Providence in 1750.

When Bristol was taken over from Massachusetts in 1747, the colony acquired a substantial minor port that was beginning to cut a figure in overseas trade. Founded in the late seventeenth century by proprietors who set a pattern for developing a waterfront very much like the one later used in East Greenwich, Bristol was sharing in the prosperity of Narragansett Bay before it came into Rhode Island. After switching jurisdictions, it began its notorious interest in the African slave trade, spearheaded by a young man named Mark Anthony DeWolf, who in 1744 immigrated from Guadaloupe on account of a new friendship with Simeon Potter of Bristol, whose sister Abigail promptly became Mrs. DeWolf and began bearing the prolific family that soon dominated the town's business. Bristol was predominantly Congregationalist and Anglican, in contrast with East Greenwich across the bay, but the difference in religion falls short of explaining the flamboyance of the older town. Perhaps the uselessness of Bristol—it tapped no hinterland to speak of and provided nothing that the bay lacked—made its commercial life so much a matter of brain and will power as to engender the profusion of eccentrics and cantankerous people of which the town became proud—more so than of the geese, onions, and pretty girls that established its wider reputation.

All the same, the outstanding success among the secondary trading centers was Providence, which advanced during the eighteenth century to the rank of competitor for Newport's supremacy. Still in 1700 a rural village beset by internal quarrels, Roger Williams' old town had already begun to conceive commercial ambitions. Just after his death in 1683 the town meeting started granting small lots—twenty feet to forty feet square—along the waterfront for warehouses or wharves. One of the earliest was given to Gideon Crawford, a Scotsman who came to pursue the career of a merchant in 1687 and prudently pursued first the hand of Freelove Fenner, daughter of Arthur Fenner, who was as close to being a merchant as any man in town. Crawford prospered but died twenty years later, after chalking up a record of acquisitiveness without many scruples. His widow carried on the business, rearing her two sons to commerce. They married daughters of another up-and-coming trader, Joseph Whipple, but died too young to give continuity to a patrician dynasty. Other newcomers kept moving to Providence to carry on commerce and ply other trades. Clearly the town was attracting people who expected it to be, as they helped it to become, a business center.

The commerce of Providence remained on a small scale, however, for several decades. Merchants there brought in imported goods from Boston directly or by way of Newport until the latter town began some shipping from Britain. By that time, Providence men could also place their orders in Philadelphia or New York, however, and so gained a measure of freedom from the mercantile community of any one major port. The pioneers in commerce slowly enlarged their trade, benefiting from the opening of roads into the hinterland in all directions, but the most successful were the members of the Brown family. Though they failed to beget heirs in a disconcerting number of cases, they managed to produce enough offspring to provide an unbroken succession through the eighteenth century. In the last decades before the Revolution there were enough to split the business into several branches, and one of them had enough capital to launch direct trade with London and Bristol.

From the start, Providence merchants understood the need for developing manufactures. In the basic ideas they were no different from their Newport competitors but had both greater zeal and a greater terrain on which to work. Newport was in the land of the windmill when it came to sources of power, while Providence was in the land of the waterwheel. The northern town also could obtain great quantities of wood, for fuel in iron smelting or forges, for distilleries, for shipyards, for export in the various forms, as well as for building and heating. Newport depended on wood brought from a smaller territory or from a greater distance. The Brown family excelled in judging when to invest in manufactures, but the principal Providence business-men were all alert to the possibilities and to the value of forming partnerships with men who could help exploit them. The result was a well balanced economic development.

By contrast, the cultural strivings were weak. Though the French immigrant, Gabriel Bernon, praised the intellect of his new neighbors in the 1720s, and a few people of cultivation were on the scene in subsequent decades, they amounted to a small coterie. A few physicians with diverse interests, a lawyer or two, the Anglican rector John Checkley, his parishioner John Merritt, a wealthy Englishman who brought his fine library and settled in town around 1746—such was the array before the College of Rhode Island was removed to the town in 1770 and the Brown brothers, Joseph and Moses, began turning their attention from business and politics to things like astronomy and technology.

Nor was education for children all that might have been expected of an ambitious young port. Schoolmasters came and went, as in rural hamlets, while anxious parents from time to time pooled money to build schoolhouses in the vain hope that such buildings would lure masters and pupils like magnets attracting so many iron filings. Somehow, nearly all the boys learned their letters and numbers—one cannot tell about the girls, although most of them probably were literate—but all the same Providence even more than Newport depended on immigrants during the last century of the colonial period to bring the more rarefied forms of learning.

The arts straggled behind the letters, sometimes forced to take abuse. The Congregationalists and then the Anglicans acquired organs and began subduing the prejudices against music. Still, when Douglass and his actors built a Histrionic Academy and began offering programs in the summer of 1762, though they carefully advertised their productions as concerts of music with a few interludes of dramatic fare thrown in gratis, there welled up a fierce hostility among the townsfolk. Some of them (who would never have bought tickets anyway) called a town meeting to demand a law against such wicked extravagance. The Assembly soon bowed to this bellicose self-righteousness, and the Academy was closed down by the sheriff, who waited from start to finish of the evening's entertainment before performing his duty. For a few years, the most the culture hounds could get away with was lectures on science, probably enlivened by sparks, booms, and bad smells. Insensibly, the frivolities of the wealthier gained toleration. By 1768 an Italian dancing master could ply his trade. Soon an elocution teacher could offer lessons and even publicly read aloud a mildly risqué play, John Gay's *The Beggar's Opera*, to an audience without being nabbed by the constable. Then the arrival of the college, an outburst of luxurious tastes among the rich, and the surprising conversion of the Baptists to magnificence turned the tide.

The shift was incarnate in architecture. With the construction of the new Baptist meetinghouse, Providence inaugurated an era of building, stalled for several years by the Revolution, that extended into the nineteenth century. A profusion of fine public buildings and dwellings, plus scores of modest houses and shops went up, transforming the town's appearance.

As Providence rose to urbanity and elegance during the eighteenth century, it gained a substantial middle class of shopkeepers and artisans. If the skills for producing luxury goods were rare compared with Newport, several of them at least were represented. The town's first print shop, a fairly good indicator of arrival of urban conditions, was opened in 1762, bringing out a newspaper almost at once. The area west of the Providence River, later the downtown district, filled with houses and shops during the 1750s and 1760s, greatly enlarging the citified area of the town.

As Providence grew, its bounds contracted. The original territory, which had included everything north of Warwick, by chunks turned into separate towns. The division in 1731 quartered the tract. Later Cranston, Johnston, and North Providence lopped off more rural zones, leaving the port city nearly alone in its jurisdiction.

The countryside thus separated was still the hinterland of Providence, however, as were also the adjoining parts of Connecticut and Massachusetts. Businessmen began dreaming of canals to extend cheap transportation up the Blackstone valley and sweep into their orbit a sizable part of what Boston regarded as its territory—and in the end managed to keep. Though the domain of Providence had no wealth or glamour to compare with the Narragansett country, it was a region of small farms and prolific families, mostly Baptists, Quakers, or irreligious, except on the Connecticut side. The land was hilly and the soil often thin, but the area abounded in small water power sites. The population turned to all sorts of small enterprises to stave off poverty. Though the hinterland presented a rather drab social spectacle, it served Providence well.

The Revolution left Providence on its feet and running, eager to plunge into trade and finance, soon ready to add spinning mills to the spate of manufacturies it was spreading across the nearby countryside. Presently there were new fortunes to dwarf the old, new families rising from homespun simplicity to urban magnificence. Though in some respects they resembled the old patriciate, they were different, their thoughts not governed by the patterns of trade in the British empire, their imaginations increasingly focused on the hill country whence many of them came rather than on the sea.

The war that left Providence poised for a new era tilted the scales against Newport and its appendages. Ravaged by occupations and a siege, the old capital never truly recovered. Soldiers quartered in the public buildings damaged some beyond repair as they, like the remaining citizens, struggled to keep warm. Fine old woodwork and family papers, the exotic trees and shrubs in the gentlemen's gardens, anything that people could live without, were likely to go into the fireplace. In the Narragansett country, foraging parties from the various armed forces ransacked the land for provisions, while the harried inhabitants fell to accusing each other of favoring the wrong side. Peace seemed at first to restore the old times, but basic economic conditions no longer made a place for Newport's commerce. The smartest men left for New York, Philadelphia, or points south. The Narragansett planters, their products no longer in great demand and their lands ever more subdivided, sank into decaying gentility. The old liveliness persisted, appearing most often in the eccentricities or remarkable wits of prominent men, but the past could not be recaptured. Manufacturing saved such fortunes as survived. The event that might serve as symbol for the end of the old Narragansett planters was the death of George II, the last crowned sachem of the Indian tribe. He wanted to enlist in the Revolutionary army, but his people objected, so he stayed with them. A short time after he made this choice, he was killed by a falling tree. With him, the Narragansett royalty came to an end.

11

INTO THE VORTEX OF
IMPERIAL WARS

Though it may not have seemed clear at the time, the major turning point in Newport's affairs came in the period of warfare between 1739 and 1763. The town had launched its rise to commercial success in the wars half a century earlier and since their end had enjoyed a happily exceptional place in the British empire. Neither confined seriously by the policies of Whitehall nor kept out of the avenues of trade open to other colonials, the Rhode Islanders had exploited their opportunities vigorously. The new conflicts began simultaneously with new measures to restrain the colony's free-wheeling use of paper currency. At British insistence, the bills issued in 1740 were intended to keep a steady relation with silver. They did not, but the attempt manifested a greater truth, that international war entangled Rhode Island more than ever in the affairs of the mother country. There would be no return to the old ways.

Nor did the citizens want to retreat into the old conditions. Imperial patriotism, expressed in eagerness for war, gushed up in Newport. Rich men there would not wait for news of an official declaration; they began fitting out privateer vessels months before the document arrived. Ordinary men flocked to enlist in the crews. Everyone wanted the glory and spoils to be had by fighting the king's foes—everyone, that is, except the substantial number of pacifists and the many who preferred to stay in their accustomed routines. The excitement, however, overwhelmed the colony's elected officials to the extent of ending privileges for

conscientious objectors and voting for mounting military expenditures. The politicians, presumably, knew what the majority of
voters wanted.

Rushing into war probably forestalled another attack on the
Rhode Island charter—and so was good policy—but nevertheless
drew the colony more intimately into imperial affairs than it
could tolerate. Newport, in effect, suffered from its own success. It
had to act like a major port and prepare to get along without its
old favored position. Judging from the behavior of its citizens,
they could not see ugly consequences in 1739, because their eyes
were dazzled by gold to be captured in Spanish ships.

The first round of international conflict, the War of Jenkins'
Ear, began over incidents in the Caribbean. Spain's efforts to
enforce her laws against smuggling and to extend territorial
waters beyond what Britain thought reasonable limits provoked
an outrage in London that was brought to a climax when
Captain Robert Jenkins displayed to a parliamentary committee
an object he said had been one of his ears, cropped as penalty for
illegal trade in Spanish waters. Never mind that he had been
caught in 1731 and had failed to call attention to the grisly relic
until seven years later. The time was right for political enemies of
Sir Robert Walpole to make a furore. Walpole dragged his heels
but finally advised George II to declare war in October 1739.
Rhode Island merchants could hardly wait. They were as
interested as anyone in Caribbean waters and trade with French
and Spanish ports contrary to local law.

At first privateering looked better than commerce. Two
months before the king signed the declaration, the General
Assembly authorized the governor to grant commissions to
private men-of-war. This step was taken in response to encouragement from London, which arrived none too soon, as three
privateers were being outfitted, provided with ammunition by
the Assembly. Two sailed on September 1, the third soon after.
One actually took prizes before hostilities officially began.
Fortunately, they were back in port when word arrived of a new
parliamentary act authorizing commissions on highly favorable
terms along with specific instructions from the Lords of the
Admiralty allowing the governor of Rhode Island to grant them.

There need be no repetition of the squabbles of Queen Anne's War.

The Newport merchants who plunged into privateering were two recent immigrants, John Bannister and Sueton Grant, along with such leading citizens as Godfrey Malbone, John Gidley, George Wanton, and the local Brown family. Their ships hurried to the Caribbean and the Bahama passage through which Spanish vessels sailed on the way east across the Atlantic. The early results, especially by Captains Charles Hall and James Hall, raised hopes of lucrative raiding.

The sheer number of privateers on both sides, however, soon led to disappointments. Merchant vessels were captured by Spanish privateers; when recaptured, they led to expensive litigation between the original owners and the men who had regained the ships from the enemy. Legitimate neutral shipping went on, and vessels of the belligerent nations carried elaborate sets of flags and fake papers to produce when caught. The Spanish prizes seldom yielded the huge values necessary to sustain investment. Quarrels between privateers under the British flag further cut profits. Soon Bannister and others prudently concluded that more was to be made by commerce.

Sea raiding revived after French entry into the war in the spring of 1744, ushering in the round known as King George's War. That year, roughly one-sixth of the vessels owned in Newport roamed on privateering cruises. The chaotic Caribbean no longer was the sole arena: the Gulf of St. Lawrence and nearby waters provided another, where almost any sail was either friend or foe, and it was relatively easy to tell which.

Enthusiasm for private sea warfare was dampened by two calamities, however. The first and more dramatic occurred in September 1744 when John Gidley, Sueton Grant, and Nathaniel Coddington, Jr., owners of *Prince Frederick*, went to inspect supplies gathered in a warehouse to fit out a privateering cruise. They were at work in the company of a custodian when a pistol was fired accidentally, touching off several casks and flasks of gunpowder, fifty grenades, and some loaded firearms. The explosion cost £1,500 and the lives of the four gentlemen, who died in agonies of burns and bruises. The second and more serious occurred over a year later. Two large vessels, of which Godfrey Malbone was chief owner, sailed on December 24 into the teeth of a blizzard. Both went down with all hands, to a total of roughly four hundred men, mostly from Newport. The port could not endure such losses.

Moreover, conditions still favored trade against raid. Instead of true privateers, merchants came to favor what have been called letter-of-marque ships. The simple privateer carried a large crew, in some years averaging one hundred men, who received no wages but signed on for shares in the prizes. The letter-of-marque ship employed a smaller crew, more nearly the normal size, for she was basically a merchant vessel, although armed and authorized to capture enemy shipping as opportunity allowed; the crew was paid wages, and the men received shares of any prizes taken as well. During the war, profits rose in commerce with the West Indies. Sea warfare imperiled shipping, which enhanced prices paid for the goods the islands wanted as well as the commodities they exported. The merchant gained two ways. Especially lucrative was the trade with the non-British ports in the Caribbean.

This trade aroused a great deal of controversy, especially during wars, so its peculiar circumstances need to be explained. To begin with, the business always required evasion of laws, even during peace. France and Spain (although not the Netherlands) forbade foreign commerce in their West Indian ports, supposedly to ensure that the home country would derive the profits from the colonies. The French and Spanish, however, neither marketed all the sugar products nor supplied all the provisions, livestock, and timber products needed by their islands. French brandy interests, furthermore, wanted to suppress the export of rum. Faced with these contradictions between laws and commercial realities, local officials in the Caribbean connived (for a price) with British colonials bringing in what the islands wanted in exchange for sugar products. This arrangement gave advantages to all concerned. It violated no British law in peacetime,* and probably

---

* Several international agreements, including the Treaty of Madrid of 1670 and the Treaty of Whitehall of 1686 and later reaffirmations of them, contained

not in wartime either, although British officials disagreed on that point. In any case, there was no reason for Britain to enforce Spanish or French regulations.

The troublesome British law was the Molasses Act of 1733, which was renewed in war as well as peace for many years. This measure was a compromise between West Indian demands for a total exclusion of foreign sugar products from the British trading realm and desires in the mother country and the mainland colonies for liberty to aggrandize as much as possible of the world's commerce. The West Indians wanted to gain a monopoly to raise their prices and compel the mainland colonials to lower theirs on the provisions and other goods they supplied to the islands. The compromise placed heavy duties on foreign sugar products, a device that was ostensibly to be prohibitive but ironically fixed the seal of legality on the traffic supposedly to be stamped out. The mainland produced more than the British islands could buy and needed more than these islands produced. Indeed, people in the British islands smuggled French sugar and molasses to sell as their own, both to meet the demand and to take advantage of the prices bolstered by the tariff. Yet the mainland merchants could not stand the full burden of the duties, so they evaded them. Besides, they preferred to do their own smuggling.

In the mainland ports several practices quickly developed to get around the Molasses Act. Either foreign sugar and molasses could be landed clandestinely, or part be landed after paying duties while the rest was unloaded secretly, or all might be brought in as British, certified so by false papers, ordinarily bought from customs officials in the Caribbean. The last of these

clauses prohibiting trade by subjects of the king of England with the colonies of Spain and France. British implementation of these clauses never went beyond toothless pronouncements and instructions to colonial officials. In 1728 the Crown's law officers gave advice to the Board of Trade, expressing what was probably the usual view of the situation: the treaties only recognized the right of France and Spain to close their colonial commerce to British subjects and take such measures for that purpose as they chose; any further action by Great Britain would have to be by parliamentary law, which had never been attempted.

was perhaps the least satisfactory. Certainly the mainland customs men preferred the others, for they received generous gratuities for taking a good-natured and understanding attitude toward the welfare of local business. Besides, it was actually legal for these officials to make downward adjustments in the rates when they thought such "compositions" were justifiable, as they generally did. The Molasses Act brought in only a trickle of revenue. The tariffs were not even collected assiduously in Great Britain.

London for several years had no firm policy on these subjects. Some officials agreed with the West Indies planters, others with the advocates of capturing and keeping all available channels of trade. Even the men in charge of the customs grew schizoid, issuing stern orders to crack down on smuggling molasses and sugar and then ignoring negligence in the customs houses. The Walpole ministry muddled through to an unofficial tolerance of what was going on in America—the traffic with the foreign sugar islands was called the "indulged trade"—while favoring rough enforcement of the Molasses Act in Britain itself. The British islands, even with their smuggling, produced only enough for the mother country, where they could enjoy a protected price. That, influential men thought, should be enough for them. The mainland colonials should serve the empire by making money from foreign sugar and molasses to buy British manufactured goods. Thus there would be suitable rewards for all.

War changed surprisingly little. A royal declaration might call on the subjects to distress the king's enemies by all possible means, but such a proclamation made trading with the enemy only a misdemeanor over which no court had jurisdiction. Parliamentary laws spelled out what trade really had to cease, and Parliament generally thought it wise to close only a few kinds of traffic, such as importing manufactures from French ports in Europe, which was already illegal for the colonials. Naval officers and West Indian planters might shout that the French and Spanish should be brought to their knees by cutting off commerce with their sugar islands, but equally strident voices maintained that such strategy would yield only a small advantage in war and would force the enemy to take up a business in peace that had previously been highly lucrative for British interests. Amid the jangle, lawyers and judges figured out the law in many different ways. Before 1756 policy in London remained unsettled on how to treat foreign sugar islands. So colonial trade with the West Indies faced no severe new legal hurdles in the War of Jenkins' Ear and King George's War. The chief effects of hostilities were to add risks to commerce, to open the alternative of taking prizes instead of carrying on trade, and to raise profits for those who escaped all the perils. Rhode Island merchants tried out raiding and found trade better.

The colony took a small part in naval warfare. At the outbreak of hostilities Rhode Island fitted out its own naval vessel, the sloop *Tartar*. Commanded at first by John Cranston, an elderly brother of the late great governor, she operated ordinarily like a short-range privateer. She was sent on various missions, however, once in consort with Connecticut's sloop, to attack enemy vessels menacing the southern New England coast. The *Tartar* also sailed more directly in the service of King George II. When an army was sent in 1740 to attack Cartagena in modern Colombia, Rhode Island furnished two hundred men for the force collected at New York. The *Tartar* assisted the convoy as far as the Caribbean. Though the assault at first seemed successful, it quickly turned into a disaster compounded by yellow fever and a desperate grab for a consolation prize in an abortive campaign on Cuba. Few of the colonials survived. The *Tartar* rushed to Jamaica whither the remains of the force had retreated.

When Britain declared war on France, the *Tartar* entered her time of glory. Under Daniel Fones as captain, she was sent on various missions to aid the combined British and New England forces attacking the French fortress at Louisbourg on Cape Breton Island. Early in this episode Fones, escorting some Connecticut troops, made a gallant assault on a French frigate, breaking up a little squadron that threatened to capture or destroy the transports. Later in 1745, the *Tartar* helped prevent French reinforcements from reaching Louisbourg. After the fortress fell, she helped guard it against attempts at recapture and occasionally seized a French vessel as prize. Compared with this service at sea, Rhode Island managed to contribute little to the campaign: after initial confusion, the colony sent three companies of fifty men apiece, but they arrived too late for the siege and served as part of an occupation garrison for a few months.

The last years of the war yielded only bitterness. In 1746 *Tartar*, under a new commander, convoyed Rhode Island troops for a projected invasion of Canada. The whole scheme proved ruinous, although the colony's share in the misery arrived with merciful swiftness. One transport was driven ashore briefly on Martha's Vineyard, the rest soon after on Nantucket. As cold weather and sickness disheartened the men, their commanders prudently gave up the campaign and sailed back to Newport, minus one transport hopelessly aground. Worse followed: troops sent to help defend Annapolis in Nova Scotia from a French attack were driven ashore at Mount Desert Island, half of the men dying by drowning or exposure. The *Tartar*, under a new commander, ended her career in disgrace when she captured a suspicious schooner off Point Judith. The schooner was engaged in nefarious activity, purportedly under some British authorization, but the Rhode Islander put in charge proceeded to unload part of her cargo of sugar illegally. The General Assembly investigated the incident, censured the *Tartar*'s officers, and sold the sloop at a public auction.

Despite the aid to the Louisbourg expedition, Rhode Island was heavily criticized by Governor William Shirley of Massachusetts, who organized the attack. He claimed that Newport privateering lured seamen from Boston and gave berths to deserters from the Royal Navy. He insisted that Rhode Island gave refuge to men from southeastern Massachusetts who wanted to elude requirements to serve in the provincial army. He was not mollified by Rhode Island's vigor in supplying a crew for a captured French man-of-war. His complaints have often been repeated as impartial judgments, but they were not. He was seeking at first to put the blame on others for the riots in Boston against the parties from royal naval vessels trying to impress men to fill up the crews. Later he was building a case against reimbursement of Rhode Island's military expenditures from the king's treasury. The Rhode Island governors, however, were probably exaggerating the local record when they replied that their colony had harbored no deserters and had done its patriotic best, even to the point of leaving its coastline unprotected in order to send men to aid the royal expeditions. Whatever the truth, when it came time to settle accounts in London, Shirley's voice was heeded.

His recriminations cost Rhode Island dearly. Wartime expenditures before the Louisbourg expedition had run to £105,000 in the colony's old tenor currency (less than a quarter of that figure if reckoned in sterling) and required a resort to taxation in addition to emission of more paper money. Louisbourg and the abortive Canada expedition required printing £180,000 more. Plans to sink this money by taxation were scrapped as soon as word arrived that the royal treasury would pick up the bill. (If the colony was rash in resorting to the printing press, it was hardly in a league with Massachusetts, which emitted over ten times as much, driving the value down sharply.) Reimbursement of the small sum spent on the Louisbourg campaign was approved easily, though the actual payment of the money was held up in London for some time. Shirley, however, managed to inspire a minute scrutiny of the Canada accounts, with royal officials finally allowing a little more than half. Even with further depreciation of the paper currency, Rhode Island could call in only about 70 percent of the special emissions.

Beyond the burdens to the colonial treasury, however, military expenditures had far-reaching effects. The war finance created a crisis that led to a thorough investigation of the currency and its administration, revealing one muddle after another. Frantic attempts to compel payment of interest and principal on the loans from the colony kept stumbling on administrative shortcomings that rendered the treasury and the colony's attorneys unable to determine who owed what or to prepare the documents (mortgages and bonds for payment of interest and installments of principal) for action in courts. When the paper work was sorted out sufficiently to launch a large number of suits, the courts proved unable to handle them all, while the officials uneasily preferred to be lenient toward the debtors. Soon the attorneys' accounts became so tangled that new investigations by committees of the General Assembly led to suits against the attorneys. Some of the debts had to be written off as impossible to collect, and some of the documents never could be explained.

The whole business of overhauling the fiscal system was carried on against a crescendo of political strife. The decision to bow to imperial requirements on paper emissions (the attempt to guarantee a fixed relation with silver) was made in 1740 after the death of Governor John Wanton had given leadership to a new rival, Richard Ward, who had been elected deputy governor in a moderate upheaval. Under Ward and his successor, William Greene, investigations continued persistently into the administrative clumsiness, if not outright corruption, in the Grand Committee. The currency reformers held sway while the war stayed at a small scale. Enlargement of hostilities in 1744 to include France as an enemy, however, plus the exuberant bellicosity behind the Louisbourg expedition, put a new face on things. A new coalition, presumably advocates of boldness, formed and brought the first major overturn to the House of Magistrates in thirty years. Gideon Wanton and a slate of cohorts nearly swept the election in 1745. Just how a partisan opposition arose to Greene remains obscure; no contemporary explanations have come to light with revelations of the goals or organization of the challengers. For three decades, leading Newport politicos had kept their squabbles on the level of family fights, but suddenly they stopped doing so. The Wantons and their allies clearly launched a general attack on the incumbents—and largely succeeded. These men rushed into military expenditures, financing them with new emissions of paper money.

When the defeated side organized for the election of 1746, it scored a great success but proceeded to outdo its rivals in support of the plans to invade Canada. The political contest probably had become, and may have been all along, a rivalry over the profits and offices spawned by the war. With the campaigns fizzling out, the Wanton forces returned in triumph at the next general election only to see the military events of the ensuing year turn out as badly. Greene then won again.

The political customs of the colony underwent a series of shocks. Intense partisanship led to new laws to prevent fraud in elections and to enforce the property requirement in voting. The five towns taken from Massachusetts in 1747 sent ten more members to the House of Deputies and created an occasion for reshuffling the usual distribution of seats in the House of Magistrates. Besides, Providence and some minor ports were on the rise, while population had virtually blanketed the colony, reaching thirty-two thousand after the added territory raised the total by almost five thousand. When rival factions formed in Newport, both sides rushed to drum up support in the other towns. Greene himself was from Warwick; his numerous family entered a lasting alliance with the Wards of Newport and their friends, including some of the remnants and sons of Samuel Cranston's associates. The Wantons, however, sought support on a wider scale and brought into high office a larger number of new men. Newport was losing its secure grip on colonial affairs. Signs of bitter contests were especially obvious within the capital's home base, as in South Kingstown.

Partisan feeling in the elections dwindled with the end of the war. The two sides lost the ardor and clarity that produced the wholesale alternations in the late 1740s. Yet, the political scene still had drama. Two episodes in 1750 cost Greene friends who later rallied his opposition. To calm a fight between East Greenwich and some Providence men, the Assembly tried slicing Kent County off of Providence, which did little but offend the north. Worse, the Assembly defied its leadership and enacted the last large paper money loan.

This measure stirred up a fierce controversy. Proponents argued that the shortage of currency resulting from retirement of old bills was making the postwar depression worse than it needed to be. The recent conversion to hard money in Massachusetts was spreading misery in all directions. If the money supply were not increased, the rural folk would end up so deeply in debt that they would have to sell their land to the rich. Moreover, people in the newly acquired towns wanted a chance to borrow money. Opponents replied that flying in the face of emphatic policy in London would provoke a new attack on the charter. Besides, the paper money excluded from Massachusetts would rush into Rhode Island, replacing any shortage with a glut. The strongest

The Rhode Island Historical Society.

objection, however, went nearly unvoiced: if Rhode Island money could not buy goods in Boston, there was no point to issuing it. As the sides lined up, most of the rural population finally swung around to favoring paper. The Newport merchants were lined up against it: they wanted to trade with Britain or the other principal colonial cities, and a strictly local currency would do them no good. By contrast, those in the rest of the colony who bought and sold in the Newport market wanted easy money.

In a bewildering succession of second thoughts, the Assembly revised its plans, removing bounties on local produce and projects for public works, toying with various means to prevent depreciation, inserting a vague clause making the new issue, and perhaps all the old ones as well, legal tender for all debts. William Greene firmly opposed the measure in any form. But the Assembly finally settled on one that offered some chance of creating a safe currency in line with British policy.

In spite of the cautious terms of the final act, a group of Newport merchants took the astounding step of opposing it by sending a petition to the king. They wanted no more loans of paper money and asked the monarch to stop the new one and prevent any measure that might lead to depreciation of the existing bills. Not content with these requests, the petitioners accused the colony of failure to impose taxes or take other action to withdraw the older bills from circulation. The accusations were correct, of course, in broad terms. Tidings of the petition got around. According to rumor, it called for abolition of the charter government. The Assembly obtained a copy of the document, however, discovering that it did not go so far. The signers were revealed to the public. Of the seventy-one, a dozen were not residents of the colony, several were men who had immigrated in recent years, two were minor officials, but a very large number consisted of Newport merchants, including a roster of illustrious names—but not a Wanton among them.

If these men did not actually call for a change of government, they provided grounds for one. They had violated the first rule of Rhode Island politics, which was never to jeopardize the autonomy under the charter. Consequently, there was an uproar. The danger to the charter was not imaginary. A similar secret move in Massachusetts had brought parliamentary action to stop the private land bank there ten years earlier, so Britain was known to be responsive to such requests. Moreover, in 1750 the officials in London were laying plans to stamp out paper money in New England.

Rhode Island's new act to emit paper money arrived in the imperial capital just as these plans were ripening and at the same time as British West Indies interests were pouring complaints before the Board of Trade over the colony's commerce with the French and Spanish islands during the recent war. Taking advantage of Rhode Island's bad reputation, the board pushed for parliamentary action on paper money. The board served up complaints from some individual Newport merchants (one of them had been a member of the Grand Committee but resigned in protest against the new measure) along with a petition from London merchants based on the one from Newport. The sugar interests were shuffled aside once their clamor had served its purpose.

The plan of forcing a rapid conversion to a currency based on silver and gold had a good chance of success in Parliament, but it was toned down at the urgent request of Massachusetts and New York. However much those provinces resented their neighbors' paper currency, they could not stand the thought of a sudden removal at a time of stagnant trade. So the final law required only a few basic rules: the New England colonies should emit no more of the bills of public credit of the old varieties; they might not postpone retirement of the existing ones or make them legal tender, yet the colonies could issue bills for current expenses as long as they made provisions for retiring them within two years or within five years under emergency conditions.

The law came too late to stop Rhode Island's issue of 1750, but it controlled fiscal policy for the rest of the colonial period. Rhode Island was forced back to regular taxation by 1754, to the mystification and annoyance of its citizens.

In the aftermath of the currency uproar, the political alignments of the late 1740s did not prevail. Erstwhile opponents gained and lost office rather at random, while Greene remained governor. A cluster of men from both sides shouldered the

Hopkins warmly endorsed the plan and tried to win the approval of Rhode Island. The General Assembly, however, feared infringement on the charter and instructed the colony's agent to lobby for postponement of action by Parliament until a full presentation could be made defending Rhode Island's privileges. The agent never had to carry out these orders. The king's ministers, who had toyed with proposals to call upon the colonies to design a system for coordinating military action, learned almost simultaneously that the Albany conference had done so and that none of the legislatures had approved its work. London decided the cause was hopeless.

As the war between Britain and France approached its full intensity, both sides committed forces to the North American theater far beyond anything in earlier conflicts. At the outset the French had the advantage, with a substantial number of troops brought over to add to the Canadians, both white and red. They fortified the forks of the Ohio River and held this strategic place against the first two attacks. The second, led by Major General Edward Braddock, ended in disaster, but it marked the beginning of British plans to send over large numbers of regular troops and recruit colonials into these regiments for continuous service in America, augmented by units raised in the various colonies. The days of gathering a force for each campaign were over.

Braddock's expedition formed part of the wide range of actions scheduled for 1755. While he was slashing slowly through the Pennsylvania forests, other British officers were deporting the French population of Nova Scotia on well-founded suspicions of disloyalty to King George II, while offshore a naval squadron failed to prevent French reinforcements from entering Canada and the fort at Louisbourg that had been given back in 1748. At the same time, Governor Shirley of Massachusetts was getting up expeditions against Niagara and Fort St. Frédéric at Crown Point on Lake Champlain. Thus from the start four areas figured in British plans—the interior of the continent west of Philadelphia, Nova Scotia, the perimeter of Lake Ontario, and the strategic zone around the southern end of Lake Champlain. The first concerned the middle colonies, the second almost exclusively the British regulars, but the battles in the third and fourth were fought by combinations of British troops and provincials from New York and New England.

Rhode Island hurried into the war. At the beginning of 1755, the General Assembly voted to raise a small force to protect the colony, but it soon responded to calls for aid to imperial designs. A few months later, it authorized recruitment of four hundred men to help the assault on Crown Point. The French would not wait to be attacked and sent a force southward to stop the Americans while they were still preparing at Lake George. In three engagements on September 8, the opposing sides each won one and scored a tie. The Rhode Island men reached the shores of Lake George in time to help prevent the barely fortified camp from being stormed. After that day, the campaign against Crown Point was abandoned and the British Americans under William Johnson settled down to build Fort William Henry at the southern tip of Lake George, but quite a few of the Rhode Islanders decided they had done enough and went home.

Before that happened, the General Assembly had already voted to send reinforcements. The new expedition, swelled by the men from the first who had returned on their own volition, marched toward Albany, while the Assembly decided on recruiting still more, raising the total to 750 for the year. So few volunteers appeared, even with promise of a bounty, that the colony resorted to conscription, as it had to do throughout the war. By the end of 1755, all the troops raised that year were discharged.

The following year was nearly a repeat of the first. The Rhode Island forces, sent at intervals to the camps north of Albany, were called upon to do nothing while a French army captured Oswego on the southern shore of Lake Ontario. The Rhode Islanders were all discharged by November, by which time an outbreak of smallpox at Albany spread the disease among the soldiers, who were greeted with suspicion when they returned home. In fact, several did carry infection and set off small local epidemics.

It was worse in 1757. Again the General Assembly sent men to northern New York, where they were stationed at Fort Edward, the chief stronghold at the head of the Hudson River, while the French under the Marquis de Montcalm captured Fort William

Henry and failed to prevent their Indian allies from butchering the wounded and attacking the retreating men, stripping to the skin such soldiers as they caught and looting the baggage. A large force raised in Rhode Island was marching across Connecticut on the way to add strength to Fort William Henry when it met news of the capture and turned around and headed home. Part of the first regiment stayed on garrison duty at Saratoga, but the rest was discharged. The British commander-in-chief, Lord Loudoun, delighted by the Connecticut turnout, over twice the strength he had called for, bitterly berated Rhode Island for sending to the campaigns of 1757 less than he wanted. He may have been venting an understandable exasperation at the general apathy in the colonies and his frustrations in all the campaigns he launched. Actually, Rhode Island supplied in the early war years almost a tenth of its males of military age, a much greater fraction than some of the other colonies.

The campaigns of 1758, when British fortunes improved dramatically in most theaters of war, drew an even larger number of men from Rhode Island. The colony supported a large contingent of regulars preparing to attack Louisbourg. (The expedition overwhelmed that fort after a painstaking siege.) The Assembly sent a thousand men, almost an eighth of the possible number, to join Major General James Abercromby in an attack on Fort Ticonderoga, recently erected by the French on the shore of Lake Champlain at the narrows south of Crown Point. The generals, deceived by reports of incredible French strength with more about to arrive, did not haul the artillery to Mount Defiance behind the fort but tried an immediate assault. The Rhode Island men were held as reserves behind the first two lines. The first line, composed of New York men and other provincials, drew the French fire, then British grenadiers advanced in several charges over the dead and wounded but were repulsed every time. Then the Rhode Island, Connecticut, and New Jersey troops advanced. They crossed the defensive trenches outside the fort but got no farther. Finally, Abercromby ordered a retreat. The French, who had suffered badly, expected a renewed attack, with artillery properly placed, and prepared to abandon the fort. Abercromby, however, withdrew to Lake George.

After this inglorious campaign, Abercromby sent some of the Rhode Island men with Colonel John Bradstreet on a daring but successful expedition. They first helped fortify the Oneida Carrying Place (near Rome, New York), then proceeded to Oswego. Though half the Iroquois who had gone with the army that far deserted there, Bradstreet loaded the rest of his force on small boats and sailed across Lake Ontario to Fort Frontenac (near Kingston, Ontario). His men vastly outnumbered the garrison, which surrendered quickly, and captured the huge quantity of supplies stored at the stronghold together with the small naval squadron based there, although the crews escaped. Bradstreet ordered the cannon of Fort Frontenac turned to destroy its very walls; he burned what remained, as well as most of the little French navy. With the rest he sailed back with the army and its booty to Oswego. Bradstreet's victory, coming after the capture of Louisbourg, helped reverse the fortunes of the French, who had to give up Fort Duquesne at the forks of the Ohio River before the campaigning season was over.

British victories continued in 1759, notably with the capture of Niagara and Quebec, but Rhode Island men once again shared little of the glory. They formed part of the army that Major General Jeffrey Amherst mobilized against Ticonderoga. Profiting from the last year's mistakes, he placed his cannon to fire upon the fort, only to discover that the French had withdrawn, except for a small garrison that stayed to blow up the fortifications before joining the retreat. Next the French destroyed Fort St. Frédéric. Instead of pursuing the enemy, Amherst put his men to work rebuilding these forts. At least Crown Point had finally fallen to the British. The next year, a new Rhode Island force, weakened by desertions, formed part of Amherst's excessively systematic campaign against Montreal. By September, the invasion of Canada finally brought an end to the French power there.

In the last years of the war, Rhode Island supplied troops to garrison northern New York and to form a small part of the

British army that invaded Cuba. The expedition captured Havana in 1762, but only half the Rhode Islanders survived, the rest falling in battle or dying of fevers. Still, the victory was genuine. Added to the others in Europe, India, and the West Indies, it crowned British success and helped win a largely satisfactory settlement in the Treaty of Paris in 1763. For New England, the French surrender of Canada and the whole of Nova Scotia meant the end of a conflict that had gone on intermittently for over a century.

The French and Indian War spawned privateering and similar seafaring as well as battles on land. Rhode Island sent out ten or twenty privateers in several years, as well as letter-of-marque ships. At times the privateer crews outnumbered the men in the expeditionary forces. Vast profits flowed into the coffers of some investors, while others, such as Henry Collins and Ebeneezer Flagg, suffered disastrous losses. Clear distinctions between private men-of-war and letter-of-marque ships became hazy and were further confused by the conduct of flag-of-truce vessels. The latter, though they served diverse purposes, ordinarily carried a few prisoners for exchange or merely to be landed at a port under their own sovereign. The comparative safety conferred by the flag of truce made it valuable for protecting an essentially commercial voyage. This advantage had been used in the last years of King George's War but became common only after 1755. In Newport as in the other northern cities, merchants paid generously for this privilege—political enemies claimed that Governor Stephen Hopkins charged up to £500. Naturally, prisoners taken in capturing enemy ships were used sparingly to allow the greatest number of flags of truce, regardless of a colonial law requiring that all in the jurisdiction be carried out on one ship whenever one sailed. Another occasion for this sort of voyage came from the impounding of enemy property in the French West Indies at the beginning of the war, a measure later relaxed. Expeditions to remove or dispose of the property could be carried on under a flag of truce. Unfortunately for clarity of classification, flag-of-truce ships sometimes seized opportunities to attack enemy vessels.

As before, trade held greater attractions than taking prize

vessels. Rhode Island merchants eagerly continued their accustomed traffic with the French sugar islands. Profits could be enormous for those who eluded wartime perils. In the recent war, Britain had tried to weigh the advantages of injuring the enemy by cutting off supplies of lumber and provisions against the danger of forcing development of alternative sources. The issue had not been resolved, and the officials tended to wink at continuation of the peacetime trade while formally condemning it.

Policy hardened, however, by 1756. Even before Sir William Pitt became the king's first minister and virtual dictator of Great Britain, the choice had been made for all-out war. One result was a genuine policy against colonial trade with the French islands, reinforced by a naval blockade. Another was an embargo on export of provisions from the northern colonies, ordered by Lord Loudoun in 1757 and supported by an act of Parliament. Of wider significance was the Rule of 1756, designed to prevent the French from perforating the blockade by licensing Dutch ships to carry on the commerce normally reserved for the French. In the face of a swarm of privateers, the neutral flag of the Netherlands could confer safety either on trade between France and her islands or, for that matter, between the islands and Dutch Caribbean ports, where sugar products could be exchanged for North American exports. The practice was legitimate under various treaties as well as the old doctrine of international law, that free ships make free goods. The British High Court of Admiralty ruled that a trade which the enemy legally closed off in peacetime could not be opened for wartime purposes and then claim protection under the old doctrine. A neutral ship would be treated as an enemy when it was trading *for*, not just *with*, the enemy. The clarity of the rule was severely mauled in litigation, but the policy remained firm in general terms.

Rhode Island merchants, like those in other northern cities, could not forego the usual commerce. War merely added new hazards and opportunities. Armed vessels could lurk outside French harbors, ready to trade or raid as might seem best. French ships could be seized on the high seas; sometimes the capture was fictitious, a cover for commerce. After enunciation of the Rule of 1756, Dutch ships might be attacked on suspicion of violating it. Even if the suspicion proved unfounded or hard to verify, the ship might be kept as a prize, as a Rhode Island skipper did now and again. Trade could go by way of Dutch Caribbean harbors or the Spanish free port on Hispaniola, Monte Cristi, until Spain became a belligerent. All the old deceptions of the earlier war, of course, came into use again, with the resulting uncertainty of which set of papers and flags found on a captured vessel was the true one. In addition, privateers from different colonies took to raiding each other's shipping on pretense of suspecting violation of wartime regulations or displaying false credentials. By 1761, British authorities were harassing or prosecuting abusers of flags of truce. Amid such risks, profits to the lucky could be huge, but surprisingly often British colonial wares glutted French island markets.

French policy did not cater to British colonials in their efforts to continue peacetime trade, in spite of acknowledging its necessity unofficially. French warships and privateers operated with devastating effect, especially in the Caribbean. In the first half of the war, Frenchmen took three times as many prizes as the British and colonials. The figures were necessarily approximate, what with the fraudulent credentials and the French resort to Dutch or other neutral ships, but Rhode Island losses corroborated the general truth of the enemy's superior success. During 1758, almost a hundred vessels were captured, according to one report; during the whole war, sixty-five from Providence. The figures may well be inaccurate, erring on the high side, but they probably express the basic truth that losses were severe.

The papers were peppered with accounts of the drastic consequences to the merchants, but the moans of the bankrupt should not drown out the cries of the dying mariners or the captives and their families. There is no way of calculating the social effects of the damage to seafaring people during the war, but it may not be farfetched to trace to this source some of the capacity for unrest and violent outbursts in the years just after. It would be feckless to preach that the sufferers faced danger voluntarily and got only what they were ready to give: for them,

Sea Captains Carousing in Surinam, painting by John Greenwood ca. 1758. Tradition in Providence maintains that the two gentlemen conversing at the rear of the table were Esek Hopkins and Nicholas Cooke. The other revelers may also have been from Rhode Island, which had long cultivated trade with Surinam. *The St. Louis Art Museum.*

as for the merchants, stopping trade and tying up the ships was an unthinkable choice of destitution.

The new war in 1754 brought back the political contests—indeed, in unprecedented bitterness—and started again the wrangles over finance. Martial zeal helped revive the Wanton side behind a new captain, Stephen Hopkins. His election as governor in 1755, along with a few partisans, brought a surge of military measures and a new issue of paper money to pay for them. The bills of credit known as "Crown Point" money were new tenor spent directly by the treasury. Like all new tenor, their value was tied to the millstone of old tenor. They frightened the rich, who refused loans to the colony or charged staggering interest. So in 1756 fiscal conservatives forced a new policy of steep taxes, issuance of "lawful money" bills (fiat money pegged to specie), and constant borrowing. The British treasury eased the burden by supplying direct payments in silver and gold to Rhode Island from time to time throughout the war.

Still, the colony plunged deeply into debt. After peace returned, the General Assembly and the citizens faced a need to go on collecting heavy taxes, to sink the old land bank bills (would they never end?), and to pay off the loans to the colony treasury. The emission of 1750, mercifully withered by depreciation, and the "lawful money" bills were refinanced contrary to the spirit and perhaps the letter of parliamentary legislation. As in 1749, so in 1764, a postwar depression made heavy taxes unwise and postponed settlement of wartime accounts. Even with delay, the levies proved cruel, and the various towns tried to use partisan politics to lighten their load by burdening their neighbors. The result was a chaotic state of public finance that put off still longer the inevitable payment for patriotic exertions.

The legacy of political strife and fiscal misery formed only part of the effects of the mid-century wars. Rhode Island had been drawn into the British empire as never before. Its commerce had been subjected to the risks of international conflicts and the confinements, however ineffective, of strategic decisions in Whitehall. Its fiscal autonomy had been nearly abolished. Willingly, for the most part, the citizens accepted the consequences of war—the gamble for gain or loss in privateering, the supply of men to the king's campaigns, the expenses to the colony's treasury. Even the conscription measures provoked no outcry. To be sure, Rhode Island was hit by few demands for seamen to man royal naval vessels. On the contrary, there may have been some truth in charges that the colony furnished a refuge for mariners fleeing the press gangs in Massachusetts. The outcome, however, had been disappointing all the same. Many men were killed, ships sank or fell prey to the enemy, some merchants were ruined. Though a febrile activity gave the appearance of wartime prosperity, and some indeed grew rich quickly, on balance the wars probably cost Rhode Island heavily.

In particular, Newport came out a loser. The damage was subtle as well as obvious. Just before the War of Jenkins' Ear, the town's leading merchants had built up the port to a point where it could enter direct trade with Great Britain and shake off the chronic dependency on Boston. John Bannister retracing the logic of Thomas Richardson a quarter century earlier, in the late 1730s undertook importation of the hardware and textiles that formed the core of imports from the mother country. His hopes were dashed by the vexations he encountered, and he turned eagerly to privateering. He survived his ventures, but some of his colleagues with similar ambitions did not. Several major mercantile firms sank hopelessly into debt as a result of losses at sea. Even Godfrey Malbone, in addition to losing his country house, suffered such reverses that he retired to his estate in Connecticut. Newport remained so dependent on the Caribbean trade that the wars raging there led to unendurable hazards. The surviving merchants, plus a few newcomers like Aaron Lopez, bravely resurrected the old plans for direct trade with London and Bristol, but the best time had passed. More than ever, Newport was at a disadvantage: it had neither the exports of Boston or Philadelphia nor New York's great influx of hard money from the royal treasury to pay for military campaigns. And of course, the old fiscal policy had been jettisoned as inimical to the commercial dealings the town aspired to. Newport had won a place as a full member in the British-American commercial web and found that there were more drawbacks than benefits.

Worse in the immediate sense was the rise of Providence, and to a lesser degree of Bristol. The one cut into Newport's hinterland by taking a great share for itself but otherwise simply duplicated Newport's trade connections. The other stepped into the role of taking big risks, such as capturing a major share of the African slave trade that had begun to figure heavily in the commercial expedients of Newport. Significantly, both rivals aligned themselves with the new political coalition formed by the Wantons, with Stephen Hopkins of Providence becoming so much the leader as to relegate his Newport friends to a secondary place. The days had gone when the Aquidneck men could vie with each other for political advantage, safely drawing in outsiders as need arose without fear of their gaining a great share of power. Moreover, the Narragansett country was on the decline in economic and political strength; it remained attached to Newport interests, but it divided as the capital did and so counted for less and less in politics.

Altogether the mid-century wars had disturbing effects on Rhode Island. Internal division, rivalry over an increasingly constricted commerce, death and debt—such were the consequences of the outpouring of patriotic bellicosity of 1739 to 1763.

12

THE WARD-HOPKINS
CONTROVERSY

Each of the eighteenth-century wars set off a political storm within Rhode Island, but the French and Indian War, the biggest of these conflicts, produced the longest and fiercest partisan strife. Queen Anne's War led to an upheaval in the Cranston administration that achieved its limited effects in one election. King George's War occasioned a conflict that raged a few years and then calmed down. The tempests that began in 1757, however, continued to shake the colony during the 1760s, being subdued at the end of that decade only to produce a few last thunderclaps at the beginning of the American Revolution. This third episode of political turbulence is often referred to as the Ward-Hopkins Controversy in honor of the protagonists of the opposing sides, Samuel Ward of Westerly and Stephen Hopkins of Providence.

The successive wars touched off political conflict in much the same way. They broke the pace of politics-as-usual by spawning military heroes, by opening and then closing opportunities for glory and profit in martial endeavors, by requiring fiscal makeshifts and then further measures to dispose of the resulting debts. Wars snared Rhode Island ever more tightly in the web of imperial policy and thus forced narrower confinements on the legislation to adjust to peace. The wars, however, did not overrule the colony's fundamental goal of economic development that had been the main purpose of government since the days of Governor Cranston. Political quarrels arose over means to reconcile the long-range policy with measures to deal with the short-range effects of the wars.

The Ward-Hopkins Controversy differed from earlier political storms not only because the French and Indian War was bigger than earlier wars, but also because the Newport patriciate could no longer keep a firm grasp on government while carrying on its internal squabbles over policies and their proceeds. Ironically, the goal of the old developmental plans had been achieved so well that the northern part of the province had grown populous and prosperous, eager for a say in public business. The political system of the colony gave no protection to the old commercial leaders and their Narragansett friends and relations. Power had to be won and kept by votes, and in elections one freeman counted as much as another. The contests within Newport inexorably expanded as each side courted support in other towns. In King George's War this practice resulted in one side backing a Warwick man, William Greene, for governor and electing him repeatedly. By the French and Indian War, the old Wanton side became so dependent on northern votes as to become a tail on the Providence kite.

These developments broke the old equation between the proper aims of the colonial government and advancing the commerce of Newport. Providence would not be content as a satellite port. It still was less than half the size of its rival, both in population and wealth, so could do no better than leap at the chance to become the dominant partner in an alliance with the weaker side in Newport. Under these conditions, who would set the course in legislation? What interests were to be served? Suddenly there was an outburst of ingenuity in devising political organizations to gather the power to answer these questions. The old rivals of the 1740s readied for combat again, but changed themselves almost beyond recognition as they struggled for advantage. Both sides built elaborate networks of agents under the direction of informal central committees to angle for every possible vote in every town. Both therefore had to heed the wishes of all the towns, rendering still muddier the alignment of parties with interests.

Partisan rivalry took on a life of its own that dismayed the leaders of the opposing sides. When the battle began early in the French and Indian War, there could be fairly simple contests over patronage and opportunities to profit from military activities. When peace returned, however, with the usual depression and puzzle of how to pay public debts, there proved to be no easy way to frame clear partisan proposals on the major questions of currency and finance. The best that could be done with these problems was to treat tax laws as a branch of the patronage system, by adjusting assessment and apportionment to reward the faithful. Deeper issues were less successfully geared to party contests. Most obviously, the two sides could keep only rough internal concord on the currency, as both were beset by genuine disagreements over the best course to take as well as by the clamors of special interests. The leaders dared not dismantle the party machines and worked them harder than ever. The anguish and lamentation of the chieftains in private and public were not insincere. They feared they had created monsters.

Actually, they had set up parties that in many vital respects were precursors of the Federalists and Republicans, because they were designed to operate under similar conditions. The goal was to gather enough local interests to make a winning combination to direct public affairs for a body politic with widely distributed voting rights and without a dominant class or interest group that could dictate the aims of government. The Rhode Island organizations foreshadowed those of later generations in technique—internal structure, use of the press, the base in a central legislature, and zeal to win every vote while relying on coalitions between a few regions to form the core of party strength. The Rhode Island parties in the times of Ward and Hopkins, however, lacked the means to formulate a full array of alternative proposals to put before the citizens, and so poured an inordinate share of their energies into the mere contest to win and distribute the modest benefits the General Assembly could bestow.

The Rhode Island leaders did not like to think they were contriving a method of political organization, however. They shared the eighteenth-century beliefs that combinations of men organized to gain office inevitably sought private rewards at the expense of the general welfare, that governmental policy was formed for the general good when it was designed by gentlemen who were able to set personal wishes aside. In the throes of party battles the leaders had to justify themselves by bemoaning partisan strife as a loathsome disease of the body politic and by denouncing their opponents as causes of the malady, schemers who had to be stopped by heroic counter-measures. At most, the leaders would avow what everyone in Rhode Island knew, that the southern towns leaned toward Ward and the northern ones leaned toward Hopkins. It was more satisfactory still to belittle the contest as a personal feud that had run out of control. There was no denying that the struggle, in addition to its other traits—a division in Newport, the challenge of Providence to the old elite, a battle over fiscal policy, and an engrossing new kind of political game—was a personal rivalry, indeed one of epic proportions.

Of the two champions, Ward, in retrospect appears the more appealing man. His personal integrity, friendly disposition, boldness, buoyancy, and sharp mind were combined with magnetism and keen political instincts. He was born into a Newport family that consistently bred intelligence and a nose for politics—at least down to his great-grandchildren, the lobbyist Sam Ward and his sister Julia who wrote "The Battle Hymn of the Republic." The Wards also had a Hapsburgian flair for marriage. Prolific, they found mates in other prolific and intelligent families. In Samuel Ward's day they had numerous connections with the Greenes of Warwick and the Rays of Block Island, as well as the Freebodys, Flaggs, and Vernons of Newport. Samuel married Anna Ray and went to live on land in Westerly that he acquired from her father. There he kept a shop part-time and raised sheep and cattle as well as a large and affectionate family. Though two of his brothers successively held their father's position as secretary of Rhode Island, neither sought to move up to the governor's chair. Instead, even before the death of Governor William Greene they had marked out Samuel as the next candidate for that office. Comparatively inexperienced—he had served in public office only by taking a few terms as deputy from Westerly—he stepped into the role of leader at the age of thirty-three as though he had long prepared for it.

Hopkins by contrast had worked his way up to fitness for high positions. Eighteen years older than Ward, he had begun his life in that part of rural Providence that was set off as the town of Scituate in 1731 and sent him to the Assembly a year later. Soon prominent in public life, he moved to Providence in 1742 to try his hand at commerce and law. He did quite well. He had an appetite for reading good books and when fairly young paid visits to the Philosophical Club in Newport. Later he led the way in forming a small public library in Providence. He was particularly fond of the writings of Jonathan Swift, but he gained a broader acquaintance with literature and history than all but the most bookish Rhode Islanders. Though he remained less than a polished gentleman, he had a tough and well-trained mind. In public affairs he distinguished himself first by a zeal for system in the colonial government, next by his grasp of law and finance. He added an urge to clarify and regulate Rhode Island's place in the British empire, first made evident when he attended the Albany conference and worked on reconciling the colony's currency to imperial regulations. Hopkins, however, could also get steamed up over quarrels and stray into dealings that exposed him to charges of corruption. Perhaps because of accidental lack of evidence, the record reveals nothing in his life to match the genial relations within the Ward family. Hopkins commanded devotion and respect rather than affection.

The two men entered their contest in 1757, when Ward, backing William Greene, wrote a pamphlet against Hopkins, who was a candidate for reelection as governor. Besides charging Hopkins with high-handedness during the previous two years, the pamphlet accused him of corruption—finding ways to get money in his own pockets and giving lucrative positions to his sons. Hopkins rushed to court accusing Ward of libel and demanding £20,000 damages. After sparring over where an impartial trial could be held, the two sides settled on Worcester, Massachusetts. Hopkins lost, appealed, but dropped the appeal and paid court costs, fuming about vengeance.

He also lost the election to Greene, but when the old gentleman died in office, the Assembly selected Hopkins to take his place. He held it for four years, then lost to Ward in 1762, again in 1765 and 1766, but came back for one last term the next year. After that the two sides joined in a coalition slate under the respected Josias Lyndon, who weakly allowed the Ward majority in the House of Deputies to take charge. Furious, the Hopkins faction refused to support Lyndon a second time, and he stood as the Ward candidate—and lost. For several years afterwards with Joseph Wanton of Newport as governor, the Hopkins forces enjoyed secure dominance, rendered palatable to the opposition by a few concessions. The two arch-rivals had stepped aside to tone down a political feud that all deplored, but none would stop.

To back the protagonists, their friends formed political parties. These organizations operated with ruthlessness, ingenuity, and unbridled zeal comparable to the best—or worst—machines of the nineteenth century. They stopped at nothing short of murder to raise the total vote for their candidates and reduce the tally for the opponents. Though both sides sought support everywhere in the province, each one found it steadily in certain areas and certain elements in the population.

The geographical pattern of support was fairly clear. Hopkins obviously had his greatest strength in Providence and the northern towns, although he also had the sizable Wanton following in Newport, a surprising number of friends in the other island towns, and some in all the rest. Ward ordinarily came out ahead in the southern towns, but he had a few bastions in the vicinity of Providence and at least a sprinkling of partisans everywhere. A few towns shifted back and forth; naturally, they received the most lavish and expensive attention from the party captains.

The two parties did not attract voters of distinct occupational groups or different levels of wealth, however. There were merchants, tradesmen, shopkeepers, great landowners, and humble farmers in both camps. In towns where precise reckonings can be made, it is clear that the two parties attracted virtually identical assortments of citizens as determined by taxable wealth.

One can discover purely accidental affiliations—perhaps the result of individual interests, friendship, spite, kinship, or unalloyed zeal. Surprisingly, however, the best general rule after the geographical was religious: Hopkins enjoyed favor among Quakers (in a very diluted way he had been one), Anglicans, and some varieties of Baptist; Ward, who was a Sabbatarian, could count on most of the other kinds of Baptists and the Congregationalists. Even these religious lines were blurred, but in general it would be fair to say that the denominations least affected by the Great Awakening were the best sources of Hopkins men. Unhappily, no one has ever figured out a significance for this generalization.

Even with the geographical and religious patterns of support established, they do not explain the obvious passions focused on the question of whether Ward or Hopkins was to be elected governor. What could Hopkins do for Providence or the Quakers and Anglicans? What could Ward do for his followers? The office of governor carried little power, having neither a veto over legislation nor a control of patronage, except for the naval officer. (By custom that gentleman split his fees with the deputy governor, who otherwise got next to nothing for serving the public.) The governor's former function of chief justice had been consigned to an officer chosen by the General Assembly. In fact, that body designated all the other judges as well and indeed all but one of the appointive officials of the colony government. The governor's discretion was small even in war, when he acted only as the head of a council of war consisting of the magistrates and some military men. Little by little the gubernatorial role had shrunk severely since the days of Samuel Cranston. About all that Ward or Hopkins could look forward to was conducting official correspondence, presiding over the House of Magistrates, and signing dozens of commissions for the appointive officials.

Why did the rivals want to be governor? The post was not even lucrative. In addition to a small salary there was a substantial income from fees for signing those commissions and performing a few similar duties. Extralegal advantages surely existed—gratuities for flag-of-truce commissions in time of war, perhaps some tokens of recognition by businessmen who appreciated the governor's role in fending off rigid application of British trade laws. Ward accused Hopkins of lust for personal gain, probably with some reason. Even so, the profits of office could not have been great. Compared with Britain or even Massachusetts, Rhode Island rewarded her public servants meagerly, whether in salaries, fees, or graft. The colony's secretary probably got the most. Surely a job like that of governor was nothing to seek by prodigious organization, bribery, and skulduggery of the most extravagant sort.

Obviously there was more to the ardent rivalry and furious partisan machinations than capturing the office of governor. Hopkins and Ward stood as the heads of opposing slates. If the governor alone had little power, that was because the Assembly had nearly all of it: the object was to put one team or another into a majority in both houses. The head of the ticket served as political leader and the symbol of the whole list. A majority in the Assembly could reward the faithful with offices—the many prestigious positions of military officers or justices of the peace, the few lucrative positions of court clerk or sheriff, the powerful positions on the bench. A majority could determine expenditures on roads and bridges; it could shift tax burdens to towns that voted for the opposition; it could favor one economic interest or another, although that proved difficult in most respects.

Of the spoils for the victors after the French and Indian War, few were as easily obtained as patronage. Such was the rivalry that both sides had partisans in every town and had to reward them in the aftermath of triumph at the polls. No longer could the colony afford to aid public works, however. Instead, the Hopkins side promiscuously granted franchises for lotteries to raise the funds the treasury could not give. Ward's friends just as impartially granted none. It was hard to find a boon that a party could confer on its loyal followers that would stay conferred and would not benefit everyone else at the same time. One reward was the location of the colony's college, which the Hopkins forces planted firmly in Providence. They looked ahead to the institution attracting business and influence to the town. Another was permission to establish an ironworks. The legal authorization was needed to dam a river and flood the nearby land upstream to get water power. The Ward side waged a long but vain struggle to

"*A* S.W. *view of the* College *in* Providence *together with the* president's house & gardens," engraving by S. Hill after a drawing by D. Leonard. The college building, now University Hall of Brown University, was constructed in 1770–1771, following a design modeled (by Joseph Brown and others) on Nassau Hall of Princeton University. *The Rhode Island Historical Society.*

Joseph Brown house on South Main Street in Providence, designed by the owner in 1774. This drawing shows the original steps. Burgeoning wealth brought urban elegance to Roger Williams' town. *The Rhode Island Historical Society.*

protect the Greene family enterprise from competition financed by Hopkins and his Providence friends. If the spoils were few and mostly ephemeral or trifling, they still kept the partisans fighting feverishly.

Of greater moment were the battles over the interlocking policies on taxation and the currency. In these controversies, party platforms were hazy at best, and party lines did not always hold firm, partly because there were more than two points of view and partly because Newport fiscal conservatives disagreed on the best way to achieve their ends. Still, in spite of the cross-currents, the most substantial conflict between the Ward and Hopkins factions concerned public finance. The legacy of the land banks had to be disposed of, and so did the debts run up in the French and Indian War. Any plan to distribute these burdens on the body politic necessarily became political tinder, ready to burst into flame. Everyone wanted to throw the weight on someone else. To make things worse, Newport commerce was ailing. If the old political conditions had prevailed, governmental policy would have been designed to cure the patient; if the old economic conditions had prevailed, the remedy would have produced few side-effects. In the 1760s, unhappily, the malady called for powerful medication, and the rest of the colony had the political strength to resist suffering the treatment.

Until the last years of the French and Indian War there was no quarrel over finance. The Ward and Hopkins measures were essentially alike, footing the bills by a combination of borrowing, taxing, and issuing treasury bills redeemable in silver or gold as short-term credits. Payments from the royal treasury allowed fairly prompt retirement of the colony's new paper. As the war ended, the debts had to be paid and measures taken to ensure a medium of exchange. Neither side proposed flouting the parliamentary prohibition on the old types of paper, but whatever the Assembly might do would favor some interests at the expense of others. It was impossible to please everyone.

Even so, some action was necessary. Chaos overtook the currency situation, portending paralysis in trade. The "lawful" bills had retained their face value and so were hoarded rather than put into circulation. By contrast the bills of the last land bank (1750) had depreciated in spite of the original legislation designed to keep them at face value in silver. There was also a lot of older paper money still in circulation, less valuable than ever, but gradually being retired. Thus a frightening currency shortage loomed in the months ahead.

The future was not the only thing to worry about, however. Debtors refused to pay lenders, cheerfully offering interest on overdue loans in the happy expectation that the cost would be more than offset by the depreciation of the paper money. More ominous still was an intricate money market that developed to make life hard in 1762 and 1763. Clever men could take advantage of regulations on retiring the old bills by making a couple of exchanges, ending with old paper that they could turn over to the treasury at a fair profit. Cagey lenders could insist on repayments that would then be enhanced through such transactions. Prudent men, moreover, had some time earlier begun stipulating in notes and contracts that payments must be made in the silver value of the paper money at the time the agreement was struck, whatever depreciation might do to lessen the value of money mentioned in the note or contract before payment fell due. Careless men neglected such precautions and then seeing the folly too late charged fraud or refused to accept payments in depreciated money. Money-lending or speculation in currencies offered so many attractions that capital threatened to go out of commerce and into financial manipulations. The colony's basic economy could not endure such a shift.

The two political parties cautiously approached this ominous situation. Hopkins presently championed an evenhanded policy of converting all the currency to a single standard backed by bullion and of stabilizing private debts according to the depreciation of the paper money as fixed by a standard scale. His forces eventually carried this policy into law, but not completely so until after a bitter fight over the related question of how to bring in the necessary revenue by taxation. Hopkins was lucky to have fairness beneficial to his backers.

The Ward side, by contrast, failed to develop a plan it could offer to the voters, whether because the leaders could not agree among themselves or because they wanted to aid Newport with measures the rural followers abhorred. When they held power, their wrangles mainly served to delay solution of the fiscal problems and prolong the fight over taxation. Ward's intimates had at heart the interests of the Newport mercantile and financial community, which they wanted to serve by tax benefits and painless retirement of the old paper money, possibly by transforming it and the war debt into interest-bearing securities of stable value. There were insinuations in the *Newport Mercury* that one plan called for restoring the 1750 bills to their original value in silver. Such a scheme would drop a windfall profit on those who had the bills, thought to be mainly in the hands of Newport financiers, and threaten ruin to the rural landowners who had originally borrowed the money from the treasury and had been counting on paying it back in depreciated value. It seems unthinkable, however, that a politician and rural land-owner like Ward could have contemplated backing this scheme. Nevertheless, his side seriously believed that the soundness of Newport commercial life was the key to the colony's economic welfare and desperately needed some support.

This consideration justified a certain amount of manipulation to roll back depreciation of the bills held by the mercantile community. Traders, it was argued, had constantly lost as the value of bills in their hands declined. There was no way to determine, however, what was a reasonable advantage for them that would not work horrendous damage to the interests of other people in the colony. Excitement raged in 1762 and 1763 until the Hopkins forces, once again in control, put through their measure.

Amazingly, the political heirs of the Wantons went over to hard money and stable values. The currency act of 1763 returned Rhode Island to the standard of current money of New England as set up in seventeenth-century Massachusetts—that is, to a silver standard one-third below sterling. The law set forth a long table of values for the different coins then in use—English shillings, Spanish dollars and pistoles, and many more. Another table specified the conversion of old tenor (and by a simple formula, new tenor) to the new single standard for each year since 1750. Thus any debt in old tenor that had fallen due and had not been paid could be discharged only by paying the value of the money when it fell due (plus 6 percent annual interest while in arrears) in whatever lawful money the debtor could come up with. The Assembly soon added a law to encourage early repayment of the loans that had floated the emission of 1750 and declared all the bills thus floated redeemable in silver at the colony's treasury, the amount of silver adjusted according to the current rate of depreciation.

The taxation controversy followed almost inevitably and became the overt partisan conflict springing from the fiscal agonies. The colony needed revenue to meet daily expenses and to uphold or retire old issues of paper money, as well as to pay the war debt. Taxation hit Rhode Island along with a stagnation of trade and a fresh crop of bankruptcies. There had already been trouble over taxes. During the recent war, Newport had balked at paying taxes because of high losses at sea. So had several other towns in Ward territory, but they were rural, mainly in the Narragansett country. If revenue was to be collected, the towns would have to be deprived of pretexts for bringing in less than the amount expected of them. The amounts had been stipulated by the General Assembly, so any revision became a political issue.

An effort to reach a fair reapportionment by eluding partisan pressures did not succeed, although both sides ostensibly favored it. To gain information needed for an equitable distribution of the tax burden the Assembly in 1761, when the magistrates had a Hopkins majority and the deputies a Ward majority, started a comprehensive reassessment of property. The Assembly appointed two assessors for each town, to join with two chosen by the town, to appraise all the property there. The resulting lists were sent to the Assembly to serve as the basis for subsequent apportionment of taxes among the towns. Seemingly beyond reproach, this procedure was not as fair as it looked because different types of property were to be assessed at various rates for computing tax obligations. Woodlands, like cargoes and vessels at sea, were reckoned at one-third actual value, money and commercial stocks at one-half, improved real estate at three-fifths, livestock and slaves at full value. This pattern favored trade and the northern country towns against the Narragansett country. Thus, the reapportionment reflected the wishes of the Hopkins side, including its vital component of mercantile interests in Bristol and the Wanton crowd in Newport.

When the Ward forces gained complete control in 1765, they undid the new apportionment and made one to suit themselves. They lightened the load on five loyal Narragansett towns by ten percent and piled the cost not on all, but on three Hopkins bastions: Cumberland, Scituate, and Providence. These northern towns then refused to pay on the grounds that the apportionment gave them unfair burdens. They vowed to resist legal actions to compel payment and looked toward the next election for redress. The Ward forces in the Assembly sued the three towns in 1766 but took no action against Newport, which had not paid either, or six other Ward towns that had paid only part of their assessed taxes. Attempts to use partisan power to rig the apportionment only produced a tax revolt.

With the return of Hopkins in 1767, the suits were dropped and the apportionment of 1761 resumed. What the three northern towns had been charged in excess of the amounts in that list was then (in a gesture of partisan recrimination) demanded of the towns that had paid less—plus interest. The Assembly, however, launched a new appraisal of property and altered the valuation system for tax purposes, declaring that all categories should be entered at full value except for manufacturing plants, which would be included at three-quarters, and vessels and cargoes at sea, which would be enumerated at two-thirds.

Even these modifications did not take taxation out of politics. Only when the Hopkins side settled into unchallenged power in 1770 did the controversy stop. If the apportionment as finally arranged was not fair beyond all question, at least it had some basis in knowledge of how the wealth was distributed. The Ward side had used guesswork. The determination of how to reckon the wealth for tax purposes, moreover, gave only moderate advantages to commerce and manufacturing, advantages that could be defended as beneficial to the public.

The tax revolt, combined with other public tumults to be

investigated later, delayed the orderly conversion to hard money currency. Once the Hopkins side won its sure grip on the government in 1769 and quelled the revolt, it turned again to fiscal matters. At last the General Assembly voted old tenor money into the grave. It was to be turned in to the colony's treasurer by the end of 1770; any left outstanding after June 30, 1771, would be worthless as far as Rhode Island was concerned. Those who brought the bills to the treasurer, however, would receive notes in the new lawful money (six shillings for £8 old tenor) to be redeemed in one year—or if later, to receive 6 percent interest beginning on January 1, 1772. Soon the receipts from a few stiff taxes made it possible to discharge in silver or gold both these notes and the older ones that had been issued to stall off meeting the old war debts. Only coin or bullion would be legal tender. Thus by 1772 Rhode Island was firmly on the way back to a hard money system.

The conversion, so long delayed and done without solicitude for Newport's ailing business world and its old hinterland, marked the victory of the Hopkins forces. Yet the victory was not merely partisan. The men in Newport who had opposed paper money for years, if they were still alive, had been backing Ward for the most part. They finally had their way in broad terms—and with Wanton backing. The painstaking officials who had spent years unraveling the snarls of land banks had been on both sides or relatively aloof from partisan contests. The main elements in the new fiscal policy were what many Ward men had long said they wanted. The fight had been over adjustment of taxation and refinancing the currency to serve different interests. Technical though the differences may seem, they were important enough to recruit vast energies in the contest.

Moreover, the rivalry of Ward and Hopkins was carried along by its own momentum. To a degree it was "pure" politics—combat for the sake of combat. This element was manifest in the almost haphazard affiliations of prominent men. Some descendants of William Harris in the vicinity of Providence resurrected their progenitor's habit of relying on Newport allies and became Ward stalwarts. So did Elisha Brown, who had fattened on public contracts under the Greene administration until his

Brick Market House at the head of Long Wharf in Newport, designed by Peter Harrison in 1761, completed in 1772. *Library of Congress.*

accounts came under scrutiny and settlement drove him into bankruptcy. The rivalry of the Wards and Wantons was a feud of long-standing; it can be traced to 1714, although it had run thin at times since then. Families were divided at random: if Elisha Brown was a Ward chieftain and gained the separation of North Providence from Providence to give him a political base, his nephews were the finance committee of the Hopkins forces. Even an occasional Wanton favored Ward. Some towns near Providence often leaned to Ward; some near Newport occasionally toward Hopkins. Obviously, underlying issues were far from overwhelming.

There were even limits to the scope of partisan conflict. The offices of attorney general and treasurer of the colony were usually left aside, even though both officials were elected by the voters along with the magistrates. Also the office of secretary proved beyond Hopkins' reach, although it was occupied by one brother of Samuel Ward, who was replaced at his death by another. The secretary wielded as much influence as the governor, but Hopkins could never summon enough votes to turn out Henry Ward.

The opposing parties waged their campaigns with vigor and cash to pile up the vital majorities in elections. Candidates and their backers made speeches, printed broadside appeals, and inspired useful items in the newspapers. The Hopkins side helped launch the *Providence Gazette* to gain an outlet for its views. The political managers treated voters with food and drink. They hired men either to earn their gratitude when the ballots (known as "proxes") were cast or to keep them busy when the voting was in progress. They rigged spurious land transactions to get poor men admitted to the suffrage. They paid the undecided to vote for their own slate and paid the dedicated opponents not to vote at all. To make sure that those who had been bought stayed bought and to discover when partisan clerks falsified their reports, the managers watched in every town as the proxes were presented and kept lists that they checked with the totals later revealed in the count.

The party managers had to control the slates of candidates with care. The lower house of the General Assembly, composed of deputies chosen by the various towns, posed one sort of problem. Sometimes it was possible to persuade a popular opponent (by cash) to abandon aspirations to office. Ordinarily, the object was to capture as many as possible of the towns that were susceptible to suasion of the various kinds. The governor, deputy governor, magistrates, and a few executive officials were elected by the voters at large. The party slate had to be known to all the freemen. For this purpose the rival captains printed proxes to distribute, so that the voter could simply use one as his ballot. The party chiefs also printed deceptive proxes, however, to trick the freemen. For instance, the entire Hopkins slate from deputy governor down might be printed under the name of Samuel Ward; the phony proxes would then be distributed in places where Ward was the favorite in the hope of garnering a few votes for the rest of the Hopkins candidates.

When the town returns were gathered at Newport for the official tally, the worst wrangles came from the custom of determining the totals at a joint session of the newly elected deputies and the previous year's magistrates. If a turnover was in the offing, the magistrates resisted. The two sides would investigate allegations of fraud, with a view to reducing the opposing votes, but in the end sheer physical control of the proxes generally was crucial. Proving fraud of some kinds or preventing tampering could be done only by the officials who had the proxes. On one memorable occasion in 1761, the governor and council had control of the ballots and held off the count until the pro-Ward deputies backed down from their highly arguable assertion that the magistrates should not rule on their own reelections. Then a bipartisan committee performed the count and found the Hopkins slate victorious by a small margin.

The zest for all this electioneering fed on itself at least as much as on the hope of reward. Major questions of fiscal policy, plus lesser ones like locating the college and authorizing an ironworks, were indeed resolved through partisan contests—and usually resolved in the interests of Providence. The parties fought, however, over many other things mainly to strengthen their own power at the elections. The faithful had to be rewarded; recruits had to receive enlistment bonuses. Hundreds of offices could change hands when one side threw out the other, yet the vast majority were positions yielding more prestige than profit and conferring little power to further partisan aims in the conduct of government—in short, these offices were mostly pure rewards for loyal men. Likewise the boons bestowed by the General Assembly on individuals and communities had little or nothing to do with other goals of the party that backed them except to encourage support at the next election.

Perhaps the ceaseless scramble for patronage and local benefits can shed some light on the surprisingly low totals in the votes. Partisan fever raged in some citizens, while others remained immune. Only about half the eligible men cast proxes. The fraction varied from 54 percent to 34 percent, according to one estimate, reaching a peak in 1765, when 4,349 eligible men voted. Some of the rest were kept away by bribes, jobs, or other inducements; some were away at sea. These absent ones were partly offset by men who were declared eligible by fraud. Still, many must have stayed home voluntarily on election day. Possibly the rivalry for patronage seemed the main ingredient in the controversy to them, and they either did not want or could not hope to get the rewards.

All the same, the excitement of the Ward-Hopkins rivalry had a vital function even if it did not clearly settle many controversies over public policy. Petty patronage and lottery franchises, centralized management of campaigns and networks of communication, even dirty tricks and systematic bribery—all brought a new species of order to political life when the old order was crumbling. The days had passed when the welfare of Newport commerce was a sufficient goal of wise policy, when the Newport patriciate could argue among itself what would best serve the trading interests. The challenge of Providence offered no radical notion of what was good for Rhode Island; it merely provoked rather special conflicts over application of the traditional policies aimed at economic development. Even so, this distortion of long-standing guide lines was enough, especially at a time when imperial policy was throttling the discretion of the colony's government, to subvert the old pattern of political action. By doing that, the Providence challenge enlivened all sorts of individual and local aspirations. By means of the vote, they could all clamor for attention. Political parties dealt with these interests so as to harness them to two organizations instead of leaving a haphazard and fluid swarm of claimants that would prevent any consistent policy by reckless vying for governmental favor.

This function of party rivalry provides the key to several mysteries of the Ward-Hopkins Controversy: the triviality of much that the two sides fought over, the apathy of half the electorate in the face of burning passions enflaming the other half, the absence of class conflicts, the rarity of sharp shifts in policy when one team turned out the other. Hemmed in by imperial regulations, the major decisions on fiscal policy could not range far beyond technical adjustments in tax assessment and currency redemption—and yet led to tax revolts. The opposing forces went to great lengths in drumming up support, yet they could not stir up the voters by planning dramatic changes in law. Nor did the two parties have a deep philosophical disagreement over how government should act; they differed on whose interests should be served. Accordingly, the strife seemed at the same time all-important and disgraceful to those who waged the party battles. They were not really hypocrites when they lamented the fight and kept on fighting.

The narrow range of political choice in the Ward-Hopkins rivalry was nowhere more obvious than in response to imperial requirements and the controversies that led up to the American Revolution. The two sides behaved in virtually the same fashion in raising troops to fight in the French and Indian War. They could no longer disagree over war finance; they could contest only certain aspects of the postwar measures to pay the debts. But when the Royal Navy began to patrol Newport harbor and Narragansett Bay, when Parliament tried to impose taxes on the colonies, for a solid dozen years the opposing parties agreed completely on resistance and vied only for patriotic credit. At most the partisans debated the ideal condition of ties to the empire and tried fecklessly to besmirch each other with accusations of embracing enthusiasts for submission. Ultimately Tories emerged in both parties, while Samuel Ward and Stephen Hopkins in reasonable amity went off to Philadelphia to speak for Rhode Island in the Continental Congress.

13

TOWARD TWO
INDEPENDENCE DAYS

While Rhode Island writhed in the mingled agonies and thrills of the Ward-Hopkins Controversy, it was also being wracked by the series of disputes over British imperial government that led to the American Revolution. The two dramas were not wholly unrelated, but they had few connections because the political parties within the province agreed substantially on fierce resistance to the new policies of the king's ministers. Internal contests raged over local matters and over the means to meet British requirements (in war and public finance) that had been made in London and accepted in Newport before 1763. When new demands arrived for confinement of Rhode Island trade and submission to direct taxation, acquiescence seemed intolerable to both colonial parties.* Only by 1775 did the leaders manifest a serious difference: Ward was for more vigorous steps, soon for pushing ahead to independence; Hopkins proceeded more cautiously, willing to delay independence if that was necessary to build a solid union among the colonies. Hopkins' thoughts on the place of Rhode Island in the British empire, long maturing, led him to see the formation of the United States as essential to his province's welfare. To his embarrassment some of his Newport backers followed similar reasoning to the conclusion that a

---

* Both parties, to be sure, contained in 1765 members of the Newport Junto, the little coterie of high Tories who were driven into exile or silence for advocating submission to the Stamp Act.

complete break with the mother country would be worse for the colony than reconciliation on distasteful terms.

As events unfolded in the drama of colonial resistance to British rule, Rhode Island played a distinctive part. Although people in the province sometimes echoed protests of other Americans against measures to control the interior of the continent, to make colonial judges serve at the king's pleasure, or to quarter redcoats in nearby colonies, these subjects were of no local concern and aroused little ardor. It was another matter when the wartime naval guard on the Atlantic coast in 1763 turned into a peacetime patrol designed to restrain commerce rigidly to channels approved by parliamentary laws, to compel payment of import duties, and soon to harass fundamentally legal shipping by peremptory searches and quixotic enforcement of impractical quirks in the statutes that had long been overlooked. Against this patrol, Rhode Island fought back with violence sooner and oftener than other commercial colonies.

Next, the British efforts to tax the Americans drew sharp resistance in Rhode Island as in other colonies. During the first dispute over taxes, the crisis over the Sugar Act and the Stamp Act, men in Providence and Newport penned the most significant argument over imperial relations that their colony produced. Though some questions were left hanging, though Stephen Hopkins displayed remarkable willingness to contemplate a role for Parliament in Rhode Island affairs, the exchange of views and insults had the effect of underscoring the traditional conviction that the charter guaranteed virtually complete autonomy under the Crown. If Hopkins was circumspect in his analysis of the situation, another Providence man was perhaps the first American in his era to question the validity of the old British trade laws. Whatever the results of the pamphlet duel, Rhode Island was second to none in repudiating the Stamp Act in every respect. Thereafter, the province's response to British taxation was less principled and decisive, but the colony was prepared to see in the British reaction to the Boston Tea Party, particularly in Parliament's attempt to change the government of Massachusetts, a threat to charter privileges that had to be met with implacable opposition and a solid union of the colonies.

Until that climactic episode began, Rhode Island more than the other provinces, had the naval patrol to preserve awareness that an ominous new turn had been taken in British imperial government. In 1763 Parliament authorized the Royal Navy to seize goods and vessels under the British flag along the coast to determine whether they were violating the trade laws. Soon ships were stationed in the major ports. The patrol ship *Squirrel* arrived in Newport before the end of the year, inaugurating a new era of acrimony. Before, during, and after the more famous controversies over taxation, Rhode Island sparred with the Royal Navy over the conduct of the patrol.

Rhode Islanders rightly saw in the patrol an abrupt change in policy, in particular an attack on existing means to make imperial regulation of commerce ineffective. For years the colony, perhaps rather better than the others, had staved off the king's power. The locally appointed naval officer exercised more supervision over commerce than the royal customs men did. After the initial quarrels, Rhode Island accepted the admiralty judges commissioned in London; these men could be tamed by influence over their selection and replacement, by pressure, and by rewarding an amiable deportment with pleasant company— and perhaps investment opportunities and bribes as well. The judges had their uses: their tribunals gave swift and reasonably fair settlements of the many conflicts cropping up in commerce, such as disputes over seamen's wages or the division of profits or costs between investors in ships and cargoes. It was better to have disagreements adjudicated promptly and get on with business than to extract the last shilling of advantage by a protracted suit in the colony's own courts. There had been little commerce to create friction with imperial authorities between the fracas over pirates and the passage of the Molasses Act in 1733. Even after that, trouble had been averted by the informal British policy of indulging importation of foreign molasses without payment of the statutory duty of six pence per gallon. Colony and mother country alike could see the mutual benefit in that trade.

The shift of policy, of course, began in the war with attempts to distress France by depriving her sugar islands of their accustomed imports from North America, but it was still a surprise when peace brought no return to the old ways. The new policy even caught the admiralty judges and the local customs officials off guard. These men had been inured to overlooking nonobservance of the Molasses Act, their consciences assuaged by annual gratuities from the merchants and a few decorous subterfuges, such as accepting false papers declaring foreign molasses to be of British sources or to be far less in quantity than it actually was. The British customs commissioners placed a notice in the *Newport Mercury* on March 19, 1764, announcing that they had heard of such "compositions" to evade the law and asking anyone who had knowledge of such practices to report them to the appropriate authorities. Perhaps the local men blushed, but no one exposed them.

Rather the patrol ships began their notorious attempts, partly to enforce the trade laws and partly to intimidate the seafaring community, and found a curious reluctance on the part of the local customs officials to lend a hand. Instead there was a stream of inflammatory incidents.

Soon after the *Squirrel* arrived, another royal vessel, the schooner *St. John*, appeared in port. Her captain, Lieutenant Thomas Hill, chased after a cargo of sugar landed illegally on the east side of Aquidneck, getting the sugar and later the *Basto*, the offending brig that had brought it. He reloaded the sugar on the brig and took them back to Newport, where he was arrested on complaint of the brig's captain while the customs collector, to Hill's astonishment, reseized the brig and cargo on the ground that the naval commander was not qualified to make the seizure. While Hill was in Boston to check up on his authority by asking a higher customs official, an event occurred that was explained in two different ways. According to Hill his junior officers sent a party to capture a deserter in Newport. Some townsfolk rescued the deserter, took the officer of the party captive, stoned the rest, and threatened worse. Later a sloop approached the *St. John*, seemingly to convey a belligerent boarding party. Aid by the *Squirrel* prevented an assault, so the Newporters headed back for the docks. But soon they had obtained an authorization from two members of the governor's council to the gunner at the fort in the harbor to bombard the *St. John* in order to prevent her from moving out of port. Cheered on by the crowd of townsmen, the gunner fired eight balls, one going through the mainsail, even though a lieutenant from the *Squirrel* ordered the gunner to desist. The *St. John* slipped under the cover of the *Squirrel*'s twenty-two guns, half trained on the fort. The bombardment ceased. The next day the *Squirrel*'s commander remonstrated with the colonial officials, who retorted "that the gunner had acted by authority, and that they would answer for it, when they thought it necessary." The officials' view was that the incident arose over thefts committed by three of the *St. John*'s crew on shore. One had been arrested, but a peace officer had been unable to persuade the naval officers to give him custody of the other two. Just before the bombardment some colonial officials approached an officer aboard the *Squirrel* to explain this grievance; that man said the offenders would be handed over, but apparently they were not. This incident was only the first in a long series.

A few months later a new naval ship, the *Maidstone*, arrived at Newport. In the spring of 1765, her captain, Charles Antrobus, sent an impressment party to find men to fill the crew. According to Governor Ward, the *Maidstone*'s men harassed fishing boats bringing their catch to market, carried off a man from a wood boat entering the harbor, and ultimately seized the entire crew of a brigantine arriving from Jamaica. Ward demanded release of the impressed men; Antrobus declined; a Newport mob seized a subordinate officer, Lieutenant Jenkins, and burned one of the *Maidstone*'s boats in June. Ward pressed his protest, asserting that when in port the naval vessels were subject to the colony's laws, not above them. After further exchanges of hot words and messages, Antrobus released the men. Ward replied to charges that his government had been behind the fracas by saying that the boat had been burnt by persons who were "of the dregs of the people, and a number of boys and Negroes." It may not have been incidental that the *Maidstone* under Lieutenant Jenkins the previous March had seized two vessels for running molasses into Providence illegally. The admiralty judge and his court advocate systematically thwarted Jenkins and the customs officers in their efforts to prosecute the offending vessels. In fact, the controversy over local men, ostensibly in the king's service, obstructing the other royal officials dragged on for two years, when it was forgotten to the relief of all concerned.

Beginning in the same year smaller naval vessels began patrolling Narragansett Bay. The *Gaspee*, later to become famous, took tours in this duty that year and a few times later before her final cruise in 1772. Her captain, Lieutenant William Dudingston, became notorious for stopping all sorts of small craft carrying on normal, legal trade between Rhode Island ports and harassing other shipping between the colony's harbors and nearby points in Connecticut and Massachusetts. Certain clauses in the trade laws, not previously enforced because they were absurd, were used as pretexts for bringing charges against such practices as conveying lumber from Connecticut without all the requisite papers. Technically, the lumber could not be loaded legally until certain forms had been procured, but these documents could be obtained only from customs officers in Newport or an inconvenient place in Connecticut, so by common consent the formalities had been attended to when the cargo reached the customs office. Accordingly, it was easy to lie in wait for entering vessels and attempt seizure of those without papers they were on the way to get.

Before harm befell the *Gaspee* and Lieutenant Dudingston, the sloop *Liberty* in 1769 had engaged in similar activities and met destruction. Captain William Reid of the *Liberty* seized two vessels arriving from Connecticut in July. The master of one of them tried to retrieve some of his personal belongings, found they had been taken to the *Liberty*, proceeded there, failed to get what he wanted, and was treated with musket fire as he rowed away. Captain Reid was ashore at the time and was prevailed upon to order all his crew into Newport "to answer for their conduct." While the men were doing so, unknown persons said to have been from Connecticut cut the *Liberty*'s cables and towed her toward a Newport wharf. The attackers cut down her mast, threw overboard "everything that was valuable," scuttled the hull, and left her to drift. She beached at Goat Island, where unknown hands set her aflame. She burned for several days. Although Governor Wanton was suspected of complicity in these doings, no British action was seriously attempted to discover the attackers.

The naval patrol from the start had interfered with smuggling

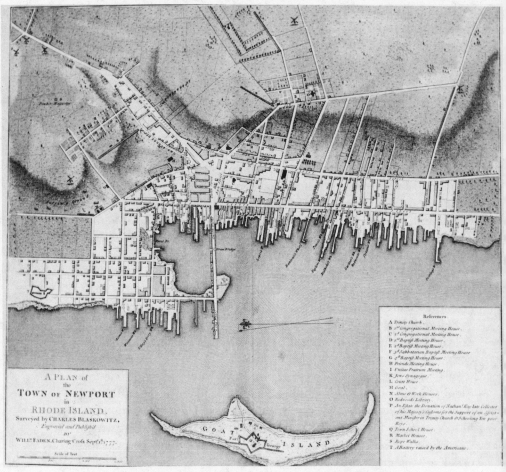

Map of Newport made by Charles Blaskowitz for the British Admiralty in 1777. The War for American Independence brought excellent cartography to Rhode Island along with death and misery. A year before Blaskowitz, the French cartographer J. F. W. de Barres drew a map that was almost as good. *Newport Historical Society.*

sugar and molasses. By 1764 news from London brought tidings of a further shift in policy on this traffic—indeed, a shift in basic thinking. Instead of watching the structure of trade and seeing the benefits of the American importation of foreign molasses, the king's ministers watched the balance sheet in the customs accounts and saw that very little revenue came in from the duty on foreign sugar products. So they planned to cut the duty in half, thinking that it might then be exacted and, though the quantities imported would be rather reduced, the tariffs would bring in the greatest practical income. The Sugar Act of 1764 was to carry these calculations into law.

Even before the new measure went on the books, Rhode Island protested. Governor Stephen Hopkins and some other Providence merchants endorsed a Bostonian objection and soon persuaded the General Assembly to send an official "Remonstrance," written by the governor, to the Board of Trade.* The colony's point of view, which remained constant, was that its commerce depended on bringing in molasses, five-sixths of it from non-British sources, for making profits from distilling rum and from the African slave trade. These profits alone made it possible to pay for imports from Great Britain. This line of thought had been in harmony with old British policy, but it was no longer persuasive. Henry Ward for partisan purposes delayed sending the "Remonstrance" and was severely blamed for it, but the delay probably made no difference.

Parliament passed the Sugar Act anyway, adding new provisions on enforcement to the change in duties. The law gave specific authorization for naval officers to make seizures of cargoes and vessels violating the trade laws (including the Sugar Act) and gave colonial admiralty courts jurisdiction over infractions of these laws. To make matters worse, the act contemplated the erection of a new admiralty court for America at which

---

* Hopkins expressed himself at greater length in *An Essay on the Trade of the Northern Colonies*, published in both Rhode Island newspapers early in 1764, as well as in papers in the other northern ports; it came out as a pamphlet in London and possibly also in Philadelphia. The author displayed wide knowledge of his subject and candor in discussing the commerce, including smuggling, with foreign sugar islands.

customs or naval officers could either start proceedings or carry them on appeal from older courts in the colonies to the south. The new judge, William Spry, set up shop in Halifax, Nova Scotia, far away from the influence Rhode Islanders had learned to exert over their local judge. There was an immediate protest. Suddenly the absence of juries in admiralty procedure loomed as a major grievance. Rhode Islanders argued that admiralty courts in England had no role in enforcing the trade laws, so they should have none in America. (Colonial protests ignored the use of other courts without juries for this purpose in the mother country.) In fact, Judge Spry had no business; his courtroom was too inconvenient for royal officials as well as their victims.

Beyond enacting the new duties and the means to enforce collection, Parliament endorsed the idea of a direct tax on the colonials by revenue stamps required for a great variety of legal documents, newspapers, playing cards, and other items. The details of the plan remained to be settled. In remarkably ambiguous fashion, George Grenville, the first lord of the treasury (the chief minister of George III), spoke of hearing colonial proposals for some other way to raise the same amount of money for the royal treasury, yet refused to say what the amount was or to discuss anything except details of the proposed stamp tax.

Rhode Island would not enter into that sort of discussion, but it sent word of its opposition to a new tax. The Assembly endorsed the ideas stated by Governor Hopkins in *The Rights of Colonies Examined*.* Though he treated all of British North America, Hopkins naturally stressed most heavily what mattered to his own province. The result was a discourse on the historical circumstances of founding the colonies and the injustice and illegality of Parliament taxing them. He dwelt on charter privileges and the lack of royal (or in many cases, any other English) financial backing or military protection for the colonies

---

* The Assembly ordered publication of the pamphlet in December 1764, and it appeared before the end of the year, although dated 1765. The London edition, under the title, *The Grievances of the American Colonies Candidly Examined . . .* , came out in 1766.

in their early years. He pointed out the damage to be done by extracting money from an area that already sent so much of its gold and silver to Britain. In characteristic American fashion he argued that the colonials enjoyed the rights of Englishmen, guaranteed in charters and other documents, including a right to freedom from taxation they did not authorize by their representatives. The British Parliament, he claimed, did not represent the people in the several colonies. They had their own legislatures, while Parliament represented only the people of Great Britain. He asked rhetorically, "can it possibly be shown that the people in Britain have a sovereign authority over their fellow subjects in America?" In answer he asserted, "In an imperial state, which consists of many separate governments, each of which hath peculiar privileges, and of which kind it is evident the empire of Great Britain is, no single part, though greater than another part, is by that superiority entitled to make laws for, or to tax such lesser part; but all laws, and all taxations, which bind the whole, must be made by the whole." Rights to liberty and security of property would be denied if one part could rule the rest.

Hopkins touched upon, but did not offer clear ideas about, the powers of Parliament outside of taxation. As was consistent with his own role in Rhode Island affairs he conceded that "money and paper credit" would need to be determined by a central authority, such as Parliament. He even conceded that the trade of the whole empire for expediency would need to be regulated by that body, yet he asked whether "the equity, justice, and beneficence of the British constitution" did not require that the different parts of the empire be represented in passing any law affecting the empire as a whole. In this query he began to contest the rights of Parliament to do many things it had been doing without American protest, such as restraining the manufacture of iron wares and woolens, as well as limiting trade in sugar and molasses. His perspective on the powers of Parliament was clearly a result of being a Rhode Islander: to him, it was natural to draw comparisons with the colonies of the ancient Greek city-states, which had not been controlled by the parent community, making this autonomy (as was Rhode Island's) the standard for judging the relation of British-American colonies to their mother country. The question for him, in other words, was to justify *any* control from London, not to justify exemptions from it.

Yet much of his essay argued the economic folly of the Sugar Act and the proposed Stamp Act. Sending hard money to London, except for buying imports, simply cut into British trade while giving the Americans hardship. Restraining the importation of molasses to the Rhode Island distilleries prevented payment for manufactures. He asked, "Is it not the chiefest interest of Britain, to dispose of and to be paid for her own manufactures? And doth she not find the greatest and best market for them in her own colonies? Will she find an advantage in disabling the colonies to continue their trade with her? Or can she possibly grow rich by their being made poor?" To Hopkins, the answers were obvious.

To George Grenville, the questions were beside the point. He saw a different set of realities. British taxpayers needed relief. Fighting the French, so heavy a charge on the royal treasury, had rendered the greatest direct benefits to the Americans. Controlling and assimilating the territory in North America taken from France and Spain required troops. Conquest of the enemies on the continent threatened to stir thoughts of independence in the old colonies. The former duties on molasses, by being evaded, had enriched venal customs collectors while draining the treasury to pay their salaries. The ramshackle colonial administration of the earlier eighteenth century was an offense to order and discipline. Altogether, the ministry believed and the majority in Parliament agreed that it was time to draw revenue from the Americans, if only to foot part of the bill for administration and garrisons in North America. So what Hopkins wrote, in the eyes of British officials, simply failed to approach the topics that mattered.

Hopkins' treatise touched off the Rhode Island phase in the pamphlet war that preceded the Revolution. (As with firing on royal ships, the colony began early; once the pamphlets of 1765 had been published, however, there were no more major ones. Rhode Island patriots had stated their ideas, and Rhode Island royalists were in flight.) Martin Howard, Jr., a lawyer who had emigrated from Britain and married into the Brenton family years earlier, replied to Hopkins in February 1765 with *A Letter from a Gentleman at Halifax, To His Friend in Rhode-Island*, generally called the "Halifax Letter." Howard had run for attorney general on the Ward ticket (and lost) four years previously, but since that time had become a leader of the Newport Junto, a band of immigrants from the mother country, mostly professional men, who thought the charter government a disgrace. They favored a royal governor, strict hard money laws, cooperation with the ministry, and a devotion to handicrafts, self-denial, and raising hemp to reduce Rhode Island's dependence on imports from the Old World.

Howard tore into Hopkins, and into James Otis of Boston, who had recently published a pamphlet called *The Rights of the British Colonies Asserted and Proved*. Otis had been Hopkins' attorney and he had relatives in Newport; Howard politely refrained from mentioning that some of them had been members of a counterfeiting ring about the time he arrived in America. He did start a tedious argument over literary skills and erudition by ridiculing what he said were ignorant and foolish passages in Hopkins' pamphlet. The most challenging point in the "Halifax Letter" was on the rights of Englishmen. Howard insisted that these rights were personal, enjoyed by individuals, not whole colonies. The political rights of colonies were defined by charters or similar documents. Nothing could be implied beyond the express words. Nor could a royal charter close out the jurisdiction of Parliament, which was "founded upon common law, . . . and was prior to any charter or grant to the colonies." The jurisdiction of Parliament followed every Englishman wherever he went. King, Lords, and Commons, the sovereign trinity, remained the "supreme head" of government in the British empire. This position of Parliament was as much a part of the rights of Englishmen as rights to "life, liberty, and estate." Moreover, Howard maintained, there were places like the Channel Islands that sent no members of the House of Commons, yet were considered to be represented there, so America might be also.

Howard's publication provoked a storm of wrath. Hopkins'

friends wanted it declared libelous. Reportedly, Deputy Governor Joseph Wanton, Jr., later a loyalist, led the pack. The General Assembly sensibly took no action, though the Superior Court grilled the printer. The controversy remained in ink.*

Howard's rebuttal forced Hopkins and Otis to hedge or qualify their statements. In a series of letters published as "A Vindication" of his pamphlet, Hopkins refined his thoughts and arrived at a moderate position that disappointed some of his friends. He claimed that Parliament *should* not tax American colonials, according to British principles of government, but that it *might*, and if it actually did so, the Americans should pay. More constructively, Hopkins wrote on the nature of representation in Parliament and on the precedents afforded by dealings with Scotland and Ireland, which showed that Parliament itself recognized limits to the propriety if not the power of taxing these kingdoms when the one was not represented and the other had a separate parliament that levied taxes. He also pursued some ideas that Howard had dwelt upon. If the authority of Parliament came from the common law, as Howard said, then it was limited by that law; the common law included the rights of Englishmen, and so Parliament could not transgress these rights.

This legalistic point bore directly on the underlying connection of the colonies with Great Britain. If the connection was "natural," then all the subjects formed one body politic and a supreme legislature could govern the whole; if the connection was "only by policy," as Hopkins claimed, then it was simply "a political relation" and was limited and definable, with the

---

* Hopkins replied to Howard in "A Vindication of a Late Pamphlet Entitled *The Rights of Colonies Examined*, . . . ," in the *Providence Gazette*, Feb. 23, Mar. 2, and Mar. 9, 1765. James Otis replied also in *A Vindication of the British Colonies Against the Aspersions of the Halifax Gentleman* . . . (Boston, 1765). An anonymous third reply, "Some Account of a Pamphlet Lately Published in Newport . . . ," appeared in the *Providence Gazette*, Feb. 23, 1765. Howard came back with *A Defense of the Letter from a Gentleman at Halifax* . . . (Newport, 1765). Hopkins continued the argument in a letter to the publisher of the *Providence Gazette*, printed on Apr. 8, 1765, and in *A Letter to the Author of the Halifax Letter* . . . (Providence, 1765). Otis got in his last and most scurrilous licks in *Brief Remarks on the Defence of the Halifax Libel, On the British-American-Colonies-* . . . (Boston, 1765).

colonials, by implication, as able to define it as Parliament. Hopkins was not drawing in his horns as much as it seemed, but his temperate and restrained statements may have cost him reelection.

The combatants presently flung moderation to the winds, however. Otis rushed to Hopkins' defense in *A Vindication of the British Colonies Against the Aspersions of the Halifax Gentleman.* In a frenzy, Otis denied believing that Parliament had no jurisdiction over the colonies—first saying that the jurisdiction could be indubitable only if the colonies sent representatives, then saying that this qualification did not matter. His slashing defense cut his friends at least as often as his enemies. Howard replied vigorously, drawing another measured response from Hopkins, but Otis descended to shrill personal attacks. The least obnoxious of these was calling Howard "that fawning, insidious, infamous parricide, Martinus Scriblerus" and Howard's friend Dr. Thomas Moffat "that mawgazeen of knowledge Dr. Mumchance." To less effect he accused them of favoring the ousted royal family of Stuart and described the Newport Junto as a "little, dirty, drinking, drabbing, contaminated knot of thieves, beggars, and transports . . . made up of Turks, Jews, and other infidels." This sort of billingsgate was futile. If Howard and his friends were supercilious snobs, they were not depraved. (Incidentally, the Ward forces had prevented naturalization of two Jewish merchants of Newport, so the logical thing would have been to attack them for using bigotry as a cover for factional schemes.)

The tone of the discussion was rescued by an anonymous writer who called himself a "plain yeoman." His letter printed in the *Providence Gazette* on May 11, 1765, only by implication made any personal attacks, well deserved ones on the literary pretensions of Hopkins and Howard. The "Plain Yeoman" forthrightly argued that Parliament had no authority to legislate for America, whether to set up a postal service or levy taxes, and protested British indignation at American petitions against the Stamp Act. He flatly proclaimed that if upholding an "argument against the levying taxes upon us without our consent" amounted to aiming at independence, then the colonials did just that—and rightly so as free English subjects and also quite consistently with their allegiance to the king. He raised the question of Parliament's authority to impose the Acts of Trade and Navigation, but set the subject aside with no more than a hint that those laws might not be legitimate in their entirety. No one knows who the "Plain Yeoman" was. The guess that he was Stephen Hopkins, recently freed from self-restraint by loss of the governor's chair, seems farfetched. About all that can be said is that the mysterious author probably lived in Providence—and was no plain yeoman.

Not that the debates in Rhode Island had any effect in London. The ministry and Parliament ignored the colony's arguments about commerce and constitutional questions, just as they ignored all other American objections to the change in imperial policy. By wide majorities the Stamp Act passed.

Naively the ministry thought it would make the measure palatable by favoring prominent colonials with positions as stamp distributors. In most places the choice fell on a man who had done something to show support for British power in America, but in Rhode Island it fell on Augustus Johnston, a popular figure, whose name graced a town set off from Providence. Johnston had been a Hopkins man, elected attorney general in 1758 and so well liked that the Ward forces often ran no candidate against him. If the choice had fallen on Howard, no one would have been perplexed, but evidently neither he nor his coterie had achieved fame in London for their royalist views when the distributors were picked. Or perhaps Grenville thought it wiser to choose a friend of the governor. Surprisingly, Johnston wanted his new job and for a time fell in with the Newport Junto.

Samuel Ward wrested the governor's chair from Hopkins in 1765 and had to face the turmoil set off by news of the Stamp Act. Composing treatises soon gave way to violence. During the summer of 1765 riots broke out in Boston against the stamp distributor, Andrew Oliver, and lesser disturbances took place in Connecticut. Rumors began to fly about in Newport of plans to hang Johnston, Howard, and Dr. Moffat in effigy. Governor Ward, though well aware that his friends, Samuel Vernon and William Ellery, were behind the plans, did little to stop them. The *Mercury* printed reports of the Boston and Connecticut incidents. Howard and Moffat, correctly fearing that the news would inspire their fellow citizens, protested in vain. The effigies appeared on August 27 and were solemnly hanged. In the evening they were cut down and buried by a crowd that had been encouraged by "strong drink in plenty with Cheshire cheese and other provocatives to intemperance and riot." Howard, Moffat, Johnston, and John Robinson, the customs collector, had prudently sought safety aboard the patrol ship *Cygnet*.

These unpopular gentlemen returned to shore the next morning, but by then news had arrived of another riot in Boston, in which a mob attacked the houses of several prominent backers of parliamentary authority. Again the news proved inspirational. In the evening a Newport crowd broke into Howard's house, destroyed the furnishings and drank his wines and liquors, then repeated the scene at Moffat's. Not content, they returned to the first site to destroy the woodwork and chimneys, and then gave the like treatment to Moffat's. Still unsatisfied, the crowd did further damage to Howard's house and cut down his locust trees. Johnston resolved to face the mob, but his friends carried his furniture and family to safety and then persuaded him to spend the evening elsewhere. Around midnight he still wanted to meet the rioters, but on his way encountered people who warned him that persuasion would not avail. He retired again to the *Cygnet*, accompanied by his host for the evening. His house escaped damage. The customs collector was less fortunate; though he took refuge also in the man-of-war, the mob took care to smash the windows of his house. Governor Ward had departed to look after his farm in Westerly. By August 29, Johnston realized that he could not wait for tempers to cool; he resigned as stamp distributor. His first statement was calculated to allow a retraction, as was seen at once by Ezra Stiles, so the leader of the protests insisted that he swear to his intent to resign.

Then suddenly the tumult took a new turn. The men who had organized the first events, Vernon, Ellery, and Robert Crook, had used as leader of the attacks a young Englishman named John Webber, who had just arrived in the colony. How they found him remains a mystery. He turned out to enjoy his role more than they liked. When they wanted to halt the violence, he

insisted on continuing and carried half the mob with him. Ellery
and Vernon caught him and got the sheriff to take him out to the
Cygnet. His half of the mob then threatened to turn on Ellery,
Vernon, and the sheriff. So they fetched him back. But he was
madder than ever and raved about pulling down their houses.
They gave him money and a new suit; they pleaded with him.
More to the point, Godfrey Malbone, Jr., began organizing a
force to combat Webber's mob. This halted the action for that
day, but Webber was up early the next to rally his forces.

Astonishingly, Webber was stopped by Augustus Johnston
himself. The ex-stamp master met the young demagogue, seized
him bodily, and with the help of some friends dragged Webber
off to jail. Peace returned. The next day Governor Ward found
that his farm in Westerly no longer needed his attention.

Newport still appeared forbidding to Howard and Moffat.
They leaped at a chance to take ship for England and were on
their way to Bristol the same day that Ward returned to his
capital. The two embittered men took their tales of misery to
London, where they agitated for overthrow of the charter and for
compensation of their losses. They managed to get the royal
treasury to hold back payment of some money due Rhode Island
for the Crown Point expedition of 1756 until the colony made
good the losses in the riots. The General Assembly would not bow
to this pressure for several years, but in 1773—too late for all
concerned—voted to pay Moffat, Howard, and Johnston out of
the money sought from the Crown.

In the aftermath of the riots in Newport, the General Assembly
convened in September. Following the lead of Virginia the
previous spring—indeed, following some of the thought and
phrasing of the House of Burgesses—the two houses passed a set
of resolutions against the Stamp Act.* Basically the resolutions
argued that the first settlers had brought with them and handed
down to their descendants all the rights of Englishmen, that these

---

* Fidelity to the Virginia example was all the more striking because some
Rhode Island towns had urged the Assembly to action, offering their own ideas
of how to proceed. In some cases, these towns called for statements on matters,
such as the abrogation of rights to trial by jury, that the Assembly passed over
in silence.

rights had been confirmed by the royal charter, that the charter had never been forfeited, that the rights included freedom from taxation except by consent, and that Parliament's attempts to impose taxes would undermine the colony's liberty. In this line of thought, the Assembly agreed with Virginia, even to the point of feigning ignorance of the events of 1685–1689. In the last two resolutions, however, the Assembly went well beyond the other colonies. It declared that the citizens "are not bound to yield obedience to any law or ordinance designed to impose any internal taxation whatsoever upon them, other than the laws or ordinances of the General Assembly." Not content with proclaiming the Stamp Act null in Rhode Island, the Assembly ordered all the officers of the government to proceed as usual, without regard for the act, promising to protect them from any harmful consequences of such conduct.

The Assembly then sent two delegates to the Stamp Act Congress to meet at New York in October. Henry Ward and Metcalf Bowler, both of the Ward side, dutifully attended and approved its doings. They may have been disappointed at the tone of its petitions and declarations—they were milder on some points than Rhode Island's, although equipped with much better thoughts about the topic of parliamentary authority—but signed them and brought them back to be approved by the Assembly.

The Stamp Act was to go into effect on November 1. For all the firmness of the official documents, no one knew what to expect when that day arrived. Some couples hurried to get married, lest a stamp be required on a license later. Merchants hustled to freight and dispatch their ships. In the last week of October, eighty ships cleared port in Newport, compared with the usual ten or a dozen. Stamps were known to exist on board the *Cygnet* in the harbor, having been brought by a sloop fittingly named *Viper*.

When the day finally arrived some people staged a funeral of "Liberty" at Newport. According to the *Mercury*, "The drowsy dawn usher'd in the gloom-ey'd morn with a sable veil!—wild horror threaten'd the wide vault of heaven!" That is, the weather was cloudy. At noon a cortege formed at the Crown coffee house to escort a coffin to the burial ground. The mourners were taking their last farewell, bemoaning the "ruin'd country," when "a groan was . . . heard, as if coming from the coffin." The supposed corpse turned out to be only in "a trance, for Old Freedom was not dead—the Goddess Britannia had order'd a Guardian Angel, to snatch Old Freedom from the jaws of frozen death, to the orb of the reviving sun, to remain invulnerable from the attacks of Lawless Tyranny and Oppression." The festivities concluded with rejoicing and huzzas for George III. It was all good eighteenth-century allegorical pageantry.

Along with its florid account of this event, the *Mercury* reported a few other important matters. Friends of John Webber, who had failed to extort his release by threatening to wreck the sheriff's house, had tried to break into the jail. After they had been foiled, the prisoner tried to hang himself, but was prevented. News was coming in from other colonies about plans to carry on in defiance of the Stamp Act. The *Mercury* itself came out regularly without using the stamped paper.

Without further prompting, Rhode Island set the pace for disregarding the Stamp Act. All the officials and the courts continued business as usual. Johnston, fearing the consequences, would not even supply the royal customs collector with stamps. When the lords of the treasury ordered Governor Ward to see that stamps got into the hands of under-distributors, however, he uneasily called on Johnston to refuse the office of distributor once more, so that it would be impossible to comply with the order. After several days Johnston gave the colony a Christmas present by renouncing the office in the amplest terms. Ward then cheerfully wrote the lords that no one would accept the office. Later, saying that he had no authority to designate a substitute for Johnston, Ward issued certificates as desired to the effect that stamps were not available.

The merchants of the colony, however, took no formal measures to cut trade with Great Britain. There was not much to cut, still the gesture was not made. If the traders did not join the boycott launched in New York, Pennsylvania, and Massachusetts, many folk went along with lesser measures that were popular elsewhere. Women spent more time on spinning, people refused to eat mutton (lest the supply of wool decrease) or wear elaborate mourning clothes. One way or another there was a good deal of spontaneous nonconsumption of British imports. At least once, a British wholesaler tried to remedy the shortcomings of a Newport merchant by putting off filling an order so as to avoid harming the political campaign to get the act repealed.

The campaign succeeded, largely through the quiet efforts of a committee of London merchants and some changes in the ministry.* News of repeal touched off a celebration in Newport. By then there was a Liberty Tree in town and a roughly organized band of Sons of Liberty to decorate it for the occasion. Cannon were fired at the fort and the ships displayed flags. Providence waited until the king's birthday on June 4, when it staged a veritable extravaganza. Bells, cannons, flags, a parade, a sermon, and a round of toasts enlivened the morning. In the evening there were fireworks, a banquet, a ball, and more toasts—to a total of thirty-four. The General Assembly sent thanks to the king, assorted others, and the committee of London merchants. (The only other colony that acknowledged the work of those men was Quebec.) But there was no public testimonial to Parliament. Aside from thinking that august body deserved no thanks for undoing its own mischief, the colony as a rule chose to ignore it and deal only with the king and his officials. Besides, the Declaratory Act, which proclaimed Parliament's "authority to make laws and statutes of sufficient force and validity to bind the colonies and people of America, subjects of the crown of Great Britain, in all cases whatsoever," was seen in Rhode Island as showing that Parliament had underlined, rather than erased, the false principles behind the Stamp Act.

---

* The background of British politics in the pre-Revolutionary years, fascinating though it is, signifies very little for the historian of Rhode Island. As perceived in the colony, British politics provided some heroes like Pitt and General Henry Conway, as well as some villains, but the ministry was a vague, sinister, mostly faceless, collection of men. They were mentioned mainly in connection with obnoxious laws and policies. Changes in the lineup were noticed, of course, but there was little attention to what lay behind them. After 1770, when Lord North began his long tenure as chief minister, there was no further need to probe political events. The leading citizens in Rhode Island may have had shallow and wrongheaded ideas about British politics, but the ideas, not the truth, guided action in Providence and Newport.

Parliament's wrongheadedness was manifest in action soon enough. It amended the Sugar Act to put a duty of one penny a gallon on all molasses, British as well as foreign, entering colonial ports. This was as smart a way as could be found to stop smuggling, because it set the duty lower than the average bribe had been to the customs officers, but the measure aimed quite blatantly at bringing in revenue. (Around Narragansett Bay, smuggling continued to be popular.) Yet the colonials did not protest. They worked up some indignation over provisions of another new act requiring the colonies to provide barracks and certain necessities to royal troops garrisoned in them. The indignation mounted when New York's refusal led to suspension of its legislature. Still, Parliament had to demand new taxes to arouse even half the resentment against the Stamp Act.

The new taxes, generally known as the Townshend duties, set off a complicated series of events. Charles Townshend proposed to raise revenue in America by duties on imports from Great Britain. The tariffs were to be exacted beginning November 20, 1767, on paper, glass, lead, painters' colors, and tea. By older trade laws, all these items had to be imported from Britain if not produced locally, so the new measure appeared like extortion. Still, there had been no American objections in principle to British duties, and the new taxes were indubitably duties. Townshend obviated one objection that had been raised against the Stamp Act, that it would take cash out of a money-short economy, by planning to use the new revenue to pay salaries of colonial officials. This, too, produced an exquisite pain, because this means of providing salaries to governors, judges, and the like, would make them dependent on Parliament and the ministry instead of the colonial legislatures. There was no plan to tamper with Rhode Island by paying its officials, however, so this aspect of the Townshend duties aroused little response there. Even so, the subsidiary administrative measures, erection of an American Board of Customs Commissioners at Boston and a spate of new superior admiralty courts on the model of Judge Spry's, threatened to make commerce more difficult in Narragansett Bay.

Rhode Island reacted strongly to Townshend's plans. The Assembly sent a petition against them to George III, who rejected it on the grounds that its claims were inconsistent with the authority of Parliament. When the Assembly learned about the rejection, it sent word to the ministry that it heartily endorsed the Massachusetts Circular Letter. That document had called for concerted protests and so offended the imperial officials that the king ordered the Massachusetts House of Representatives to rescind it (which they would not do) and the royal governors in the other colonies to dissolve the legislatures if they proposed to deliberate on the letter. Rhode Island was intentionally offensive.

Public discussion of the Townshend duties brought out more strenuous and sweeping condemnation than had greeted the Stamp Act, but opinion was divided. Old points were scored again about the legislature of Great Britain, as the representatives of one body politic having no authority over the colonies, which were separate bodies. This time the arguments drew added support from theories of human equality. Silas Downer, at the dedication of the Liberty Tree in Providence, went through the whole catalogue of parliamentary legislation from the post office law passed under Queen Anne, as well as the trade laws beginning in the seventeenth century, denouncing the lot as "infractions on the natural rights of men" and therefore without force. Less strident voices, however, could also be heard. There was not the prompt, reflexive union against the Townshend measures that there had been against the Stamp Act.

Confusion and double-dealing appeared all over America in efforts to organize a nonimportation agreement to repeat the economic pressures that had just worked so well. In Rhode Island, the towns once more talked up frugality and domestic manufactures and called on merchants to stop trade with Britain. The merchants proclaimed their zeal for the cause. Yet their brave talk gave way to equivocation, following the lead of Boston, where traders had no wish to ruin themselves by stopping commerce and letting the other ports grow rich. Mutual distrust among the American merchants bespoke a knowledge of widespread lukewarmness toward a trade stoppage. In most places importers wanted to delay nonimportation until they had stocked up. The result was a ragged and fractious boycott. When Boston, Philadelphia, and New York finally agreed to stop bringing in

East India goods and either all or most European manufactured wares, Newport and Providence gave only lip service.

Until forced to do otherwise, the Rhode Island merchants, like some in other places that were jealous of the three leaders, took the occasion as one for capturing a share of their neighbors' business. This course of action invited reprisals. By 1769 the New York merchants were cutting off trade with Rhode Island, and the Bostonians and South Carolinians threatened to follow suit. Providence merchants hastily drew up a nonimportation agreement. The Newporters, to stave off commercial isolation, agreed to their own nonimportation plan, only to arouse indignation in New York and Philadelphia for confining their self-denials to British and East India products, thus leaving the port open to manufactures of all sorts from other ports or countries of Europe. Some modification mollified the critics, and Newport saved its coastal trade. Even so, the merchants did not abide by their own promises.

When Parliament in 1770 repealed all the Townshend duties except that on tea, colonial merchants revealed in many ways how little they liked the boycott. The repeal satisfied nobody, but it was a gain. So the weak wall of nonimportation began crumbling. Newport cheerfully declared an end to its participation, again enraging the other ports. Merchants from Maine to Delaware cut off trade with Rhode Island. (The Providence merchants self-righteously denounced Newport, but they would have scrapped nonimportation if the town meeting had let them. Besides, it was no secret that the Providence men were no more faithful to their promises than the Newporters.) Recriminations broke out within the colony. Some Newport men blamed failure of the nonimportation plan on the Jewish merchants, especially Aaron Lopez.* A quarrel nearly split the Hopkins political forces by alienating the Providence Browns from the Newport Wantons. Luckily, news arrived that New York merchants were going

---

* It is well known that Lopez went on importing from Bristol, in fact, from Henry Cruger, a leading advocate there of the trade stoppage. Lopez owed Cruger so much money that neither man could afford to halt trade. But there was no occasion for making scapegoats of the Newport Jews: Lopez' situation was only an extreme case of the troubles many others faced.

back on their promises. Soon the nonimportation movement had nothing left but shrill seers who maintained that it could have forced repeal of the tea duty if kept up a little longer.

By the middle of 1770, the nonintercourse efforts were things of the past, trade resumed as usual, and the duty on tea was paid fairly regularly; in most colonies an interval of calm set in, but hardly in Rhode Island. The new customs collector, Charles Dudley, tried like his predecessors to do his job and learned like them to do it in accord with local tradition. Soon he was receiving tokens of appreciation from grateful merchants, but he tried to maintain a veneer of integrity. Probably the effort cost him the beating meted out to him in April 1771. He lived, but royal officials demanded that Governor Wanton see to it that the laws were more faithfully observed. Wanton explained away the incident as an attack by "drunken sailors," not native Rhode Island men, when Dudley alone boarded a vessel in the dark of night. The governor added some complaints about the conduct of customs officers in the colony.

The conflict over the naval patrol of Narragansett Bay had become chronic, moreover, and was headed toward its climax. The schooner *Gaspee*, commanded by Lieutenant William Dudingston, had cruised the bay a few times earlier, but arrived for an extended stay in March 1772. Dudingston contemptuously ignored his duty to show his commission to the governor and began harassing shipping. He stopped anything afloat, even if patently engaged in trade between ports in the colony. He fired on small vessels. His men stole livestock from coastal farms. Governor Wanton protested to his superior, Rear Admiral John Montagu, in Boston, who backed up Dudingston and sent the sloop *Beaver* to help him. Dudingston further enraged Wanton and the mercantile community by sending a vessel loaded with rum, belonging to the Greene family of Warwick, to be condemned at the superior admiralty court in Boston. On June 9, when pursuing a vessel that Dudingston had reason to believe was carrying smuggled goods, the *Gaspee* ran aground on what then was called Namquit Point, later renamed in honor of the royal schooner.

Perhaps the Rhode Island merchants had been planning an

Portrait of Abraham Whipple (1733–1819), privateer captain,
merchant captain in the service of the Browns of Providence,
commander of the attack on *Gaspee*, and hero of the Continental
Navy, as painted by Edward Savage in 1786. *Courtesy of the United
States Naval Academy Museum.*

attack on the *Gaspee*, perhaps just daydreaming of it, but the opportunity had arrived. John Brown of Providence seized the chance. He quickly organized a party of men who rowed down the bay in longboats with muffled oars. Brown joined in the expedition but left actual command to Abraham Whipple. Hailed by a sentinel, the attackers did not reply, but Dudingston appeared on deck wanting to know what was happening. Whipple yelled that he was the sheriff of Kent County and had a warrant to arrest Dudingston. Someone grew impatient and shot Dudingston before Whipple had finished. The attackers then stormed the *Gaspee*, taking care to dress Dudingston's wound. They removed everyone from the schooner and set her afire. She burned slowly, slowly to the water's edge.

Providence went about its business the next day without revealing a sign that unusual events had taken place, but the incident could not pass unnoticed. Deputy Governor Darius Sessions began an inquiry into the destruction of the *Gaspee*, and Governor Wanton soon offered a reward of £100 for information leading to conviction of the perpetrators of the "atrocious crime." Admiral Montagu fumed. A few weeks later officials in London heard the news and decided that something must be done. They could not vent official wrath by words alone when the Rhode Islanders had burnt a second naval vessel. Parliament had recently passed an act making it a felony punishable by death to set fire to one of his majesty's ships and allowing colonials accused of the crime to be tried in England. There being no established way to proceed under this law, the Privy Council resolved upon a secret board of inquiry to gather evidence and take such action as seemed wise.

The Privy Council chose five men to serve on this special commission. In addition to Governor Wanton, they were the admiralty judge at Boston and the chief justices of Massachusetts, New York, and New Jersey. These gentlemen were all old hands in colonial government, disposed to keep the *Gaspee* incident from touching off a fresh outbreak of American hostility to Great Britain. The commission was to have remained inconspicuous— absolute secrecy was unthinkable for a board calling witnesses— but Governor Wanton reported the planned inquiry to the

General Assembly, and the *Providence Gazette* published news about it by the end of October. Though they could have guessed that the commissioners wished to smooth things over, people in Rhode Island still feared that they would act ruthlessly.

For over four months the colony dreaded what was to come. From October until the end of 1772, when the commissioners assembled at Newport, there was a lot of useless trembling, bravado, and perfervid talk about privileges and principles. Allegedly Admiral Montagu was smacking his lips over the opportunity "to gratify his rancor" against the colony and had orders to line its harbors with small craft to catch suspects. Three regiments of redcoats were said to be poised for a descent on Rhode Island. "Americanus" in the *Newport Mercury* solemnly announced: "To be, or not to be, that's the question: Whether our unalienable rights and privileges are any longer worth contending for, is now to be determined." At last "the tools of despotism and arbitrary power" had found their chance to overthrow the right of trial by jury and reduce the Americans "to a miserable life of slavery, in chains, under a pack of worse than Egyptian tyrants, whose avarice nothing less than your whole substance and income will satisfy."

Anticipation of a "court of inquisition, more horrid than that of Spain and Portugal," proved unfounded. The commissioners brought no bloodhounds, they set up no racks. When they marched to the council chamber in the Colony House at Newport on January 5, 1773, they had their commission read aloud and then went into conclave. The wording of the commission proved surprising. Not only did it authorize the board of inquiry to investigate the alleged wrongs done by naval officers in Narragansett Bay as well as the destruction of the *Gaspee*, but it also was ambiguous on what was to be done with men suspected of perpetrating the attack on the royal schooner.

In the conclave the commissioners were joined by two men who had just rushed down from Providence, Chief Justice Stephen Hopkins and Deputy Governor (then acting governor) Sessions. Hopkins offered his services to issue warrants, so that the commissioners need not "usurp an executive jurisdiction within the colony." The seven talked over possible causes of the outrage. Soon the commissioners intimated that they would not hand over anyone to be held by Admiral Montagu for possible delivery to a British court without approbation of Hopkins' Superior Court. It also became clear to Sessions that the commissioners disliked their task. He reported that Judge Frederick Smythe of New Jersey, the only British-born commissioner, made a point of saying "he was come to judge according to law and right, and not to be the executioner of ministerial vengeance." Hopkins had been wise in counseling the General Assembly to raise no objections to the legality of the commission but to remain in session awaiting developments. He had promised the Assembly to do everything in his power to hinder capture of anyone for trial in Britain; his methods may have been indirect, but he was succeeding beautifully.

The commissioners conferred often, awaiting the arrival of Admiral Montagu, who was to present witnesses. He was surprisingly reluctant to leave Boston, and when he did, traveled by way of Taunton to avoid risking his safety in Providence. From Taunton he proceeded by water to Newport, entering the harbor late on January 12. The next day he went ashore, with his admiral's flag flying while the five naval vessels there honored him with salutes. The colony's fort neither hoisted a flag nor fired a gun. (Montagu dashed off a note reporting this insult to his superiors at London.) The admiral wasted time exchanging disrespects with Governor Wanton, but produced his "witnesses."

These turned out to be an anticlimax. One was a deranged and dipsomaniacal young man from Smithfield, who was angry at the town council for declaring him *non compos mentis* and at a court for refusing to dock the entail placed on the family lands by his prudent father. The commissioners decided his testimony was "not to be relied on." The other was one Aaron Briggs, described as a mulatto because his father was black and his mother Indian. Like many other offspring of Indians, he had been classified as indigent and bound into servitude until the age of twenty-four. He was crossing Narragansett Bay in flight from his master when he was picked up by a naval patrol. The captain threatened to whip him or hang him from the yardarm if he did not name the culprits in the burning of the *Gaspee*. Briggs named a lot of names. His testimony counted for little when he was found to contradict himself, and other people brought evidence that demolished all claims that he had been an eyewitness. Beyond these men, Montagu could offer only names of six Providence residents.

The commissioners heard evidence from crewmen of the *Gaspee* and assorted others and wrote the six Providence men asking them to testify. No subpoena was issued to any of them. Four who were lawyers replied that they were too busy attending court for their clients. The tavernkeeper whose house had been the site of planning the attack on the *Gaspee* indignantly refused to go to Newport. The sixth did not reply at all. Discouraged, the commissioners adjourned until May. Admiral Montagu departed inconspicuously.

Their second session achieved little more. Some of the Providence men did appear. Other witnesses were examined. After a while, the commissioners presented their findings to Acting Governor Sessions and the Superior Court. These gentlemen quite accurately concluded that the evidence justified no arrests. Aside from Briggs's forced testimony only one other witness offered a name—someone "by the name of Greene"— that was too vague to track down among the numerous members of that family. Commissioner Daniel Horsmanden of New York scratched his aged head and could do no better than conclude that the *Gaspee* had been burnt by "a number of bold, daring, rash, enterprising sailors, collected suddenly from the neighborhood," but he could not find out who they were or who had organized them. He could have figured out that much by reading his newspaper back home. The commissioners were all remarkably complacent in the face of Providence people who professed complete ignorance of the event. Prudently the board of inquiry balanced the lassitude of its investigation with almost total apathy in probing the conduct of naval officers in Narragansett Bay. When the commissioners gave up and went home, Ezra Stiles commented, "They have done so very little and have finished with so much stillness that we scarcely know what they have done."

If the commissioners carried on their business in a fashion that probably was calculated to consign the *Gaspee* incident to oblivion, they nearly succeeded, but not quite. Nothing could eradicate the fear of ministerial malevolence that had welled up before January 1773. If no attempt had been made that time to hustle American suspects to kangaroo courts in Britain, conceivably the commissioners' forbearance had been a ruse to lure the colonials into accepting the authority of the commission so that on a later occasion drastic measures would have the strength of precedent behind them. Fired by a probably ungrounded apprehension of sinister designs in London, people in Rhode Island fell to criticizing those who appeared before the commission and seeking support from other colonies to repel invasion of their liberties. When the *Gaspee* faded in memories elsewhere, it continued to keep passions intense around Narragansett Bay.

There were a few protests against the commission outside Rhode Island. Some of these were made before it got down to work. Between its sessions, however, the Virginia House of Burgesses declared the board of inquiry a "flagrant attack upon American liberty" and called for an investigation of its "principles and authority." To carry the project forward, the Burgesses named a Committee of Correspondence to communicate with the other colonies. In response to the Virginia efforts, there rapidly spread a web of such committees, often joined with the earlier and looser web of Sons of Liberty, to form the basic fabric of a revolutionary organization. In Newport, Ezra Stiles correctly predicted that the Committees of Correspondence would lead to "a general congress."

Parliament helped make Stiles a prophet by passing the Tea Act of 1773. Designed to help the stockholders of the East India Company by letting the company negotiate direct sales of tea to American importers and escape a tax in the process, the act provoked unexpected wrath in the colonies. Though many merchants privately may have been irate at the thought of others getting favored treatment by the company, in public everyone denounced the scheme as trickery to seduce the colonials into paying the tea tax left over from the Townshend duties. Though

no Rhode Island merchants were tempted with special consignments of tea from the company, a great many people in the
colony foreswore the beverage.

The destruction of the tea consignments at Boston in December 1773 touched off an outburst of town actions in Rhode Island
against the Tea Act, and the excitement soon stepped up. News
of the Coercive Acts passed by Parliament in response to the
Boston Tea Party found the towns and the General Assembly
aroused and ready to join in sending relief to Boston and
representatives to an intercolonial congress to arrange concerted
protest. Before any other public call for a congress, Rhode Island
had advocated one and had chosen her delegates: Stephen
Hopkins and Samuel Ward. The Assembly provided them with
instructions to urge a remonstrance to King George III, to
ascertain the rights of the colonies, to pursue whatever means
seemed likely to get a redress of colonial grievances, and to
advocate an "annual convention of representatives from all the
colonies to consider of proper means for the preservation of the
rights and liberties of the colonies." Significantly, the Assembly
also began approving plans to form new military companies in
Rhode Island. It even proclaimed June 30, the day the Coercive
Acts were to take effect, a day of "public fasting and prayer."
The closure of the port of Boston by one of these acts must have
seemed less than an unmixed evil in the colony, but the
companion law to change the government of Massachusetts
could only inspire horror. If Parliament could alter one colonial
charter, it could alter any.

At the First Continental Congress in Philadelphia, the Rhode
Island delegates carried out their instructions and joined in plans
they knew their constituents would applaud to stop trade with
Great Britain. The embargo, specified in the Articles of Association, was indeed adopted with an alacrity and success far greater
than the nonimportation plans of earlier years. The organization
of committees to enforce the stoppage proved quite effective.

As American politicians, Hopkins and Ward manifested some
differences. Hopkins was cautious and unwilling to declare that
Parliament had no authority to enact regulations of trade. After
years of doubt on this point, he resolved it in a way that

harmonized with his acceptance of parliamentary authority to prohibit Rhode Island paper currency. Ward, however, forthrightly repudiated Parliament's power over colonial trade. Hopkins also favored the Plan of Union offered by Joseph Galloway of Pennsylvania, providing for an American house of Parliament to add to the Lords and Commons for deciding on laws affecting the colonies. This too was consistent with Hopkins' older ideas. As a delegate to the Albany Congress in 1754, he had advocated the plan of union recommended by that body. Ward rejected Galloway's plan and advanced into the ranks of the aggressive patriots in Congress. An admiring constituent, perhaps with local bias, soon rated him third in importance behind the Adamses of Massachusetts.

Ward had enthusiastic backers at home. By the end of 1774, the colony's two newspapers began publishing arguments that even the king's authority was conditional on his acting as the servant of the people. When neither king nor Parliament reacted to the Continental Congress with anything but sterner measures, the publishers were prepared to say that the subjects would be absolved from their allegiance and bound to resist if George III acted to damage their welfare. Though the editors did not speak for all Rhode Islanders by any means, they voiced a widespread readiness to combat British repression.

Those of a different mind began learning the strength of the zealots by the end of 1774. Vigilantes with tar and feathers or the General Assembly with citations for contempt bore down on defenders of British authority. Remnants of the old Newport Junto, royal customs officers, and stray men of loyalist principles found life growing difficult. Based at Newport the naval patrol, enlarged to ten vessels, shielded Tories in the old capital, but elsewhere only defenders of American liberty could be safe. By degrees, certain of the colony's own officials aroused the suspicions of the hotheaded patriots. Joseph Wanton, Jr., the Newport leader of the Hopkins faction, formerly deputy governor and later a deputy, fell an early victim to charges of Tory views. His political friend Walter Chaloner, sheriff of Newport County, was often accused.

But the elderly Joseph Wanton, Sr., the governor himself,

became the leading suspect. It was enough to say that he drank
tea and that Stephen Hopkins drank it with him. There was no
ground for believing that Wanton intended to subvert the
colony's charter or that he had ever been lukewarm in defending
it, yet somehow he manifested a reluctance to support the last
degree of American resistance to Britain well before he displayed
it openly. The suspicions proved justified in 1775. Just after he
had been reelected once more, the Assembly voted to raise a force
of 1,500 men to protect the colony and aid other colonies if
necessary—in essence, the plan was to help draw the ring around
British forces in Boston after the battles of Lexington and
Concord—and Wanton protested against the decision. Though
he had the company of Deputy Governor Sessions, two assistants,
and the Newport deputies, Governor Wanton drew the patriot
fire. He refused to sign the commissions of officers for this force
and so became a marked man. The Assembly voted to strip the
governor of nearly all his powers and to prevent him from taking
the oath or engagement of office except in its presence and with
its consent. The consent, one may be sure, was contingent on his
changing his mind about resistance to Britain. Deputy Governor
Sessions thereupon refused to enter a new term and was replaced
by Nicholas Cooke, an old Hopkins man from Providence who
had been moderate enough in his politics to earn the goodwill of
Ward.

Wanton stayed in Newport waiting for the Assembly to come
to its senses and give up either its rash measures or its annoyance
at himself. He believed that he had prudently preserved the
colony's self-government under the royal charter and that the
surest way to overthrow it was to take arms against the king. (He
was resoundingly wrong: the charter remained in force until
1842, and overthrowing it took something close to an internal
revolution.) Hopeful that tempers had calmed, he met the
Assembly in June, expecting to be installed for the rest of his new
term. But the members refused him. Baffled, he returned to
Newport and began to show open cordiality to the commander of
the naval patrol, Captain James Wallace. The Assembly in
November resolved the constitutional dilemma by moving Cooke
into the governor's chair and appointing William Bradford of

Bristol as deputy governor. Thus in Rhode Island the main political event of the revolution took place in rather drawn-out fashion during 1775. Still, the deposed magistrate kept the colony's charter and other documents customarily entrusted to the governor. Finally in March 1776, the Assembly sent the sheriff of Newport County to demand these things. Wanton refused to surrender them, but pointedly stepped into another room, allowing the sheriff to carry away the chest containing these symbols of office.

Governor Wanton and his son became Tories, but they were not of like mind with the royalists of earlier years. Heirs of a long tradition of Rhode Island political maneuvering in the British empire, the Wantons not only knew how to carry it forward but also believed that the province needed to continue the ties with the mother country. "The prosperity and happiness of this colony," Wanton argued to the unmoved Assembly, "is founded on its connection with Great Britain." All he could see as the consequences of armed resistance were "ruin and destruction," followed by "universal bankruptcy." He would enthusiastically support all sorts of defiance of royal authority, but only up to the point where it might be wholly rejected. When he balked at further defiance, he moved firmly into opposition to the course his constituents were taking.

Everyone had to take a side when the naval patrol fleet under Captain Wallace systematically began to assert royal power. By May 1775 the customs house had closed, the collector allowing clearance of ships only when approved by Wanton's naval office rather than the one created to supersede it by the Assembly. Within a few weeks, Wallace's men were menacing not merely shipping in Narragansett Bay but also the town of Newport itself. Rumor had it that he threatened to bombard and burn it. The population began to flee. By the fall, royal naval parties were foraging and looting, a few shots were fired at Newport, Bristol and Portsmouth received a regular cannonade, and Wallace was stopping wood boats and ferries to Aquidneck. He demanded that his men be allowed ashore, that his fleet be supplied with provisions, and that the Rhode Island troops, raised during the summer, be removed from the island. George Washington advised that Wallace's demands be met; the town of Newport pleaded for concessions to the navy. Finally the colonial officials allowed negotiation of a truce: Wallace might buy provisions at Newport, provided he ceased interfering with small craft bringing necessities into town, and the colonial militia stationed there would be moved out. The truce prevented a winter of misery, but it did not stop sparring between the opposing sides.

Resistance to British intimidation took many forms. When Wallace captured someone, his opponents caught one of his men to hold for exchange. All around the bay, men were building forts. Military forces were assembled in every town. Fast-moving farmers whisked livestock beyond the reach of foraging parties from Wallace's fleet. One Newporter strode out on Long Wharf and showed his backside to the British. Refugees straggled inland from there and the other exposed areas along the southern shores of the bay.

Toward the end of 1775, fear of the Tories spread in the colony. Though open defenders of British policy were few, advocates of accommodation were reasonably numerous. By the time almost half of the population of Aquidneck had fled, the remaining men could conceivably elect deputies to the General Assembly who would oppose resistance to the king. Or they might do even worse. Fear inspired measures to exact an oath of fidelity to the American cause on pain of death. Suspected opponents were arrested, but even those who refused the oath were scarcely punished; none was executed. Almost a hundred were rounded up on one occasion in Newport, all but eleven managing to satisfy the Assembly of their conscientious objection to war or their inclinations to the patriotic side.

In Philadelphia the Second Continental Congress was embroiled with the problem of framing policies for the colonies. It applauded Rhode Island's early steps against loyalists, it endorsed revolutionary regimes in several colonies, parried each attempt by the imperial authorities to restrain American defiance or set conditions for ending the conflict, and it began negotiations for French and Spanish aid. But the Congress could not take drastic steps for many months, even though its army forced the British evacuation of Boston in March 1776, because the middle colonies as a block remained uncertain over the wisdom of measures that might foreclose reconciliation. Samuel Ward had concluded by November 1775 that independence should be declared, but Hopkins had doubts. Actually, the slow process of fomenting overthrow of the proprietary government of Pennsylvania, the keystone of the colonial arch, proceeded steadily. Ward, however, died of a particularly severe case of smallpox in March, before he could see the culmination a few weeks later. Hopkins wrote home for instructions as the Congress approached the time when a declaration of independence would be feasible politically.

Rhode Island lost patience with the machinations of the middle colonies. The General Assembly defiantly reasserted its admiralty jurisdiction, abandoned over seventy years earlier, to commission privateers to take British ships engaged in any way in operations against the United Colonies and to erect a court (with a jury) to hear claims to prizes. The election of 1776, for all the fears, hardly changed the membership in the Assembly. Governor Cooke was reelected by a landslide, some British sympathizers lost office, and no Tory majority appeared in Newport. Heartened by this uneventful outcome, the General Assembly proceeded to a dramatic step on May 4, 1776. It voted to repudiate allegiance to George III. According to the preamble to this act, the king, "forgetting his dignity, regardless of the compact most solemnly entered into, ratified and confirmed to the inhabitants of this colony by his illustrious ancestors," had entirely departed "from the duties and character of a good king." Instead of protecting his American dominions, the Assembly proclaimed, he is "endeavoring to destroy the good people of this colony, and of all the United Colonies, by sending fleets and armies to America, to confiscate our property and spread fire, sword, and desolation throughout our country, in order to compel us to submit to the most debasing and detestable tyranny." For that reason, Rhode Island must resist with all its power. The Assembly went on to alter the forms of commissions for public officials and the oaths or engagements to take office or give evidence in court. Henceforth, none of these governmental ceremonies was to invoke the name or authority of the king. Rhode Island had severed her slender ties with the mother country.

In later years, May 4 would be celebrated as Rhode Island Independence Day, yet in 1776 there was no public excitement. The citizens of the new state, in a practical mood, awaited the decision of the Continental Congress. As far as the state's remaining delegate was concerned, the Assembly had given him instructions. When it sent an additional representative, William Ellery, a Ward stalwart from Newport who had tried to brand Hopkins a Tory, the old statesman may not have found the company beguiling, but the political message was clear. Rhode Island's delegates solidly backed the resolution passed in the Congress to declare independence. The news got back to their state soon, inspiring a wave of patriotic enthusiasm. The General Assembly met a week later; on July 18, it voted to take out the word, "colony," from the name of the jurisdiction and insert the word, "state." Two days later it endorsed the Declaration of Independence—one dissenter raised his voice and was expelled— a vote that launched preparations for a public celebration. The declaration was proclaimed from the statehouse in Providence on July 25. The theme of the event, as of much of the earlier enthusiasm, was the union of the thirteen former colonies. Four divisions of cadets and light infantry "fired thirteen vollies, then the Artillery Company fired thirteen cannon, and thirteen cannon were fired at the bridge [across the Providence River] and the ships *Alfred* and *Columbus* also fired thirteen each." There followed a public entertainment featuring "thirteen patriotic toasts."

The two decisions to repudiate allegiance to the king spoke for two equally vital traditions in Rhode Island. The state's own action, seemingly rash and impetuous, voiced the old spirit of independence, the readiness to follow conviction to the limit. The move was not really brash, for the colony had been fighting the British navy for some time. Fittingly, Samuel Ward had been the foremost advocate of independence. The public forbearance, waiting for news from the Congress before the cheering began, reflected Rhode Island's early and resolute call for union of the rebellious colonies. This had been the goal of Stephen Hopkins. May 4 was Ward's day, July 4 was Hopkins'. Happily, he was still alive to rejoice.

14

EPILOGUE: IN, OUT, AND FINALLY IN THE UNITED STATES

Officially, the history of colonial Rhode Island ended with the assertion of independence in 1776, but that is true only because the United States managed to survive the ensuing war and establish a durable federal union. Accomplishing these things took a dozen years. Rhode Island and its citizens had more than their share of the fighting; although the state was the scene of only a single sizable battle, and that one of secondary importance, there were skirmishes throughout the war. Moreover, Rhode Island men in great numbers fought on land and sea from the siege of Boston to the capture of Cornwallis at Yorktown. The state was a much more conspicuous actor in the drama of creating a strong federal government. Indeed, as the states drifted toward disunion after 1782, Rhode Island was the extreme case: it figured initially as the stone wall that stopped the first effort to enlarge the powers of Congress, next as a prime example of a state seeking its own fortunes regardless of the rest, then as the firmest opponent of the Constitutional Convention, and finally as a completely independent commonwealth. Rhode Island and Providence Plantations suddenly became in 1789 as independent as in 1642. Again the complete autonomy was short-lived. There was little thought of remaining aloof from England in the seventeenth century; there was practically none of remaining outside the United States in 1790.

Even though Rhode Island was never the scene of crucial engagements during the War for American Independence, yet the people there had a taste of virtually everything that went on in the conflict. There were battles and raids on land and at sea. There was a British occupation, leading to recruitment of a small loyalist unit for service under King George. There were privateer cruises out of Narragansett Bay and regiments of the Continental Army raised in the state. There were paper money problems, shortages, profiteers, Tories and hysterical fears of Tories, fortifications, blockades, soldiers who were underpaid, under-armed, and underfed; there was a French expeditionary force; there were deaths, maimings, and upstart merchants who found out how to turn a profit amid chaos. All in all, Rhode Island missed only a few major ingredients in the war, notably a battle in which George Washington commanded the Continental Army. The course of the conflict turned into an ugly train of events that reversed Rhode Island's early enthusiasm for a union of the states.

The excitement over declaring independence provided an inspiriting interlude in a war already under way. Much had happened before July 1776. Fighting with the Royal Navy had expanded from the occasional skirmish to a running battle that did not end even with the departure of Captain Wallace and the patrol vessels in April 1776. People had been sending out privateers and fortifying the coast of Narragansett Bay. Rhode Island had fitted out a small navy, begun organizing forces to guard the coasts, and had sent men to serve around Boston. At first a collaborative effort of the New England colonies, this force became the Continental Army in June 1775, when the Continental Congress adopted it and sent George Washington to be its general. Stephen Hopkins in the Congress had carried Rhode Island's call for a continental navy, had won appointment of his brother as its first commodore, and had secured for his home state contracts for building two of the thirteen frigates planned as the core of the fleet. Brother Esek Hopkins had put a number of friends and relations in command of the first few vessels fitted out at Philadelphia and then set sail on a cruise to raid stores of ammunition in the Bahamas for the benefit of Washington's army. Thus his fleet had to make deliveries in southern New England, which were finished just as Captain Wallace left

Narragansett Bay, allowing Hopkins to establish his base at Providence. So the guns of the United States Navy helped greet the Declaration of Independence in that city.

The early phase of the war came to a promising end in the spring of 1776, but no one dared hope that there would not be a second phase. The main action had been around Boston, where the siege culminated in success on March 17, 1776, the day the British forces evacuated the city, leaving the rebellious colonies almost free of the king's men. The question was where British troops would land on their return.

Washington correctly guessed New York, but Rhode Islanders feared that it would be Newport. Wallace had kept a toehold there after the evacuation of Boston, and it might look like a good base for a second attempt to restore domination over rebellious New England. In fact, the British commanders did think of Newport, both as a gateway into New England and a guard over the seaways to New York, but decided to put off seizing it until December 1776. By then Manhattan had been secured and efforts had failed to knock down the revolutionary cause by negotiating surrender or showing Washington that the king's forces could put the Continental Army into flight whenever they attacked.

Sir Henry Clinton and his men entered Newport without opposition on December 8 and settled in for a long, dreary stay. As it turned out, they could keep Hopkins' fleet bottled up for a while but in the long run could neither occupy the nearby mainland nor stop the revolutionaries from using ports up the bay. The British could not even count on buying supplies locally; most had to be shipped in, although foraging parties with hard money could often find sellers in the Narragansett towns. Firewood became particularly scarce in Newport, leading people to burn anything that was not absolutely necessary, such as woodwork and old papers. Faced with shortages, the British commanders cheerfully allowed refugees to leave town and encouraged the city fathers to send out the paupers.

While the main action of the Continental Army remained in the Middle Atlantic states, Rhode Island kept trying to get help in expelling the British from Newport. The Congress and

General Washington thought other things were more important. Even if a significant number of naval vessels languished immobilized at Providence, soldiers could not be spared from campaigns in New York, New Jersey, and Pennsylvania to uncork Narragansett Bay by recapturing Aquidneck. Esek Hopkins was blamed for his predicament and slowly relieved of his command. All the Congress would do was encourage the generals in charge of forces in New England to improvise an army out of state units whenever a likely time arrived for an attack on Newport.

Three such times appeared. The first was in February 1777, just after Clinton withdrew half his troops. The second was in the following October. On both these occasions, the New England states sent a few thousand men who could scarcely be prevailed upon to stay, let alone be formed into a unified army. On the third occasion, in the summer of 1778, the Congress and Washington backed a stronger assault. General John Sullivan spent months gathering men and ammunition, preparing for the arrival of units of the Continental Army under the Marquis de Lafayette and Rhode Island's own General Nathanael Greene. The attackers were to get additional help from a French squadron with a contingent of marines, one of the first benefits of the recent alliance with Louis XVI. The Continentals and the French arrived late. Sullivan could hardly wait to attack. The French naval commander, Admiral Charles Hector, Comte d'Estaing, was almost as impatient, because his fleet was running low on fresh water and provisions. Still, there had to be conferences on strategy and final preparations, which delayed things until a British squadron appeared. D'Estaing called back his marines and sailed off to give battle, leaving Sullivan's men in the act of laying siege to Newport.

For eleven days the attack continued, in spite of a hurricane on August 12. Sullivan's men forced their way to the last ring of fortifications around their target. Then d'Estaing returned and announced that he could not stay: his ships had been damaged so severely by the storm that he had to get them repaired. His orders required him to sail to shipyards at Boston. Nothing the generals could say would persuade him to use the facilities in Narragansett Bay. So Newport lay open to reinforcement.

Sullivan's numerical superiority, about eight thousand men to six thousand, was narrow enough to begin with. He had to retreat. As he fell back, the British attacked and suffered defeat. He thought of resuming the siege, hoping for d'Estaing's return, but Clinton brought in four thousand men and a naval force that sealed off the bay once more.

Sullivan withdrew to safety but hoped to try again. The Continental troops waited for months near Providence, while the generals bickered over who was to blame for their failure and supplies ran short as neighboring states tried to curtail shipments across their borders. After a mutiny among the men, the concentration of forces in Rhode Island had to be given up. Washington still believed that he should devote all his resources to capturing New York City; nothing Rhode Island could say would persuade the Congress to do more than authorize a special bonus plan to help raise a state army of fifteen hundred men and recommend that neighboring states lift their embargoes on provisions. Actually, the British evacuated Newport in October 1779 when a new naval commander, Admiral Marriott Arbuthnot, decided that holding the place gave him no advantage, and Clinton decided the occupation force could be more useful in the south.

Newport was occupied a second time in July 1780, but then by a friendly force from France. The Comte de Rochambeau with six thousand men and a small supporting fleet of warships waited there for an opportunity to aid Washington. The British blockaded the mouth of Narragansett Bay most of the time, allowing the French only a few chances to slip out and attack the enemy ships or support military action in Virginia. At least the French stymied Clinton's plans for retaking Newport. Finally Rochambeau marched across Connecticut to join the Continental Army in June 1781, leaving the squadron to escape when it could. Luckily, the opportunity arrived just after Washington and Rochambeau had deceived Clinton and set out for Virginia, where they were to meet a much stronger French fleet commanded by the Comte de Grasse. Washington chose to attack the small British army under Lord Charles Cornwallis, then near Yorktown, and defer the assault on New York City still longer.

The action in Virginia proceeded smoothly, little aided by the squadron that escaped Newport to lend a hand. Cornwallis surrendered, giving the revolutionary cause a victory that proved decisive, although Washington at the time still believed he must retake New York City by force. He was bitterly disappointed when de Grasse refused to join in an attack there. Rochambeau and his men returned to Rhode Island for a short stay, but the state soon saw the last of foreign soldiers.

Rhode Island was a small theater of war, where a great local effort brought no dramatic results, although men from the state served in the forces that saw action elsewhere on land and sea. The first troops sent to Boston in 1775 were taken into the Continental Army as three regiments. After that year, the state supplied two regiments until they were consolidated into one in 1781. The men served mainly in New York and New Jersey, distinguishing themselves especially in the defense of Fort Red Bank across the Delaware from Philadelphia in October 1777. The next year one of the regiments was restored to full strength by recruiting free blacks and slaves, the General Assembly buying the freedom of the slaves from their erstwhile owners. The two regiments, one largely composed of black men, formed part of Sullivan's army in the siege of Newport but later returned to New York while General Greene went off to earn fame by his brilliant Fabian strategy in the Carolinas. The consolidated regiment went with Washington to share in the glory at Yorktown.

Rhode Island maintained its own army, as did other states, to form a home guard, aided by the militia. The old train bands had to supply men for active duty for short stints on a rotational basis. The local Tories formed miniature counterparts of these forces. The loyalists, though hardly numerous, defy easy generalization: they included all sorts of people, ranging from bellicose royalists to Quakers who were as conscientious in remaining faithful to the king as they were in refusing to take up arms for him. Conspicuous among the Tories were prominent citizens, especially professional men who were British-born, of Aquidneck and the Narragansett country. Eighty of the more ardent men joined the Loyal New Englanders in 1777, and a greater number later formed the Loyal Newport Associates to defend the city against the revolutionaries.

In naval affairs the early efforts of Esek Hopkins to take the United States Navy home with him came to grief behind a British blockade. His son and his brother-in-law, Abraham Whipple of *Gaspee* fame, kept skirting disgrace, as did the other local men whom Hopkins put in command of United States vessels. Virtually the only captain of unsullied reputation was an army man, Silas Talbot of Providence, who now and then got command of a ship. His greatest exploit took place in October 1778 when he attacked the British schooner blocking the mouth of Sakonnet River east of Aquidneck. The jib boom of Talbot's sloop plunged into the rigging of the British vessel, holding her tight while Talbot's men overran her. Actually, Whipple managed to serve illustriously for most of his naval career and even displayed a talent for strategic fleet action as well as the capture of enemy ships that American officers really preferred. The New England captains generally drew complaints for acting essentially as privateers did, seeking prizes and squandering time on shore grasping for larger shares of the profits. Naval policy veered from endorsing to opposing such ways. There was a good case to be made for using the navy to prey on enemy shipping: prizes helped the revolutionary cause in many ways, while there could be no hope of matching British seapower in fleet engagements. Still, the Congress in its vacillation tended to want strategic use of the navy or none. When this became obvious, a number of captains resigned to command privateer cruises.

Rhode Island shippers rushed into privateering early in the war with results that were only a variation on what had happened in the two previous wars. The initial burst of activity came to a halt with the closing of Narragansett Bay. Thereafter Rhode Island investors and seamen had to operate from bases at New Bedford or Boston for the most part, often merging their ventures in the plans of men living in those ports. Toward the end of the war privateering returned to Providence and Newport in a small way but never attained great proportions. The seafaring communities had to keep active to escape poverty, and many lost their lives or fortunes all the same.

Commerce based in Rhode Island, like privateering, went through an early burst of activity, to be forced into other channels by independence and the British occupation of Newport. Though vessels could get in and out of Narragansett Bay by stealth and expert seamanship, the risks were great and traffic shifted to less perilous ports in Massachusetts. By expensive overland transportation, Providence merchants usually managed to keep stocks of most basic imports at fancy prices that enriched the lucky few. Even before Lexington and Concord, far-sighted men began looking to continental European markets. With hostilities against Great Britain closing off accustomed sources, merchants sought connections in France and Spain, which proved hard to make, and in the Netherlands, where huge central marketing cities not only offered a great array of goods but also by clandestine traffic supplied the wares previously bought in London and Bristol. Similar business developed in the Caribbean, most extensively at the Dutch island of St. Eustatius, where British exporters as well as other Europeans took cargoes to sell to Americans. In spite of such expedients, however, Rhode Island merchants rejoiced at the end of hostilities and rushed to resume their voyages to British ports.

To supplement the proceeds of commerce and to aid the revolution, Rhode Island men turned to new kinds of business. Contracts for the armed forces proved lucrative to some, while others lost heavily. Wartime scarcities made profits possible in manufacturing, such as a cannon foundry, that would have failed in peacetime. Providence and vicinity tried a number of enterprises that enjoyed an ephemeral prosperity.

Public finance in the revolutionary war necessarily had a makeshift quality. Rhode Island, released from the restraints of British law, reflexively resorted to paper currency. After a fleeting effort to support the value by promising interest, the state joyfully embraced the congressional plan to foot military bills in a unified way by the creation of continental dollars. Though Rhode Island intermittently printed small additional amounts of paper, it endorsed the reasoning that issuance of a United States currency, at first as fiat money and only later to be supported, would eventually distribute the costs of revolution equitably, regardless of where battles took place. Rhode Island held its share of the burden firmly in the early years, taxing its citizens more than most states and compelling them to subscribe to federal loans when the Congress began borrowing. This zeal cooled when the United States repudiated most of the continental currency in 1780 and went over to a system of requisitions on the states to supply men, arms, provisions, uniforms, and everything else needed to fight a war.

The War for American Independence kept quenching Rhode Island's initial ardor for a union of the states. The failure of a fiscal system that could finance the war and lead to a reasonable distribution of the costs was only one trouble. The Congress consistently relegated the recapture of Newport to low priority and never made serious efforts to supply protection to the New England coast. When the United States launched a navy, local enthusiasm suffered the blows of official displeasure at what Hopkins regarded as bad luck, condemnation of the basically predatory approach to fighting at sea that Rhode Island skippers thought natural and logical, and then abandonment of all efforts to maintain naval strength. The state rushed to ratify the Articles of Confederation in 1778 but thereafter grew distrustful of the Continental Congress.* Men who had schooled themselves in the ways to use their colonial government to watch out for local interests and head off centralization of authority in London naturally resisted centralization in Philadelphia and sought to use state power even more extensively than colonial.

The armies and navies vanished over the horizons in 1781. Surprisingly, they never returned. The battle of Yorktown turned out to be the decisive event of the war, although the patriots did not realize it at first. Washington still thought he had to storm New York City and sought French help. The British government, however, saw in Cornwallis' surrender the proof that stamping out the Revolution would be so long and expensive as to be politically impossible. Reluctantly, George III accepted Lord North's resignation and turned to long-time opponents of the American war to form a new ministry and end the conflict.

---

* Rhode Island adopted the unusual practice of letting the voters choose the representatives in the Congress at the annual general election.

Even more rapidly, Rhode Islanders sensed the end of hostilities. Before Rochambeau decamped, they were preparing for peace. Forced by Congress to assume the burden of supporting military measures in 1781, cheered by the gold the French used to buy what they wanted, Rhode Island took steps to manage its own commercial future. The plan for a federal impost, a tariff of 5 percent *ad valorem* intended to give the Congress a revenue of its own, promised fewer benefits than an independent policy on trade. Accordingly the state chose to levy its own duty, to put a discriminatory burden on British shipping, and to favor the local merchants with a rebate on taxes paid on wares they reexported. The goal was to make the state a center of importation and distribution of goods destined for its neighbors.

Rhode Island's refusal to approve the federal impost thwarted the plan at some cost to good relations with the other states. Under the Articles of Confederation, the tariff could not be imposed without an amendment, which required unanimous consent of the states. Merchants of Newport and Providence wanted to stop the scheme, but they wanted a second state to join the opposition, so they used delaying tactics. Local advocates of a strong federal government, led by James Mitchell Varnum, argued the case for the impost in the newspapers. Writers on the other side, notably David Howell and Theodore Foster, presented the case for states' rights, use of western lands as a fund to pay for the Revolution, and for straightforward interpretation of the Articles to forestall efforts to read into the document implications that the Congress might do whatever was likely to help carry out the powers explicitly given it. The Rhode Island enemies of the impost particularly resented proposals for the Congress to appoint its own revenue agents in the states. There was some basis for this feeling: the state in the past had been fairly diligent and successful in gathering taxes to meet congressional requisitions.

Whatever the merits of the question the impost went down to defeat in 1782. The Congress sent men to plead for it, Thomas Paine wrote newspaper articles defending it, but the General Assembly heeded local merchants. Howell and two like-minded men were sent as delegates to face congressional wrath. Fresh efforts to sway the Assembly were launched but quickly given up when Virginia rescinded her approval of the amendment permitting the tariff. Rhode Island belatedly had the desired consort in opposition. Later attempts to concoct a substitute proposition that would meet the objections raised in 1782 fared little better, crashing on opposition in various states—and not always in Rhode Island.

The delay and debate over the federal tariff, in addition to inspiring a praiseworthy analysis of the issues, served to let businessmen reap profits from speculation in currencies. Some patriots in Providence, burdened with congressional securities, let rumors of likely ratification of the impost boost the value of their holdings until it was attractive to sell for debased state notes, which rose in price once Rhode Island's intransigence became obvious.

New England state paper money and bonds gained value as the governments behind them took steps to insure their worth. Rhode Island joined in these efforts fairly strenuously. The state began assuming its citizens' claims on the Congress. Though far from complete, the process converted several types of federal bonds and bills into state notes and certificates of indebtedness. At first the result appeared to be a sound and stable fiscal system, which was what the trading interest wanted, but soon the expense of paying interest and principle mounted up so as to impose an intolerable weight of taxes on the populace beyond what the import duties brought in.

Before popular resentment reached a dangerous level, the fiscal policy provided favorable conditions for commerce, for rebuilding social institutions, and for repairing wartime damage. Merchants rushed to reestablish trade even before the peace treaty was signed in 1783. They imported so much as to glut the market and force the usual postwar depression. The crisis was not the same as earlier ones, however, because there was a new set of conditions to be faced. British policy naturally treated the United States as foreign territory, posing a novel challenge to men who had learned business inside the imperial commercial web. Besides, American consumers still liked the wares available from London and Bristol. Rhode Island importers could resume only

John Brown house on Power Street in Providence, designed by Joseph
Brown in 1786, now headquarters of the Rhode Island Historical
Society. *The Rhode Island Historical Society.*

some of the old exchanges. Most significant was the shift in British policy to exclude them from the accustomed business in the West Indies. It became necessary to use at British ports the extralegal maneuvers formerly developed to carry on trade with the French islands. Less hampering were tax arrangements to favor British shippers in their home ports against Americans. After all, Rhode Island had gained authority by the Revolution to retaliate with its own discriminatory laws.

There was a whole world outside the British empire, moreover. If trade with France had been crippled by misunderstandings and red tape, the possibility remained that patience and knowledge would in time win success. Or there were other European countries, notably the Netherlands and the Baltic nations, where lucrative business might be carried on. More hazardous, but potentially more profitable, was direct trade with exotic ports where one could get tea, silks, fine cottons, porcelain, or spices. Rhode Islanders cautiously sought out these formerly forbidden territories, but many prudently put their capital in the familiar slave trade from West Africa even after the state forbade fitting out slaving voyages. The perils and disappointments in commerce inspired much lamentation and hand-wringing, but traditional shrewdness and sharp practice served the merchants well. Some, such as John Brown of Providence, prospered and built imposing new houses befitting the opulence they knew was within their reach.

Business was stimulated by the need to replace houses, shops, wharves, and ships destroyed during the revolutionary war, yet peace also spoiled certain economic ventures. In Newport and at various points along the coast, buildings had to be replaced or repaired. The British occupation, with the attendant shortage of firewood, had left many houses and public buildings in bad shape. It took several years to put Newport's churches and meetinghouses to rights. Providence suffered little, but in the 1780s resumed a building boom interrupted by the war. All the ports wanted to get merchant fleets afloat with the least possible delay. By liberal and widespread credit, construction could be undertaken, giving employment to workmen who made the ships or buildings with which to carry on business.

Nevertheless, the rush into construction and commerce could not spread prosperity evenly. Wartime manufacturing enterprises and their workers often faced hard times as cheaper competitive products flowed in again from foreign suppliers. Merchants suffered from a loss of customers, especially so because the state's population had dropped by one-eighth during the war, most of the decline in Newport. Peace brought a return of refugees, soldiers, and sailors, but not all who still lived came back. Some found new homes in other states, a few fled the country altogether. The most famous tories, Joseph Wanton senior and junior, had died in New York, but others remained in exile. In one respect fewer people seemed desirable; local opinion held that Rhode Island had been unable to grow enough food for the inhabitants before the war. This may well have been true, though hard to prove. Certainly wartime wrestling with the problems of provisioning the additional men who came as soldiers, small though the numbers may appear to later generations, showed that the farms in a wide belt of southern New England had to be drawn upon to provide supplies. With the return of peace, the need to rely on sources across the borders seemed likely to create a dependency that could hamper commercial progress. When the population returned to the prewar level in 1786 and kept on growing, the dependency seemed to be imminent.

Reconstruction was necessary also in the social institutions. The Redwood Library, for instance, had fallen into disarray. The books had been scattered, the organization disbanded. Devoted men had to hunt down the missing volumes and get the General Assembly to authorize reconstituting the membership into a self-perpetuating corporation. Churches had to be set up again, their property repaired, their endowments in some cases disentangled from the estates of departed loyalists. The college in Providence had to be put back into action. Charities had to be reorganized. Especially in Newport the social fabric had been so torn that reweaving required much time and money.

Elsewhere repair was less extensive and there was more fresh construction. Quakers were energetically trying to provide sectarian schools for their children, gentlemen in the Kingstowns at last wanted to improve a legacy of one of the Pettaquamscut purchasers to endow an academy. There was even a new religion, curiously reminiscent of the old Antinomian movement. Jemima Wilkinson, a Quaker from Cumberland who had defected to the New Light Baptists, after a severe illness became convinced that she had died and that her body had been taken over by a spirit named the Publick Universal Friend. Her preaching and powerful personality attracted numerous followers, enough in East Greenwich to finance a meetinghouse. Scoffing and hostility so depressed her that she sent her converts to western New York in 1788, joining them a couple of years later. After that she ceased to disturb her native state. In more substantial, if less definable, ways there was a ferment of activity to build an indigenous civilization, to found cultural and financial institutions, to pioneer in industrialization, and in general to prove that America deserved to be on the map.

Rhode Island opponents of slavery began organizing to abolish bondage by law. After some years of agitation the General Assembly voted for gradual emancipation in 1787. Enthusiasts, many of them Friends, undertook private efforts to provide education for the newly free and otherwise to set them on the way to becoming self-supporting members of their communities. Stopping the slave trade proved harder. In a risky commercial recovery, merchants cherished a traffic with relatively certain profits and evaded state laws against fitting out slaving voyages. Rhode Island almost entirely excluded open slave dealing within its borders, but this hardly hurt the traffic because the merchants did not want to bring in black people anyway, only to take them where slavery flourished.

The difficulties of regaining commercial prosperity to some people justified the energetic fiscal measures to assume the state's share of the federal debt and create a stable money system. The effects of this policy, however, grew so severe as to generate a fierce opposition. The revenue needed to support the fiscal measures quickly outgrew the proceeds of the import duties and forced resort to steep taxes on property. The very success of the new Rhode Island dollar caused trouble, because people hoarded the state's money. A currency shortage then made it hard for the

rural people to pay taxes or even to borrow the money they
needed for daily affairs. Farmers feared loss of their property.
Towns fell behind in collecting taxes. Bitter and clever men
began examining the fiscal measures and concluded that they
had been contrived to benefit a few, who had large holdings in
certain kinds of securities issued during the war, at the expense of
many others, who had held different kinds in smaller face value
amounts.

Genuine misery and accusations of favoritism gave support to
a characteristic Rhode Island plan: a new land bank. To
promote the scheme a new political party formed, called the
Country Party. The most conspicuous leader was Jonathan J.
Hazard, dubbed "The Oracle" by an enemy. Although he came
from a prominent family in South Kingstown, he had important
aides from many places, including lesser merchants in the cities.
The candidate for governor was one of the latter, John Collins of
Newport. Hazard drew directly on knowledge of the paper
money plans and the party machines of the colonial period, but
in political technique he advanced beyond Ward and Hopkins.
Counter-organization fared ill because the desultory remains of
the prewar parties slowed a coalescence of enemies of the
Country Party; and besides, Hazard had a scheme to benefit
nearly everybody. He and some friends talked it up with great
success in 1785.

The idea was to make the state's debt and its obligations to
support the local dollar vanish in a few years of strenuous fiscal
action. The state would lend paper money in the old fashion, tax
property heavily to bring the money into the treasury, use it to
buy back the state's securities, and then tax the money back to
the treasury again and burn it. The pace could be regulated
according to the ability of the populace to tolerate the taxation,
but the outlook was favorable for a rapid operation because the
loans would put money in people's hands, and landowners could
endure high taxes for a few years if they could see the end of such
burdens.

By contrast there was a minority naturally opposed to Hazard.
The major owners of securities could look forward to losing them
in exchange for dubious paper, a loss hardly to be compensated

by an end of steep taxes, although it might have seemed a
reasonable price for safety against social revolution. Merchants,
by 1785 making headway in restoring commerce and finding
new trade routes, feared disruption of the currency and introduction of a money that would not circulate far outside Rhode
Island. Those whose livelihood was directly dependent on export
trade could likewise conclude that a new land bank would hurt
them by paralyzing commerce. Still, even in Providence and
Newport, the Country Party had nearly half the vote. In the
rural towns it drew huge majorities.

Hazard and his cohorts swept the elections in 1786 and
promptly began to carry out their plan. The best the opponents
could do within Rhode Island—and that was not very good—
was to attack the soundness of the new paper money by refusing
to accept it. Hazard had insisted that it would not depreciate if it
circulated freely, and his friends passed various laws designed to
insure that everyone should use it. Some measures were knocked
down when the Superior Court ruled for a Newport butcher
named John Weeden who had refused to take the new bills in
payment from a cabinetmaker named John Trevett. The court
spoke, technically, only on its power to hear the suit, but some of
the judges made it clear that they regarded a Country Party law
as unconstitutional, because it allowed trials without a jury in
disputes over receipt of the money. The court's decision in 1786
was enough to force Hazard to different measures and to hasten
the depreciation of the new notes. Their loss of value, ironically,
speeded up the retirement of the state debt by making steep taxes
easier to pay. There was no question of the state's legal power to
force owners of securities to choose between having them
repudiated and selling them to the treasury. Nor was there any
challenge to the measures to remove public backing of certain
private contracts and promissory notes, a device used mainly to
intimidate those who were reluctant to use the paper money.

However limited the power of the opposition inside the state,
Hazard's enemies could and did spread propaganda against the
Country Party and its measures throughout the rest of the United
States. The campaign went to such lengths that a delegate in the
Congress, though himself an opponent of the paper money plan,

felt he had to protest stories printed in New York as libels against his state. The vilification, along with news of Shays's Rebellion in Massachusetts—just the sort of thing that had menaced Rhode Island before the Country Party launched its plan—served to gain support for those who wanted to alter the federal government. In the end the success of the moves to adopt a new constitution for the United States, not local opposition by itself, brought the downfall of Jonathan J. Hazard.

The Country Party had a firm grip on the state's political machinery. It won elections by landslides. It brought fresh talent into public life. It maintained astounding party discipline in the General Assembly—so much as to make its secret caucuses a substitute for genuine public deliberation. It maintained its strength by the practice of calling on the towns for instructions to their representatives. The result was almost a system of government by plebiscite. The representatives scrupulously observed their constituents' orders. Of course, the representatives took care to influence the framing of instructions, but they sometimes did not get what the party leaders wanted, and felt bound all the same. Indeed, when faced with the problem of ratifying or rejecting the new federal Constitution, Hazard and his friends found opposition to the new document so prevalent and durable in rural Rhode Island as to hamper the party's freedom to maneuver and to pursue the course Hazard really thought best, finishing the fiscal overhaul and then ratifying the Constitution. In the end, he got his way on this strategy, but to get it took time, labor, and fast footwork. The only major question on which the party leadership was actually stymied was amending the state's constitution to cut down the representation of the original towns in the General Assembly, which was sought because three of the four usually sided with the opposition.

Firmly in control, the Country Party proceeded with its fiscal measures. The state treasury began buying back securities in the spring of 1787. By then the paper money was worth a seventh or less of its face value. Some major owners refused to sell and preferred to let their securities be declared worthless, thus enabling the government to call in the rest more rapidly than planned. The process was nearly finished by the end of 1789.

State property taxes ceased, with adequate revenue flowing into the treasury from tariffs, excises, and interest from the loans that had floated the paper money. The state was out of debt. Hazard's scheme appeared to have been a huge success.

A large majority of the citizens agreed that the fiscal magic had worked splendidly. To be sure, many people had qualms about elements in it. It entailed temporary interference with trade across the borders while governmental power tried to uphold the paper money as legal tender. It remained to be seen whether the end of state debt and high taxes would bring the predicted gush of commercial prosperity. Some who paid off debts in depreciated paper believed they were cheating their creditors and, when better times came, voluntarily paid the difference between the value of the paper and the sum originally borrowed.

The minority, however, was fiercely unreconciled. Hazard's opponents believed the Country Party was tampering with civil liberties and the safety of property rights. Obviously, the owners who chose to take nothing rather than the state's new money disliked the whole scheme and in a sense were quite right in thinking it was designed to confiscate their investments. The other side of the question, however, had merit too: the state was paying more for the securities than could be obtained for them on the open market. That view of the case persuaded most owners. The others, the ones with the largest holdings, in effect gambled on the arrival of a new method to restore full face value to their securities.

A new method began to look like a distinct possibility when steps were taken to create a new federal government that might recapture control of fiscal policy from the states and restore value to securities representing the public debt. Timing of the steps could scarcely have been worse for the Country Party and ultimately ruined the political careers of Jonathan J. Hazard, John Collins, and most of the other party chieftains. They refused to send delegates to the Constitutional Convention in 1787 and thereafter sent no representatives to Congress except for roughly a year before Washington's inauguration as president, and during that time denounced Congress for endorsing the new

Constitution, because it was not legal under the Articles of Confederation. Hazard quite rightly insisted that Rhode Island must not interrupt its own fiscal measures once they had started.

To prevent interference he in effect over-sold his followers on the need to resist the new Constitution. He predicted that ratifying it would at the very least buy taxation at the price of liberty, foster a strangling bureaucracy, and subject Rhode Island to domination by the large states. By rejecting the new federal government, the state could be completely independent and thrive in commerce, in the fashion of the Netherlands, attracting business from ports where United States taxes and regulations would make goods more expensive. The Country Party in 1787 had the backing of the Quakers, the only other solid bloc on the political scene, who opposed a federal government that would countenance slavery. The campaign to arouse popular opposition to the Constitution worked beautifully, and Hazard systematically used measures to keep ratification a matter of popular vote. Still, he and Governor Collins favored ratifying when their fiscal policy had been carried out. So determined was the opposition to the Constitution among their followers that this strategy could hardly be mentioned in public, let alone propagated among a large number of the voters.

Unfortunately for the Country Party, the question of ratifying could not be put off for long. Gloomily the leaders received news that state after state endorsed the new document, that the new government was organized in New York, that Congress planned to treat Rhode Island as a foreign country in commercial dealings. Local pressures built up. Advocates of the Constitution warned that if delay continued an angry United States would invade Rhode Island and partition it between Connecticut and Massachusetts. This prediction had no foundation; it was used purely to frighten people. So in all likelihood was the secessionist talk in Providence, which spread to Newport and all the towns in between.

Hazard and his friends had to do something. They steered through the General Assembly a resolution calling a ratifying convention to meet on March 1, 1790. Even this action barely succeeded over the opposition of the party faithful and cost

Governor Collins his good name when he broke the tie in the upper house. Inconspicuously the advocates of ratification within the Country Party began showing their colors, allowing some force to the arguments they had so recently opposed. The Quaker leadership simultaneously broadcast second thoughts on the Constitution, declaring that it was highly satisfactory for the most part, that a well-formed United States government would be advantageous, and that the clauses on slavery should not determine the question because the Constitution did after all permit ending the slave trade as early as 1808.

The convention met and would have turned down the Constitution if a vote had been taken at once. The party leaders, convinced that ratification was necessary and could be done soon, steered the convention to proposing amendments, then to adjournment in order to let the citizens in the towns express their views. During the recess the Country Party safely won the spring election, replacing Governor Collins with the enigmatic Arthur Fenner, the party chief in Providence. Frantic efforts turned a few towns to favoring the Constitution, Congress added a kick by threatening to cut off all commerce with Rhode Island, but still when the convention met again the majority was opposed. More hectic machinations, including the whip of party discipline and some impromptu consultations in various towns, resulted in a bare majority for ratification by May 28—but at the price of such obvious bending of the party's principles on obeying the will of the people as to bring into the open the internal quarrels among the leaders. The Country Party did not survive very long.

Once the convention had finished its work, Governor Fenner rushed word to President Washington and summoned the General Assembly to make the necessary arrangements for restoring Rhode Island to a place in the United States. Everything was done speedily, and President Washington planned a goodwill tour a few weeks later. Upon his arrival in Providence on August 19, the city staged something like a repeat of the celebration that had greeted the Declaration of Independence. Cannon boomed, bells pealed, dignitaries declaimed laudatory salutations. Graciously the first president replied to the address of the Assembly, "it affords me peculiar pleasure to observe that the

The King's County courthouse at Little Rest (now home of the Kingston Free Library in Washington County), scene of the Rhode Island convention that met in March 1790 and finally ratified the Federal Constitution on May 29. Detail of a map of South Kingstown by Henry F. Walling, 1857. *The Rhode Island Historical Society.*

completion of our Union, by the accession of your state, gives a strong assurance of permanent political happiness to the people of America."

Outwardly everything was jubilation, but in state politics a storm was brewing. In the race for the seat in the United States House of Representatives, three Country Party stalwarts opposed each other, and one of their opponents won a majority of the votes. The Assembly refused to send Jonathan J. Hazard to the Senate, virtually ending his political career. Governor Fenner instead engineered selection of his own brother-in-law, a well-liked Federalist. In fact, the previously vague or inscrutable Fenner was shaking up the political alignments to finish off the Country Party and gain a backing that would keep him and his son in office for years to come.

Fenner's new coalition even undid Hazard's fiscal manipulations as part of a general revision of public finance. When the Congress voted to assume state debts, it allocated only a small sum to Rhode Island. Political tactics to revise it upward had some success but did not raise the total high enough to cover all the securities that Rhode Island had bought up, the ones its citizens had refused to sell, and the amount due to its citizens for payment of additional claims against the federal treasury (principally for wartime damages and purchases) that Congress finally decided to honor. So Fenner sponsored legislation that returned to the owners those securities the state had bought, adding an endorsement that the owners had received one-fifteenth of the value—the paper currency had fallen to that point in depreciation—and rescinded the repudiation of the securities that people had refused to sell to the state. Rhode Island was back in debt and resumed taxation to pay off what the congressional appropriation did not cover, a process that was mostly completed during the 1790s, although it dragged on for several years afterwards. This expensive, but evenhanded, policy avoided the political perils of the years just after the Revolution, when the state shifted from one extreme to another, and so prevented the revival of old contests. All the same, it brought to a close the freewheeling fiscal adventures that had characterized Rhode Island public policy in the eighteenth century.

After a century and a half of bucking the outside world, the people around Narragansett Bay submitted to the bridle of the United States. Their ancestors had risked their lives rather than fall into line with the Puritans of Massachusetts. They had preserved their little communities for decades against neighboring colonies that wanted to subdue the pariah settlements. In the generations of Walter Clarke and Samuel Cranston, the leaders of Rhode Island steered it past the perils of internal discord, predatory neighbors, and energetic imperial government to a secure autonomy under the British Crown. As they did so, they fostered the commercial and fiscal system that lifted Newport to such prosperity and size that it could become a serious rival to Boston. As daring in finance as it had been in religious doctrine, Rhode Island cheerfully continued to offend its neighbors and the mother country. The monetary policy called down the wrath of Great Britain by 1751, bringing an early forerunner of restrictions that came thick and fast after 1760. If the officials in Newport at first thought it wise to accept the confinements imposed by London, to take the consequences of achieving a prominent place in the British commercial world, there were second thoughts when the naval patrol began in 1763 and the Parliament began attempts at direct taxation soon after. Remaining in the British empire, to all but a few leading citizens, seemed intolerably constricting by 1775. The only question then was one of timing, whether the colony should assert its independence when it saw fit or wait for the others to join in a general declaration. As events worked out, Rhode Island tried it both ways, reserving the public celebrations for action by the Continental Congress. Even after that, adherence to the United States remained uncertain, with attitudes shifting according to the advantages or lack of them that the state derived from the connection. The old spirit of separatism and independence did not subside easily.

What had been the value of clinging to autonomy for so many years? The benefits were mainly for people in the colony; outsiders rarely saw more than the superficial attractions of the place. Long after the establishment of the United States, the old condemnations of Rogues' Island and its founders were often repeated. Some, like Samuel Gorton, have never gained renown. By the twentieth century, however, it became fashionable to canonize Roger Williams as a saint of American democracy, to praise him for rescuing government from interference by religion, for upholding freedom of worship, for dealing magnanimously with the Indians, for resisting tyranny and the priesthood in Massachusetts. Eventually Anne Hutchinson was rehabilitated as a champion of religious liberty and later still of women's rights. These two, it has been said, were ahead of their times, pioneers of modern ideas and values, and therefore misunderstood and reviled in their own day.

The zeal to pluck heroes out of the past is surely not an evil one, but it commonly has been practiced without a sense of proportion. The people of colonial Rhode Island were all truly of their own times, not later ones. They lived their own lives, not rehearsals for posterity. Roger Williams' quarrel with the authorities in Boston was a quarrel among Puritans. If he concluded that church and state must be held apart, it was first for the sake of purifying the church. The dramatic events of 1636 flowed from religious convictions that seem as idiosyncratic now as they did to John Winthrop then. These notions have naturally tended to fade out of sight. The enduring results of these events came in the later development of Williams' wisdom. The headstrong reasoner turned into the politician and patriarch, leading in secular rather than ecclesiastical affairs, reconciling squabbling neighbors, searching for ways to make self-government effective, damping his brother's outbursts of enthusiasm for theoretically pure democracy as well as fighting William Coddington's schemes for personal authority.

In dealings with fellow settlers in Rhode Island, to better effect than in arguments with other Puritan ministers, Williams explored the meaning of the "soul liberty" he had sought. He soon decided that for the time being a pure church was unattainable, that God's chosen were destined to live scattered among the rest of humanity; thus he came to a practical policy of working or praying with people of all persuasions. He and his neighbors so disagreed on religion that they virtually had to concur on building a wall between church and state if govern-

ment was to exist at all—and even then, some people kept trying
to tear it down. Religious freedom, which certainly was attained
in early Rhode Island, became as much the policy of prudence as
of conviction.

By making the best of what he learned as events dashed his
original hopes, Williams proceeded to ideas more congenial to
modern views. Religious liberty was necessary for the welfare of
mankind because people would surely have different persuasions,
not because they could attain one perfect understanding. Williams concluded that the heathenism of the Narragansetts, which
he abhorred, was as good for them as Christianity was for most
Europeans—that is, little more than a weak curb on wickedness
and a dim guide to some basic truths. He deplored the failure of
the early Rhode Island settlers to preserve intellectually respectable religion, yet he resigned himself to the conviction that
religious freedom must allow ignorance, error, and even irreligion. This extent of liberty was protected by law in his colony.

In the seventeenth century, full exercise of soul liberty
necessarily included repudiation of the traditional clergy.
Though Anne Hutchinson was no builder, though William
Coddington demeaned himself by clutching for high status, they
dared to take the last big step in the Reformation by rejecting
even the intellectual authority of the priesthood. Williams
argued against them but joined them in preserving the right of
anyone to follow their example and the right of men to do so
without affecting their standing in the body politic. This was
indeed a thoroughgoing dedication to religious freedom, not
religious toleration such as English sectaries were gaining then at
the price of tacit promises to remain obscure and powerless.
Though nobody proclaimed it with fanfares, Rhode Island in the
seventeenth century was unique in giving complete participation
in secular affairs to men of all religious views, in eradicating
religious tests and ceremonies from the conduct of government.

It would be agreeable to conclude that the "lively experiment"
in religious liberty that Charles II authorized in the charter was
a complete success. But in the terms that John Clarke proposed
in his petition for that document, the experiment was mostly a
failure for half a century. Religious liberty flourished indeed, yet

it neither conduced to "a most flourishing civil state" nor "true loyalty" to the king of England. Neither did it yield domestic peace. It merely provided religious liberty. The temporal blessings of wealth and respite from sectarian bickering, as far as they were enjoyed, came in the eighteenth century, along with imperial patriotism. Before then, soul liberty, beyond its own benefits, did little for Rhode Island except prevent the citizens from adding religious persecution to each other's woes. That was quite enough to justify the policy.

Likewise it is wrong to judge early Rhode Island as a shining light of fairness in dealings with the Indians. It was as good as any, but no colony deserved a halo. Williams may be praised justly for treating Indians as fellow human beings and for honorable diplomacy to prevent bloodshed between European immigrants and American natives. Yet his behavior was not entirely saintly—his diplomacy was more to preserve the English than the Indians—nor did his views prevail among his fellow settlers. They sometimes had a decent regard for the goodwill of the sachems who had opened a place of refuge to Massachusetts dissidents; more important, the outcasts knew that they would be fools to antagonize the Narragansetts, who outnumbered them. They lived in fear, and probably on that account acquiesced when the neighboring colonies stirred up a war and pulverized the Wampanoags and Narragansetts. Even Williams, as a soldier in King Philip's War, made sure he got his share of the captives who were to be sold into servitude. His fellow citizens scrambled to make sure they got as much as they could of the Indians' land.

The separatist colony, then, in the times of its founders, should not be regarded as a band of legendary heroes any more than as a nest of crackpots and villains. The people who went to the settlements around Narragansett Bay may have held radical religious beliefs but they displayed an assortment of human traits and virtues—daring, courage, greed, magnanimity, resolution, obstinacy, hospitality, quarrelsomeness, duplicity, independence of spirit—and all in human dimensions. Their success in working out a policy of religious freedom that later generations have found admirable was as much an adjustment to unforeseen necessities as the implementation of high ideals. Their explora-

tions of ways to create self-government, ingenious and inventive
as they were, took them into all the possibilities the mind has
ever thought of, but did not yield the desired results. Though the
record is a fascinating spectacle of what ordinary people could do
with a little intellectual preparation, an uncommon measure of
mental boldness, and the pressure of necessity, it is nevertheless a
record of failure to achieve order.

It is more difficult to assess the significance of the long stretch
of the colonial period after the founders passed from the scene.
Since that time people have often ignored this turbulent and
interesting period, even though the surviving artifacts and
buildings help the imagination to picture life in the eighteenth
century much more than anything can do for the early years.
The conflicts over land and local government, over keeping a
separate Rhode Island, over wars and paper money—these have
seemed like tedious and sterile contests that could interest only
the participants, happenings that later generations can cheerfully consign to the file of things over and done with. Even the
striking figures of those days have been nearly forgotten, except
by the genealogist who pries into their procreative exploits.

Patient inquiry, however, can nourish even the appetite for
heroes and villains. The commercial and maritime derring-do
that built the wealth of colonial Newport, properly appreciated,
should provide a treasure of exciting narratives. Unfortunately,
some of the best, such as the early triumphs of the Wantons, are
nearly impossible to reconstruct. The political events brought
fascinating personalities into action, notably Samuel Cranston
and the Ward dynasty. Among the preachers also there were
outstanding characters. Creative people in culture, especially the
ones who designed buildings or made the magnificent furniture,
are being discovered as memorable men. Lately attention has
turned to the women who managed print shops, Anne Franklin
in Newport and Sarah Updike Goddard in Providence.

Still, what these people did before the celebrated events
leading up to the Revolution has not seemed to have a large
significance. Perhaps that is because what they accomplished has
been taken for granted. For instance, the mere preservation of
Rhode Island as a distinct colony was no easy task, yet because it

was done the outcome appears foreordained by some vague whim of fate or nature. Only the very naïve presume to ask why there is such a tiny state.

The adjustment to religious diversity, too, appears unremarkable to people who regard the condition as ordinary. Yet in the eighteenth century, this had to be managed in the presence of a much wider assortment of faiths than before when the Anglicans, Congregationalists, and Jews were added to the radical sects of the seventeenth century. The first two of these newly arrived denominations did not regard as ordinary the soul liberty of Rhode Island. They had to learn to live under conditions determined by neighbors whose views they despised. The neighbors also had to revise their notions to let them all exist together in something like tranquillity. The success was so great as to make it appear to have required little effort, yet the people of Rhode Island were the first under the British flag, perhaps in the whole area dominated by western civilization, to make a go of religious freedom in a body politic containing no dominant religion. The eighteenth century, far more than the seventeenth, made the "lively experiment" a success.

In the secular order as well, the achievements of the eighteenth century consisted of arranging affairs in ways that now seem normal. The special purposes of that period, fending off British control and fostering Newport's trade, were pursued by centralizing authority in the colony's government and using the resulting power ingeniously. The General Assembly brought order to the military system by imposing a rational chain of command, defined the functions of towns by law, and regulated the business of the landowning syndicates to prevent their growth as bastions of autonomous power. With public affairs thus rescued from rampant localism, the colony could make headway in fiscal and economic measures for the general good. Military support of the monarchy and taxation of the citizens became feasible. The colony could also patrol commerce, extend a network of transportation, and manipulate currency for local advantage against the well-established commercial web centered at Boston.

All of this may seem today like a species of common sense, yet it was almost as innovative in public policy as was peaceful coexistence of half a dozen discordant sects of roughly equal size. The pioneering was the more significant because centralization of secular authority and extension of law to regulate the affairs of the colony were done not by an absolute monarchy, as was the case in some European states of that day, but by elected officials who preserved individual liberties and expected that a large proportion of the men in the jurisdiction would have to approve the conduct of public business. If the system was not democracy in a strict sense, if the interests of commercial Newport dictated much of what the government did, the result could reasonably be said to have enjoyed the consent of the body politic. Surely the voters and the political chiefs never hesitated to battle in the elections. In the end, the power potentially to be wielded by the ordinary man even made possible the precocious organization of political parties recognizably like those of the later United States.

The people of the colony generally gave warm approval to its form of self-government and let others think what they would. Outsiders deplored colonial Rhode Island as a licentious republic, royal officials in London became exasperated at its insistence on charter privileges and its high-handed resistance to imperial policies, some insiders groaned over the political squabbling and the refusal of ordinary citizens to honor their social superiors by letting them have their way in running the public business. Altogether there were many complaints, but the bulk of the citizens prized the governmental system they had created, although they might bemoan excesses in the political strife, and wanted to keep it.

There was no question, then, of Rhode Island failing to resist increased efforts by Great Britain to regulate American affairs. The king's ministers had very few friends in the heretic colony. There had been acquiescence in the need to cooperate in imperial wars, to accept vice admiralty courts and royal customs officers, even to submit to restraints on fiscal policy, once it became to Newport's taste to submit. In broad terms, Stephen Hopkins and the last Wantons championed a policy of sensible adjustment to changing realities in the structure of the empire and Rhode Island's place in it. Even the Hopkins party, however, reacted violently against the naval patrol, the Sugar

Act of 1764, and the next year's Stamp Act. They would adjust only so far as had been required under conditions prevailing in the previous two decades. Direct royal control and taxation were intolerable. Only a few men, like the Joseph Wantons, were driven to the conclusion that further compromise of Rhode Island autonomy would be better than revolution—and they reached this conclusion late and reluctantly. (Ironically, the elder Wanton was right in thinking that severing the ties with Great Britain would be suicide for Newport trade.) The events leading up to the Revolution in Rhode Island may have been dramatic, but not because the issues of the day turned the citizens against each other.

So deeply ingrained was the devotion to colonial self-government that Rhode Island could scarcely give up any of its independence for the sake of the United States. Led by Hopkins, whose appreciation of larger political systems far exceeded that of most of his compatriots, the state vociferously joined the new federal republic, but lost its enthusiasm as benefits from the connection seemed harder and harder to find. By the close of the War for American Independence Rhode Island was resuming resistance to a superior central government, this time confidently relying on constitutional law to give effect to its refusal to accept taxes and tax collectors imposed from outside.

The result of this defiance was the high point in Rhode Island's saucy independence. First the business interests insisted on using state power to support the value of the public debt and the currency, to create commercial law designed at last to give local shippers an advantage over British, but at the cost of ruinous taxation. This venture into making the state an economic realm of itself proved so disastrous politically as to bring on the still more extreme policies of the Country Party, designed to clear away the debt and taxes in one grand act of fiscal legerdemain. Unluckily this magic began when the United States was being reconstituted, so Rhode Island briefly chose total independence rather than abandon its plans in mid-career. The internal strife in the years between 1782 and 1789, however, reached such bitterness—beyond even the Ward-Hopkins Controversy—as to burn out some of the devotion to autonomy.

Arthur Fenner, the erstwhile Country Party captain in Providence, easily put together a new political combination to take Rhode Island firmly and finally into the United States.

While giving up some of the old independence, Rhode Island saved a portion. It even kept the precious old charter as its constitution for another half century. Submission to government under the new federal Constitution had its attractions. It was finally clear that the state could not get along as an economic unit by itself. The federal government would have to win commercial concessions from foreign nations. It would surely guarantee state boundaries, which was appealing after the long fights over them, and assure the free flow of interstate commerce, which had loomed as a new problem. The state would be represented in Congress, as it had never been in the British Parliament, and so would have a voice in the national affairs. Besides, some of the old purposes of autonomy, notably protection of religious freedom, no longer had to be fought for. In public policy toward religion as in securing individual rights and the formation of political parties, the United States was catching up with Rhode Island.

Maybe some sentimental tears were shed over the end of a century and a half of brash defiance—of Massachusetts and Connecticut, of sound money morality and the New England canons of decency, of Great Britain and the United States of America—but Rhode Island merged genially into the new nation once it decided to do so. The old commerce slowly dried up, but the state pioneered in spinning mills, followed by a whole textile industry, finance, insurance, metalworking, and the production of machinery. The people around Narragansett Bay continued to be noticeably otherwise-minded, yet they sallied forth to make their mark on the United States. The Browns of Providence, by their money from investments throughout the land, added their name to a college that became a national university. The Wards practiced their political skills in the lobbies of Congress or in the stirring verses of "The Battle Hymn of the Republic." The Ellerys and Channings sired leaders of learning and liberal religion. Later generations of Hazards won new fortunes in the mills of South Kingstown. Obscure pioneers gave the name What Cheer to a town in Iowa. Roger Williams became a hero of a nation he never dreamed of, celebrated for advocating a liberty of conscience that in his own lifetime had changed from a protection of piety to a guarantee of individual freedom. Americans in recent times have seen in his heroism, like that of Anne Hutchinson, inspiring examples of the individual conscience refusing to bow before the massed forces of society. The events that propelled these eccentric Puritans to the shores of Narragansett Bay have seldom been understood. Yet the unyielding determination of these heroes to chart their own courses has been understood reasonably enough to stand for the special spirit of colonial Rhode Island and what it gave to the United States.

BIBLIOGRAPHY

No extensive modern bibliography exists for guidance to materials on colonial Rhode Island. Some help may be obtained from John R. Bartlett, ed., *Bibliography of Rhode Island. A Catalogue of Books and Other Publications Relating to the State of Rhode Island* (Providence, 1864); Clarence S. Brigham, ed., *Bibliography of Rhode Island History* (Boston, 1902); and John Eliot Alden, ed., *Rhode Island Imprints, 1727–1800* (New York, 1949). Brigham's compilation may also be found in Edward Field, ed., *State of Rhode Island and Providence Plantations at the End of the Century; A History*, 3 vols. (Boston, 1902), vol. III, pp. 654–681. Still quite useful is Clarence S. Brigham, "Report on the Archives of Rhode Island," in American Historical Association, *Annual Report*, 1903, vol. I, pp. 543–644, which covers all public documents, town and court, as well as colony and state. Most of the documents are still where Brigham found them, though some are not, as will be explained later. To fill the lack of a large general bibliography, one must consult the references in secondary works, the most useful of which are mentioned herein.

PRIMARY SOURCES

GENERAL WORKS

The most valuable documents are to be found at the State Archives in the State House at Providence. The collection is distressingly incomplete for the years before 1730: few file papers exist; even some records of proceedings of the General Assembly exist only in transcripts (of reports sent to the towns) made over a century after the event—and there are gaps still. Though the Archives have been somewhat rearranged since 1903, Clarence S. Brigham, "Report on the Archives of Rhode Island," in American Historical Association, *Annual Report*, 1903, is a useful guide. The late archivist, Mary T. Quinn, made a wealth of indexes and checklists to aid in finding things at the State Archives.

Those who are not in a position to visit the State Archives ordinarily approach the history of Rhode Island before 1792 through the ten volumes customarily called *Rhode Island Colonial Records.* Actually the title was *Records of the Colony of Rhode Island and Providence Plantations in New England* for volumes I–VII (Providence, 1856–1862; reprinted New York, 1968), covering the years 1636 to 1776, and *Records of the State of Rhode Island and Providence Plantations* for volumes VIII–X (Providence, 1863–1865; reprinted New York, 1968), covering the years 1776–1792. These volumes were edited by John Russell Bartlett, a noted bibliographer with quite a supplementary career as an army officer, but his work was of extremely uneven quality. The main text is composed of the formal records of the central organ of the colonial government—the Court of Commissioners and then the General Assembly—but there are numerous other documents incorporated to fill out the record. The first volume contains materials pertaining to the towns and the Aquidneck commonwealth prior to the founding of the first legislature. There are various basic land conveyances, documents such as those reporting the work of the several royal commissions, and official correspondence of the General Assembly and the governors. Much of the supplementary material came from British repositories and was transcribed for Bartlett in the Public Record Office or other archives; the transcriptions are in the John Carter Brown Library at Brown University. By modern standards the transcriptions are casual, especially in spelling and punctuation. These documents, as well as the others Bartlett included, should be consulted in the original whenever possible or in W. N. Sainsbury *et al.,* eds., *Calendar of State Papers, Colonial Series, America and West Indies* . . , 44 vols. so far, covering 1574 to 1738 (London, 1860–1969). Bartlett's treatment of the main corpus of the General Assembly records was also deficient by modern standards. He left out more and more over the span of years and never indicated omissions. At first prone to include anything military, he even abandoned that penchant. For the years after volumes of published laws were available, he commonly omitted the text of such laws in the *Colonial Records*, inserting (but not always) citations to the volume of statutes where the laws could be found. He prepared the text for the printer by making penciled marks on the original manuscript, which was then delivered to the typesetter. As a result, the compositor had inordinate responsibility for the published text. All the same, the first three volumes (to 1706) were surprisingly successful. The whole project, however, should be done over.

To supplement the *Colonial Records*, one needs the several volumes of published laws. These were printed as *Acts and Laws of His Majesty's Colony of Rhode Island and Providence Plantations in America*, with minor variations in the title, in 1719, 1730, 1744, 1752, and 1767, with supplements in other years. The first publication was in Boston, the later ones in Newport. They are all rare. Beginning in 1747, the decisions of the General Assembly were printed after each session under various titles. These "schedules" have been compiled in different ways, such as in annual volumes, so the researcher should be prepared to find them as luck may allow. The published laws and schedules were reprinted in facsimile editions (also rare) toward the end of the nineteenth century. The man responsible for this project, J. Harry Bongartz, provided a *Check List of Rhode Island Laws . . .* (Providence, 1893). Shortly thereafter appeared Sidney S. Rider, ed., *Laws and Acts of Her Majesties Colony of Rhode Island, and Providence Plantations Made from the First Settlement in 1636 to 1705* (Providence, 1896), which contains a facsimile of the manuscript compilation of 1707, a transcript of it in typography to resemble the later publications of laws, and an introduction by Rider. Citations of other official publications may be found in John Eliot Alden, ed., *Rhode Island Imprints, 1727–1800* (New York, 1949). Of the colony's central court records, only a small portion has been published, apart from extracts that appear here and there. Two slim volumes of *Rhode Island Court Records; Records of the Court of Trials of the Colony of Providence Plantations*, one covering 1647–1662 and the other, 1662–1670 (Providence, 1920, 1922) have not been the beginning of anything extensive, perhaps because the material is as thin as the books, lacking the file papers that have disappeared almost completely for cases heard prior to about 1720.

For the early years of the colony Howard M. Chapin, ed., *Documentary History of Rhode Island*, 2 vols. (Providence, 1916, 1919) can be useful. The documents are well explained, a few are available nowhere else, but not all the texts are the best to be had. Some came from the early and unreliable publications of the Winthrop Papers at the Massachusetts Historical Society, in that organization's *Collections*, 4th Ser., vols. VI and VIII; 5th Ser., vols. I and VIII; and 6th Ser., vols. III and V. These volumes also contain many other items pertaining to Rhode Island, as do the "Trumbull Papers" in Massachusetts Historical Society *Collections*, 5th Ser., vol. IX. Fortunately the Massachusetts Historical Society has begun a better publication, currently existing as *Winthrop Papers, 1498–1649*, 5 vols. (Boston, 1929–1947). More may be expected. Chapin also drew upon John Winthrop's diary, which may be consulted in its entirety in any of three editions. Of the two prepared by James Savage, the second, *The History of New England from 1630 to 1649*, 2 vols. (Boston, 1853), is generally regarded as the better. Less reliable but easier to read, apart from the nauseating "Introduction," is the edition by James K. Hosmer, *Winthrop's Journal "History of New England" 1630–1649*, 2 vols., in John F. Jameson, ed., *Original Narratives of Early American History* (New York, 1908). A compilation that deals with much that took place in the seventeenth century is the "Harris Papers," Rhode Island Historical Society *Collections*, vol. X (Providence, 1902), which was very well edited, although not as complete as claimed in the preface; additional documents exist in manuscript at the Rhode Island Historical Society itself as well as other places.

Documents of a general nature pertaining to the eighteenth century have not been published extensively. The State Archives, skeletal before 1730, contain numerous items for the remainder of the colonial period, most of them well indexed in finding aids of some sort. Gertrude S. Kimball, ed., *Correspondence of the Colonial Governors of Rhode Island, 1723–1775*, 2 vols. (Cambridge, Mass., 1902–1903), supplements the material in *Rhode Island Colonial Records*. One judicial record has been published: Dorothy S. Towle, ed., *Records of the Vice-Admiralty Court of Rhode Island, 1716–1752* (Washington, 1936). Gertrude S. Kimball, ed., *Pictures of Rhode Island in the Past, 1642–1833* (Providence, 1900), offers a garland of descriptions. C. Edwin Barrows, ed., "The Diary of John Comer," Rhode Island Historical Society *Collections*, vol. VIII (Providence, 1893), reports many events transpiring in the colony during the 1720s. Carl Bridenbaugh, ed., *Gentleman's Progress; The Itinerarium of Dr. Alexander Hamilton, 1744* (Chapel Hill, 1948), is valuable. Of surprisingly broad use are the writings of Ezra Stiles: Franklin B. Dexter, ed., *Literary Diary of Ezra Stiles*, 3 vols. (New York, 1901) and *Extracts from the Itineraries and Other Miscellanies of Ezra Stiles . . .* (New Haven, 1916). These volumes provide a great deal of firsthand information and also report some of Stiles's inquiries into Rhode Island antiquities.

The newspapers, *Rhode-Island Gazette* (Newport, 1732–1733), *Newport Mercury* (1758–1928; variant names), *Newport Gazette* (1777–1778), *Gazette Francaise* (Newport, 1780–1781), *Newport Herald* (1787–1791), *Providence Gazette* (1762–1825; variant names), *American Journal* (Providence, 1779–1781), and *United States Chronicle* (Providence, 1784–1804), provide a great deal of information. Events prior to 1758 are reported in the Boston papers.

For the revolutionary period, fortunately, documents are more readily available. Bernard Bailyn, ed., *Pamphlets of the American Revolution*, four volumes projected (Cambridge, Mass., 1965–   ), vol. I, contains the most important contributions of Rhode Islanders to the pre-revolutionary debate. Others may be found in Edmund S. Morgan, ed., *Prologue to Revolution; Sources and Documents on the Stamp Act Crisis, 1764–1766* (Chapel Hill, 1959); Merrill Jensen, ed., *Tracts of the American Revolution, 1763–1776* (Indianapolis, 1967); and the newspapers of the day. For more extensive bibliographical guidance, consult Thomas R. Adams, "American Independence, The Growth of an Idea, A Bibliographical Study of the American Political Pamphlets Published Between 1764 and 1776 Dealing with the Dispute Between Great Britain and Her Colonies," Colonial Society of Massachusetts *Publications*, vol. XLII (Boston, 1966; this volume contains "Transactions, 1956–1963"), pp. 4–202, and David S. Lovejoy, "Bibliographical Essay," in *Rhode Island Politics and the American Revolution 1760–1776* (Providence, 1958), pp. 221–236. A generous, if not scrupulously edited, compilation of sources may be found in William R. Staples, ed., *The Documentary History of the Destruction of the Gaspee* (Providence, 1845), to which should be added John R. Bartlett, *A History of the Destruction of His Britannic Majesty's Schooner Gaspee . . .* (Providence, 1861), and Samuel W. Bryant, ed.,

"HMS *Gaspee*—The Court-Martial," *Rhode Island History*, vol. XXV (1966), pp. 65–72. Bernhard Knollenberg, ed., *Correspondence of Governor Samuel Ward, May 1775–March 1776* . . . (Providence, 1952), deals mainly with the Continental Congress. Further documents on Rhode Island's transactions with the Congress are in Worthington C. Ford, *et al.*, eds., *Journals of the Continental Congress, 1774–1789*, 34 vols. (Washington, 1904–1937), and Edmund C. Burnett, ed., *Letters of Members of the Continental Congress*, 8 vols. (Washington, 1921–1938). Two books are especially helpful in giving British views on the war: William Willcox, ed., *The American Rebellion; Sir Henry Clinton's Narrative of His Campaigns, 1775–1782, with an Appendix of Original Documents* (New Haven, 1954), and Bernhard A. Uhlendorf, trans. and ed., *Revolution in America; Confidential Letters and Journals 1776–1784 of Adjutant General Major Baurmeister of the Hessian Forces* (New Brunswick, N.J., 1957). A variety of other documents has been published concerning the revolutionary war, with a new project launched to print the papers of General Nathanael Greene, but by all odds the most magnificent publication is Howard C. Rice, Jr., and Anne S. K. Brown, trans. and ed., *The American Campaigns of Rochambeau's Army, 1780, 1781, 1782, 1783*, 2 vols. (Princeton and Providence, 1972). See also "Revolutionary Correspondence from 1775–1782," Rhode Island Historical Society *Collections*, vol. VI (Providence, 1867), pp. 105–300; "Revolutionary Correspondence of Governor Nicholas Cooke, 1775–1781," American Antiquarian Society *Proceedings*, New Ser., vol. XXXVI (1926), pp. 231–353; Alverda S. Beck, ed., *The Correspondence of Esek Hopkins, Commander-in-Chief of the United States Navy, 1775–1777* (Providence, 1932), and *The Letter Book of Esek Hopkins, Commander-in-Chief of the United States Navy, 1775–1777* (Providence, 1932); and Mary Almy, "Mrs. Almy's Journal. Siege of Newport, R.I., August, 1778," *Newport Historical Magazine*, vol. I (1880–81), pp. 17–36.

Post-revolutionary events are revealed in several publications, notably William R. Staples, ed., *Rhode Island in the Continental Congress: With the Journal of the Convention that Adopted the Constitution, 1765–1790* (Providence, 1870); Irwin H. Polishook, ed., "Peter Edes's Report of the Proceedings of the Rhode Island General Assembly, 1787–1790," extracted from the *Newport Herald* and serialized in *Rhode Island History*, vols. XXV and XXVI (1966–1967); James M. Varnum, *The Case, Trevett against Weeden: On Information and Complaint, for Refusing Paper Bills in Payment for Butcher's Meat, . . . Tried before the Honourable Superior Court, in the County of Newport, September Term, 1786. Also, The Case of the Judges of Said Court, Before the Honourable General Assembly, at Providence, October Session, 1786, on Citation for Dismissing Said Complaint.* . . . (Providence, 1787); and Robert C. Cotner, ed., *Theodore Foster's Minutes of the Convention held at South Kingstown, Rhode Island, in March, 1790, Which Failed to Adopt the Constitution of the United States* (Providence, 1929).

Manuscript sources are sparse for the seventeenth century, so the printed versions account for a substantial portion of those extant; but for the years after 1730 the manuscripts are voluminous. Outside the State Archives and other governmental repositories, the most important collections are those at the Rhode Island Historical Society (at Providence) and the Newport Historical Society. In both these institutions the holdings are arranged under a variety of collections and series. Therefore, the investigator must be prepared to search widely without expecting the names of the compilations to afford guidance in many cases; only the institutional and business records commonly stand as distinct items identifiable by their names. Lesser collections may be found at the John Carter Brown Library and the Special Collections Department of the John Hay Library, both at Brown University; the New York Public Library; the Houghton Library at Harvard University; and the Massachusetts Historical Society in Boston. The State Archives of Massachusetts and Connecticut contain documents pertaining to Rhode Island, also.

COUNTY AND TOWN

Counties, created only in the eighteenth century, were officially no more than judicial districts. The courts seldom dealt with matters of county-wide significance. Nevertheless, circumstances made Washington County (formerly King's, but long known as South County) a region of itself; Providence County, consisting of the original territory of the town of Providence, once Kent was set off, had something of a collective existence; and commercial historians, by putting together county histories, fostered the notion that these units were suitable for study.

Fundamentally, county records are court records. The information in Clarence S. Brigham, "Report on the Archives of Rhode Island," in American Historical Association, *Annual Report*, 1903, vol. I, is mostly pertinent to the situation today, as to the descriptions of the documents. Court records have been relocated in several cases, however. King's (later Washington) County documents, like most of the Bristol County ones, have been taken to the Providence County Court House. The King's County materials have been terribly damaged, as a result of a leaking roof where they were formerly stored, and ought not to be touched by anyone except an expert for the purposes of preparing them for filming. The Providence Superior Court documents (and a few others) have been removed to new quarters by the State Department of Records Management.

There are, however, other primary sources pertaining to county units. Records of the Narragansett Proprietors, declared unofficial after a long controversy, were published as James N. Arnold, ed., *Records of the Proprietors of the Narragansett, Otherwise Called the Fones Record* (Providence, 1894). In spite of governmental repudiation, these records contain much that pertains to Washington County. Many documents concerning the same region, together with commentary, were published in Elisha R. Potter, *The Early History of Narragansett; with an Appendix of Original Documents* (Providence, 1835). This was Volume III of the Rhode Island Historical Society *Collections*; the book was reprinted with additional notes and material in 1886. A document of extremely partisan nature has been published far oftener than it deserves: Francis Brinley, "A Briefe Narrative of that Part of New England Called the Nanhiganset Country," Rhode Island Historical Society *Publications*, New Ser., vol. VIII (1900–1901), pp. 72–96, or in Massachusetts Historical Society *Collections*, 3rd Ser., vol. I, pp. 209–228, or in *Narragansett Historical Register*, vol. VIII (1890), pp. 176–199. A similar treatment of the subject by Brinley, with more order and documents, appears as "A Brief Account of the Several Settlements and Governments in and about the Lands of the Narragansett-Bay, in New England," in Massachusetts Historical Society *Collections*, 1st Ser., vol. V, pp. 216–252.

Records of Providence County are synonymous with the records pertaining to the town of Providence up to 1730, the Providence proprietors and their subdivisions, the Westconnaug proprietors, the Meshanticut proprietors, and the litigation and intrigues carried on by these organizations against each other. See particularly the "Harris Papers," Rhode Island Historical Society *Collections*, vol. X (Providence, 1902).

Town records were kept ordinarily in several sets of ledgers, supplemented with collections of file papers. Town meeting records, town council records (sometimes with probate records segregated in a separate series), and "land evidence" records (deeds and the like, although sometimes mortgages to the colony and other documents pertaining to the land banks were recorded in special volumes) were the basic elements, but they were not always separated in the early years. The Block Island records piled everything together, for instance. Vital records and earmark registrations were commonly inserted wherever blank space could be found, although ultimately separate volumes were used in several towns.

Few town records have been published. The twenty-one volumes of Horatio Rogers *et al.*, eds., *Early Records of the Town of Providence* (Providence, 1892–1915), along with five reports of the record commissioners (Providence, 1892–1897) provide a great deal of information on that place, but the project was abandoned at a time when little had appeared beyond the seventeenth century. The texts were excellent. Mercifully the Rhode Island Historical Society reprinted the rare Volume XXI in 1950 and an *Index to the Early Records of the Town of Providence* (Providence, 1949). Clarence S. Brigham, ed., *Early Records of the Town of Portsmouth* (Providence, 1901); Howard M. Chapin, ed., *Early Records of the Town of Warwick* (Providence, 1926); and Howard M. Chapin, ed., *Records of the Court of Trials of the Town of Warwick, 1659–1674* (Providence, 1922), cover even shorter spans of time, but were also prepared with a passion for accuracy. The early records of Newport, such as there are, appear in the first volume of the *Colonial Records*.

To find more town documents, it is necessary to consult manuscript originals. The Providence Town Papers, running over a hundred volumes, as well as other collections at the Rhode Island Historical Society, should supplement the records kept at different offices in the city hall. Newport records suffered a bath in sea water during the Revolution, from which they emerged in bad shape. What remains has been entrusted to the Newport Historical Society. A fair amount of the town meeting records from 1679 on has survived. A transcript made about 1860, probably by Benjamin B. Howland, contains nearly all that can be deciphered. The surviving town council records are bound in a jumbled state. The land evidence volumes are somewhat better. Regular town records, begun after the damage had been done to the old ones, may be found either at the Newport Historical Society or at city hall. A fire severely impaired the North Kingstown records in the nineteenth century, burning away the edges of many volumes that survived. Miscellaneous accidents have overtaken various items in Warwick. Otherwise town records are roughly where they should be, except when they are in a town hall where one does not expect to find them, or in the State Archives, as is the case in recent years of the West Greenwich records. Clarence S. Brigham, "Report on the Archives of Rhode Island," in American Historical Association, *Annual Report*, 1903, vol. I, provides descriptions of the various town records that are still accurate for the most part.

Many towns kept plats and miscellaneous file papers that frequently are very valuable. As with the Providence papers, quite a few Warwick and West Greenwich ones have found their way to the Rhode Island Historical Society. Those remaining in town halls often are hard to find, except for probate papers.

Unlike Massachusetts, Rhode Island did not ordinarily treat records of proprietors of common lands as town responsibilities. Indeed, in many towns there was no such proprietary organization concerned with land neatly contained within the town boundaries. Except in some towns taken from Massachusetts in 1747, therefore, town archives do not have full collections of such documents. (Neither do they have ecclesiastical records except when a church has deposited some in a town vault.) Providence proprietors' records appear in the published *Early Records*, the Town Papers, the Harris Papers (published and unpublished), a small separate collection in the Rhode Island Historical Society, and a few other places. Most were burned in the nineteenth century. The Harris Papers contain material on several other organizations, as do the Warner Papers at the Rhode Island Historical Society. Some East Greenwich and West Greenwich proprietors' records, originals or copies, are at the town hall in East Greenwich. Some of the Jamestown proprietors' records are at the town hall, others at the Newport Historical Society and in the Elisha R. Potter Papers in the Rhode Island Historical Society, but many have vanished. Some of the Westerly materials survive in the Elisha R. Potter Papers. Such Pettaquamscut purchasers' records as remain are scattered in the Rhode Island Historical Society. Most of the extant Newport proprietors' records are at Middletown town hall. Portsmouth proprietors' decisions appear in other town records. Block Island proprietors' transactions are scattered in the town records but are far from complete. A copy of some Westconnaug records has been published as "The Minutes of the Westconnaug Purchase," serialized in Rhode Island Historical Society *Collections*, vols. XXV–XXVII (1932–1934).

Records pertaining to territory ultimately in Rhode Island are contained in Thomas W. Bicknell, *Sowams. With Ancient Records of Sowams and Parts Adjacent* (New Haven, 1908). Many proprietors' records have disappeared completely.

RELIGION AND CHURCHES

The prominent founders of the Rhode Island towns were, of course, involved in religious controversies. Their extant writings and documents pertaining to their lives deal mainly with religious matters, except for some of the letters of Roger Williams. Most of Williams' surviving writings may be found readily in the six volumes of the Narragansett Club *Publications* (Providence, 1866–1874), which were republished with an added volume as *The Complete Writings of Roger Williams* (New York, 1963). Unhappily, many letters were omitted, others come to light occasionally, and a full publication has yet to be made. Long extracts from Williams' works, embedded in an interpretive commentary, were published in Perry Miller, *Roger Williams; His Contribution to the American Tradition* (Indianapolis, 1953). The answer to Williams' polemic against the Quakers was George Fox and John Burnyeat, *A New-England-Fire-Brand Quenched, Being Something in Answer unto a Lying, Slanderous Book, Entituled; George Fox Digged out of his Burrows, &c . . .* 2 vols. (London, 1678).

The Antinomians left behind a slimmer documentary record. A fascinating collection of documents has been admirably compiled and presented in David D. Hall, ed., *The Antinomian Controversy, 1636–1638; A Documentary History* (Middletown, Conn., 1968). Various Coddington letters appear in the Winthrop Papers; there is also his remonstrance, written after he became a Quaker, called *A Demonstration of True Love unto You the Rulers of the Colony of Massachusetts . . .* (n.p., 1674).

The writings of Samuel Gorton are long, obscure, and hard to find. His version of his dealings with Massachusetts is *Simplicities Defence Against Seven-Headed Policy. Or Innocency Vindicated, . . .* (London, 1646; republished in 1835 and edited by William R. Staples in vol. II of Rhode Island Historical Society *Collections*). The polemical pieces, *Saltmarsh Returned from the Dead, . . .* (London, 1655) and *An Antidote Against the Common Plague of the World . . .* (London, 1657), the latter described as an answer to the former, tell what Gorton opposed. To learn more of his beliefs one must consult the incomplete and untitled manuscript at the Rhode Island Historical Society, which poses as an exposition of the Lord's Prayer. The other side of the Gorton case is presented in Edward Winslow, *Hypocrisie Unmasked; . . .* (London, 1646) and *New-Englands Salamander, . . .* (London, 1647).

The tribulations of Dr. John Clarke are explained in his *Ill Newes from New-England: Or A Narrative of New Englands Persecution. Wherein is Declared that while Old England is Becoming New, New-England is Become Old . . .* (London, 1652). For an answer to Clarke, see Thomas Cobbet, *The Civil Magistrates Povver in Matters of Religion Modestly Debated, . . .* (London, 1653).

A reasonably impartial eyewitness account of circumstances in the early

Rhode Island towns may be found in Thomas Lechford, "Plain Dealing: or, Newes from New England," in Massachusetts Historical Society *Collections*, 3rd Ser., vol. III, pp. 55–128 (also annotated by J. Hammond Trumbull and published as a book in 1867, which version was reprinted with an introduction by Darrett B. Rutman in 1967).

Documents pertaining to the history of the Baptists in Rhode Island are not voluminous; indeed there are almost none for the seventeenth century. A good guide to what there is may be found in Historical Records Survey, Division of Community Service Projects, Work Projects Administration, *Inventory of the Church Archives of Rhode Island; Baptist* (Providence, 1941). The compilation was incomplete, some of the items reported as in existence have never been found, but it remains highly useful and a small testimonial to the valuable service performed by the oft-maligned WPA.

Religious affairs in the seventeenth century are especially obscure. After the documentation on the founders, there is little to turn to until the results of Comer's efforts to collect documents. His work is to be found mostly at the Newport Historical Society in the records of the churches with which he was associated.

Records in greater quantity survive from the eighteenth century, most conspicuously from the Newport Baptist churches, which are at the Newport Historical Society. A few controversial items are in print, notably William Claggett, *A Looking-Glass for Elder Clarke and Elder Wightman, And the Church Under their Care* . . . (Newport, 1721), and *A Letter From Sundry Members Belonging to a Church of Jesus Christ, in Newport* . . . *Under the Pastoral Care of Timothy Packcom* . . . (Newport, 1741). Many of the papers collected by Isaac Backus in preparation for writing his *History of New England* (for full citation, see p. 396 herein) are at the Rhode Island Historical Society.

The Seventh Day Baptists are somewhat apart from the others. Copies of their records may be found at the Newport Historical Society and the Rhode Island Historical Society. The interesting journal of an early devotee may be found as Samuel Hubbard, *Samuel Hubbard's Journal Circa 1633–1686* . . . (Providence, 1940), with additional information in "Extracts from the Letter Book of Samuel Hubbard," serialized in *Magazine of New England History*, vols. I and II (1891, 1892). No one has been able to trace the originals of these documents.

Quaker records are mostly on deposit at the Rhode Island Historical Society, but a few are at the Newport Historical Society. The bibliography, Historical Records Survey, Works Progress Administration, *Inventory of the Church Archives of Rhode Island: Society of Friends* (Providence, 1939), is no longer accurate as to location of documents but quite useful in telling what is extant.

In the controversial literature concerning the Quaker invasion of New England, a few items are of special interest to Rhode Island, notably George Bishope, *New England Judged, Not by Man's but the Spirit of the Lord:* . . . (London, 1661) and George Fox, *Something in Answer to a Letter* . . . *of John Leverat Governour at Boston,* . . . *wherein John Leverat Justifies Roger Williams's Book of Lyes* (London, 1677).

Documents on the short-lived Huguenot church are to be found in L. Effingham de Forest, trans. and ed., "Records of the French Church at Narragansett, 1686–1691," *New York Genealogical and Biographical Record,* vol. LXX (1939), pp. 236–241 and 359–365; vol. LXXI (1940), pp. 51–61.

Congregationalism in colonial Rhode Island has not been investigated extensively. Records of churches and societies may be found at the Rhode Island Historical Society, the Newport Historical Society, and in the hands of the several congregations.

More has been done to make available documents on Anglicanism. See George C. Mason, ed., *Annals of Trinity Church, Newport, Rhode Island, 1698–1821* (Newport, 1890), and James MacSparran, *A Letter Book and Abstract out of Services Written During the Years 1743–1751* . . . , ed. Daniel Goodwin (Boston, 1899). There are published sermons by James Honeyman. Other documents remain in manuscript in the hands of churches at Providence, Wickford, and Bristol. There are digests of a few important documents in William W. Manross, *The Fulham Papers in the Lambeth Palace Library; American Colonial Section Calendar and Indexes* (Oxford, 1965; this calendar serves as a finding aid to transcripts at the Library of Congress). The writings of George Berkeley pertaining to his American sojourn may be found in A. A. Luce and T. E. Jessop, eds., *The Works of George Berkeley Bishop of Cloyne,* vols. VII–IX (London, 1955–1957).

EDUCATION AND CULTURE

Very little of substance has been published in the way of documents pertaining to education and culture. Reuben A. Guild, *Early History of Brown University, Including the Life, Times, and Correspondence of President Manning. 1756–1791* (Providence, 1897) contains copious documentary inclusions. George C. Mason, *Annals of the Redwood Library and Athenaeum, Newport, R.I.* (Newport, 1891), provides basic documents and helpful notes. Beyond these, one must search out the fugitive items in newspapers, miscellaneous compilations of manuscripts, and governmental records.

COMMERCE AND THE ECONOMY

Original sources pertaining to commerce are voluminous. Great quantities of merchants' pepers—letter books, account books, and so forth—may be found at the Rhode Island Historical Society, the Newport Historical Society, the John Carter Brown Library at Brown University, and other places. Beyond these there are numerous fragments in governmental and even ecclesiastical documents. Unfortunately, the surviving mercantile papers are usually incomplete and hard to evaluate by reason of the absence of any way to determine whether what exists is representative of the commercial life of its period. The Brown papers at the John Carter Brown Library are perhaps the closest thing to a complete set of papers of a mercantile firm of the colonial period. Published sources include Peleg Sanford, *The Letter Book of Peleg Sanford of Newport . . . 1666–1668* (Providence, 1928); Bruce M. Bigelow, ed., "The Walter Newbury Shipping Book," Rhode Island Historical Society *Collections*, vol. XXIV (1931), pp. 73–91; and *Commerce of Rhode Island, 1726–1800*, in Massachusetts Historical Society *Collections*, 7th Ser., vols. IX and X, which contain mainly selections of the Redwood and Champlin papers, more of which may be found in manuscript at the Newport Historical Society and the Rhode Island Historical Society, along with great quantities of correlative documents.

In connection with trade, see the records of the proprietors of Long Wharf at Newport, manuscripts of which are at the Newport Historical Society.

Documents on privateering are scarce but naturally less so than those on piracy. For a selection concerning both subjects, consult John Franklin Jameson, ed., *Privateering and Piracy in the Colonial Period: Illustrative Documents* (New York, 1923). Rhode Island records of local privateers are surprisingly sparse. In the State Archives several items may be found in the Notarial Records, Admiralty Papers, Marine Bonds, and Petitions to the General Assembly. Some of these have been printed in Howard W. Preston, *Rhode Island and the Sea* (Providence, 1932).

SECONDARY SOURCES

GENERAL WORKS

General studies of the history of Rhode Island began with John Callender's *Historical Discourse on the Civil and Religious Affairs of the Colony of Rhode Island and Providence Plantations . . .* (Boston, 1739), which dealt mainly with the seventeenth century. As Callender reckoned the founding as having taken place in 1638, this was a centennial celebration. As such it was printed a century later as Rhode Island Historical Society *Collections*, vol. IV (1838). Some interesting material is to be found in William E. Foster, ed., "Early Attempts at Rhode Island History, Comprising those of Stephen Hopkins and Theodore Foster," Rhode Island Historical Society *Collections*, vol. VII (Providence, 1885), pp. 5–134. The next historical work still often consulted is Isaac Backus, *A History of New-England with Particular Reference to the Denomination of Christians called Baptists* (in the second and third volumes the title was changed to *Church History of New-England*), 3 vols. (vol. I: Boston, 1777; vol. II: Providence, 1784; vol. III: Boston, 1796). The second edition, going back to the first title, 2 vols. (Newton, Mass., 1871), had notes by David Weston, including long extracts from documents used by Backus. Backus treated Rhode Island quite broadly, because he regarded the colony as the homeland of Baptists in America.

Libraries often have one or more of five multivolume sets. Oddly, the most useful is Samuel Greene Arnold, *History of the State of Rhode Island and Providence*

Plantations, 2 vols. (New York, 1859–1860). The oldest of the five, this work was cast in the deplorably humdrum form of annals. Arnold reported chiefly what he found in the State Archives, which made his books seem to take the affairs of the colonial central government as a theme. In actuality, however, he had no theme. Arnold's accuracy and convenient arrangement make the work a handy reference for scholars. By contrast they have less respect for Edward Field, ed., *State of Rhode Island and Providence Plantations at the End of the Century; A History*, 3 vols. (Boston, 1902), which has a systematic arrangement and a balanced distribution of topics. Some of the authors did well, but most of the work is pedestrian. A similar set, Thomas W. Bicknell, *History of the State of Rhode Island and Providence Plantations*, 5 vols. (New York, 1920), is positively hazardous. Bicknell, though a fanatic for accuracy in editing documents and in writing about some of his favorite topics (e.g., why Dr. John Clarke should get the honor lavished on Roger Williams), was so slipshod in much of this history as to leave the reader unable to trust anything in it without checking elsewhere. A better reputation is enjoyed by Charles Carroll, *Rhode Island, Three Centuries of Democracy*, 4 vols. (New York, 1932). The only work in this group that combines insight with accuracy is Irving B. Richman, *Rhode Island, Its Making and Meaning*, 2 vols. (New York, 1902). Alas! it takes the subject only to 1683.

Shorter treatments of early Rhode Island may be found in Irving B. Richman, *Rhode Island, A Study in Separatism* (Boston, 1905); William B. Weeden, *Early Rhode Island, A Social History of the People* (New York, 1910); Clarence S. Brigham, *History of the State of Rhode Island and Providence Plantations* (n.p., 1902; a separate publication of a portion of Field's multivolume work); and the episodic volume by Bertram Lippincott, *Indians, Privateers, and High Society; A Rhode Island Sampler* (Philadelphia, 1961). Again, Richman's work is especially appealing, although some admire Weeden's. On a still smaller scale, there is the excellent treatment of the seventeenth century in Charles M. Andrews, *Colonial Period of American History*, 4 vols. (New Haven, 1934–1938), to be found in vol. II, pp. 1–66. Much less valuable are the relevant portions of Herbert L. Osgood, *American Colonies in the Seventeenth Century*, 3 vols. (New York, 1904–1907) and *American Colonies in the Eighteenth Century*, 4 vols. (New York, 1924–1925).

THE COLONIAL PERIOD

Detailed treatment of chronological segments of Rhode Island history has rarely been done with much success. An obvious exception to this comment is the lively little book by Carl Bridenbaugh, *Fat Mutton and Liberty of Conscience; Society in Rhode Island, 1636–1690* (Providence, 1974). The best discussion of negotiations behind the charter of 1663 is in Richard S. Dunn, "John Winthrop, Jr., and the Narragansett Country," *William and Mary Quarterly*, 3rd Ser., vol. XIII (1956), pp. 68–86, an article that was partly reprinted in a book that contains more that is pertinent to Rhode Island: Dunn's *Puritans and Yankees; The Winthrop Dynasty of New England, 1630–1717* (Princeton, 1962). Douglas Edward Leach, *Flintlock and Tomahawk; New England in King Philip's War*

(New York, 1958), has good chapters on the Rhode Island phases. An introductory analysis of the early eighteenth century is in Sydney V. James, "Colonial Rhode Island and the Beginnings of the Liberal Rationalized State," in Melvin Richter, ed., *Essays in Theory and History* (Cambridge, Mass., 1970), pp. 165–185. Lawrence L. Lowther, "Rhode Island Colonial Government, 1732" (Ph.D. dissertation, University of Washington, 1964), attempted to portray things as they stood in a single year but necessarily had to provide information about the surrounding years.

More is to be found pertaining to the years after 1760. David S. Lovejoy, *Rhode Island Politics and the American Revolution, 1760–1776* (Providence, 1958), is an able piece of scholarship but suffers from the attempt to find a closer relationship than exists between the book's two subjects. Mack E. Thompson, "The Ward-Hopkins Controversy and the American Revolution in Rhode Island: An Interpretation," *William and Mary Quarterly*, 3rd Ser., vol. XVI (1959), pp. 363–375, promptly offered a somewhat different view; but more insight is to be gained from the analysis of political groupings in William Nisbet Chambers, *Political Parties in a New Nation; The American Experience, 1776–1809* (New York, 1963), chapter ii, though Rhode Island scarcely figures in it.

There are few studies of particular aspects or episodes in the history of colonial Rhode Island, and fewer good ones. This shortage may be explained by the pronounced localism of the colony (for all its small size), the significance of certain salient topics, and the happenstance of what evidence survives. Among the most valuable works are: John Blanchard MacInnes, "Rhode Island Bills of Public Credit, 1710–1755" (Ph.D. dissertation, Brown University, 1952); Marguerite Appleton, "Richard Partridge: Colonial Agent," *New England Quarterly*, vol. V (1932), pp. 293–309; Patrick T. Conley, "Rhode Island Constitutional Development, 1636–1841: Prologue to the Dorr Rebellion" (Ph.D. dissertation, University of Notre Dame, 1970); P. T. Conley, "Rhode Island Constitutional Development, 1636–1775: A Survey," *Rhode Island History*, vol. XXVII (1968), pp. 49–63, 74–94; and John Hutchins Cady, *Rhode Island Boundaries, 1636–1936* (Providence, 1936).

There are several fine treatises that deal with Rhode Island as well as other places. Richard Pares, *War and Trade in the West Indies, 1739–1763* (Oxford, 1936) and *Colonial Blockade and Neutral Rights, 1739–1763* (Oxford, 1938), are illuminating studies of the period of the mid-century wars. Pares used a considerable number of Rhode Island documents in his work, so the reader can often pick out matters of local concern and can be confident that the general statements have been framed to take Rhode Island into account. Howard H. Peckham, *The Colonial Wars, 1689–1762* (Chicago, 1964), in brief and Lawrence H. Gipson, *The Great War for the Empire* (vols. VI–VIII of *The British Empire before the American Revolution*; New York, 1946–1953) at much greater length give more comprehensive narratives of the mid-century wars. An excellent study of Connecticut, Richard L. Bushman, *From Puritan to Yankee: Character and the Social Order in Connecticut, 1690–1765* (Cambridge, Mass., 1967), offers some valuable insights into Rhode Island.

There are quite a few books and articles dealing with the imperial connections and international affairs that affected Rhode Island during the colonial period. Among the more useful are: Charles M. Andrews, *The Colonial Period of American History*, 4 vols. (New Haven, 1934–1938), vol. IV, bearing the subtitle: *England's Commercial and Colonial Policy*; Max Savelle and Margaret Anne Fisher, *The Origins of American Diplomacy: The International History of Angloamerica, 1492–1763* (New York, 1967); Michael Kammen, *Empire and Interest; The American Colonies and the Politics of Mercantilism* (Philadelphia, 1970); I. K. Steele, *Politics of Colonial Policy; The Board of Trade in Colonial Administration, 1696–1720* (Oxford, 1968); Thomas C. Barrow, *Trade and Empire; The British Customs Service in Colonial America, 1660–1775* (Cambridge, Mass., 1967); and James A. Henretta, *"Salutary Neglect"; Colonial Administration under the Duke of Newcastle* (Princeton, 1972).

THE REVOLUTIONARY ERA

There are many writings on the revolutionary era, defined as the period beginning with the imperial crises from 1763 to the Revolution proper and its aftermath. In addition to Lovejoy's book mentioned on p. 398, the following are useful treatments of events in the years 1763–1776: Frederick B. Wiener, "The Rhode Island Merchants and the Sugar Act," *New England Quarterly*, vol. III (1930), pp. 464–500; relevant passages in Edmund S. Morgan and Helen M. Morgan, *The Stamp Act Crisis, Prologue to Revolution* (Chapel Hill, 1953); relevant passages in L. H. Gipson, *The Triumphant Empire* (vols. IX–XII of *The British Empire before the American Revolution*; New York, 1956–1965); Larry R. Gerlach, "Charles Dudley and the Customs Quandary in Pre-Revolutionary Rhode Island," *Rhode Island History*, vol. XXX (1971), pp. 53–59; William G. Roelker and Clarkson A. Collins III, "The Patrol of Narragansett Bay (1774–1776) by H. M. S. *Rose*, Captain James Wallace," serialized in *Rhode Island History*, vols. VII–IX (1948–1950); Carl Bridenbaugh, *Silas Downer, Forgotten Patriot* (Providence, 1974); David S. Lovejoy, "Henry Marchant and the Mistress of the World," *William and Mary Quarterly*, 3rd Ser., vol. XII (1955), pp. 375–398; and the relevant portions of Arthur M. Schlesinger, *The Colonial Merchants and the American Revolution* (New York, 1918). There is a spate of pieces on the *Gaspee* affair: Eugene Wulsin, "The Political Consequences of the Burning of the Gaspee," *Rhode Island History*, vol. III (1944), pp. 1–11, 55–64; William R. Leslie, "The Gaspee Affair: A Study of its Constitutional Significance," *Mississippi Valley Historical Review*, vol. XXXIX (1952–53), pp. 233–256; Samuel W. Bryant, "Rhode Island Justice—1772 Vintage," *Rhode Island History*, vol. XXVI (1967), pp. 65–71; Lawrence J. DeVaro, Jr., "The Gaspee Affair as Conspiracy," *Rhode Island History*, vol. XXXII (1973), pp. 106–121; and DeVaro's "The Impact of the Gaspee Affair on the Coming of the Revolution, 1772–1773" (Ph.D. dissertation, Case Western Reserve University, 1973).

Unfortunately, the leading treatment of the War for Independence, as it concerned Rhode Island, remains Benjamin Cowell, *Spirit of '76 in Rhode Island*

. . . (Boston, 1850). See also William B. Willcox, "Rhode Island in British Strategy, 1780–1781," *Journal of Modern History*, vol. XVII (1945), pp. 304–331. On the internal consequences of the Revolution, see Joel A. Cohen, "Democracy in Rhode Island: A Statistical Analysis," *Rhode Island History*, vol. XXIX (1970), pp. 3–16; J. A. Cohen, "Rhode Island Loyalism and the American Revolution," *Rhode Island History*, vol. XXVII (1968), pp. 97–112; J. A. Cohen, "Rhode Island and the American Revolution: A Selective Socio-Political Analysis" (Ph.D. dissertation, University of Connecticut, 1967); and relevant portions of Irwin H. Polishook, *Rhode Island and the Union, 1774–1795* (Evanston, Illinois, 1969).

The rest of Polishook's book deals with Rhode Island during the Confederation period. Other works to consult on that era include: Frank G. Bates, *Rhode Island and the Formation of the Union* (New York, 1898); Forrest McDonald, *We the People; The Economic Origins of the Constitution* (Chicago, 1958) and *E Pluribus Unum; The Formation of the American Republic, 1776–1790* (Boston, 1965); Allan Nevins, *The American States During and After the Revolution* (New York, 1927); Jackson T. Main, *The Upper House in Revolutionary America 1763–1788* (Madison, Wis., 1967); Franklin S. Coyle, "The Survival of Business Enterprise in the American Revolutionary Era (1770–1785)" (M.A. thesis, Brown University, 1960); and Patrick T. Conley, "Rhode Island in Disunion, 1787–1790," *Rhode Island History*, vol. XXXI (1972), pp. 99–115. William Winslow Crosskey, *Politics and the Constitution in the History of the United States*, 2 vols. (Chicago, 1953), contains a valuable analysis of *Trevett* v. *Weeden*; so does Irwin H. Polishook, "Trevett vs. Weeden and the Case of the Judges," *Newport History*, vol. XXXVIII (1965), pp. 45–69; the treatment by Julius Goebel, Jr., in *Antecedents and Beginnings to 1801*, vol. I of Paul A. Freund, ed., *History of the Supreme Court of the United States* (New York, 1971) is shallow, perfunctory, and inconclusive except in the analysis of Varnum's arguments, where it is partly wrong.

Rhode Island and Rhode Islanders figure in the following: Paul F. Dearden, "The Siege of Newport: Inauspicious Dawn of Alliance," *Rhode Island History*, vol. XXIX (1970), pp. 17–35; J. G. Rosengarten, "The German Soldiers in Newport, 1776–1779, and the Siege of 1778," *Rhode Island Historical Magazine*, vol. VII (1886–87), pp. 81–118; Jack Coggins, *Ships and Seamen of the American Revolution—Vessels, Crews, Weapons, Gear, Naval Tactics, and Actions of the War for Independence* (Harrisburg, Pa., 1969); Fred Anderson Berg, *Encyclopedia of Continental Army Units, Battalions, Regiments, and Independent Corps* (Harrisburg, Pa., 1972); the splendid book by Howard I. Chapelle, *The History of the American Sailing Navy, The Ships and Their Development* (New York, 1949); and Benjamin Quarles, *The Negro in the American Revolution* (Chapel Hill, 1961). Noel P. Conlon, "Rhode Island Negroes in the Revolution: A Bibliography," *Rhode Island History*, vol. XXIX (1970), pp. 52–53, provides references to works on both Rhode Island blacks and the siege of Newport.

In many respects the Revolution has been approached most successfully through biography. For instance, one finds a fine discussion of Esek Hopkins and the early years of the United States Navy in Samuel Eliot Morison, *John Paul Jones, A Sailor's Biography* (Boston, 1959). William H. Foster, "Stephen Hopkins: A Rhode Island Statesman," two parts, *Rhode Island Historical Tracts*, No. 19 (Providence, 1884), and William M. Fowler, Jr., *William Ellery: A Rhode Island Politico and Lord of the Admiralty* (Metuchen, N.J., 1973), discuss political figures of the revolutionary period without much insight. Four military men are presented in Edward Field, *Esek Hopkins, Commander-in-Chief of the Continental Navy During the American Revolution, 1775 to 1778* (Providence, 1898); Theodore Thayer, *Nathanael Greene, Strategist of the American Revolution* (New York, 1960); Charles P. Whittemore, *A General of the Revolution, John Sullivan of New Hampshire* (New York, 1961); and Arnold Whitridge, *Rochambeau* (New York, 1965). Several naval officers are presented in William James Morgan, *Captains to the Northward; The New England Captains in the Continental Navy* (Barre, Mass., 1959).

LOCAL HISTORIES

There are three county histories: J. R. Cole, *History of Washington and Kent Counties, Rhode Island* (New York, 1889); Richard M. Bayles *et al., History of Newport County, Rhode Island* (New York, 1891); and Richard M. Bayles *et al., History of Providence County, Rhode Island*, 2 vols. (New York, 1891). They are neither as informative nor as reliable as might be desired.

There are several volumes on the Narragansett country (Washington or South County) of some interest: Esther Bernon Carpenter, *South County Studies of Some Eighteenth Century Persons Places & Conditions* . . . (Boston, 1924); Edward Channing, "The Narragansett Planters: A Study of Causes," in *The Johns Hopkins University Studies in Political and Social Science*, vol. IV (Baltimore, 1886), pp. 105–127; William Davis Miller, "The Narragansett Planters," in American Antiquarian Society *Proceedings*, New Ser., vol. XLIII (1933), pp. 49–115; Caroline Hazard, *Anchors of Tradition*, . . . (New Haven, 1924); and Daniel B. Updike, *Richard Smith, First English Settler of the Narragansett Country* (Boston, 1937).

There are not many good general histories of Rhode Island towns. For Barrington, the publications of Thomas W. Bicknell, *History of Barrington* (Providence, 1898) and *Sowams* (New Haven, 1908), must do. Samuel T. Livermore, *History of Block Island* (Hartford, Conn., 1877); Daniel H. Greene, *History of the Town of East Greenwich and Adjacent Territory, from 1677 to 1877* (Providence, 1877); William R. Staples, *Annals of the Town of Providence, from its First Settlement to the Organization of the City Government, in June, 1832* (Providence, 1843; also issued as vol. V of Rhode Island Historical Society *Collections*); Thomas Steere, *History of the Town of Smithfield from its Organization, in 1730–1, to its Division, in 1871,* . . . (Providence, 1881); Guy M. Fessenden, *The History of Warren, R.I. from the Earliest Times* (Providence, 1845); Oliver P. Fuller, *History of Warwick, Rhode Island* (Providence, 1875); and Frederic Denison, *Westerly (Rhode Island) and Its Witnesses for Two Hundred and Fifty Years, 1626–1876* (Providence, 1878), are old volumes of some use. The authors of most of them, like most of their modern successors, neglected one of the basic tasks of the local historian, the attempt to present the subject as a place with its own character and inner life. Writers of town histories generally have taken for granted the existence of the subject and have sought out colorful individuals or incidents, reported events of formal significance (e.g., official creation of a jurisdiction or change of boundaries), collected lists of officials and ministers, and lavished attention on matters that connected the town to national affairs, such as supplying soldiers or congressmen. The effect is to imply that the town's importance lay in its meager offerings to national history. For the most part, however, there is no attention to the effects of the major events in national history on the life of the town. The reader would never guess, furthermore, that town elections were contested, that people committed crimes or faced economic struggles, that there were religious or social animosities, or that the rich men may have been anything but paragons of rectitude who were universally beloved. All change was progress, all wealth admirable; all employers were social benefactors, all employees insignificant.

Rather more entertaining is Charles Comstock, *A History of South-Kingstown; with a Particular Description of the Hornet's Nest Company, and the Cats Let Out of the Bag* (Newport, 1806), but its value as local history is oblique at best.

Bristol has been fortunate. Not only is there a useful old book, Wilfred H. Munro, *The History of Bristol, R.I., The Story of the Mount Hope Lands* (Providence, 1880), but two more, both of which suggest that it is possible to write about the internal development of a town: M. A. DeWolfe Howe, *Bristol, Rhode Island, A Town Biography* (Cambridge, Mass., 1930), and George Howe, *Mount Hope, A New England Chronicle* (New York, 1959).

There is a valuable manuscript history of Scituate, Cyrus Walker, "The History of Scituate, R.I., from the Acquisition of the Territory in 1659, to the Close of the Nineteenth Century," reportedly at the Scituate town hall, but more conveniently consulted at the Rhode Island Historical Society on microfilm. Walker was the last person to make use of the full corpus of the Providence proprietors' records, destroyed by fire in 1888, and he used them carefully, so his work contains information of great importance to the study of early Providence as well as Scituate.

Two manuscripts on the territory originally embraced by Warwick (Warwick, West Warwick, and Coventry) are to be found at the Rhode Island Historical Society. They are about land divisions but of rather broad interest: Frank Greene Bates and Charles W. Perry, "The Shawomet Purchase in the Colony of Rhode Island and Providence Plantations in New England" (n.d.; donated in 1953); and the nine Harrison S. Taft notebooks with assorted titles or none at all (probably the product of research ending in the 1940s). These works present roughly as much as can be learned about the land system begun by the Gortonians.

A few modern town histories have been published. Walter Leon Watson, *History of Jamestown on Conanicut Island in the State of Rhode Island* (Providence,

1949), is useful. Much less successful are Mary Agnes Best, *The Town that Saved a State, Westerly* (Westerly, R.I., 1943), and Martha R. McPartland, *The History of East Greenwich, Rhode Island 1677–1960 With Related Genealogy* (East Greenwich, R.I., 1960). George A. Levesque, "Coventry: The Colonial Years 1741–1783" (M.A. thesis, Brown University, 1969), would be appreciated if it were more easily available.

The literature is richer when one turns to studies of special phases of local history.

A few discontinued periodicals contain many small items on local history, albeit of uneven quality. Sidney S. Rider's *Book Notes* (1883–1916) and *Rhode Island Historical Tracts* (1877–1896) include a great deal of argumentative and polemical work as well as dispassionate antiquarianism. The second of these series contains some substantial work of enduring value; two of these pieces appear elsewhere in this bibliography. There are useful items also in *Magazine of New England History* (1891–1893), *Narragansett Historical Register* (1882–1891), and the publication begun under the title of *Newport Historical Magazine* (1880–1884) and continued as *Rhode Island Historical Magazine* (1884–1887).

The serial publications of the Newport Historical Society, its *Bulletin* (1912–   ), and the Rhode Island Historical Society, its *Collections, Proceedings, Publications,* and now *Rhode Island History,* also have numerous items.

Noteworthy publications include: Gertrude S. Kimball, *Providence in Colonial Times* (Boston, 1912), which is a series of topical studies, done with more research than appears at first glance; Antoinette F. Downing and Vincent J. Scully, Jr., *The Architectural Heritage of Newport Rhode Island, 1640–1915,* 2nd ed. (New York, 1967), a magnificent book, although it has a few dreadful misprints, such as the reversal of the maps on pages 19 and 20; John Hutchins Cady, *The Civic and Architectural Development of Providence, 1636–1950* (Providence, 1957); Ralph E. Carpenter, Jr., *The Arts and Crafts of Newport Rhode Island 1640–1820* (Newport, 1954); Carl Bridenbaugh, *Peter Harrison, First American Architect* (Chapel Hill, 1949), which tells a great deal about Newport in the course of reporting Harrison's career; Carl R. Woodward, *Plantation in Yankeeland: The Story of Cocumscussoc, Mirror of Colonial Rhode Island* (Wickford, R.I., 1971), which concerns Smith's trading post near Wickford and what happened there later; Bradford F. Swan, *Gregory Dexter of London and New England 1610–1700* (Rochester, N.Y., 1949) and *The Case of Richard Chasmore alias Long Dick* (Providence, 1944), which is quite enlightening on life in Providence in the 1650s; Elisha R. Potter, *Memoir Concerning the French Settlements and Settlers in the Colony of Rhode Island* (Providence, 1879); William Davis Miller, *Notes and Queries Concerning the Early Bounds and Divisions of the Township of East Greenwich As Set Forth in William Hall's Plat, 1716* (Providence, 1937); Dennis A. O'Toole, "Democratic Balance—Ideals of Community in Early Portsmouth," *Rhode Island History,* vol. XXXII (1973), pp. 3–17; John Demos, "Families in Colonial Bristol, Rhode Island: An Exercise in Historical Demography," *William and Mary Quarterly,* 3rd Ser., vol. XXV (1968), pp. 40–57; Edward H. West, "The

Lands of Portsmouth, R.I., and a Glimpse of its People," *Rhode Island Historical Society Collections*, vol. XXV (1932), pp. 65–85; E. H. West, "New Interpretations of the Records of the Island of Rhode Island," *Rhode Island Historical Society Collections*, vol. XXXII (1939), pp. 107–115; George C. Mason, *Reminiscences of Newport* (Newport, 1884); and Carl Bridenbaugh, "Colonial Newport as a Summer Resort," *Rhode Island Historical Society Collections*, vol. XXVI (1933), pp. 1–23.

Of some interest is a cluster of argumentative pieces on early Providence: Sidney S. Rider, *The Forgeries Connected with the Deed Given by the Sachems Canonicus and Miantinomi to Roger Williams of the Land on which the Town of Providence was Planted* (Providence, 1896); George T. Paine, *A Denial of the Charges of Forgery in Connection With the Sachems' Deed to Roger Williams* (Providence, 1896); Henry C. Dorr, "The Proprietors of Providence, and Their Controversies With the Freeholders," *Rhode Island Historical Society Collections*, vol. IX (1897); and Sidney S. Rider, *The Lands of Rhode Island as They Were Known to Caunounicus and Miantunnomu When Roger Williams Came in 1636* . . . (Providence, 1904).

Careful research into the history of Newport has finally gotten under way. So far, one project has been finished: Sheila Skemp, "Social and Cultural History of Newport, Rhode Island, 1720–1765" (Ph.D. dissertation, University of Iowa, 1974). Others are in progress. For the time being, however, one may learn a great deal about the city by consulting the most recent editions (complete with notes and corrections for the first time) of Carl Bridenbaugh, *Cities in the Wilderness: The First Century of Urban Life in America, 1625–1742*, 3rd ed. (London, 1971) and *Cities in Revolt: Urban Life in America, 1743–1776*, 2nd ed. (London, 1971).

GEOGRAPHY AND ABORIGINES

The geological underpinnings of Rhode Island are amply explained in Nathaniel Southgate Shaler, *et al.*, *Geology of the Narragansett Basin* (Washington, 1899).

The native inhabitants before the seventeenth century are not well known. Alden T. Vaughan, *New England Frontier: Puritans and Indians 1620–1675* (Boston, 1965), supplies information and references to sources and anthropological studies, as well as a pro-Puritan narrative of events. Rhode Island partisans will find his treatment of Miantonomi and the Narragansetts particularly unpalatable. William Scranton Simmons, *Cautantowwit's House; An Indian Burial Ground on the Island of Conanicut in Narragansett Bay* (Providence, 1970), is a fascinating anthropoligical study of a small subject—anthropologists often write like that—but carries its implications far, although scrupulously. The citations are particularly useful guides to anthropological literature. Howard M. Chapin, *Sachems of the Narragansetts* (Providence, 1931), is helpful, though unimaginative. It begins with the legendary past and continues to the extinction of the royalty in the late eighteenth century. An extraordinary amount has been written on the Wampanoags and the Narragansetts in connection with early explorations and settlements, especially the Plymouth Colony. Vaughan's book is superior to most of this literature. Douglas E. Leach, *Flintlock and Tomahawk; New England in King Philip's War* (New York, 1958), continues the narrative to the point where most modern readers lose interest—the point when these nations had been reduced to shreds. James N. Arnold, *A Statement of the Case of the Narragansett Tribe of Indians,* . . . (Newport, 1896), offers an indignant exposé of the means whereby the tribal lands were acquired by white men in the eighteenth century.

EXPLORATIONS

Explorations before 1600 are admirably presented in Samuel Eliot Morison, *The European Discovery of America: The Northern Voyages A.D. 500–1600* (New York, 1971). Morison is particularly judicious on the alleged Norse activities in Narragansett Bay (see pages 72–75) and Verrazzano (pages 303–308). For examples of believers in the Norse colonization of Narragansett Bay, see Philip Ainsworth Means, *Newport Tower* (New York, 1942), and Hjalmar R. Holand, *America 1355–1364, A New Chapter in Pre-Columbian History* (New York, 1946).

On the explorations between 1600 and 1636 a great deal has been written, mostly in connection with Puritans and Pilgrims. See the references in Vaughan, *New England Frontier*, and Charles H. Levermore, ed., *Forerunners and Competitors of the Pilgrims and Puritans; or Narratives of Voyages Made by Persons Other than the Pilgrims and Puritans* . . . *1601–1625* . . . , 2 vols. (Brooklyn, N.Y., 1912); W. M. Williamson, *Adriaen Block* . . . (New York, 1959), which is a brief pamphlet; and Charles K. Bolton, *The Real Founders of New England* . . . (Boston, 1929).

RELIGION AND CHURCHES

Illuminating introductions to Puritanism may be found in Edmund S. Morgan, *The Puritan Dilemma, The Story of John Winthrop* (Boston, 1958); Samuel Eliot Morison, *Builders of the Bay Colony* (Boston, 1930); Darrett B. Rutman, *American Puritanism, Faith and Practice* (Philadelphia, 1970); Alan Simpson, *Puritanism in Old and New England* (Chicago, 1955); and Perry Miller, *Orthodoxy in Massachusetts, 1630–1650* (Cambridge, Mass., 1933). An important article on dissident strands in Puritanism is James F. Maclear, " 'The Heart of New England Rent': The Mystical Element in Early Puritan History," *Mississippi Valley Historical Review*, vol. XLII (1955–56), pp. 621–652. With the exception of Morison's book, these items bear directly on the place of Rhode Island offshoots of Puritanism within the movement as a whole.

For further investigation of modern studies of Puritanism, a convenient guide is Michael McGiffert, "American Puritan Studies in the 1960's," *William and Mary Quarterly*, 3rd Ser., vol. XXVII (1970), pp. 36–67. The base line from which recent scholarship has proceeded may be found in the magisterial tomes by Perry Miller, *The New England Mind; The Seventeenth Century* (New York, 1939), and *The New England Mind; From Colony to Province* (Cambridge, Mass.,

1953). In many ways just as important were William Haller, *The Rise of Puritanism* . . . (New York, 1938), and *Liberty and Reformation in the Puritan Revolution* (New York, 1955); these volumes deal with England. In the rich literature that has come after these seminal works, the following are especially enlightening for those interested in early Rhode Island: Edmund S. Morgan, *Visible Saints: The History of a Puritan Idea* (New York, 1963); Darrett B. Rutman, *Winthrop's Boston* (Chapel Hill, 1965); Norman Pettit, *The Heart Prepared: Grace and Conversion in Puritan Spiritual Life* (New Haven, 1966); Geoffrey F. Nuttall, *The Holy Spirit in Puritan Faith and Experience* (London, 1947); and Larzer Ziff, *Puritanism in America: New Culture in a New World* (New York, 1973).

There is a vast literature on the Puritan dissidents who settled Rhode Island, particularly on Roger Williams. A useful survey may be found in LeRoy Moore, "Roger Williams and the Historians," *Church History*, vol. XXXII (1963), pp. 432–451. Two biographies remain the most helpful: Ola E. Winslow, *Master Roger Williams* (New York, 1957), and Samuel H. Brockunier, *The Irrepressible Democrat, Roger Williams* (New York, 1940); Winslow's pleases those who like to think of Williams as a religious hero, but Brockunier's (in spite of tendentious terms that disfigure the generalizations and some of the interpretation) has much more to say about the subject as a founder of Rhode Island. Brockunier is generally quite accurate, although not to be trusted in the explanation of Williams' contest with William Harris. Alan Simpson, "How Democratic Was Roger Williams?" *William and Mary Quarterly*, 3rd Ser., vol. XIII (1956), pp. 53–67, answered himself and Brockunier, "Not very," but the evidence is more on Brockunier's side. A fine brief appraisal is to be found in Lawrence C. Wroth, "Roger Williams, Marshall Woods Lecture, in Sayles Hall October 26, 1936," *Brown University Papers*, XIV (Providence, 1937). Modern study of Williams' thought began with Mauro Calamandrei, "Neglected Aspects of Roger Williams' Thought," *Church History*, vol. XXI (1952), pp. 239–258, which insisted that Williams was emphatically a Puritan. Perry Miller, in his interpretive commentary in *Roger Williams; His Contribution to the American Tradition* (Indianapolis, 1953), strongly endorsed Calamandrei but strenuously advanced the view that an interest in the mode of scriptural exegesis known as typology was the hidden key to Williams' thinking and his controversy with the other Massachusetts ministers. This proposition has been examined in Sacvan Bercovitch, "Typology in Puritan New England: The Williams-Cotton Controversy Reassessed," *American Quarterly*, vol. XIX (1967), pp. 166–191. See also Jesper Rosenmeier, "The Teacher and the Witness: John Cotton and Roger Williams," *William and Mary Quarterly*, 3rd Ser., vol. XXV (1968), pp. 408–431; and LeRoy Moore, "Religious Liberty: Roger Williams and the Revolutionary Era," *Church History*, vol. XXXIV (1965), pp. 57–76. A brilliant and balanced interpretation of Williams' thought is to be found in Edmund S. Morgan, *Roger Williams, The Church and the State* (New York, 1967).

Anne Hutchinson and her followers have been the subjects of several studies, the best being Emery Battis, *Saints and Sectaries; Anne Hutchinson and the Antinomian*

Controversy in the Massachusetts Bay Colony (Chapel Hill, 1962). As the title
indicates, little is included about the settlement at Portsmouth. See also Lyle
Koehler, "The Case of the American Jezebels: Anne Hutchinson and Female
Agitation during the years of the Antinomian Turmoil, 1636–1640," *William
and Mary Quarterly*, 3rd Ser., vol. XXXI (1974), pp. 55–78. William Coddington
has been given slight attention by historians. Emily Coddington Williams,
William Coddington of Rhode Island; A Sketch (Newport, 1941), is amateurish but
the best available treatment. Rabid fans of John Clarke will be delighted by
Thomas W. Bicknall, *Story of Dr. John Clark, the Founder of the First Free
Commonwealth of the World on the Basis of "Full Liberty in Religious Concernments"*
(Providence, 1915), but no one else will be.

The best modern treatments of Samuel Gorton are both short: Kenneth W.
Porter, "Samuel Gorton, New England Firebrand," *New England Quarterly*, vol.
VII (1934), pp. 405–444; and Robert E. Wall, Jr., *Massachusetts Bay: The Crucial
Decade, 1640–1650* (New Haven, 1972), chapter iv.

The history of the Baptists in Rhode Island was sketched first by Callender
and Backus, both of whose works are mentioned on p. 396. A great deal has
been written since; most of it worthless. For a good guide to important works as
well as the many dull recitals of skeletal information about different churches,
see Historical Records Survey, Division of Community Service Projects, Work
Projects Administration, *Inventory of the Church Archives of Rhode Island: Baptist*
(Providence, 1941). Backus is the subject of a fine short biography: William G.
McLoughlin, *Isaac Backus and the American Pietistic Tradition* (Boston, 1967). The
biography touches Rhode Island fleetingly, as does McLoughlin's monumental
New England Dissent, 1630–1833; the Baptists and the Separation of Church and State, 2
vols. (Cambridge, Mass., 1971). There is very little of value on the Seventh Day
Baptists; see Ray Greene Huling, "Samuel Hubbard of Newport, 1610–1689,"
Narragansett Historical Register, vol. V (1887), pp. 289–330, and D. Burdett Coon
et al., Seventh Day Baptists in Europe and America; A Series of Historical Papers . . . 2
vols. (Plainfield, N.J., 1910).

Secondary works on Rhode Island Quakerism include relevant portions of
Rufus M. Jones *et al., The Quakers in the American Colonies*, 2nd ed. (New York,
1966); Mary H. Jones, *The Standard of the Lord Lifted Up; a History of Friends in New
England from 1656–1700, Commemorating the First Yearly Meeting Held in 1661* (n.p.,
1961); Arthur J. Worrall, "New England Quakerism 1656–1830" (Ph.D.
dissertation, Indiana University, 1969); Jerry William Frost, *The Quaker Family
in Colonial America, A Portrait of the Society of Friends* (New York, 1973); Virginia
Lee Frank, "Quaker Reading and Education in Eighteenth Century Narragansett" (M.A. thesis, Brown University, 1964); Caroline Hazard, *The Narragansett
Friends' Meeting in the XVIII Century, with a Chapter on Quaker Beginnings in Rhode
Island* (Boston, 1899); and Zora Klain, *Educational Activities of New England
Quakers; A Source Book* (Philadelphia, 1928). Klain's volume is useful more for
the documents it publishes than for the explanations of them. Virginia Lee
Frank, unfortunately, has not made available all her important discoveries
about East Greenwich and South County Quakers.

For the later eighteenth century, particularly the Quaker revival, three works contain useful material: Mack Thompson, *Moses Brown, Reluctant Reformer* (Chapel Hill, 1962); Sydney V. James, *A People Among Peoples; Quaker Benevolence in Eighteenth-Century America* (Cambridge, Mass., 1963) and "The Impact of the American Revolution on Quakers' Ideas About their Sect," *William and Mary Quarterly*, 3rd Ser., vol. XIX (1962), pp. 360–382.

Very little has been written about Congregationalism in colonial Rhode Island. An early publication of some value is Benjamin Bourne, *An Account of the Settlement of the Town of Bristol . . . And of the Congregational Church Therein . . .* (Providence, 1785). Modern studies include Felix G. Davis and Grace Stafford Durfee, *The History of Amicable Congregational Church, 1746–1946* (n.p., n.d.); and Arthur E. Wilson, *Weybosset Bridge in Providence Plantations 1700–1790* (Boston, 1947). Still, the best information on the denomination is to be found in Edmund S. Morgan, *The Gentle Puritan, A Life of Ezra Stiles, 1727–1795* (New Haven, 1962), and in the brief biographies of Harvard men who lived in Rhode Island, scattered in Clifford Shipton, *Sibley's Harvard Graduates*, vols. IV-XVI (Cambridge and Boston, 1933–1972). For the general background of Congregationalism in New England, Williston Walker, *The Creeds and Platforms of Congregationalism* (New York, 1893), is still useful. On Samuel Hopkins, see Frank H. Foster, *A Genetic History of the New England Theology* (Chicago, 1907), especially chapters vi, vii, and viii; Oliver Wendell Elsbree, "Samuel Hopkins and His Doctrine of Benevolence," *New England Quarterly*, vol. VIII (1935), pp. 534–550; the "Memoir" by Edwards Amasa Parks in the first volume of *The Works of Samuel Hopkins . . .* , 3 vols. (Boston, 1852); Stephen West, ed., *Sketches of the Life of the Late, Rev. Samuel Hopkins, D.D., Pastor of the First Congregational Church in Newport, Written by Himself; . . .* (Hartford, Conn., 1805); and relevant passages in Alan Heimert, *Religion and the American Mind from the Great Awakening to the Revolution* (Cambridge, Mass., 1966).

Anglicanism may be approached with some success through Wilkins Updike, *A History of the Episcopal Church in Narragansett, Rhode Island*, 2nd ed., 3 vols. revised and enlarged by Daniel Goodwin (Boston, 1907). The visit of George Berkeley is treated in A. A. Luce, *The Life of George Berkeley Bishop of Cloyne* (London, 1949), and Benjamin Rand, *Berkeley's American Sojourn* (Cambridge, Mass., 1932). For the controversies over an American episcopate, see Arthur L. Cross, *The Anglican Episcopate and the American Colonies* (New York, 1902), and Carl Bridenbaugh, *Mitre and Sceptre: Transatlantic Faiths, Ideas, Personalities, and Politics, 1689–1775* (London, 1962). There are pertinent sections in E. B. Carpenter, *South County Studies*; Gertrude S. Kimball, *Providence in Colonial Times*; and W. H. Munro, *History of Bristol*, mentioned on pp. 401, 402, and 403.

By far the best information about Jews in Rhode Island is to be found in Jacob R. Marcus, *The Colonial American Jew, 1492–1776*, 3 vols. (Detroit, 1970). The arrangement is topical. By contrast, Morris A. Gutstein, *The Story of the Jews of Newport* (New York, 1936), is slipshod and credulous.

The current authority on Jemima Wilkinson and her following is Herbert A.

Wisbey, Jr., *Pioneer Prophetess: Jemima Wilkinson, the Publick Universal Friend* (Ithaca, N.Y., 1964).

EDUCATION, CULTURE, AND SOCIETY

Education in colonial Rhode Island has not been studied extensively—perhaps it cannot be—except in connection with the Quakers and the college that became Brown University. The early years of the college may be examined at length in Reuben A. Guild, *Early History of Brown University, Including the Life, Times, and Correspondence of President Manning* (Providence, 1897), or more succinctly in Walter C. Bronson, *The History of Brown University, 1764–1914* (Providence, 1914). See also Mack Thompson, *Moses Brown, Reluctant Reformer* (Chapel Hill, 1962), chapter iii.

In the treatment of cultural matters, Antoinette F. Downing, *Early Homes of Rhode Island* (Richmond, Va., 1937), is quite good. Less enlightening are: Joyce E. Mangler and William Dineen, "Early Music in Rhode Island Churches," serialized in *Rhode Island History*, vol. XVII (1958), and Henry W. Rugg, *History of Freemasonry in Rhode Island* (Providence, 1895). The relevant portions of Carl Bridenbaugh, *The Colonial Craftsman* (New York, 1950), are useful. See also various titles mentioned earlier under "Local Histories."

The arts and crafts are treated in many other places, including numerous periodicals, local historical studies, and biographies. *Rhode Island History*, in particular, has carried many helpful articles and pictures. The fascinating material in "Boston Prints and Printmakers 1670–1775," Colonial Society of Massachusetts *Publications*, vol. XLVI (1973; this was a volume of "Collections"), should not be overlooked. Joseph K. Ott, *The John Brown House Loan Exhibition of Rhode Island Furniture* (Providence, 1965), is the most authoritative general work on the subject.

There are four biographies of part-time Rhode Islanders who were artists: Carl Bridenbaugh, *Peter Harrison, First American Architect* (Chapel Hill, 1949); Henry W. Foote, *John Smibert, Painter* (Cambridge, Mass., 1950); H. W. Foote, *Robert Feke, Colonial Portrait Painter* (Cambridge, Mass., 1930); and Charles M. Mount, *Gilbert Stuart, A Biography* (New York, 1964).

An interesting foray into the discouraging thickets of Rhode Island population trends is Herbert A. Whitney, "Estimating Precensus Populations: A Method Suggested and Applied to the Towns of Rhode Island and Plymouth Colonies in 1689," *Annals of the Association of American Geographers*, vol. LIX (1965), pp. 179–189.

Interesting glimpses into eighteenth-century life are afforded by Caroline Hazard, *Thomas Hazard son of Rob* call'd College Tom; A Study of Life in Narragansett in the XVIII*th* Century* (Boston, 1893); and Nancy P. Chudacoff, "Woman in the News 1762–1770—Sarah Updike Goddard," *Rhode Island History*, vol. XXXII (1973), pp. 99–105.

THE ECONOMY

Information on commercial affairs in Rhode Island has not often been developed systematically. The brilliant work of Bernard Bailyn, *The New England Merchants in the Seventeenth Century* (Cambridge, Mass., 1955), explains the context for the trifling trade of the early years. His volume written in collaboration with Lotte Bailyn, *Massachusetts Shipping 1697-1714; A Statistical Study* (Cambridge, Mass., 1959), sheds some light on the beginnings of shipbuilding around Narragansett Bay. Useful in various ways are: Bruce Macmillan Bigelow, "The Commerce of Rhode Island with the West Indies before the American Revolution," 2 vols. (Ph.D. dissertation, Brown University, 1930); Richard Pares, *Yankees and Creoles; The Trade Between North America and the West Indies before the American Revolution* (Cambridge, Mass., 1956); Stanley F. Chyet, *Lopez of Newport, Colonial American Merchant Prince* (Detroit, 1970); the monumental work of James B. Hedges, *The Browns of Providence Plantations, Colonial Years* (Cambridge, Mass., 1952); and relevant portions of Oliver M. Dickerson, *The Navigation Acts and the American Revolution* (Philadelphia, 1951), and Robert A. East, *Business Enterprise in the American Revolutionary Era* (New York, 1938).

Studies of privateering and piracy, for want of sufficient documentary evidence, are sketchy and inconclusive. See William P. Sheffield, *An Address Delivered . . . Before the Rhode Island Historical Society* (Newport, 1883); Howard M. Chapin, *Privateer Ships and Sailors; the First Century of American Colonial Privateering 1625-1725* (Toulon, France, 1926); Howard M. Chapin, *Rhode Island Privateers in King George's War, 1739-1748* (Providence, 1926); Howard W. Preston, *Rhode Island and the Sea* (Providence, 1932), which explains governmental machinery, includes some interesting documents and gives lists of privateer ships known to have been active during the wars of the mid-eighteenth century; and Edgar Stanton Maclay, *A History of American Privateers* (New York, 1899). On piracy, see George Francis Dow and J. H. Edmonds, *The Pirates of the New England Coast, 1630-1730* (Salem, Mass., 1923); Edward Rowe Snow, *Pirates and Buccaneers of the Atlantic Coast* (Boston, 1944); and Hugh F. Rankin, *The Golden Age of Piracy* (New York, 1969).

A useful book on the slave trade is George Francis Dow, *Slave Ships and Slaving* (Salem, Mass., 1927).

Rhode Island paper money and its counterfeiting have been examined by John Blanchard MacInnes, "Rhode Island Bills of Credit, 1710-1755" (Ph.D. dissertation, Brown University, 1952); Elisha R. Potter and Sidney S. Rider, "Some Account of the Bills of Credit or Paper Money of Rhode Island: From the First Issue in 1710, to the Final Issue, 1786," *Rhode Island Historical Tracts*, 1st Ser., No. 8 (Providence, 1880); Richard LeBaron Bowen, *Rhode Island Colonial*

Money and Its Counterfeiting 1647–1726 (Providence, 1942); and Kenneth Scott, *Counterfeiting in Colonial Rhode Island* (Providence, 1960).

LAW

A number of treatises on the legal history of Rhode Island, or on legal history in which Rhode Island had an important place, have been written, including the following: Marguerite Appleton, "Rhode Island's First Court of Admiralty," *New England Quarterly*, vol. V (1932), pp. 148–158; Frederick B. Wiener, "Notes on the Rhode Island Admiralty, 1727–1790," *Harvard Law Review*, vol. XLVI (1932), pp. 44–90; Zechariah Chafee, Jr., "Records of the Rhode Island Court of Equity, 1741–1743," in Colonial Society of Massachusetts *Publications*, vol. XXV (1951; this volume consisted of "Transactions 1942–1946"), pp. 91–118; Harold D. Hazeltine, "Appeals from Colonial Courts to the King in Council, With Especial Reference to Rhode Island," in American Historical Association, *Annual Report*, 1894, pp. 299–350; and Joseph Henry Smith, *Appeals to the Privy Council from the American Plantations* (New York, 1950), which is the standard work on that subject.

INDEX

INDEX

Acts of Trade and Navigation, 72, 159, 328, 335

Adams, John, 198–99

Admiralty courts and jurisdiction, 116–18, 124, 128–29, 132–33, 268–69, 316–17, 321–22, 334, 349

Africa. *See* Slave trade

Agriculture, 49–51, 146, 160, 252, 257–58; regulation of by towns, 146–47, 149. *See also* Animal husbandry

Albany Congress (1754), 282–83

Almy, Christopher, 112

Amusements, 14, 232–33, 243–45, 252–53, 264

Andros, Sir Edmund, 107–9

Angell, John, 37

Anglicanism, 121–22, 189–97, 226, 234–35, 252, 261, 300. *See also* Church of England

Animal husbandry, 49–50, 160, 252–53

Antinomians, 20–30, 33–36, 38–40, 50, 52, 234

Aquidneck (R.I.), 1–2, 8, 25–28, 39, 59–60, 63, 77–78, 129, 231–32, 250

Aquidneck commonwealth, 53–54, 60, 62

Architecture, 216, 238–43, 264

Arnold, Benedict, 4*n.*, 82

Arnold family, 50, 259

Articles of Confederation, 360–61, 371

Aspinwall, William, 25, 38–39

Awashonks, 98

Bannister, John, 237, 240, 269, 292

Baptists, 34, 36, 37, 41–47, 188, 205, 207, 211–16, 227, 248, 252, 261, 265, 300; Five Principle or Calvinist, 42, 212–14; Six Principle or General, 43–44, 46, 206; Seventh Day, 34, 42, 211, 214–15

Barclay, Robert, 218, 221, 223

Bass, John, 205

Bellomont, Richard Coote, Earl of, 124–26, 128, 141, 189

Berkeley, George, 191–93, 218–21

Bernon, Gabriel, 193

Bills of exchange, 162

Black people, 255–56, 357, 366. *See also* Slavery

Blackstone, William, 2

Blagrove, Nathaniel, 137

Blathwayt, William, 129, 134

Block, Adriaen, 5